Record Your Presentations

Get Personalized Feedback

More than 69% of employers look for candidates with high-caliber communication skills.[1] Verbal communication may be one of the hardest skills to improve, but there is one simple way to become an incredible presenter fast: video.

According to research, recording your presentations and reviewing the footage afterwards is the secret to better presentations. This record-and-critique method helps presenters change their habits quickly, set goals for improvement, and measure their progress reliably.[2] Along with video, immediate in-context feedback from your professor is the most scientifically effective way to reinforce learning and develop new skills quickly.[3]

To help you become a stand-out presenter, this textbook includes access to a one-of-a-kind video tool: GoReact. Using GoReact to record and review your own presentations will . . .

- Boost your self-awareness.
- Allow your instructor to give you immediate time-coded feedback.
- Reduce your presentation anxiety over time.
- Help you practice and improve faster than any other method!

We're excited and honored to be a part of your journey.

"Students improved more in one week with GoReact than they usually do in an entire semester."

Anne Grinols,
Baylor University

"Before GoReact, students would get 6–8 written comments. With GoReact, they probably get 20–30 each, and they're much more specific and targeted."

Bill Baker,
Brigham Young University

1. NACE's *Job Outlook 2016* survey.

2. Knight, Jim, et al. "Record, Replay, Reflect: Videotaped Lessons Accelerate Learning for Teachers and Coaches. *Journal of Staff Development*, 33.2 (2012): 18–23.

3. Shute, Valerie J. "Focus on formative feedback." *Review of Educational Research* 78.1 (2008): 153–189.

seventh edition

PUBLIC SPEAKING
ESSENTIALS FOR EXCELLENCE

Shawn T. Wahl | LeAnn M. Brazeal | Mark J. Butland

Missouri State University   Missouri State University   Austin Community College

With contributions by Gail E. Mason and John J. Makay

Kendall Hunt
publishing company

Book Team

Chairman and Chief Executive Officer   Mark C. Falb
President and Chief Operating Officer   Chad M. Chandlee
Vice President, Higher Education   David L. Tart
Director of Publishing Partnerships   Paul B. Carty
Senior Developmental Coordinator   Angela Willenbring
Vice President, Operations   Timothy J. Beitzel
Senior Permissions Editor   Caroline Kieler
Cover Designer   Jenifer Fensterman

Cover image © Shutterstock.com

Kendall Hunt
p u b l i s h i n g   c o m p a n y

www.kendallhunt.com
Send all inquiries to:
4050 Westmark Drive
Dubuque, IA 52004-1840

This book was previously published by Harcourt Brace College Publishers
Copyright © 1998, 2000, 2008, 2012, 2017 by Kendall Hunt Publishing Company

ISBN 978-1-5249-1599-5
Text ISBN 978-1-5249-1601-5

Published in the United States of America

BRIEF CONTENTS

CONTENTS

Chapter 3 – Being Audience-Centered 72

Chapter 6 – Organizing and Outlining Your Ideas 174

PREFACE

A new edition, a new look, a new journey for this book. We are pleased to share the seventh edition of *Public Speaking: Essentials for Excellence* with you. **Our mission** in writing this book was to focus on theory, research, and application of knowledge related to public speaking so that it can easily be covered in one term across delivery formats (e.g., traditional, online, hybrid). We recognize the diversity from one college or university to the next.

In response to our goal of focusing directly on the individual student experience related to the study of public speaking, we developed an **organizing theme** (the ESSENTIALS FOR EXCELLENCE theme described below), which we believe will help instructors guide students across public speaking contexts.

Organizing Theme: Essentials for Excellence

We believe that developing an organizing theme lends clarity to a textbook. The **organizing theme** running throughout the text is ESSENTIALS FOR EXCELLENCE, a theme aimed at developing students' oral communication skills.

Overview of the Book

In this text, we provide 14 focused chapters in which the best material is explored with relevance to the study of public speaking.

By providing complete and thorough coverage of the study and practice of public speaking, the seventh edition offers students theory and practical skills, presenting public speaking as an art form for transactional communication between speaker and audience.

Our goal in writing this text is to make it one that will prepare students to become effective public speakers in any of the various speaking situations they may encounter in their lives. Whether they are presenting in a professional capacity, speaking as a community leader, offering a tribute to a retiring colleague, eulogizing a friend, delivering a commencement address, or sharing views as a concerned citizen, these and other public speaking situations will result in an effective message to the audience.

The text comprises three parts:
Part I: Public Speaking in Our Lives
Part II: Preparing and Presenting Your Speech
Part III: Types of Public Speaking

Part I: Public Speaking in Our Lives

Public speaking is an essential activity that begins at an early age. Part I explores the role of public speaking in our lives and prepares students to present, while discussing the role of ethics in speech. The importance of listening and evaluating speeches is also a key element of Part I.

Chapter 1: Public Speaking: Essentials for Excellence

This chapter focuses on public speaking as a valuable activity that influences career and community success. The basic elements of the communication process are outlined and defined to provide the foundation for growth and understanding.

Chapter 2: Ethics in Public Speaking

An essential element of every speech, ethics is defined and explained through guidelines to promote speaker credibility. Points for avoiding unethical practices are also included in this chapter.

Chapter 3: Being Audience-Centered

Knowing your audience is key to presenting a successful speech. This chapter discusses how to adapt to different audiences and situations. It explains how to create the speaker-audience connection by doing such things as using humor, encouraging participation, and getting to the point of your speech quickly.

Chapter 4: Listening and Critiquing Speeches

As crucial as the skills for speaking are to a presenter, just as important are listening skills to the audience. Understanding how you listen helps improve the process. Eight steps promote fine-tuning your listening skills. Criteria for speech evaluation are discussed as well.

Part II: Preparing and Presenting Your Speech

The focus of Part II is the actual work of planning, researching, and delivering your speech. This section offers numerous strategies for the stages of preparing and presenting, from the beginning ideas of who the audience will be and what kind of message will captivate them, through to the most effective delivery techniques as you present.

Chapter 5: Research and Supporting Material

Research is the raw material that forms the foundation of your speech, and this chapter helps you develop an effective research strategy as well as provides guidelines for using various methods of supporting your speech.

Chapter 6: Organizing and Outlining Your Ideas

Organizing your speech helps your audience follow your points and understand your message. This chapter concentrates on developing the body of your speech, including selecting, supporting, and organizing your main points. It also discusses how to create effective outlines and speaker's notes to best serve you as you present.

Chapter 7: Introducing and Concluding Your Speech

This chapter approaches introductions and conclusions in relation to how your speech can make a lasting impression. It discusses both how to engage your audience at the beginning of the speech so they will want to listen, and then how to remind your audience at the end of what you said and why it was relevant. Techniques and suggestions, including common pitfalls for introductions and conclusions, are offered.

Chapter 8: Language

It is important to remember to consider how words affect your listeners. In this chapter, we identify characteristics of spoken language and provide guidelines for using it more effectively. We also address pitfalls, which are aspects of language that a speaker should avoid. The use of humor is also discussed.

Chapter 9: Confidently Delivering Your Message

Your ability to communicate information, persuade, and entertain is influenced by the manner in which you present yourself to your audience. Chapter 9 discusses methods of delivery and offers specific strategies for vocal delivery and physical delivery so your message is favorably enhanced by the way you convey it, with a focus on what communication apprehension is and strategies you can use to control it.

Chapter 10: Presentational Aids and Technology

Exploring the different types available and offering criteria for their use and display, this chapter focuses on the benefits of using presentation aids and technology. Your decision to include an aid should be based on the extent to which it enhances your audience's interest and understanding. Guidelines are presented for determining what to incorporate and how to use it.

Part III: Types of Public Speaking

In Part III, we discuss specifically the kinds of different speeches intended to inform, persuade, and entertain or inspire your audience. Another common scenario is speaking in a small group situation, and this section offers suggestions for all types of public speaking environments.

Chapter 11: Informative Speaking

The intent of an informative speech is to communicate information and ideas in a way that your audience will understand and remember. The different types of informative speeches are identified, and goals and strategies for informative speaking are presented. The ethics of informative speaking are also discussed.

Chapter 12: Persuasive Speaking

Persuasion is intended to influence choice through appeals to your audience's sense of ethics, reasoning, and emotion. This chapter explores the goals of persuasive speaking and discusses elements, reasoning, appeals, and arguments as well as the ethics of persuasive messages.

Chapter 13: Special-Occasion Speaking

Beginning with general guidelines for special-occasion speeches, this chapter discusses how to present effectively in the most common situations wherein a brief speech is appropriate. Chapter 13 addresses topics such as speeches of introduction, speeches of presentation, speeches of acceptance, commemorative speeches, the keynote speech, and after-dinner speeches.

Chapter 14: Presenting to and Working with Small Groups

Small groups are a part of life and you may have opportunities to speak in a variety of professional, academic, and community situations in a small group setting. This chapter discusses role responsibilities, working and presenting in a small group, and small group formats. It also presents guidelines for group problem-solving and presenting.

Features of the Textbook/New to This Edition

We provide several unique pedagogical features to help students understand and apply the concepts and theories introduced in the text. The features help reinforce the book's themes and promote critical thinking in readers.

Chapter Outlines detail the organization of each chapter, while the **What You'll Learn** feature highlights chapter learning outcomes to help students prioritize information so that they can learn more efficiently.

Communication ethics is emphasized in all chapters with a feature called **Ethics Matter**, which connects the topic to an ethical perspective—a key essential for public speaking excellence.

We include **Reflect Questions** that instructors may use as a means of generating class discussions about chapter content, as actual assignments, or as thought-provokers for students to consider on their own time.

All chapters include new **Review Questions** designed to help students practice for exams.

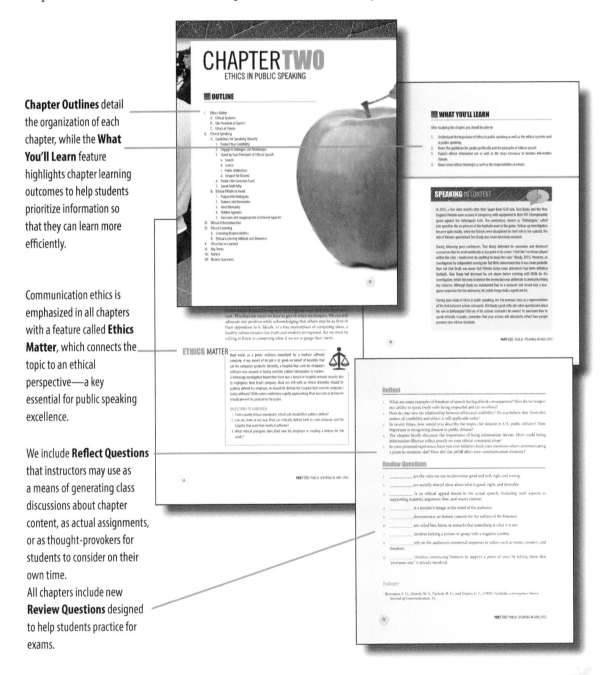

Complete **References** to the research base cited within the text appear at the end of the book and are organized by chapter. Students may find these references useful as they prepare assignments and/or conduct their own research projects. Instructors may use the references to gather additional material for their own research or to supplement instruction.

New **Speaking in Context** vignettes introduce each chapter with a contemporary example drawn from the real world.

All chapters also include a new feature called **What You've Learned**, designed to promote reading comprehension and serve as a guide to help connect chapter concepts to learning objectives. **Key Terms** highlight the important concepts discussed in each chapter and where to find them.

The **Engaging in Community** feature in all chapters encourages civic engagement and communication activism related to public speaking.

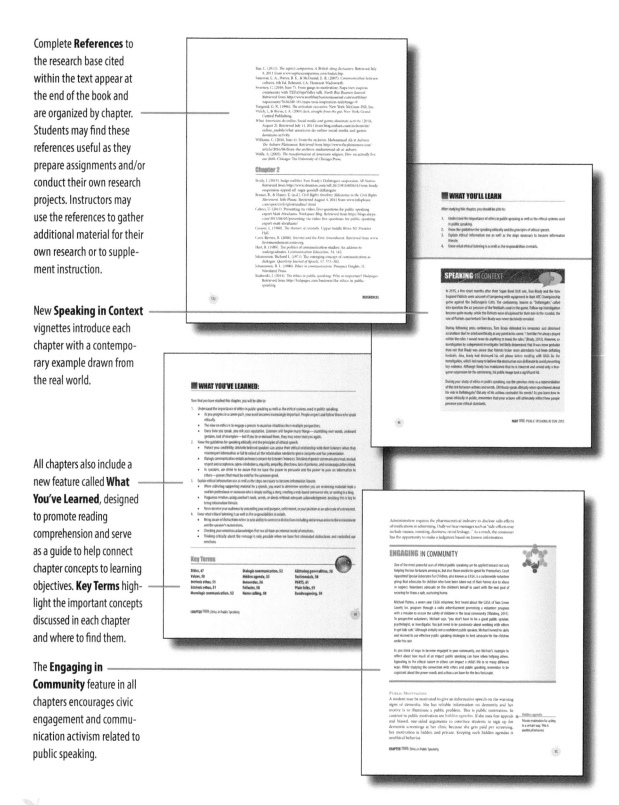

The **Speaking Excellence in Your Career** feature connects public speaking to a variety of professional contexts, industries, and occupations.

The **Speaking Well with Technology** feature provides tips and best practices related to presentation aids and new media.

Speaking tips and best practices are emphasized in a feature called **Essentials for Excellence** that appears at the end of each chapter.

Updated photo program throughout every chapter.

Instructional Supplements

On adoption of the text, an online Instructor's Manual (IM) is provided through the publisher. Designed for both community colleges and 4-year universities, the IM contains chapter outlines that can serve as class notes for instructors or students, PowerPoint slides containing outlines and graphics for each chapter, and activities/exercises to enhance instruction and stimulate class discussion. An online Test Bank that includes multiple-choice and short-answer questions is available for instructors' use. Materials from the IM support **distance education** and are easily loaded to systems such as Blackboard, making them useful to **traditional, online, and hybrid delivery formats**. The IM can support **large courses** and departments using graduate teaching assistants or adjunct instructors—both the textbook and IM provided by the publisher support departments needing either instructional flexibility or consistency in the way persuasion courses are delivered across sections.

Student Oriented Pedagogy

Because we recognize the importance of assessing student learning, we have included features in each chapter that facilitate student learning and help instructors measure learning outcomes.

- **Chapter Outlines** serve as a map to guide students through the content of the chapter and focus on key points.
- **Bold-faced Key Terms** throughout the chapter include clear definitions for each term.
- **Real-world Examples and Strategies**, including international examples, illustrate chapter theories and concepts, as well as help students apply those concepts in their own work.
- **Questions for Study and Discussion** encourage students to further explore the concepts they learned in the chapter.
- **Glossary of Terms** serves as a helpful reference tool at the end of the text.

Instructional Online Enhancements

Both students and instructors have access to online content that is integrated chapter by chapter with the text to enrich student learning. The web access code is included on the inside front cover of the textbook. Look for the web icon in the text margins to direct you to various interactive tools.

Student Web Content

- **Poll Questions** draw students into the subject matter of the chapter by asking questions relevant to students and the chapter theme.
- **Video** brings the chapter content to life, clearly illustrating theory by showcasing actual student speeches.
- **Interactive Video Exercises** reinforce chapter concepts by incorporating chapter content with an actual speech example to illustrate the application of the concept.
- **Applications** offer real-world scenarios to key terms so students can apply them effectively.
- **Interactive Flashcards** reinforce definitions of key terms.

Instructor Web Content

- **Chapter Outlines** highlight central ideas for each chapter and can serve as lecture notes.
- **Activities and Worksheets** further explore chapter content and can be made accessible to students.
- **Extensive Teaching Tips** enhance the textbook content to aid student understanding.
- **Comprehensive Test Bank** offers several different types of questions to better assess student comprehension.

Acknowledgments

This project has been both exciting and challenging. Thus, there are many people we would like to acknowledge. We wish to thank the team at Kendall Hunt, who all offered great assistance, feedback, and encouragement.

We are grateful to our colleagues and friends in the field of communication whose advice and encouragement helped inform our decisions during the revision process of this text. Reviewers include

Kenneth Albone
Rowan University

Tim Anderson
Elgin Community College

Christa Brown
Minnesota State University – Mankato

Sabrina Caine
Erie Community College – City

Eric Carlson
Collin County Community College

Scott Christen
Tennessee Technological University – Cookeville

Kathryn Dederichs
Minneapolis Community & Technical College

Linda Desjardins
Northern Essex Community College

Sally Deuermeyer
Blinn College

Anie Dubosse
Norwalk Community College

John Edwards
Fayetteville Technical Institute

Steven Epstein
Suffolk County Community College – Brentwood

Barbara Franzen
Central Community College – Hastings

Karrie Gavin
Temple University

Steven Ginley
Morton College

Debbi Hatton
Sam Houston State University

Kim Higgs
University of North Dakota

Karen Huck
Central Oregon Community College

Mark Johnson
Rhodes State College

Bernadette Kapocias
Southwestern Oregon Community College

Michele King
College of William and Mary

Kara Laskowski
Shippensburg University

John Luecke
*University of Wisconsin –
Whitewater*

Edie MacPherson
*Suffolk County Community College
– Selden*

Diane Matuschka
University of North Florida

Jamie McKown
College of the Atlantic

Shawn Miklaucic
Pace University – New York

Mike Milford
Tarleton State University

Emma Rollin Moore
Santa Barbara City College

Beverly Neville
*Central New Mexico Community
College*

Tushar Oza
Oakland University

Joyce Pauley
Moberly Area Community College

Matthew Petrunia
University of New Mexico

Kelly Rocca
St. John's University

Marybeth Ruscica
St. John's University

Nick Russell
*California State University – Long
Beach*

Cindy Stout
Midlands Technical College

Darren Sweeney
Manchester Community College

Charles Tichy
Creighton University

Mike Wartman *Normandale
Community College*

Sharon Waters
Tidewater Community College

Trent Webb
Nassau Community College

Richard West
University of Texas – San Antonio

Thanks also to our colleagues, friends, and students at Missouri State University and Austin Community College. We are especially grateful to Travis Covill, Tucker Robinson, and Shaley Moore for their contributions to the research-gathering process, photographic selections, permissions, and assistance with instructional supplements.

Finally, we thank our family and friends for their support and belief in this book and our passion for teaching and studying communication.

—Shawn T. Wahl
—LeAnn M. Brazeal
—Mark Butland

ABOUT THE AUTHORS

Shawn T. Wahl (PhD, University of Nebraska, Lincoln) is a Professor of Communication and Head of the Department of Communication in the School of Communication Studies at Missouri State University (MSU). Prior to MSU, he served as head of the Department of Communication, Mass Media, & Theatre at Angelo State University and as the Director of Graduate Studies at Texas A&M University, Corpus Christi. He is coauthor of *The Communication Age: Connecting and Engaging*, *Nonverbal Communication for a Lifetime*; *Business and Professional Communication: KEYS for Workplace Excellence*; *Persuasion in Your Life*; *Communication and Culture In Your Life*; and *Public Relations Principles: Strategies for Professional Success*. Shawn has published articles in *Communication Education*, *Communication Research Reports*, *Communication Teacher*, *Journal of Family Communication*, *Basic Communication Course Annual* and more. Shawn was a faculty participant in the National Communication Association Learning Outcomes in Communication project and was the 2016 President of the Central States Communication Association. In addition, Shawn has worked across the nation as a corporate trainer, communication consultant, and leadership coach in a variety of industries. Outside of his professional work, he enjoys spending time with his family and two Chinese pugs (Jake and Bentley).

LeAnn M. Brazeal (PhD, University of Missouri, Columbia) is an Associate Professor and Director of the Basic Course in the Department of Communication at Missouri State University, a position she previously held at Kansas State University. She is co-author of *The Primary Decision: A Functional Analysis of Debates in Presidential Primaries*, and has published numerous articles and book chapters in outlets such as *Communication Quarterly*, *Argumentation and Advocacy*, *Communication Studies*, and *Basic Communication Course Annual*. An award-winning teacher and veteran course director, LeAnn writes and speaks on a variety of pedagogical issues, including graduate assistant training, academic integrity and plagiarism, civic engagement and civility, information literacy, teaching methods, and the first-year experience. Her work on public speaking and civic engagement has been recognized by the National Endowment for the Humanities. LeAnn's outside interests include travel, sports, tea, and wonderful meals with family and friends.

Mark Butland is Professor of Communication Studies at Austin Community College. His teaching experience in Communication includes graduate and undergraduate courses at Baylor University, Central Texas College, Texas State University, National American University, and Austin Community College. He is an award-winning researcher and has received accolades for excellence in teaching. He was an innovator in distance learning and the founder and director of the Austin Community College Honors Program. He has authored, co-authored, and contributed to over a dozen books in his field. In addition to his service as a college professor, Mark is active as a corporate trainer and professional speaker, and is pleased to have these frequent opportunities to practice what he professes. His interests include traveling, hiking, and "food adventuring." Mark and his son live in Austin and greatly enjoy being active in their community.

PART**ONE**

PUBLIC SPEAKING IN OUR LIVES

2 Former heavyweight boxing champion Muhammad
Ali gave numerous electrifying public speeches throughout his career.

CHAPTER ONE
PUBLIC SPEAKING: ESSENTIALS FOR EXCELLENCE

OUTLINE

I. Public Speaking: Essentials for Excellence
- A. Public Speaking Is a Valuable Activity
- B. Public Speaking Influences Success in College
- C. Public Speaking Teaches Critical Thinking Skills
- D. Public Speaking Skills Influence Career and Community Success
- E. Public Speaking Skills Are Key to Leadership
- F. Public Speaking Skills Complement Technology
- G. Public Speaking Is a Part of Our Democratic Tradition

II. Eight Elements of the Communication Process
- A. Sender/Receiver
- B. Receiver/Sender
- C. Message
- D. Channel
- E. Feedback
- F. Noise
- G. Occasion
- H. Cultural Context

III. Five Steps for Preparing to Speak
- A. Select and Narrow an Audience-Centered Topic
  1. Know the Speaking Assignment
  2. Understand the Audience
  3. Choose an Appropriate Topic
  4. Determine the General Purpose, Specific Purpose, and Thesis Statement
  5. Demonstrate Ethical Behavior Throughout the Process
- B. Develop Content Through Research and Sound Support
  1. Research
  2. Support Your Ideas
- C. Draft the Introduction, Body, and Conclusion
  1. Introduction
  2. Body
  3. Conclusion

▰ WHAT YOU'LL LEARN

After studying this chapter, you should be able to:

1. Explain how public speaking teaches critical thinking skills.
2. Understand how technology can complement public speaking
3. Identify the purpose and expectations for drafting a speech introduction, body, and conclusion.

SPEAKING IN CONTEXT

On July 3, 2016, former heavyweight boxing champion Muhammad Ali passed away after fighting a respiratory illness. Ali is widely remembered not only for his skill in the boxing ring, but also for his charismatic personality and ability to electrify audiences with his speeches. Over forty years ago Ali was invited to give a speech in Alabama, which at the time was a major battleground of the Civil Rights movement.

"It is refreshing to see so many people of all nationalities and races all here in unity in a place like Alabama," Ali said in his speech at Auburn University in May 1973. "I've never been to Alabama and was shook up when I got the invitation to speak in Alabama. Some people down here don't like the way I talk."

In Ali's speech "The Intoxications of Life," the heavyweight champion discussed how people can be distracted in life by countless activities—not only drugs and alcohol

(Gattis, 2016). Ali stressed that education did not come solely from the classroom. "People like Napoleon, Jesus Christ and Malcolm X, men who had no schooling, were some of the wisest men in the world. Their education came from traveling and talking, worldly education ... and that's where I get mine." (Duncan, 1973).

Through the course of this book, you will examine many theories, studies, and strategies that will guide you into becoming a more effective public speaker. Keep in mind, however, the words and advice of Muhammad Ali. Becoming great at public speaking and presentations goes beyond what is written in any book; remember that your interactions and travels with others are useful tools for developing your speechcraft as well.

Welcome to your study of public speaking! This book focuses on how to present yourself and your messages in a way that increases the odds of getting what you want in an efficient and ethical way. While our primary focus will be on the more formal presentations life brings each of us, many of the ideas we develop may be applied to other, less formal messages you create and share, such as online profiles, text messages, phone conversations and conference calls, an avatar for your favorite game, and simple face-to-face conversations.

This first chapter lays a foundation for the rest of the book by showing you how important and relevant public speaking is to several aspects of your life. We introduce a model that clarifies the parts of the communication process and how the parts interact to help, and sometimes hurt, our communication effectiveness. Then we turn our attention to the steps to take to create your first speech.

Public Speaking: Essentials for Excellence

Public speaking can be a *powerful tool* for an effective speaker who wishes to present new information, or for the individual who wishes to advocate for a particular position or persuade an audience to take action. Power is inherent in effective public speaking—power to communicate facts and emotions, convictions and attitudes, and values and beliefs—in a way that leaves a lasting, and often unequalled, impression on the audience.

Public speaking is also a *creative activity* that includes both mental and physical aspects. The mental aspect involves connecting thoughts and ideas in an original or innovative manner while centering on the audience's needs and interests. Delivering the speech is the physical aspect of the creative process, which includes knowing when to look at the audience, where to pause, where to place emphasis, using appropriate gestures and body movement, communicating ethically, and expressing self-confidence. Effective speakers have learned the *art* of public speaking and are able to design and deliver a speech that resonates with listeners through careful word choice, organization, supporting material, appropriate eye contact, and meaningful gestures. This art is audience centered, and its core is the message.

Public speaking is also a *decision-making process*. While taking your public speaking class, you will have to determine your interests, analyze your audience, decide where to look for information, figure out the best way to organize your information, make decisions about word choice, and decide how to deliver your speech most effectively.

As viewers watch speakers on TV, it's easy to find examples of poor decision making. We watch professional athletes come across poorly on TV because they were unprepared to comment on their performance. Late-night TV comedians, such as Trevor Noah of the *Daily Show*, regularly lampoon politicians for awkward gestures, odd word choice, and lack of logical reasoning. As authors, our task is to help you think about all the decisions you make when developing and delivering a speech and to guide you to be effective as a speaker and as a listener.

Trevor Noah is one of many entertainers who lampoon public figures for poor public speaking performances.

Public Speaking Is a Valuable Activity

It is fair to ask what value successful public speaking has in your life. Gaining self-confidence in front of an audience, learning how to make the best use of the time allowed, and being active when given an opportunity to express what you know and how you feel are genuine benefits to be gained from success as a public speaker.

Public speaking skills are important for success in school, career advancement, and for increasing self-confidence. Learning to communicate in a public setting is valuable for many reasons, including the six identified as follows.

Public Speaking Influences Success in College

Since you are currently in college, it makes sense to note that the first reason to learn and practice the essentials of public speaking is because they may influence your success in college. Oral presentations in English, philosophy, political science, or environmental science are all considered public speaking events. Normally, part of your grade is based on your presentation skills.

In addition to making presentations in your classes, any involvement in extracurricular activities may also be influenced by your ability to speak in public. If you are comfortable and possess the skills to address an audience, it will be possible to run for student body president, to present your point during an organizational meeting, or to be part of a film criticism workshop.

SPEAKING EXCELLENCE IN YOUR CAREER

When taking a public speaking course in college, a common question arises for many students: why is this class necessary, and how will I even use this outside of school? To begin answering this question, it's important to note that exposure and practice can help familiarize you with any body of knowledge (especially public speaking!). Researchers Karla Hunter, Joshua Westwick, and Laurie Haleta studied the effectiveness of public speaking courses on decreasing public speaking anxiety.

Participants were enrolled in a standardized basic public speaking course at a midsized Midwestern university. Using James McCroskey's (1970) 34-item Personal Report of Public Speaking Anxiety (PRPSA), students were asked to assess their anxiety before and after completing the class. The results of the assessments indicated that public speaking anxiety can be reduced through a well-designed public speaking class. Compared to the PRPSA's pretest average of 114.83 on the public speaking anxiety (PSA) scale, students reported a PSA reduction average of 12.63 points after completing the class (Hunter, Westwick, & Haleta, 2014). The findings of this study give a strong indication of the effectiveness of basic public speaking courses, especially when used in conjunction with speech lab assistants.

Throughout this textbook, you will examine numerous research articles and their application to the study of public speaking. These comprehensive analyses will prove invaluable to your education as a communication professional. Remember to use these resources whenever the opportunity presents itself.

Public Speaking Teaches Critical Thinking Skills

Critical thinking

The application of the principles of reasoning to your ideas and the ideas of others.

A second reason for studying public speaking is that it teaches **critical thinking**—the application of the principles of reasoning to your ideas and the ideas of others. Generally, teachers of all subjects are concerned that students learn to think critically. Some argue that of all the skills you will learn in college and thereafter, none is more important than critical thinking. *Critical thinking enables you to evaluate your world and make choices based on what you have learned.* It is the intellectual tool necessary to make critical decisions at work (Do I recommend or discourage a new product line?), at home (Should I encourage my children to learn to read before entering kindergarten?), and in your roles as a consumer and citizen (Should I believe what the auto sales representative tells me or do my own independent research?). The critical thinking skills required to answer these questions can be developed, in part, through public speaking.

Critical thinking skills are used in many ways every time you prepare a speech. When choosing a topic, for example, you may decide that, although a speech describing how to fix a car's transmission would be right for a group of auto mechanics, it would be too technical for your public speaking classmates. Because the world's oil reserves are finite, you may decide to persuade your classmates to trade in their old cars for newer, hybrid cars. As everyone in your audience is probably a driver, this topic could be more appropriate.

When researching a speech, you must decide what kinds of supporting material, or evidence, best enable you to express your views and develop your arguments. You use critical thinking skills to build, advance, and assess arguments. And you must make choices about language and expression.

Listener

Perceives through sensory levels and interprets, evaluates, and responds to what he or she hears.

Critical thinking is necessary to the development of an effective speech, and it's important in your role as **listener**. A listener perceives through sensory levels and interprets, evaluates, and responds to what he or she hears. Critical thinking skills are essential as you listen to and evaluate the messages of other speakers. As an audience member, your analysis will focus on several factors, including the purpose and organization of the speech; whether the speaker has accomplished his/her goal to persuade, inform, or speak appropriately on a special occasion; and whether he/she has satisfied your needs as an audience member. As your critical thinking skills develop, you will be able to say effectively what you mean as well as assess another speaker's effectiveness.

Public Speaking Skills Influence Career and Community Success

A third reason to study public speaking is that your public speaking skills may influence your success in career and community settings. Upward movement in the corporate hierarchy may depend on your ability to speak to groups at business conferences and at public presentations. Public speaking skills are an essential part of most professional interactions, including sales presentations, campaigns for public office, teaching and training programs, presentation of research findings at conventions, employee recruitment campaigns, and awards ceremonies. People who can speak on their feet, are articulate in meetings, and engage in good conversation have clear advantages. People involved in business, politics, religious organizations, and community activities who promote their ideas also promote themselves and what they represent, whether this is their intention or not. Few professionals can avoid public speaking.

In your community, unexpected events may move you into the public arena. For example, in a largely rural region of the Midwest, an international company attempted to acquire scenic land for use as a place to deposit waste materials. Many residents believed this would threaten— if not destroy—much of their rural setting. Citizens left their homes to rally and form a grassroots organization. Through the power of its most effective spokespersons, the organization provided enough resistance to persuade the company to cease its effort to acquire and use the land.

© Lee Snider Photo Images/Shutterstock.com

New York City Council Speaker Melissa Mark-Viverito uses her public speaking skills to promote environmental awareness in her city.

ENGAGING IN COMMUNITY

For many college students coming directly from high school, speaking in front of an audience can be a daunting task (especially when you have little to no experience at your disposal). However, this didn't stop Kimberly Jessica Ramirez Gonzales from telling her life story at TEDxNapaValley's annual Student Speak-Off.

Ramirez Gonzales, a senior at Napa High School, talked about the subject of success, and how people define it. She talked about overcoming alcohol and drug abuse, as well as belonging to a gang (Sweeney, 2016). Ramirez Gonzales is now two years sober, and is credited with forming a support group for Hispanic girls at her school called Girls United. Despite her achievements, however, Ramirez Gonzales stressed that self-accomplishment is not enough. She believes using her own experiences with pain, anguish, and struggle should be used to inspire others.

"Because that's what success is. Use what you've got," said Ramirez Gonzales. "Everyone has something. Everyone. Use that. Help someone. Inspire someone. Save someone. Change someone's life. Success is helping other people."

Kimberly's experience highlights the first of countless ways you can learn how to use public speaking skills to better your community. As you learn about other examples of community engagement in this book, remember Kimberly's words: everyone has something. Combine the information and skills you learn from public speaking with the tools you already have, and reflect on the different ways you personally can engage in community.

Public Speaking Skills Are Key to Leadership

A fourth reason public speaking is valuable is that it is a key to leadership. In his book *The Articulate Executive*, corporate communication consultant Granville Toogood (1996) discusses the relationship between effective speaking and coming across as a leader. He advises, "You've got to be able to share your knowledge and information (perhaps even your vision) with other people. It is not in any job description, but you've got to be a translator (explaining the law or technology to neophytes, for example), a teacher, and, eventually, a leader. The only way you can ever be a leader is to learn to speak effectively" (p. 10).

President Barack Obama emerged as an articulate spokesperson from the U.S. Senate, Hillary Clinton became Secretary of State for the United

States, Steve Jobs made Apple Computers profitable, and since leaving Washington, Colin Powell has traveled the globe giving speeches on leadership from his perspective. Each of these individuals is a leader who demonstrates considerable public speaking skills. A skill all of these leaders possess is the ability to appear before audiences with well-prepared speeches and deliver them with authority, sincerity, enthusiasm, and self-confidence.

Public Speaking Skills Complement Technology

A fifth reason we find public speaking skills important is that they complement technology. Through Internet access, we can access billions of facts, but those facts may not be as impressive without the added human element. Speeches are supported by computer-generated graphics, supporting material is discovered on electronic databases, and images can easily be projected while a speech is being delivered.

Public Speaking Is Part of Our Democratic Tradition

The sixth and most important reason public speaking is valuable is that speaking is part of our democratic tradition. The drive for change often begins with the spoken word. Indeed, from our founding as a nation, and especially since the First Amendment to the U.S. Constitution guaranteed free speech in 1791, public speaking has served an important purpose in our democratic processes and procedures. Citizens have gathered at our nation's capital to listen to abolitionists, suffragettes, and leaders of the civil rights, women's, and gay rights movements. We have witnessed peace marches, Million Man marches, and anti-war protests.

As you speak to your classmates, keep in mind that your speeches are rhetorical opportunities to show your understanding of and commitment to an idea and your ability to communicate your thoughts and feelings to others. If you use your public speaking class as a training ground to develop and refine your skills as a communicator, these learning experiences will serve you well throughout your life. Moreover, the confidence you develop here will allow you to speak forcefully within your community.

Public Speaking and the Communication Process

Communication

The creation of shared meaning through symbolic processes.

Communication is the creation of shared meaning through symbolic processes. You communicate your thoughts and feelings to your audience with the intent of generating knowledge and influencing values, beliefs, attitudes, and actions. Often, your purpose is to reach mutual understanding. As you speak in public, you use the shared symbols of communication to achieve a specific purpose.

The speeches you deliver fall into three general categories: *to inform, to persuade,* and *to entertain*. Sometimes you may want to share information and create a clear understanding with an audience. Other times you may want your audience to change their attitude and/or follow a different course of action. On special occasions, your task may be to entertain, inspire, or celebrate. Each of these three categories is treated in separate chapters to explain fully what is required for success. No matter what type of speech you deliver, your speaking objective is to elicit a response from your audience by sharing meaning with them.

Eight Elements of the Communication Process

The communication process involves at least eight elements: sender, receiver, message, channel, feedback, noise, occasion, and cultural context. These elements are discussed briefly here but they are explored in more detail throughout the book. Models provide insight into how things work and provide a go-to list when things go wrong. (See **Figures 1.1** and **1.2**.)

1. Sender/Receiver

Static variables

Those things that remain stable from speaking situation to speaking situation.

Dynamic variables

Those things that are subject to change.

Each speaker brings something unique to the occasion. As the speaker, you may have an interesting perception of an issue because of static and dynamic variables. Static variables are those things that remain stable from speaking situation to speaking situation. These include biological aspects such as race, sex, and age. Experience and knowledge are also considered static, because one does not change experience, knowledge, health, and personality based on the speaking situation. Dynamic variables are variables that are subject to change. They include decisions you make about a particular speech, word choice, the structure you choose to support your points, and aspects of appearance that are easily changed (clothing, hair, accessories). In your role as a speaker, remember two things:

1   YOUR IMAGE MAKES A STATEMENT. Keep this in mind. The image your audience has of you will be shaped with each comment you make. If you are a member of an athletic team or a frequent performer in plays on campus, your reputation may precede you and determine, in

FIGURE 1.1 Communication Model (Ideal)

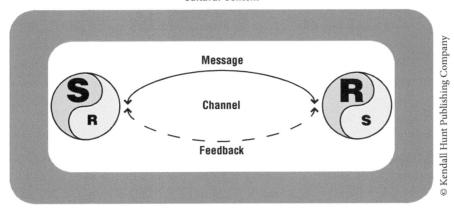

FIGURE 1.2 Communication Model (Actual)

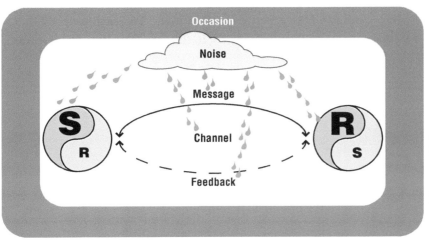

part, how your audience responds. However, speaking in front of the class or from your seat as a member of the audience also plays a role in the construction of an image of you and, as a public speaker, you must deal with your audience's preconceived notions. When you speak, your words and style of delivery communicate your involvement with your topic, and your listeners need only a few moments to pass judgment on your confidence, knowledge, integrity, and skill.

2   THE SPEAKER AND THE AUDIENCE BOTH HAVE NEEDS. The speech is about you *and* your audience. Through the communication exchange,

speakers seek from their audience a response that can satisfy certain needs. Depending on the situation, speakers need to be understood, to have influence, to bring about action, to be liked, or to be respected. For example, a common practice among financial advisers is to invite clients and potential clients to evening seminars where informative sales presentations are made. The speakers' needs are to produce results in the sale of their financial products and services. After the presentation, the successful speaker will meet the needs of his/her audience, which in this case involves helping clients meet both immediate and long-term financial needs.

In our model, whether you are speaking or are a member of the audience, you are always playing the dual role of sending and receiving messages. As sender, the speaker initiates the message in public speaking. The impact of the speech is affected by whether the receivers find the speaker to be believable, trustworthy, competent, sincere, and confident.

For example, if an audience is receiving a lethal dose of PowerPoint, they will likely send messages of boredom through yawns, murmurs, and possibly nodding off. An effective speaker monitors this audience reaction, or feedback, and adjusts appropriately. In this secondary sense, the sender is also a receiver.

2. Receiver/Sender

In the communication process, the receiver is the target of the message. In public speaking, the receiver is the collection of individuals gathered to hear the speaker. We underscore the primary importance of the receiver or audience in public speaking situations. An effective speaker focuses on having some meaningful impact on our receivers. Listeners (receivers) bring their own frames of reference, which are influenced by the same variables found in the speaker: race, gender, age, health, personality, knowledge, experience, and so on. These variables influence how the audience responds to a speaker's message.

Although audience members may hear every word a speaker says, they can miss shades of meaning or may attribute meanings that have little or nothing to do with the speaker's intent. Because the potential for misunderstanding always exists, it is critical to plan every speech with your audience in mind. In the classroom, use terms and language your classmates can understand and find engaging but not offensive. Use examples that touch their lives.

Both the speaker and members of the audience share the responsibility of achieving mutual understanding. As such, listening as a necessary skill is mentioned frequently throughout our text. Ron Hoff (1998), a consultant and author on making speeches, explains: "By coming to your presentation, by simply showing up, your audience is expressing a need for help, counsel, wisdom, inspiration—maybe even something that can change its life … If truth be told, the audience arrives on the scene with the ardent hope that the presenter knows something that it does not" (p. 9).

Listening to the speaker and interpreting the speaker's message is the receiver's primary role in the communication process. However, receivers also send messages nonverbally while the speaker presents his/her message. They clap, laugh, yawn, talk to each other, text, frown, and smile. All of these behaviors communicate some message to the speaker. The receiver's feedback is relevant, although one should avoid distracting the speaker. The audience may send cues to the speaker that it is time to wrap up, that the speech is funny, or that something is confusing. The receiver is not a passive participant in the communication process.

3. Message

The message is what is communicated by the speaker and perceived by the audience. Public speaking is a meaning-centered process. Theorists have long recognized that *the essence of the message lies not only in what the speaker intends, but also in the meaning ascribed to the message by the listeners.* A speaker may intend to send a certain message, such as knowledge about a movie. But the speaker may also send an unintentional message, such as superiority or a faulty memory. Likewise, a speaker may choose to send a message via YouTube, only to later discover that audiences become bored more easily when watching streaming video.

A fundamental task of the speaker's message is to maximize understanding. Clarity is imperative. You are challenged to make your speech as clear as possible—through your words, lines of reason, and delivery. The message is constructed from your knowledge, feelings, and additional research.

4. Channel

The channel is the medium through which the message is sent. In the previous example, the message was sent from speaker to audience through face-to-face communication. Students could respond nonverbally,

Social media is now one of the major channels to send and receive messages.

© Twin Design/Shutterstock.com

displaying disagreement or agreement and understanding or confusion through their facial expressions and body movement. In our wired and wireless society, a speaker's message can be sent by a variety of channels, including a public address system, radio, TV, the Internet, recordings, the use of smart phones, and text messages.

Despite the improved quality of video, we maintain that the richest channel for communication is still face-to-face. You are in the same room with the speaker, you have the advantage of experiencing the speaker firsthand. You are in a better position to judge the intangible qualities, including the speaker's honesty, ethical stance, commitment to the topic, trustworthiness, and sincerity. Those qualities can be communicated through eye contact, gestures, and the speaker's voice. When you listen to a speech through a less direct channel, your ability to judge these qualities is diminished.

5. Feedback

In the public speaking transaction, feedback refers to the messages the audience sends back to the speaker. Feedback may be immediate or delayed. **Immediate feedback** may include applause, yawns, laughter, verbal comments, and even boos. A speaker may choose to ignore the feedback or he may change his message in response to the feedback. For example, if the audience looks confused, you may want to slow down,

Immediate feedback

Audience response as the speech is performed.

elaborate more fully, or give additional examples. Immediate feedback is difficult for speakers to interpret accurately at first, but with practice, interpreting feedback becomes easier.

Delayed feedback may come in the form of letters, emails, phone calls, formal evaluation, or votes. For example, it was discovered that a politician had plagiarized much of a speech delivered in a local campaign. A report of the incident was noted in the local newspaper, and the politician lightly dismissed his use of someone else's words without acknowledgment. Subsequently, a letter to the editor of the newspaper was sent by an irate citizen. The published letter was a form of delayed feedback.

Delayed feedback
Audience response after the speech is performed.

6. Noise

In an ideal world, noise would not exist. However, the potential for multiple sources of noise exists within every communication transaction. Speakers should not ignore it. Noise is defined as anything that interferes with the communication process. Noise can be physical, physiological, psychological, or semantic in nature.

Physical noise includes anything in the environment that distracts the speaker or listeners. Examples include cell phones going off, the microphone not working well, people talking in class, students kicking chairs or clicking pens, people talking outside the classroom, thunder, noisy cars, heating that kicks on and off, and lights that make buzzing sounds. Physical noise does not actually have to be heard to be considered noise. The classroom may be too cold, the lights may be too dim, the listener may be seated too far from the speaker, or the room may have distracting artwork. Generally, some physical noise always exists and both speaker and listeners are aware of physical noise. To minimize the effects of physical noise, we suggest working to filter it out by staying focused on the message.

Physical noise
Anything in the environment that distracts the speaker or listeners.

Physiological noise occurs when our senses fail us in some way. If we have hearing loss or poor vision, for example, we might become frustrated when we cannot hear or see adequately. Likewise, a speaker may grapple with physiological challenges of stuttering, lisping, or tics beyond their control. Maybe the formation of cataracts has diminished the ability to read note cards in the dim lighting often accompanying public speaking. When our senses fail us, typically they are accompanied by another kind of noise as well, that being psychological. Our mind sends us silent, distracting messages of frustration.

Physiological noise
A result of our senses failing us in some way.

Psychological noise exists in the individual's mind. The speaker could be having a bad day and is not happy to be there or it may be near lunch

Psychological noise
A distraction that exists in an individual's mind.

time and the listeners are thinking about how hungry they are. One listener may be thinking about a fight she just had with her boyfriend, and another listener may be thinking about the project that is due next period. Or, the listener may not like the speaker. Understanding psychological noise is more difficult than understanding physical, physiological, or semantic noise. It is easy to tell that the auditorium is cold or that there is too much noise in the hallway. It is not possible to see or hear what affects people psychologically. Sitting in the same row may be one person who is happy to be there, another who is distracted by relationship problems, and a third who is worried about his or her future career.

Semantic noise

The disconnect between the speaker's words and the listener's interpretation.

Semantic noise refers to a disconnect between the speaker's words and the listener's interpretation. This disconnect may result from the use of inappropriate or offensive words, misunderstanding or misinterpretation, or disagreement on the meaning of words. Your professor may use words you do not know, or you may experience cultural differences. For example, even though Australians, British, and Americans all have English as their native tongue, many words are different and cause confusion.

7. Occasion

The situation for public speaking is often referred to as the *occasion* and is composed of the time, place, event, and traditions that define the moment. Before a speech begins, an audience already has an expectation of what they would like to hear from you. At a recent college commencement ceremony, the usual speakers gave their speeches in the five- to seven-minute range. Then it was time for the invited speaker to present. She spoke for 25 minutes about her background and experience. After about 10 minutes, audience members started shifting in their chairs. After 20 minutes, the audience's annoyance was clear to everyone but the speaker. The invited speaker failed to recognize that the commencement ceremony is an occasion designed to focus on the students graduating, not their stamina. She violated their expectations and lost the listening audience because she did not consider the demands of the occasion carefully.

Physical surroundings help define the speaking occasion. As a speaker, you should know in advance whether you are speaking to five people or several hundred and whether you will be speaking from an elevated platform or from an easy chair surrounded by an audience of listeners also seated in easy chairs. Be aware of the order of your speech in the day's events. Are you the first or last speaker? Is your speech scheduled right before or after lunch? Knowing the circumstances of your speech helps you prepare better to meet the needs of the occasion. For example, if your speech is scheduled at the end of the day, a short speech is more appropriate than a long one.

8. Cultural Context

Every speaking occasion operates within a broader cultural context that affects the entire experience. **Culture** is defined in terms of norms, the rules people follow in their relationships with one another; values, the feelings people share about what is right or wrong, good or bad, desirable or undesirable; customs accepted by the community of institutional practices and expressions; institutions; and language. Culture often determines the common ground between speaker and audience.

As a speaker, one should recognize that cultural differences exist between audiences. Cultural similarities and differences exist not only between nations, but also between co-cultures that exist within our own population. Therefore, adaptation is necessary. A nearby university hired a new president who was familiar with the corporate culture of a large business organization. When he sought to impose standards from the culture with which he was most familiar, there was considerable opposition to his efforts. At a faculty meeting, one exasperated department chair stood up, faced the new president, and declared: "With all due respect for your new position, you need to understand that this is a different culture than the one you have worked in, and what you found to be successful rules there are not going to work here."

An effective speaking style in the United States may not be viewed as such by members of a different culture. If we want to be successful speakers, knowledge of our audience's cultural norms is crucial. Failure to adapt can result in a loss of credibility, and prevent you from achieving the purpose of your speech.

Finally, do not forget that the eight elements of the communication process are also relevant in a mediated situation, such as a video

> **Culture**
>
> The rules people follow in their relationships with one another; values; the feelings people share about what is right or wrong, good or bad, desirable or undesirable; customs accepted by the community of institutional practices and expressions; institutions; and language.

Meetings between international leaders rely heavily on tactful intercultural communication.

© Drop of Light/Shutterstock.com

conference, live streaming of a speech, or recording a speech for later playback. The speaker presenting in a mediated situation needs to create a background conducive to listening, and take care to avoid external noises, such as noises in the hall or construction noise outside. When the channel is mediated, video should be clear, and care should be taken to make sure the speaker can be heard and seen. Taping a speech in your dorm room with all of your "stuff" around can be distracting, just as having a stationary camera might not be effective. We provide more suggestions in our chapter on presentational aids.

Once you understand the communication process and its elements, you are ready to incorporate your analysis of these elements in your first speech. There are five steps you need to follow when developing any speech.

Five Steps for Preparing to Speak

1   Select and narrow an audience-centered topic.
2   Develop content through research and sound support.
3   Draft the introduction, body, and conclusion.
4   Develop the language of the speech with care.
5   Practice!

1. Select and Narrow an Audience-Centered Topic

A difficult task for students beginning the study and practice of public speaking is selecting a topic. You and some of your classmates may already be thinking of possible topics for all your speeches during this term. Some students find a topic within five minutes of hearing about the assignment; for others, it may take weeks of reflection. This section is designed to make topic selection a productive experience for you.

Know the Speaking Assignment

Before considering topics, *know the constraints of the speaking assignment.* In addition to knowing the general purpose, which is addressed shortly, you need to know the following:
•   Time requirements for the speech (3–4 minutes? 4–6 minutes? 5–7 minutes?)
•   Time-frame for preparation (one week? one month? six weeks?)

- Type of source materials acceptable (print? Internet? interviews? personal experience?)
- Timeliness of research (last five years? last 10 years?)
- Number of sources required (three sources? five? eight?)
- Note cards (Can I use note cards? How many?)
- Media (Will a computer be available? PowerPoint? Multimedia possibility? Smart Board?)

Knowing the guidelines for the assignment helps you get started. Whether it's a speech for class, a speech at a fundraiser, or a briefing at work, understanding what is expected of you is the place to begin.

Understand the Audience

As stated throughout our book, public speaking is an audience-centered activity. Your reason for presenting a speech is to communicate your message to others in the clearest, most convincing way. *An effective speaker analyzes and adapts to the audience.* This involves finding out as much as possible about your audience in advance, such as their demographics (age, race, gender, religious affiliation, political affiliation, etc.), their level of knowledge about your topic, and their point of view. Critical thinking skills are valuable here as you determine these parameters.

The initial way to approach your responsibility as an audience-centered speaker is to find out as much as possible about the audience. In the chapter on the speaker–audience connection, we discuss audience analysis in depth. Before you gather research or develop main points you should find out the following:

- What does the audience know about me?
- What does the audience know about my topic?
- What are the audience's views on my topic and purpose?
- How do audience members define themselves as an audience?
- How do the setting and occasion influence my audience?
- What other factors might affect how the audience responds?

Outside the classroom, you may become a spokesperson for an issue, a cause, or an organization. Generally speaking, your audience will have some basic information about you. In college, characteristics such as age, gender, race, and level of education are easily known, but you may need to include relevant background information at the beginning of your speech. For example, if you wanted to talk about the problems associated with children of state and federal prisoners and your father worked in the prison system, it would be helpful to note this as you begin your speech.

The amount of supporting material you include and the extent to which you explain or elaborate are influenced by the expertise or knowledge of your audience. If you are speaking to a group of cardiologists on the need to convince pregnant women to stop smoking, you can assume far greater audience knowledge than if you were to deliver the same message to a group of concerned citizens.

The views of your audience should influence your choice of main points, the supporting material, and the way you develop your speech. Attitudes can be more important than information in determining how your audience responds to a message. It's natural to expect some preconceived attitudes about what you are hoping to accomplish.

Audience members may be present at your speech as a result of how they define themselves at that particular moment. At a city council meeting that addresses housing regulations in your community, you might be with several college students attending as tenants of rental property. At another city council meeting, you might gather with other college students because the council is discussing changing the bar entry age in the city. Though the same people might be in the audience, how you identify or define yourselves differs from situation to situation. In one instance, you and the other college students identify yourselves as renters. In the second situation, you are with college students who are interested in expanded entertainment options.

The setting and occasion are important considerations for any speaker. The speech may take place in an indoor gymnasium or an outdoor stadium. The occasion may be a graduation ceremony or a funeral service. It helps a speaker to plan carefully when she or he learns in advance what the general feeling is about the setting and the occasion for the presentation. Members of a congregation during a Christmas Eve service may start to get restless if a member of the clergy drifts off from the main message and begins talking about old family gatherings when her audience is expecting to hear about the story of the birth of Jesus and what this event means in our present day.

Captive audience

Those who are required to attend.

Voluntary audience

Those who choose to attend.

Remember, it's harder to reach a captive audience (those who are required to attend) than a voluntary audience (those who choose to attend). Students who attend a guest lecture on campus simply to obtain extra credit to boost their grade in a class may feel somewhat indifferent, if not bored, while those who chose to attend because of a keen interest in the speech and speaker will feel differently. As a speaker, you need to obtain some helpful information about audience attitudes toward the setting and occasion that will bring everyone together for the speech.

Many factors influence how an audience responds to a speaker. Are you the first speaker of the day? The last speaker? Are you speaking at a convention in Las Vegas at 8:00 a.m.? Were the participants out late? Are you one of six students to give a speech during a graduation ceremony? If you have knowledge of any factor that may influence your listeners' attentiveness, you can plan in advance ways to increase the likelihood that they will listen carefully. You can shorten the speech, include more vivid examples, and/or work to make your speech even more engaging.

As time goes by, you get to know your classmates and their concerns. Use that information to create interest and engage their attention. Reflect on the six questions identified above and then adapt your topic, language, support, and delivery based on what you decide.

Choose an Appropriate Topic

Some instructors may give you a topic while others may provide strict limitations on what you may speak about. If you are allowed to choose, the best place to begin your search for a topic is *yourself*. When the topic springs from your own interests, personal experience, or work experience, you bring to it the motivation and information necessary for a good speech.

If no ideas come to you when thinking about a speech topic, try the following. Write down two or three broad categories representing subjects of interest to you, and divide the categories into parts. You might begin, for example, with the broad areas of politics and sports. From these general topics useful lists will emerge.

POLITICS
1   Campus politics
2   Political corruption
3   Contemporary political campaign tactics

SPORTS
1   Learning from participation in sports
2   The challenges facing student athletes
3   Why NASCAR races are increasingly popular

As your list of choices grows, you will probably find yourself coming back to the same topic or a variation of it. For example, "Football after college" could be added to "The challenges facing student athletes."

Perhaps your brother played college football and then attempted to join a professional football team. You could talk about his experiences, including successes and failures. Now you have your topic.

While choosing a topic you are familiar with is the best place to begin, carefully consider what your *listeners* might want to hear. You may be an Agriculture Management major who is interested in artificial insemination of chickens. Trust us, most audiences do not want to know! Ask yourself if your topic would create murmurs of interest or gasps of horror. If you lean toward the topic less traveled, can you create a motive for your audience to care? What can you tell them early on to convince them of the importance of your chosen topic? Remember, a topic should fit the speaker and audience.

You may know something about your classmates' interests, backgrounds, or group affiliations. You may want to develop a list of general topics by thinking about your audience. For example, in a college classroom, you might consider one or more of the following:

1 Music
2 Politics
3 Current events
4 Hobbies

Once you've thought about general topics of interest to your audience, you add to the list related possibilities:

1 Music
    • Grammy Awards
    • Country music
    • Musicals
    • *Hamilton*
2 Politics
    • Tea Party
    • Unethical behavior
    • Campaign spending
3 Current events
    • Trouble in Syria
    • Trouble in Somalia
    • Social networking and political action
4 Hobbies
    • Collecting
    • Selling on eBay
    • Video games

Once you've developed a list that your audience may have interest in, you can select a few that might be worth exploring in more depth.

Finally, in addition to selecting topics that *you* have interest in or your *listeners* want to hear, you can work to find a topic through **research**. You could ask friends to brainstorm with you for topics, or you can try looking up topics on the Internet. For example, you could search "current events," "top headlines," "sports," or "politics." Broad topics will lead you to other topics. Following are several possible topics:

- Acupuncture
- Biodiesel fuel
- Cyberspace regulation
- Dream analysis
- Education cuts
- Facebook fraud
- Ghosts
- Home schooling
- Joining organizations
- Minimum wage
- Natural foods
- Organ donation
- Prison reform
- Reincarnation
- Surrogacy
- Teacher competency tests
- Volunteering
- World religions
- Zero-tolerance policies

Do not assume, however, that any topic is relevant. Some topics have been used so often that there is not much left to say in the short amount of time you will have. If you are interested in a topic such as "smoking," think about your approach. Ask yourself, Is this something they have heard hundreds of times before, or is there a new or creative approach I can take? If you cannot think of some new approach, then you might want to delete smoking as a topic. If you have a wealth of information, determine what must be left out. If you know about the background of your audience, you can decide what information is most relevant and how much time should be spent on each point.

Research

The raw material that forms the foundation of your speech.

Determine the General Purpose, Specific Purpose, and Thesis Statement

The time you spend preparing your speech may be of little value if you do not determine what you want your speech to accomplish. Now that you have selected a topic, clarify the general purpose, specific purpose, and thesis statement. How you conceive of each will help you clarify and narrow your topic.

GENERAL PURPOSE. There are three general purposes for speeches:

1 To inform
2 To persuade
3 To entertain or inspire

If you want to explain the differences between classical ballet and modern dance, the general purpose of your speech would be "to inform." If you think having a scooter or bicycle on campus is more beneficial to students and the environment than driving a car, your general purpose would be "to persuade." If you hope to make people laugh after eating a good meal, your general purpose is "to entertain." If you want to motivate your fellow graduates at the commencement ceremony, your general purpose is "to inspire."

Keep in mind, however, that it's difficult to deliver a speech that is *only* informative, *only* persuasive, or *only* entertaining. Often, in the perception of listeners, the purposes may converge or overlap. For example, as a speaker informs her audience about options for eating a healthy breakfast each day, some audience members may interpret her speech as an attempt to persuade them to change their daily behavior.

SPECIFIC PURPOSE. Once the general purpose is set for your speech, determine the specific purpose. This is the precise response you want from your audience. Specific purpose statements should be expressed as an infinitive phrase that includes the general purpose as well as the main thrust of your speech. The specific purpose also identifies who the intended audience is. Here are two examples of specific purposes:

1 To inform the class of differences between the operations of an on-campus political club and an off-campus political party
2 To persuade the Student Senate that requiring all college students to participate in service-learning projects benefits the student, college, and community

Because the specific purpose identifies the audience who will hear your speech, it guides you in speech preparation. A speech on health care reform given before a group of college students should be constructed differently than a speech on the same topic given before an audience of retirees. Obviously, the second audience has a more immediate need for reform than the first group of listeners.

Following are two specific purpose statements written differently. See if you can pick out which is correct.

Steve Jobs, co-founder of Apple Computers, was a master of both persuading and informing in his public presentations.

TOPIC 1A: To persuade my audience that the Federal Drug Administration (FDA) should regulate dietary supplements

TOPIC 1B: To persuade my audience that the FDA should regulate dietary supplements and print more warning labels on prescriptions

TOPIC 2A: To inform my audience of the negative aspects of the Barbie doll

TOPIC 2B: To inform my audience of the positive and negative aspects of the Barbie doll

A specific purpose statement should be written with one goal in mind. With the first topic, "A" is correct. "B" is incorrect, because there are two topics: dietary supplements and warning labels on prescriptions. Also, a specific purpose statement must be clear to all readers. It is possible that "FDA" is not known to all; therefore, it makes sense to spell out the name first and put the initials in parentheses. With the second topic, statement "A" is a persuasive speech that has been falsely identified as an informative speech. With little exception, without presenting both negative and positive aspects, your speech is inherently persuasive.

THESIS STATEMENT. While the general and specific purpose statements set the goals for your speech, the thesis statement, or your core idea, focuses on what you want to say. The thesis statement is the central message you want listeners to take with them. It distills your speech to one sentence, summarizing your main idea. A well-defined thesis is critical to your speech's success. The following examples show how one moves from a topic to a thesis statement.

Topic: Study abroad

General purpose: To inform

Specific purpose: To explain to my class what is involved in the study abroad options available at our university

Thesis statement: Students interested in earning college credit while studying abroad have several options that differ in terms of academic content, location, length of stay, potential number of credit hours, and cost.

Topic: Study abroad

General purpose: To persuade

Specific purpose: To convince my class that studying abroad would be a life-changing experience

Thesis statement: Studying abroad can be a life-changing experience because students gain knowledge in an academic area, face the unfamiliar, and interact with individuals from a different culture.

As you can see, although the topic is "study abroad," there are different aspects of studying abroad that one could address. The above example shows choices for an informative speech and a persuasive speech. A speech with the general purpose to entertain could include humorous examples of the gaffes made while studying in a foreign land.

Remember that your speech has one of three general purposes, which on your outline should be stated in the infinitive. The specific purpose is an infinitive phrase, not a sentence. It should express one goal, not multiple goals. The thesis statement is one idea, and should be stated as one cohesive thought written in one complete sentence.

Demonstrate Ethical Behavior Throughout the Process

A consideration of ethics is important in virtually all aspects of speech development, including, but certainly not limited to, how you approach a topic, where you get information, how you edit or interpret information, word choice, and distinguishing between your own ideas and those that need to be cited. **Plagiarism** involves using another's work, words, or ideas without adequate acknowledgment, according to Plagiarism.org (2011).

Ethics are being discussed within the context of many disciplines, including medicine, psychology, business, and communication. Stories of ethical breaches appear almost daily in the newspapers and online.

Plagiarism
Using another's work, words, or ideas without adequate acknowledgment.

© Drop of Light/Shutterstock.com

Joe Biden saw his 1988 presidential hopes ruined over accusations of plagiarism.

Unethical behavior in many contexts and situations has heightened our sensitivity to the need for honesty from all sources, including public speakers. Use accurate and current information, rely on sound reasoning, and present a speech that is your own, based on your independent research and views. Remember to cite sources and to quote and paraphrase correctly when you present information or ideas that are not your own.

2. Develop Content Through Research and Sound Support

The next step is to research your topic to develop and support your ideas. Each point delivered to an audience should be backed up by research and sound support. Most of your time will be spent on this step.

Research

Now, armed with a focused topic and main points in mind, you are ready to do some research. Before you hit the Internet, though, consider what a time-consuming activity that can be. It is easy to search one topic, check out links to another closely related topic, then follow links to yet another topic, and find yourself engaged in research for an evening but not much closer to preparing your speech. You need a better research plan.

ETHICS MATTER

Hunter is a college student enrolled in a public speaking course at his university. For his first public speaking assignment, Hunter has been assigned an "icebreaker" speech—an informal presentation in front of his classmates over any topic of his choice. Because he is a fan of basketball, Hunter decides to give his presentation on the creation of the National Basketball Association (NBA). Hunter owes much of his knowledge to sportswriters and basketball historians; most of his presentation involves talking about the information researched by these professionals. Although his teacher explicitly stated that students must correctly cite all their sources, Hunter is intimidated by the amount of citations he would need to research. Knowing that his teacher is not a basketball fan, Hunter is confident he can get away with citing only a handful of his sources. Because this presentation is informal and his first, Hunter debates the idea of leaving out the majority of his citations.

QUESTIONS TO CONSIDER:
1. What ethical breaches would Hunter commit by omitting many of his sources?
2. What (if any) are the positive and negative aspects of this approach to public speaking?
3. With regards to the policy of academic honesty, are Hunter's actions more related to plagiarism or collaboration?

Although you *can* begin your research by seeking out some search engine, we encourage you, even with all the technology available to you, to begin with a visit to your college library. If you are taking an online course from a remote location, this is not possible. And clearly, much research is available to students from the comfort of their own computers. However, the library can be a productive resource for research. You can ask experts for advice, and check out books that may not be available online.

Once there, seek out reference librarians and tell them about your assignment, your topic, thesis, and specific purpose. They will likely have some great ideas and resources at their immediate disposal, including search engines and databases. Librarians will help you find even more materials that are both relevant and credible. After you drain the reference librarian of all useful information, look around. Could there be a journal article, newspaper story, book chapter, DVD, or audio track of interest? Quickly scan for the facts, statistics, quotations, and expert testimony that relate to your main points. Be sure to take good notes of the source for all the information you find. You will need to cite sources orally in your speech and may be required to turn in a reference page.

Next in your research plan, consider the benefit of interviewing. Do you know an expert or someone with knowledge or experience on your topic? One student met with a local chiropractor. He outlined his plans for his informative speech and she was enthusiastic. She told the student several funny anecdotes involving cracking and popping, let him borrow an expensive model of the human spine, and gave him a myth-vs.-fact sheet to share with his audience.

One warning: Be careful about the credibility of any information you find, and also watch that you don't lose too much time in the process.

Support Your Ideas

Each point made before an audience should be backed up with reliable supporting information and sound reasoning. For example, if you want to persuade your audience that the sales tax should be used to fund education instead of the real estate tax, concrete evidence will be necessary to support your specific purpose. Later in the book we devote an entire chapter to research and supporting materials, but briefly, we want to point out ways you can provide support.

USE FACTS. One way to provide support is to use facts. Facts are verifiable. They hold more weight than opinions. If your specific purpose was "To demonstrate how political campaigns have changed dramatically over the last several decades," you might include the following facts:

- In 2016 Hillary Clinton established a website and numerous social media accounts (e.g., Facebook, Twitter) that included numerous ways to contribute to her presidential campaign.
- In 2016 Donald Trump used Twitter as his primary communication medium.

These facts support the speaker's claim and show how candidates have attempted to reach the masses over time. Do not forget to cite sources as you provide facts.

PROVIDE STATISTICS. A second form of support involves providing statistics. This can offer strong support to your speech. Statistics inform with numbers, and when they are made relevant and understandable to an audience, statistics can startle and convince.

Keep in mind, however, that your speech should not be a laundry list of statistics. Carefully select only those statistics that you are able to make relevant, interesting, and meaningful. After offering a statistic, summarize what it is intended to demonstrate. Some audience members are easily confused or bored with numbers. By summarizing before you move on, you are less likely to lose them.

ILLUSTRATE USING EXAMPLES. A third form of support is examples that illustrate a point or claim. Illustrations, especially detailed and current ones, clarify points and they may leave a lasting impression on your audience. If the purpose of your speech is "To convince the class that voters are influenced by the Internet," you might use the following illustration:

> The use of computers by members of the general public has increased considerably in recent years. Even my 78-year-old Uncle Elmer and his friends use their computers for gaming, social networking, and word processing. Elmer meets regularly with a group of friends who, like him, have retired after years of working in a nearby assembly plant. As they developed their computer skills, each browsed the Internet more and began to pay attention to political news and advertisements. This led to new insights on issues of interest to the group, and often served as the subject of their informal get-togethers leading up to the election. They reported to their friends and family that what they learned from the Internet influenced how they voted.

This example, along with other forms of support such as facts and statistics, demonstrates to the audience the increasing use and effectiveness of the Internet in political campaigns. As an audience-centered speaker, you want to think of the best way to keep the attention of your audience and provide support that is best suited to them. Chapter 5 elaborates on the use of examples.

INCLUDE TESTIMONY. A fourth form of support is the use of testimony, which involves quoting someone's experience or opinion. Testimony can be a powerful form of support because everyone pays attention to an expert. Courts of law frequently call on the testimony of expert witnesses; televised news programs broadcast the observations of experts on newsworthy stories; and, from time to time, even commercials provide the endorsement of experts rather than celebrities to confirm the reliability of a product or service. So to prove, reinforce, or clarify a point, a public or presentational speaker often quotes or paraphrases statements of a recognized expert on a subject.

CONSTRUCT ANALOGIES. Using analogies is a fifth form of support. This involves making comparisons to clarify or prove a point. Analogies lend support by encouraging listeners to think in a novel way. **Figurative analogies** compare different kinds of things, and **literal analogies** compare similar categories.

If you compare an argument with a sporting event, you are using a figurative analogy, but if you compare one college with another college, you are using a literal analogy. For example, in a speech about studying abroad, a student could use the following figurative analogy.

> Studying abroad is like your first week in college. You're unfamiliar with the environment, you don't know the people around you, and you're not quite sure what to expect. But as the week goes on, you start to make friendships, your environment becomes more comfortable, and you start to get into some kind of predictable routine. Keep in mind, anytime you have a new experience, you'll experience some uncertainty.

Then, the literal analogy:

> Studying abroad is similar to studying at this or any other university. You attend classes and take exams. You have a place to live and dining options. You have to study and you also have free time. The difference is, you're far from home, you aren't familiar with your environment, and people may speak a different language.

Think of support material as adding interest and texture to your speech. Oftentimes, someone from your audience will recall a story, example, or analogy you offered because of its striking nature. We strive not only to be clear and concise, but also to be colorful as speakers, and the color comes from our use of a variety of support materials that engage our listeners.

3. Draft the Introduction, Body, and Conclusion

If you spend days researching your first speech but little time organizing your ideas, the result is likely to be a speech that fails to present your message in a focused way. To be effective, speeches require an easy-to-follow organizational plan that makes it possible for others to receive and

Figurative analogy

Drawing comparisons between things that are distinctly different in an attempt to clarify a concept or persuade.

Literal analogy

Drawing comparisons between things that are similar in an attempt to clarify a concept or persuade.

understand your message. As you will see in future chapters, the logical way to organize your speech is to divide it into three parts: introduction, body, and conclusion.

As you draft your speech, lay it out into the three parts. Construct a comprehensive, full-sentence outline and work to tie the sentences into a coherent whole. Then, reduce these sentences to key words and phrases and transfer them onto speaker's notes, which will serve as your guide when you deliver your speech. A well-thought-out, clearly constructed outline and speaker's notes greatly increase the potential for success. The following paragraphs highlight important aspects to consider as you develop your first speech.

Introduction

The introduction should capture the attention and interest of your audience, establish your credibility as a speaker, and preview your speech. You can accomplish these aims in many ways, such as humorous anecdotes or a dramatic or startling statement. For his informative speech, Jesse started with the following:

> You walk into a bar, sit down, and notice something oddly unfamiliar. Where are the beer taps? Where are the liquor bottles? All you see are fish, tentacles, and an assortment of brightly colored items that are not familiar. You've walked into a sushi bar, my friend.
>
> I fell in love with sushi years ago, and so have millions of other Americans. Sushi has become increasingly popular over the past several years, and it has become a major force in the restaurant industry and culinary arts. My passion with sushi began when I started managing a sushi lounge in downtown Memphis called Bluefin. Throughout my three years at Bluefin, I learned quite a bit about the art form of making sushi. To appreciate sushi, it helps to understand its history, the different styles, and common terms and ingredients associated with sushi.

In his introduction, Jesse captures our attention through his vivid description of the bar. He establishes credibility by noting his work experience. Finally, in his last sentence, he presents a preview statement, which lets his audience know what he intends to cover in the body of his speech. He accomplishes the three goals of an effective introduction.

Body

The body of your speech contains your key ideas and relevant supporting material. It's the most time-consuming aspect of speech development. Frequently, speakers work on the body before the introduction, because gaps in logic or information may be discovered as the body is developed. Main points should flow from the thesis statement in some logical pattern. Chapter 7 discusses organizing and outlining your ideas. You have at least five patterns of organization to consider: chronological, topical, spatial, cause-and-effect, and problem–solution. To help your audience follow your ideas and to avoid a disjointed series of points, the body also makes use of transitions. These are well-crafted statements that let our audience know we are moving on to our next point.

Conclusion

Your concluding remarks have three purposes: (1) to reinforce the message, (2) to summarize the main points, and (3) to provide closure in some way that relates your message to your listeners' lives. We focus briefly on creating closure here. Closure may take the form of a quotation, a statement, or a question that reinforces or even broadens the purpose of your speech. The conclusion of a persuasive speech may also describe the specific actions you want your listeners to take. Jesse accomplished the goals of a conclusion this way:

> Now when you walk into a bar and see all the brightly colored fish and seafood, you have a better idea of what you just walked into. With knowledge of the history of sushi, its different styles, and common terms and ingredients, you can steer your palate in the right direction. I urge even the timid to try sushi, and try it more than once to experience the different flavors, textures, and styles. Sushi is not a fad, and sushi will make its way to your neck of the woods soon enough if it hasn't already. Impress your date with a bit of knowledge when you go to the new trendy sushi spot. I bet you'll look like quite the gourmet.

4. Develop Language and Presentation Aids Carefully

An enthusiastic young woman looked out into the audience of almost 1,500 people on her graduation day and was overwhelmed with the spirit that marked this important occasion. A hush fell over the crowd as she began her address as president of the senior class: "You guys are all terrific! Awesome! This has been an awesome four years for us, right? Like, we have really made it! Wow!" As she proceeded, reflecting on the events of the past four years, her comments were laced with slang that may have been suitable for the coffee shop or gatherings with friends, but not for such a momentous occasion.

The words you choose to convey your message reflect your personality, your attitude toward your subject, occasion, and audience, and your concern for communicating effectively. Words are your primary vehicle for creating meaning. They set forth ideas, spark visions, arouse concerns, elicit emotions, but if not used carefully, produce confusion. The following four guidelines will help you choose your words with care.

Use Plain English

Let simple, direct language convey your message. Your audience should not need an interpreter. You could say "contusion" or "ecchymosis," but most audiences would find the word "bruise" clearer. Also, it's generally best to avoid slang or jargon.

Remember That Writing and Speaking Are Different Activities

While in a written report the terms "edifice," "regulations," and "in the eventuality of" may be acceptable, in public speaking the words, "building," "rules," and "if" are far more effective. Writing, in general, is a more formal process than speaking. While the spoken word should sound more conversational, we still want you to pronounce words correctly and articulately (avoid "I'ma go now" for "I'm going to go now").

Relate Your Language to Your Audience's Level of Knowledge

If you are describing drug testing in professional sports, do not assume your audience understands such terms as "false positives," "chain of custody," and "legal and individual safeguards." If you use unfamiliar terms in your speech, you should define them to keep the message clear.

Recall the audience analysis you have already done and review your words with your intended audience in mind.

Use Language for Specific Effect

Assume you are giving a speech on the plight of America's working poor. Here are two possible introductions:

> INTRODUCTION #1: "Although millions of Americans work a full day, they cannot pay their bills or provide for their families."

> INTRODUCTION #2: "Millions of Americans come home each day, exhausted and covered with a layer of factory filth or kitchen grease. Their backbreaking labor has given them few rewards: They cannot pay their rent, buy shoes for their children, or eat meat more than once a week."

The first example is not incorrect, but it may be ineffective: The second introduction is more powerful. It paints memorable word pictures. Keep your audience in mind as you choose effective language for communicating your ideas.

Be Culturally Sensitive

Inappropriate cultural references do harm to others and should be eliminated from your speech. Besides, there is always a chance that negative remarks will inflame an audience. At the very least, you will lose credibility. Being culturally sensitive in a global sense includes nationality and race. "Arabs" and "Middle Easterners" are nowhere near synonymous terms. Culture can also refer to regions and groups of people. All Democrats are not liberal, and all Republicans are not conservative. People on welfare are not inherently "lazy," just as people from New York City are not

On the campaign trail, 2016 presidential candidate Donald Trump came under fire for what many perceived to be culturally insensitive remarks.

© Andrew Cline/Shutterstock.com

all "brusque." Avoid stereotyping, and avoid making comments about the audience or audience members that may be offensive.

Determine Where to Incorporate Technology and Presentational Aids

You have several decisions to make when it comes to the use of technology. First, not all speeches are enhanced by technology. Some may be too short to warrant its use. Second, PowerPoint should not be the default use of technology. Using PowerPoint to outline the major points of your speech may not be necessary or effective. Third, if you don't have time to practice your speech using the technology, you may be faced with a disastrous series of difficulties. Your flash drive may not work, the setup may not be easy to figure out, and the technology you hope to use may not be available or functioning correctly. Carefully weigh the risks versus the rewards of using technology in this speech.

If you choose to use technology, determine where it will be most effective. For example, in a speech on world population growth, a speaker might begin with a computer-projected image of the current world population count, and at the end of the speech, refer to it again, to show the growth in population over the brief time it took to deliver the speech. In a speech on hurricanes, you may want to show a picture from Hurricane Andrew of a piece of plywood stuck *through* the trunk of a tree (see weathersavvy.com) or a YouTube clip of a hurricane hunter being thrashed by hail.

Using technology could involve something as simple as clicking on a relevant website, using PowerPoint slides, or showing a clip. You might use multiple forms of media, and have music, video, and slides. Whatever you choose, it should enhance your message in some way, and not substitute for content.

5. Rehearse and Deliver Your Speech

How important is practice? Consider what professional speaker and author Bill Bachrach said on the subject: "Practice! Practice by videotaping, audiotaping, or role-playing with friends and colleagues. Be so comfortable with what you are going to say that you don't have to think about it. This frees your thoughts to be totally in tune with your [audience]" (McRae & Brooks, 2004).

Speaking Well with Technology Is an Essential for Excellence

Whatever feelings you have about social media, it's impossible to deny its impact on popular culture. More and more often, companies are using social media platforms to announce, generate buzz, and promote events to the public. Concerts, charity drives, community rallies, and countless other cultural events are being changed by the immediate impact social media can bring to the table. Jamie Michaels, head of brand strategy for Twitter Canada, offers three tips on how to amplify events and attract virtual audiences to your content.

To build momentum, promote a single hashtag.

Focusing on a single hashtag can start the conversation about your event while also serving as an invitation for your virtual audience to join the conversation. It provides a clear designation for your event on social media, and allows countless people across the globe to talk about it.

To ensure consistency, define your social voice prior to creating content.

Think about what you want to be known for as a social media brand. From there, develop a content strategy that can shape your message, communication, and visuals (Michaels, 2016). Remember to ask yourself before any content decision, "does this reflect the brand I'm trying to create?"

To measure the true impact of your social media efforts, use the power of social media analytics.

Platforms like Twitter allow you to gauge your event's performance in real time, thus helping you gain valuable insight into what does (and doesn't) work for your audience. Tools like this can be indispensible when creating a marketing strategy.

Without practicing your speech, it's difficult to know whether the speech flows and the material "works" for you. Sometimes, the outline looks good, and appropriate transitions, main points, and supporting material have been developed, but when you speak aloud, you find that the speech is choppy. You discover your word choice needs tweaking. You may have particularly long words, names of authors, websites, or organizations that you stumble over the first time you try. Practicing reduces such surprises during your speech and, of course, demonstrates to your audience that you are prepared.

Much of what you need to know about practicing is found in the chapter on delivery. The biggest benefit of practicing is that it builds confidence and reduces your nervousness. Keep in mind that practicing allows you to work with your note cards, determine where to pause, and decide when to emphasize certain words and ideas and to think about where it is appropriate to incorporate technology (Welch & Byrne, 2001).

ESSENTIALS FOR EXCELLENCE

In this chapter, you've been given an introduction to the strategies needed to be an effective public speaker. If you spend significant time online, you may be familiar with TED (Technology, Entertainment, Design) Talks. TED is a global set of conferences that specializes in having public speakers spread a wide variety of ideas across the world, often quite effectively. TED head curator Chris Anderson offers several tips on becoming a great public speaker.

A speaker's job is to give, not to take.
Try not to frame your speech as a sales pitch; it makes for terrible presentations. Ask what you are gifting to your audience with your talk.

Slash back your topics to a single big idea and connect every point to that theme.
Don't let yourself or your presentation get distracted. Don't be afraid to cut out things you like if it doesn't help promote what you want your gift to the audience to be (Phillips and Demuro, 2016). Always focus on the subject of your presentation.

Get personal.
People crave a sense of connection with others, whether it's family, friends, or a speaker they are listening to. Connections can come from unexpected places, like fear, humor, or vulnerability (Anderson, 2016). Don't be afraid to share vulnerability with your audience, and remember to park your ego; it's a connection killer.

Start strong, end stronger.
Once you get your audience hooked with a great opening and kept them engaged with your big idea, don't allow your ending to fizzle. Make sure whatever point you end on sticks with your audience long after.

![] WHAT YOU'VE LEARNED:

Now that you have studied this chapter, you will be able to:

1. Explain how public speaking teaches critical thinking skills.
   - Critical thinking skills are used in many ways every time you prepare a speech.
   - When researching a speech, you must decide what kinds of supporting material, or evidence, best enable you to express your views and develop your arguments.
   - Critical thinking skills are essential as you listen to and evaluate the messages of other speakers. As an audience member, your analysis will focus on several factors, including the purpose and organization of the speech; whether the speaker has accomplished his/her goal to persuade, inform, or speak appropriately on a special occasion; and whether he/she has satisfied your needs as an audience member.

2. Understand how technology can complement public speaking.
   - Through the Internet we can access billions of facts, but those facts may not be as impressive without the added human element.
   - Speeches are supported by computer-generated graphics, supporting material is discovered on electronic databases, and images can easily be projected while a speech is being delivered.

3. Identify the purpose and expectations for drafting a speech introduction, body, and conclusion.
   - The introduction should capture the attention and interest of your audience, establish your credibility as a speaker, and preview your speech.
   - The body of your speech contains your key ideas and relevant supporting material; it's the most time-consuming aspect of speech development.
   - Your concluding remarks have three purposes: (1) to reinforce the message, (2) to summarize the main points, and (3) to provide closure in some way that relates your message to your listeners' lives.

Key Terms

captive audience, 22
communication, 11
critical thinking, 8
culture, 19
delayed feedback, 17
dynamic variables, 12

figurative analogy, 33
immediate feedback, 16
listener, 8
literal analogy, 33
physical noise, 17
physiological noise, 17

plagiarism, 28
psychological noise, 17
research, 25
semantic noise, 18
static variables, 12
voluntary audience, 22

Reflect

1 How can public speaking skills help you achieve your personal career goals?
2 Think of some of the major institutions in society, including government, schools, the judicial system, and organized religion. What role do public speakers play in each of these settings and what do you see as their strengths and their weaknesses?
3 Why is it important to consider the elements of occasion and cultural context when developing your speech? How might your approach to convincing people to vote change based on these two elements?
4 What factors should you keep in mind when choosing a topic and framing a purpose for speaking?
5 How do you think your experience doing research at a library differs from that of doing research in your room on your personal computer? What are the benefits and disadvantages of both?
6 Discuss with members of your class the relationships among a speaker's link to a topic, choice of a purpose, amount of information available, and the needs of the audience.

Review Questions

1 A _____ perceives through sensory levels and interprets, evaluates, and responds to what he or she hears.

2 _____ is the creation of shared meaning through symbolic processes.

3 _____ are things that remain stable from speaking situation to speaking situation.

4 _____ are things that are subject to change.

5 _____ refers to audience responses after a speech is performed.

6 _____ involves anything in the environment that distracts the speaker or listeners.

7 _____ is a result of our senses failing us in some way.

8 _____ involves distractions that exist in an individual's mind.

9 _____ is the disconnect between a speaker's words and the listener's interpretation.

10 _____ are the rules people follow in their relationships with one another; values; the feelings people share about what is right or wrong, good or bad, desirable or undesirable; customs accepted by the community of institutional practices and expressions; institutions; and language.

11 _____ is the raw material that forms the foundation of your speech.

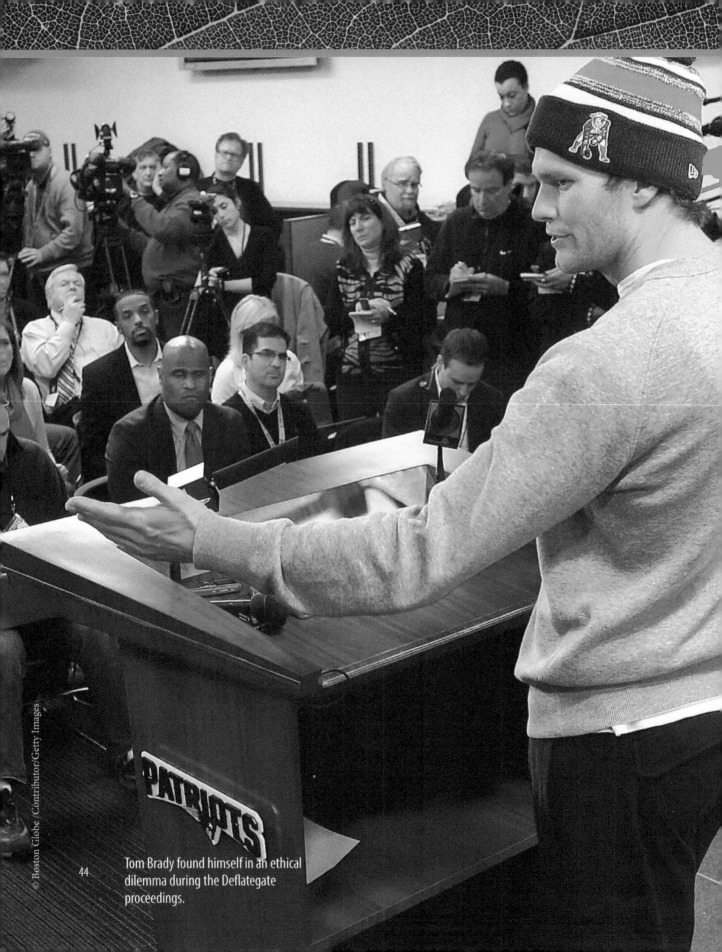

Tom Brady found himself in an ethical
dilemma during the Deflategate
proceedings.

CHAPTER TWO
ETHICS IN PUBLIC SPEAKING

OUTLINE

◼ WHAT YOU'LL LEARN

After studying this chapter, you should be able to:

1. Understand the importance of ethics in public speaking as well as the ethical systems used in public speaking.
2. Know the guidelines for speaking ethically and the principles of ethical speech.
3. Explain ethical information use as well as the steps necessary to become information literate.
4. Know what ethical listening is as well as the responsibilities it entails.

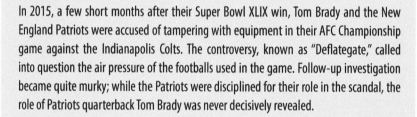

SPEAKING IN CONTEXT

In 2015, a few short months after their Super Bowl XLIX win, Tom Brady and the New England Patriots were accused of tampering with equipment in their AFC Championship game against the Indianapolis Colts. The controversy, known as "Deflategate," called into question the air pressure of the footballs used in the game. Follow-up investigation became quite murky; while the Patriots were disciplined for their role in the scandal, the role of Patriots quarterback Tom Brady was never decisively revealed.

During following press conferences, Tom Brady defended his innocence and dismissed accusations that he acted unethically at any point in his career. "I feel like I've always played within the rules. I would never do anything to break the rules." (Brady, 2015). However, an investigation by independent investigator Ted Wells determined that it was more probable than not that Brady was aware that Patriots locker room attendants had been deflating footballs. Also, Brady had destroyed his cell phone before meeting with Wells for the investigation, which led many to believe the destruction was deliberate to avoid presenting key evidence. Although Brady has maintained that he is innocent and served only a four-game suspension for the controversy, his public image took a significant hit.

During your study of ethics in public speaking, use the previous story as a representation of the link between actions and words. Did Brady speak ethically when questioned about his role in Deflategate? Did any of his actions contradict his words? As you learn how to speak ethically in public, remember that your actions will ultimately reflect how people perceive your ethical standards.

◼ Ethics Matter

The Tom Brady Deflategate example gets us thinking about the importance of ethics in public speaking. How do we know what is right and wrong? Sometimes the answer is obvious: it is wrong to steal or it is right to help others in need. But sometimes the world presents more murky waters. Communication in public situations often calls into play our sense of ethics—the subject of this chapter (Wahl & Maresh-Fuehrer, 2016).

Ethical Systems

When there is no obvious ethically right position, then what? Most commonly, we trust and follow those before us. What has been the traditional response to ethical situations like this one by those we admire? But sometimes tradition becomes a barrier to needed change. Consider change in response to racism, sexism, and other discriminatory practices in employment opportunities. Just because a firm had never hired "someone like that" before was no reason to continue such unethical practices. When common sense and tradition fail us, we might consider how the wisest have historically approached ethical dilemmas. Aristotle suggested discovering the middle ground or "golden mean" between two extreme alternatives. He reasoned that between most choice options lies a happy medium. When faced with an aggressive act, we might respond with fighting or fleeing (extremes) or discussion and negotiation (golden mean). Christianity suggests the "golden rule," that we should treat others as we would like to be treated ourselves if we were on the receiving end of the choice. Philosophers Jeremy Bentham and John Stuart Mill suggested using utilitarianism as a yardstick in ethical decision making. They suggested that the greater good is that which serves the greatest number of people involved.

More recently, the view on ethics is to engage a process to examine situations from multiple perspectives. Having a nuanced and complex view of ethical questions allows for a deeper understanding and stronger responses.

Professional organizations create and adhere to codes of ethics. These codes provide ground rules of ethical behavior within the context of that profession. Such directives as avoiding conflicts of interest, providing accurate and timely information, not abusing power of position for personal gain, preserving confidentiality and due process, honoring all laws and regulations, and operating in a transparent and forthright manner

Ethics

The rules we use to determine good and evil, right and wrong. These rules may be grounded in religious principles, democratic values, codes of conduct, and bases of values derived from a variety of sources.

are good examples. Professional organizations with excellent codes of ethics include the National Communication Association Credo for Ethical Communication (see Figure 2.1); The Code of Ethics of the American Sociological Association; Code of Ethics of the Education Profession of the National Education Association Representative Assembly; Ethical Principles of Psychologists and Code of Conduct from the American Psychological Association; and the Statement on Professional Ethics by The American Association of University Professors.

FIGURE 2.1	National Communication Association Credo for Ethical Communication

**NATIONAL COMMUNICATION ASSOCIATION
CREDO FOR ETHICAL COMMUNICATION**
(Approved by the NCA Legislative Council in 1999)

Questions of right and wrong arise whenever people communicate. Ethical communication is fundamental to responsible thinking, decision making, and the development of relationships and communities within and across contexts, cultures, channels, and media. Moreover, ethical communication enhances human worth and dignity by fostering truthfulness, fairness, responsibility, personal integrity, and respect for self and others. We believe that unethical communication threatens the quality of all communication and consequently the well-being of individuals and the society in which we live. Therefore we, the members of the National Communication Association, endorse and are committed to practicing the following principles of ethical communication:

- We advocate truthfulness, accuracy, honesty, and reason as essential to the integrity of communication.
- We endorse freedom of expression, diversity of perspective, and tolerance of dissent to achieve the informed and responsible decision making fundamental to a civil society.
- We strive to understand and respect other communicators before evaluating and responding to their messages.
- We promote access to communication resources and opportunities as necessary to fulfill human potential and contribute to the well-being of families, communities, and society.
- We promote communication climates of caring and mutual understanding that respect the unique needs and characteristics of individual communicators.
- We condemn communication that degrades individuals and humanity through distortion, intimidation, coercion, and violence, and through the expression of intolerance and hatred.
- We are committed to the courageous expression of personal convictions in pursuit of fairness and justice.
- We advocate sharing information, opinions, and feelings when facing significant choices while also respecting privacy and confidentiality.
- We accept responsibility for the short- and long-term consequences for our own communication and expect the same of others.

Every time you speak, you risk your reputation. Listeners will forgive many things—stumbling over words, awkward gestures, lack of examples—but if you lie or mislead them, they may never trust you again. We believe that common sense, tradition, wisdom, codes, and personal reflection are all parts of being a responsible and ethical person. This chapter will help you become a more ethical speaker, consumer of information, and listener.

Our Freedom of Speech

American citizens have the First Amendment right of freedom of speech. As a U.S. student, you have opportunities to speak before your class about issues of concern. As a citizen, you have the right to support publicly the political party of your choice. As a community resident, you have the right to speak before the city council or the local school board to express agreement or disagreement with their policies.

While we enjoy these freedoms, periodically attempts are made to censor both our public and private lives. As First Amendment lawyer Robert Corn-Revere (2007) notes, the "seemingly simple command" of the First Amendment becomes "exceedingly complex" when applied to electronic media. Openly recruiting for a terrorist group via online blogs, for example, suggests the appropriateness of some censorship. Ultimately, limitations to our freedom of speech are decided by the U.S. Supreme Court. For example, the Supreme Court has ruled that dangerous speech, like shouting "Fire!" in a movie theatre, is not protected by the First Amendment.

First Amendment rights to freedom of speech are rooted in the discussion of ethical issues and dilemmas.

© Cheryl Casey/Shutterstock.com

Freedom of expression comes with responsibility. In class, each speaker has the ethical responsibility to communicate accurately with sound reasoning and to decide what is said and best not said. This responsibility requires a speaker to be truthful without hesitation. As listeners, we are also given a responsibility: to respect the opinions of others, even those different from ours.

In a public speaking class, you have a forum to talk about those things you feel are right or wrong, desirable or undesirable. You can speak out against homelessness or remain silent. Though you might hesitate to speak out, you may be surprised by how many others agree with you. Inherent to a discussion about ethics in public speaking is the concept of values and how they ground us. **Values** are socially shared ideas about what is good, right, and desirable. They propel us to speak and act.

Ethics of Choice

Freedom of expression is balanced by freedom of choice. In most situations, listeners have the ultimate power to listen or to focus elsewhere. It is the freedom to pursue our individual interests that keeps the freedom of speech of others in check. Yet this is not always a perfect system. There are times when the audience is captive and has no real choice, such as your classroom, when an attendance policy may require students to be there. It becomes the ethical responsibility of the speaker and host (your instructor) to monitor more carefully and on occasion censure inappropriate material on behalf of the captive audience. We begin by discussing the connection between ethics and public speaking.

Ethical Speaking

Your integrity is important now. As you progress in a career path, your word becomes increasingly important. People respect and follow those who speak ethically. Let's see how you might preserve or enhance your own ethical high ground when speaking by offering five ethical guidelines for speakers and suggesting common ethical pitfalls worth avoiding.

Values
Socially shared ideas about what is good, right, and desirable; deep-seated abstract judgments about what is important to us.

Guidelines for Speaking Ethically

Protect your Credibility

It may surprise you to learn that the ethics of public speaking has been systematically studied for over 2,000 years. In his text *Rhetoric*, Aristotle discussed the term ethos, meaning "ethical appeal." In a translation by Lane Cooper (1960), we find that Aristotle defined ethos in terms of the intelligence, character, and goodwill a speaker communicates during a speech:

> *Speakers are untrustworthy in what they say or advise from one or more of the following causes. Either through want of intelligence they form wrong opinions; or, while they form correct opinions, their rascality leads them to say what they do not think; or, while intelligent and honest enough, they are not well disposed [to the hearer, audience], and so perchance will fail to advise the best course, though they see it.*

Intrinsic ethos

Ethical appeal found in the actual speech, including such aspects as supporting material, argument flow, and source citation.

Aristotle believed speakers can abuse their ethical relationship with their listeners when they misinterpret information or fail to collect all the information needed to give a complete and fair presentation, and when self-interest leads them to dishonesty and lack of goodwill.

Extrinsic ethos

A speaker's image in the mind of the audience.

Since Aristotle's time, scholars have made the distinction between intrinsic ethos and extrinsic ethos. Whereas **intrinsic ethos** is the ethical appeal found in the actual speech, including such aspects as supporting material, argument flow, and source citation, **extrinsic ethos** is a speaker's image in the mind of the audience. Extrinsic aspects include how knowledgeable, trustworthy, and dynamic the speaker is perceived to be. Both intrinsic and extrinsic ethos contribute to a speaker's credibility. Communication theorists McCroskey and Young (1981) tie credibility to the audience's perception of the speaker as an expert, as a person to trust, and as a person with positive and honest intent. If you are too casual, unprepared, or do not provide support for your claims, your credibility may work against you.

© MidoSemsem/Shutterstock.com

Aristotle's teachings about ethics is foundational to the practice of public speaking.

Engage in Dialogue, not Monologue

Monologic communication

From this perspective, the audience is viewed as an object to be manipulated and, in the process, the speaker displays such qualities as deception, superiority, exploitation, dogmatism, domination, insincerity, pretense, coercion, distrust, and defensiveness.

Dialogic communication

Demonstrates an honest concern for the welfare of the listeners.

Monologic versus dialogic communication tendencies is one clear indicator of ethical speaking. Author-centered speakers engage in **monologic communication** (Johannesen, 1974). They view the audience as an object to be manipulated and freely use deception, superiority, exploitation, dogmatism, domination, insincerity, pretense, coercion, distrust, and defensiveness—all qualities considered unethical.

In contrast, **dialogic communication** entails an honest concern for listeners' interests. This kind of speech "communicates trust, mutual respect and acceptance, open-mindedness, equality, empathy, directness, lack of pretense, and nonmanipulative intent. Although the speaker in dialogue may offer advice or express disagreement, he or she does not aim to psychologically coerce an audience into accepting his/her view. The speaker's aim is one of assisting the audience in making independent, self-determined decisions" (Johannesen, 1971). Whereas monologic speakers attempt to force an issue, dialogic speakers are interested in creating a fair, honest dialog with their audience. The dialogic speaker does have a goal toward which he/she is attempting to move the audience but is concerned with doing so ethically.

Stand by Four Principles of Ethical Speech

As you recognize the importance of your credibility and project firm ethical standards as a speaker, we encourage you to reflect on the following four principles of the ethical speaker (Wallace, 1955).

SEARCH

Search refers to putting forth an effort to learn enough about your topic to speak knowledgeably. As you speak before your class, you are responsible for presenting a message that reflects thorough knowledge of the subject, sensitivity to relevant issues and implications, and awareness that many issues are multifaceted. If your search is half-hearted or incomplete, you might mislead others and cause harm.

JUSTICE

Justice reminds us to select and present facts and opinions openly and fairly. Instead of attempts to distort or conceal evidence, just speakers offer the audience the opportunity to make fair judgments. The Food and Drug

Administration requires the pharmaceutical industry to disclose side-effects of medications in advertising. Daily we hear messages such as "side-effects may include nausea, vomiting, dizziness, rectal leakage..." As a result, the consumer has the opportunity to make a judgment based on known information.

ENGAGING IN COMMUNITY

One of the most powerful uses of ethical public speaking can be applied toward not only helping the less fortunate among us, but also those unable to speak for themselves. Court Appointed Special Advocates For Children, also known as CASA, is a nationwide volunteer group that advocates for children who have been taken out of their homes due to abuse or neglect. Volunteers advocate on the children's behalf in court with the end goal of securing for them a safe, nurturing home.

Michael Patton, a seven-year CASA volunteer, first heard about the CASA of Tom Green County Inc. program through a radio advertisement promoting a volunteer program with a mission to ensure the safety of children in the local community (Walding, 2015). To prospective volunteers, Michael says, "you don't have to be a great public speaker, psychologist, or investigator. You just need to be passionate about working with others to get kids safe." Although initially not a confident public speaker, Michael honed his skills and learned to use effective public speaking strategies to best advocate for the children under his care.

As you think of ways to become engaged in your community, use Michael's example to reflect about how much of an impact public speaking can have when helping others. Appealing to the ethical nature in others can impact a child's life in so many different ways. While studying the connection with ethics and public speaking, remember to be cognizant about the power words and actions can have for the less fortunate.

Public Motivation

A student may be motivated to give an informative speech on the warning signs of dementia. She has reliable information on dementia and her motive is to illuminate a public problem. This is public motivation. In contrast to public motivation are hidden agendas. If she uses fear appeals and biased, one-sided arguments to convince students to sign up for dementia screenings at her clinic because she gets paid per screening, her motivation is hidden and private. Keeping such hidden agendas is unethical behavior.

Hidden agenda

Private motivation for acting in a certain way. This is unethical behavior.

As a speaker, consider whether your motives are personal or reach beyond individual concerns. Ethical speakers reveal personal motives as well as the sources of their information and opinion. Such full disclosure and transparency assists the audience in weighing any special bias, prejudices, and self-centered motivations in a message. Avoid concealing information about your source materials and your own motives because the effectiveness of your message is weakened if they are suspect.

RESPECT FOR DISSENT

Respect for dissent allows for and encourages diversity of argument and opinion. It involves seeing a different point of view as a challenge rather than a threat. It means being open to accepting views different from one's own. This does not mean we have to give in when we disagree. We can still advocate our position while acknowledging that others may be as firm in their opposition to it. Ideally, in a free marketplace of competing ideas, a healthy debate ensures that truth and wisdom are exposed. But we must be willing to listen to competing ideas if we are to gauge their merit.

ETHICS MATTER

Brad works as a public relations consultant for a medical software company. A key aspect of his job is to speak on behalf of hospitals that use his company's products. Recently, a hospital that used his company's software was accused of losing sensitive patient information to hackers. A following investigation found that there was a breach in hospital network security due to negligence from Brad's company. Brad was left with an ethical dilemma: should he publicly defend his employer, or should he defend the hospital that used his company's faulty software? With a press conference rapidly approaching, Brad was torn as to how he should present his position to the public.

QUESTIONS TO CONSIDER:
1. From a purely ethical standpoint, which side should Brad publicly defend?
2. Can you think of any way Brad can ethically defend both his own company and the hospital that used their medical software?
3. What ethical principles does Brad owe his employer in creating a release for the public?

Protect the Common Good

Have you ever watched a commercial and decided you had to have that product? Have you been in church when a minister tells about a needy homeless shelter, and you felt compelled to donate at that moment? Have you heard a message about environmental hazards created by plastic bottles and tossed your next empty bottle of water in the recycle bin? These examples illustrate that speaking is an influential activity.

Speakers travel to campuses across the country to address a wide range of issues related to race, ethnicity, poverty, public health, alcoholism, immigration, and national security, to name a few. Some speakers are recruited by organizations on campus; others advertise their expertise in the hopes of being allowed to speak. These people understand the power of the podium. They know they can inform audiences, they can move them emotionally, or they can move them to act.

Some speakers may have national forums through the media or through their positions, such as members of Congress, the military, or even celebrities. Some abuse that power. As speakers, we strive to be aware that we have the power to persuade and the power to pass on information to others—powers that must be used for the common good.

Speak Truthfully

Whenever you speak before an audience, be certain of your facts. When your listeners realize your facts are wrong, they will trust you less. For

Politicians are charged with protecting the common good of their constituents.

© Joseph Sohm/Shutterstock.com

example, if you give a speech on campus thefts and you blame students for the majority of crimes, when, in fact, most thefts are committed by city residents, you will lose credibility with listeners who know the facts. Here are a few common pitfalls to keep in mind:

Ethical Pitfalls to Avoid

1. Purposeful Ambiguity

When we leave out specific detail, we can paint a misleading picture. Choose words carefully to communicate your point. Realize, for example, that references to "hazing abuses" may conjure images of death and bodily injury to some, while others may think of harmless fraternity pranks. Similarly, choose your supporting materials carefully. Ambiguities often stem from inadequate or sloppy research.

2. Rumors and Innuendos

It is unethical to base your speeches on rumors. Rumors are unproven charges, usually about an individual. By using them as facts, you can tarnish—or ruin—a reputation and convey misleading information to your audience. It is also ethically unacceptable to use innuendo to support a point. Innuendos are veiled lies, hints, or remarks that something is what it is not. Innuendo frequently surfaces in the heat of a strongly contested political race. The exaggerated rhetoric of opponents results in observations ranging from misstatements about events to hints about improprieties in the alleged behavior of the political opponent. An ethical speaker avoids any use of rumor or innuendo when preparing a speech.

Innuendos
Veiled lies, hints, or remarks that something is what it is not.

3. Herd Mentality

Speaking in support of the public good implies a willingness to air a diversity of opinions, even when these opinions are unpopular. According to Roderick Hart (1985), professor of communication, we must "accept boat rocking, protests, and free speech as a necessary and desirable part of [our] tradition" (p. 162). Your goal as a speaker can be to encourage the "ideal of the best ideas rising to the surface of debate" (p. 46). Despite the tradition of free speech in Western society, taking an unpopular stand at the podium is not easy, especially when the speaker faces the threat of repercussions.

4. Hidden Agendas

Joyce is a real estate agent in a community suffering from too few buyers. To attract potential homebuyers, Joyce gives a series of speeches in a nearby city, praising her community. Although much of what she says is true, she also bends facts to make her homes seem more attractive and affordable. For example, she tells her listeners that jobs are available, when, in fact, the job market is weak (the rosy employment figures she used are a decade old). Joyce also mentioned that the community schools are among the top in the state, when, in fact, only one in five is ranked above the state average. If asked, Joyce would offer that her goal is restoring her community to its former economic health and feels justified in this manipulation. She likely would not admit that it is the only way she can sell a house in the declining community. An ethical speaker is transparent while offering the strongest possible legitimate arguments, allowing each listener to evaluate the argument on its merits.

5. Excessive and Inappropriate Emotional Appeals

Some speakers prey on our fears or ignorance and rely heavily on the use of excessive and inappropriate appeals to emotion. In our chapter on persuasive speaking, we examine further the nature of emotional appeals. However, following are four circumstances that create ethical concern.

DECEPTION. Your speech creates a need in your audience through deception and requires an action that will primarily benefit you. For example, it is manipulative and unethical to try to convince a group of parents that the only way their children will succeed in school is to purchase an educational program that is comprehensive in detail, according to the company you represent.

MANIPULATION. This emotional appeal is aimed at taking advantage of those particularly susceptible to manipulation. A bit of channel surfing late at night will bring the viewer to quite a number of infomercials full of emotional appeals to persuade the viewer to purchase expensive programs that are supposed to lead them to considerable wealth, health, or both.

CONFUSION. Emotional appeals are part of a sustained plan to confuse an audience and make them feel insecure and helpless. If, as a community leader, you oppose the effort to establish group homes for developmentally challenged adults by referring repeatedly to the threat these residents pose to the neighborhood children, you leave your listeners feeling vulnerable and frightened. Fear can become so intense that homeowners may dismiss facts and expert opinions that demonstrate developmentally challenged persons are neither violent nor emotionally unstable.

FALLACIES. Instead of relying on facts to convince listeners, the speaker disguises messages and deceives listeners to achieve his or her goal with specific strategies including the following fallacies: name calling, glittering generalities, testimonials, plainfolks, and bandwagoning.

Name calling involves linking a person or group with a negative symbol. In a persuasive speech, if your purpose is to convince your audience that abortion is morally wrong, you would be engaging in name calling if you referred to individuals who support a woman's right to choose as "murderers" and "baby-killers." You may believe these labels are truthful, but they are emotionally charged names that will arouse emotions in your audience, and many listeners may tune you out.

Glittering generalities rely on the audience's emotional responses to values such as home, country, and freedom. Suppose the real issues of a campaign are problems associated with the growing budget deficit, illegal immigration, and dependence on foreign oil. If a candidate avoids these issues and argues for keeping the Ten Commandments in front of courthouses, reciting the pledge of allegiance more often, and amending the Constitution to prevent flag-burning, that particular candidate is likely relying considerably on glittering generalities. Although it is acceptable to talk about these latter concerns, manipulating the audience's response so that critical judgments about major issues are clouded in other areas is unethical.

Testimonials can be both helpful and destructive. People who have had their cholesterol levels improve because of a particular prescription medicine may lead others to success. People who love their hybrid cars may help others make the decision to buy one. However, we are also bombarded by celebrities touting products including shampoo, sports drinks, and phone services because they are paid to do so, not because they have expert or first-hand knowledge of those products.

Fallacies
Appealing to audience emotions to disguise the deficit of the speaker's logic not holding up under scrutiny.

Name calling
Linking a person or group with a negative symbol.

Glittering generalities
Rely on the audience's emotional responses to values such as home, country, and freedom.

Testimonials
Statements testifying to benefits received; can be both helpful and destructive.

© carrie-nelson/Shutterstock.com

Peyton Manning regularly does testimonials for Papa John's pizza, but also owns many of the pizza chain's stores himself.

Plain folks are statements crafted to create false identification with the audience. Be cautious when a speaker tells an audience, "Believe me, because I'm just like you." Speakers who present themselves as "plain folks" may be building an identification with their audience appropriately (something speakers often want to do), or they may be manipulating their listeners. Consider an investment adviser who told his audience of senior citizens

> *One main reason I chose this career path is because my own parents, not unlike you gathered here tonight, did not have the opportunities I am offering you. I discovered that they are struggling in their retirement years to make ends meet on a monthly basis. Like you, they worked hard throughout their careers. However, what was available to them to live on when they left their work was modest.*

This speaker appeared believable, but in fact, his parents retired with considerable funds acquired from owning a successful business for 30 years. The emotional tactic of using plain folks as an emotional appeal was simply to gain sales. It amounts to lying and deception.

Bandwagoning is another unethical method of deception. Often listeners are uncomfortable taking a position no one else supports. Realizing this reluctance, unethical speakers may convince their listeners to support their point of view by telling them that "everyone else" is already involved. As a speaker, try to convince others of the weight of your evidence—not the popularity of your opinion. In the case above, the speaker should not be asking everyone to jump on the bandwagon, but should be explaining to people why a certain course of action is a positive thing.

Bandwagoning

Unethical speakers may convince listeners to support their point of view by telling them that "everyone else" is already involved.

Ethical Information Use

The way we find, use, and credit our sources of information is important to consider in our discussion on ethics as well. Ethical speakers, writers, researchers, and students must develop the skills of information literacy if their work is to be trusted. And when the best, most appropriate information is used, it must be credited appropriately to avoid all appearances of plagiarism. We take a closer look at information literacy and plagiarism next.

Become Information Literate

Certain sources have more credibility than others. If you are researching the need for college students to update vaccinations with booster shots, an article in *The New England Journal of Medicine* or *Science* would be preferable to an article in *Newsweek* or *Time*. Although the latter publications are generally reliable, scientific journals are the better choice for this specific type of information. Wikipedia may be informative, but is generally not considered a reliable source on its own, and your instructor may not approve using it as a source. When collecting supporting material for a speech, you want to determine whether you are reviewing materials from a credible professional or someone who is simply writing a story, creating a web-based commerce site, or ranting in a blog. This is not as difficult as it might seem once you understand all the parts of the process.

Speaking Well with Technology Is an Essential for Excellence

Advances in multimedia technology have made it possible to give public presentations to people without physically being in the same room as them. Many of you will even have classes that take place online, using some type of web software to remain engaged with the professor and other students. One of the more popular platforms currently is Skype, an application that provides video chat and voice call services. Skype is used extensively in both academic and professional contexts. Public speaking expert Matt Abrahams answers several questions about how to speak effectively via video presentations:

How do you prepare differently for a video presentation compared to one delivered in person?
Think about the "theater" of the video. People will see your face clearly, so be conscious of nonverbal facial cues. Practice talking directly to the camera so you can make eye contact (Cebeci, 2013).

What should a presenter via video ask of their audience?
Set expectations before the presentation. Be sure to let your audience know what you will be covering and what their role will be.

> **Are there any types of presentations you should never give via video?**
> *Use common sense as a guide. Ask yourself, if you were part of the presentation's audience, would you be ok receiving it via video?*

Information literacy implies consuming information wisely and appropriately. A handy way to ensure your information literacy is found in the acronym PARTS.

POINT OF VIEW. Recognize whether there is a point of view or bias. Is the information making every attempt at being objective or is it likely biased to serve a special interest? Even if a source claims to be "fair and balanced," you may not be getting an unbiased view from any one reporter of that organization. Discerning the point of view is critical to consuming information intelligently.

AUTHORITY. Consider the credentials of both the author and publisher. Are they recognized as experts and/or leaders in the field? Does the author hold a terminal degree such as Ph.D. or M.D.? Is the publisher a scholarly or reputable news source? The issue of authority is challenging online. The person who is responsible for content on some web pages and blogs is not always clear. In these cases, it is best to look for independent confirmation in other locations to ensure accuracy.

RELIABILITY. Even if the point of view seems unbiased and the source checks out, consider whether you can believe in the accuracy and treatment of the information. Reliability is related to the credibility, or believability, of the source. For example, recent research has shown that there are health benefits to eating chocolate and drinking a glass of red wine each day. Now, if the wine or cocoa industries commissioned those studies, one might question the reliability of the findings. If the science community came to these conclusions after independent tests, the information has greater credibility. An ethical speaker will look for the most recent, authentic, and unbiased information.

TIMELINESS. Timeliness refers to how current the information is. In some cases, information as recent as last year may be outdated. Consider this: If you want to inform your class on the latest technology for diabetes

> **PARTS**
> A mnemonic for building your information literacy through consideration of the point of view, accuracy, reliability, timeliness, and scope of your sources.

management, a simple search may lead you to the insulin pump. However, by probing a little further and finding more recent information, you should find articles about the insulin inhaler, which has more recently hit the market. Bottom line: Evaluate how important recent information is to your topic as you gather information.

SCOPE. Scope refers to the extent of your research. Check to see that your research has both depth and breadth appropriate for the topic and audience. Does the information create an overview or develop a narrow portion of your topic? Who is the information intended for, and is any information too technical or too basic? Is the information appropriate for a college audience?

Our world is changing rapidly. Old facts are often wrong facts, especially in such volatile areas as public safety, science, technology, and even our civil liberties. As you prepare your speech, take into consideration all the PARTS of information literacy. If you find credible evidence that appears to undermine your position, be honest enough to evaluate it fairly and change your position if warranted. Throughout this process, keep in mind your ethical obligation to present accurate information to your listeners.

Plagiarism

We learned in Chapter 1 that plagiarism is using another's work, words, or deeds without adequate acknowledgment. The word plagiarism is derived from the Latin *plagiarius* which means to kidnap, abduct, or take hostage. Here we take a closer look at what plagiarism is and develop four common kinds of plagiarism we see in student work. Unless you invented the information yourself, it needs to be cited and credited to the person(s) who did. Otherwise, you have kidnapped the ideas and committed an act of plagiarism. According to the Merriam-Webster Online Dictionary, to plagiarize means:

- To use [another's production] without crediting the source
- To commit literary theft
- To present as new and original an idea or product derived from an existing source
- To steal and pass off [the ideas or words of another] as one's own

Most institutions of higher learning specify what consequences will accrue to the student who plagiarizes. Plagiarism is unethical, and it can result in academic punishment, public embarrassment, or damage to your career. These consequences underscore the importance of doing your own work and giving credit to sources.

2016 presidential candidate Ben Carson was accused of plagiarism in his 2012 book *America the Beautiful.*

© Albert H. Teich/Shutterstock.com

Plagiarism can be categorized in two subgroups based upon intent of the plagiarizer. Intentional plagiarism takes place when the intent is to deliberately swipe someone's work as a shortcut. A whole industry is built upon this common, unethical practice. Students can purchase whole papers online. Such venders even guarantee their content to be safe from discovery. In response, academic types use increasingly sophisticated software to discover the use of such materials. Paying for papers is the extreme in intentional plagiarizing, but any time you knowingly take or use someone else's work as your own, you are guilty of purposeful, intentional plagiarism. By contrast, unintentional plagiarism occurs by accident. This can happen because individuals do not know better, don't completely understand what constitutes plagiarism, come from a different culture where such practices are acceptable, or think they are crediting the sources they use but do so in an incorrect or incomplete fashion. Unintentional plagiarism is far more common and more easily understood, but still is an unacceptable ethical breach.

We can further understand what it means to plagiarize by considering the most common types of plagiarism. We have already mentioned one—buying a paper—but there are more. Buying, stealing, or borrowing a complete paper or speech, hiring someone to write your work for you, or copying sections from multiple sources and pasting them together into a composite of others' work and calling it yours, are all clearly acts of plagiarism. A less obvious and far more common type of plagiarism is incremental plagiarism. This is when a student selects passages or paragraphs from different print sources and various web sites and assembles them into one paper or speech, but fails to credit the sources of the information used. Such "grip and rip" speech and paper composition is also unethical. What is missing is correctly and consistently crediting the sources for the good ideas being used. In our chapter on supporting material we will explore the best ways to credit sources both orally and in writing.

You may be wondering if citing so many sources in your own work makes it seem less original or somehow not your own. In academic writing, the premium is on integrating thoughts from various sources in new and provocative ways. When you cite others in your work, you are in fact enhancing your own credibility by showing that you have done your research, and you are placing your own work into the context of that broader, global discussion. By citing sources, you are publicly joining an academic discussion that was happening before your work, and will continue beyond you, but may in some ways be influenced or colored by you. When you cite sources in your speeches, your listeners will recognize you as more competent and knowledgeable, which will increase the impact of your message in the minds of your listeners.

Unethical Research and Delivery Practices

After making the commitment to maintain ethical standards as a speaker, you should ensure that your research and speech delivery reflect your commitment. The following questions will help you avoid unethical practices (Johannesen, 1990).

RESEARCH
- Have I used false, fabricated, misrepresented, distorted, or irrelevant evidence to support my arguments or claims?
- Have I intentionally used unsupported, misleading, or illogical reasoning?
- Have I oversimplified complex situations into simplistic either–or, bipolar views or choices?

DELIVERY
- Will I represent myself as informed or as being an "expert" on a subject when I am not?
- Will I deceive my audience by concealing my real purpose, self interest, the group I represent, or my position as an advocate of a viewpoint?
- Will I distort, hide, or misrepresent the number, scope, intensity, or undesirable aspects, consequences, or effects?

SPEAKING EXCELLENCE IN YOUR CAREER

While transitioning from college to the professional workplace, it is still critical to be aware of plagiarism during public speaking presentations (Quintanilla & Wahl, 2016). Researchers Daniel Martin, Asha Rao, and Lloyd Sloan examined the link between academic plagiarism and its connection to potential workplace plagiarism and white-collar crime (Martin, Rao, & Sloan, 2009). The researchers' findings concluded that there are strong relationships between dispositions for plagiarism and overall workplace deviance.

Think about how you practice academic honesty in your career as a college student. Will you apply the same rigorous university standards to your professional workplace? Public speaking, by its nature, can offer very tempting opportunities to plagiarize another's speech to complement your own. However, the consequences for being caught in the act of plagiarism are just as (if not more) severe in the professional workplace than in college. Most professional jobs will require at least some degree of public speaking and presentation. As a professional communicator, remember to always act ethically when preparing your speeches; one instance of plagiarism can ruin your credibility in the workplace.

- Will I use emotional appeals that lack a supporting basis of evidence or reasoning or that would not be accepted if the audience had time to examine the subject themselves?
- Will I pretend certainty where tentativeness and degrees of probability would be more accurate?
- Will I advocate something in which I do not believe myself? (p. 254)

Ethical Listening

We have focused on our ethical responsibilities as speakers and information consumers, but we also have responsibilities as listeners. Because communication is a transactional process, we depend on listeners to receive our messages and help create meaning with us. Some listeners are more ethical in their listening habits and tendencies than others. You will be listening to many speeches and other presentations in this course on public speaking. We encourage you to be an ethical listener.

Listening Responsibilities

It is your responsibility to decide when to tune in or dismiss a message that is being presented to you. As noted earlier, freedom of speech is balanced by freedom of choice. But how do we know what to give our attention to? Simply put, there is an ethical process that assures we as listeners are doing our part. Communication professor and scholar Ernest Bormann and colleagues argue that for the communication process to work effectively listeners should be aware of distractions, check our emotions, and think critically about the message.[1] Let's take a closer look at each of Bormann's suggestions.

BE AWARE OF DISTRACTIONS refers to your ability to overcome distractions including extraneous noise in the environment and the speaker's mannerisms. When we decide the relative worth of a message is low because we don't like the person who is speaking or the way it is being presented, we miss the point of the message. First in our process of ethical listening is to tune in to the message.

CHECK YOUR EMOTIONS acknowledges that we all have an internal world of emotions. Various emotional states ebb and flow within us throughout the day and are influenced by what we perceive within and around us. This is normal. It also poses a challenge. Maintaining emotional control and perspective, not being overly aroused or turned off by emotional appeals, and not allowing emotionally charged past experiences with the topic to distract us are all possible. The key is to maintain an objective distance from the subject and messenger.

THINK CRITICALLY ABOUT THE MESSAGE. Critical thinking is possible only when we have first eliminated distractions and controlled our emotions. Now we are free to focus on the structure of what we are hearing. Particularly helpful here is to discern main points, kinds and quality of support materials, and what logical arguments are being used. If the message itself cannot stand up to your critical thinking, it is ethical to tune out.

Tragedies like the one in Ferguson, Missouri challenge public speakers to control their emotions.

© a katz/Shutterstock.com

Ethical Listening Attitude and Behaviors

As a listener you are a key part of the communication event. You shape how things unfold by your attitudes and actions. If your intent is to get the best, most useful interactions with those you are listening to, you can increase the likelihood by what you do. Adopting an attitude of empathy for the speaker and finding compassion for their situation and interest in their message, even if you suspect you might disagree, communicates that you are interested in dialogue and are open minded. To that empathetic attitude you may add supportive nonverbal behaviors like strong eye-contact, head nods, and a smile. Such cues help ease speakers so they can give you their best. Think about this: when you are speaking to a group, you are most distracted by the person showing open, hostile disagreement or clearly not paying attention at all. When our attitudes and actions either purposefully or accidentally derail someone's message, we are being unethical listeners in the communication interchange.

ESSENTIALS FOR EXCELLENCE

In this chapter, you have learned the strategies necessary to become an ethical public speaker. Placing your education into practice, however, can be daunting for communication professionals. Author James Kudooski offers several practical tips for ethical public speaking.

Show respect for your audience.

One of the most important things you need to learn as a public speaker is showing respect for your audience. It does not show respect to talk down to your audience in relation to their gender, religion, ethnicity, race, educational, or social status. If getting your point across requires making practical examples, avoid using ones that will belittle your audience or harm their reputation (Kudooski, 2014).

Be honest and don't mislead your audience.

Ethics in public speaking demand that you're honest and accurate with the information you present to your audience. Never mislead your audience intentionally, or distort facts to suit your aim. If you are unsure about a piece of information or a fact/statistic, don't use it.

Ensure your objective is ethical.

If the objective of your speech is to motivate people to get involved in harmful or illegal activities, then you are not observing the ethics of public speaking. Remember to constantly reflect over your message, and ensure that what you are asking of the audience is never malicious or self-serving.

WHAT YOU'VE LEARNED:

Now that you have studied this chapter, you will be able to:

1. Understand the importance of ethics in public speaking as well as the ethical systems used in public speaking.
   - As you progress in a career path, your word becomes increasingly important. People respect and follow those who speak ethically.
   - The view on ethics is to engage a process to examine situations from multiple perspectives.
   - Every time you speak, you risk your reputation. Listeners will forgive many things—stumbling over words, awkward gestures, lack of examples—but if you lie or mislead them, they may never trust you again.
2. Know the guidelines for speaking ethically and the principles of ethical speech.
   - Protect your credibility; Aristotle believed speakers can abuse their ethical relationship with their listeners when they misinterpret information or fail to collect all the information needed to give a complete and fair presentation.
   - Dialogic communication entails an honest concern for listeners' interests. This kind of speech communicates trust, mutual respect and acceptance, open-mindedness, equality, empathy, directness, lack of pretense, and nonmanipulative intent.
   - As speakers, we strive to be aware that we have the power to persuade and the power to pass on information to others—powers that must be used for the common good.
3. Explain ethical information use as well as the steps necessary to become information literate.
   - When collecting supporting material for a speech, you want to determine whether you are reviewing materials from a credible professional or someone who is simply writing a story, creating a web-based commerce site, or ranting in a blog.
   - Plagiarism involves using another's work, words, or deeds without adequate acknowledgment; avoiding this is key to being information literate.
   - Never deceive your audience by concealing your real purpose, self interest, or your position as an advocate of a viewpoint.
4. Know what ethical listening is as well as the responsibilities it entails.
   - Being aware of distractions refers to your ability to overcome distractions including extraneous noise in the environment and the speaker's mannerisms.
   - Checking your emotions acknowledges that we all have an internal world of emotions.
   - Thinking critically about the message is only possible when we have first eliminated distractions and controlled our emotions.

Key Terms

Ethics, 47
Values, 50
Intrinsic ethos, 51
Extrinsic ethos, 51
Monologic communication, 52

Dialogic communication, 52
Hidden agenda, 53
Innuendos, 56
Fallacies, 58
Name calling, 58

Glittering generalities, 58
Testimonials, 58
PARTS, 61
Plain folks, 59
Bandwagoning, 59

Reflect

1   What are some examples of freedom of speech having ethical consequences? How do we temper our ability to speak freely with being respectful and fair to others?
2   How do you view the relationship between ethics and credibility? Do you believe that Aristotle's notion of credibility and ethics is still applicable today?
3   In recent times, how would you describe the respect for dissent in U.S. public debates? How important is recognizing dissent in public debates?
4   The chapter briefly discusses the importance of being information literate. How could being information illiterate reflect poorly on your ethical communication?
5   In your personal experience, have you ever failed to check your emotions when communicating a point to someone else? How did this pitfall affect your communication dynamic?

Review Questions

1   _____ are the rules we use to determine good and evil, right and wrong.

2   _____ are socially shared ideas about what is good, right, and desirable.

3   _____ is an ethical appeal found in the actual speech, including such aspects as supporting material, argument flow, and source citation.

4   _____ is a speaker's image in the mind of the audience.

5   _____ demonstrates an honest concern for the welfare of the listeners.

6   _____ are veiled lies, hints, or remarks that something is what it is not.

7   _____ involves linking a person or group with a negative symbol.

8   _____ rely on the audience's emotional responses to values such as home, country, and freedom.

9   _____ involves convincing listeners to support a point of view by telling them that "everyone else" is already involved.

Endnote

[1] Bormann, E. G., Howell, W. S., Nichols, R. G., and Shipiro, G. L., (1969). Symbolic convergence theory. *Journal of Communication*, 35.

Dave Chappelle has been open about the use of code-switching his communication throughout his career.

CHAPTER THREE

BEING AUDIENCE-CENTERED

◾ WHAT YOU'LL LEARN

After studying this chapter, you should be able to:

1. Know how to analyze your audience and tailor your speech to their wants, needs, and interests.
2. Understand the best practices for obtaining audience information and tailoring your presentation to their expectations.
3. Speak with confidence, use humor effectively (and appropriately), and create a personalized experience for your audience.
4. Learn how to adjust your message as you present it, and also encourage participation from your audience.

SPEAKING IN CONTEXT

When being audience-centered, it's important to speak with your audience in a way that they can recognize and relate to. For example, the way a politician delivers a speech in Texas could be drastically different from the same speech delivered to residents of New York. Radio host Jennifer Guerra identifies this type of public communication as "code switching" (Guerra, 2014). Code switching involves alternating between two or more languages (or language varieties) in the context of communication.

Guerra notes several different celebrities who admit to utilizing code switching. Several years ago when comedian Dave Chappelle was interviewed on *Inside the Actors Studio*, he discussed the code switching African-Americans practice among their community and the professional environment. "Every black American is bilingual. We speak street vernacular and we speak job interview. There's a certain way I gotta speak to have access...." (Guerra, 2014).

Code switching is a dynamic, constantly evolving skill; there is no empirically "correct" way to apply it. The ability to switch codes to adapt to your audience is something that comes with observation and practice. Alter your communication too strongly, and you risk coming off as insincere or even insulting to your audience. What is important is that you keep your own voice while still being able to relate to your audience.

As you study more about the importance of being audience-centered, remember to think reflexively about your presentation. Practice code switching before your speech and then place yourself in the audience's shoes; would you perceive your speaking to be authentic and sincere? Also, remember the importance of ethics in public speaking. The goal is not to shamelessly pander to your audience, but to educate and motivate them to a course of action.

Whether in a large auditorium, a corporate boardroom, or a classroom, audiences are usually self-centered. Listeners want to know "What's in it for me?" That is, they want to understand what they can learn from a speech or how they can take action that will, in some way, enhance their lives. If you show your audience you understand their needs and help them achieve their goals, they will want to listen. Being audience-centered and adapting to their needs are critical factors in creating effective presentations. These two concepts are the focus of this chapter.

Audience-centered

Showing your audience you understand their needs and want to help them achieve their goals.

Adapting

Making your speech fit the audience's needs.

Know Your Audience

How do you prepare and deliver a speech that will mean enough to your audience to capture their attention and convince them to listen? Begin by learning as much as you can about your listeners so you can identify and focus on their concerns.

Audience-Centeredness

Making your intended audience central in your message formation will result in a stronger, more tailored speech that resonates with your listeners. This is desirable because you can feel and respond positively to the energy and enthusiasm that a receptive and captivated audience exudes. In essence, if you are audience-centered, both you and your audience benefit greatly.

© Joseph Sohm/Shutterstock.com

Favreau's slogan, "Yes we can," was an effective tool for President Obama's presidential campaign.

Early in your speech, telling your audience what's in it for them and letting them know they were front and center in your mind as you worked on your message is a great way to help establish your credibility, common ground, and build their interest in your topic. Knowing what your audience needs is the first step to being audience-centered.

Audience Analysis

You need not be a presidential speechwriter to understand your audience. All speakers can create a sketch of their listeners by analyzing them in terms of key demographic and psychographic characteristics.

Demographics include age, gender, race and ethnicity, education/knowledge, group affiliation, occupational group, socioeconomic status, religious background, political affiliation, and geographic identifiers. Depending on your general and specific purposes, certain demographics may be more important than others for any given speech.

Demographic Analysis

You need to craft a good fit between the various aspects of your speech, such as supporting material, thesis, and main points, and your audience's characteristics. Depending on the speaking situation, ascertaining demographics may or may not be easily accomplished. Following are 10 key demographics you should strive to identify.

1   AGE. Try to determine the age of your audience and if there is a large or a small variation in age. Examples and stories you provide need to relate to your audience. Think about how you might foster a feeling of inclusion among all ages present. Ask yourself, "How does my age potentially impact my audience's perceptions of me?" Perhaps certain stereotypes exist based solely on their assessment of your age. If you believe your age may influence their response to you, reflect on how you might make these assumptions work in your favor instead of against you.

When taking into consideration your age and the age(s) of your audience, we suggest the following:
- Avoid assumptions about the average age of your audience.
- Focus on your speech, not your age.
- Avoid dating yourself with references or language.

Demographics

Age, gender, race and ethnicity, education/knowledge, group affiliation, occupational group, socioeconomic status, religious background, political affiliation, and geographic identifiers of listeners.

2   GENDER. Consider the composition of your next audience. Is it mixed or is there a majority of males or females? Also, while we do not identify sexual orientation as one of the 10 demographics, it is closely related. Every audience will likely contain members who are gay, lesbian, bisexual, or transgendered. Maintaining this awareness by using sensitive and inclusive language and examples goes a long way toward fostering common ground, inclusiveness, and a more positive response your message.

Avoid unfairly categorizing or stereotyping members of the audience. For example, airlines no longer have "stewardesses," but "flight attendants." Departments on college and university campuses are no longer headed by a "chairman" but rather by a "chair" or a "chairperson." For the most part, speakers should avoid relying on the masculine pronoun and find ways to include men *and* women in their audiences.

3   RACE AND ETHNICITY. Long ago, the image of the United States as a melting pot gave way to the image of a rainbow of diversity—an image in which African Americans, Hispanics, Asians, Greeks, Arabs, and Europeans define themselves by their racial and ethnic ties as well as by their ties to the United States. Within this diversity are cultural beliefs and traditions that may be different from your own (Wahl & Scholl, 2014).

Hurricane Katrina was one of the worst natural disasters in U.S. history, and polarized the nation regarding race relations.

As you develop your speech, we ask that you avoid invoking stereotypes related to race, ethnicity, or nationality, even if these groups are not present in your audience. Even when couched in humor, such comments are deeply offensive and unethical. Appreciation of different people and ways can help you avoid several critical errors in your speech. Any of these gaffes will surely compromise the connection you are trying to create.

Understand also that ethnocentrism, which is the belief that one's own culture is superior to other cultures, comes into play when we express a bias for the way we do things. Unfortunately, some or many individuals who might be identified as ethnocentric have little experience with other cultures. Therefore, an accurate comparison is difficult to make. A speaker should try to avoid being offensive or unfair by examining his/her language usage as well as the examples, stories, and illustrations he/she is contemplating incorporating into a speech.

4   EDUCATION/KNOWLEDGE. Are the members of your audience high school or college graduates, experts with doctorates in the field, or freshmen taking their first course? Knowing the educational level of your audience will aid in the construction of your message. If you're speaking to elementary students about the *Challenger* explosion, you can safely assume they need to be provided with some historical

The *Challenger* explosion remains the worst space program disaster in U.S. history.

© Everett Historical/Shutterstock.com

background. But to an older group of adults who witnessed the tragedy on television such information would not be necessary.

In addition to determining what type of background information or explanation is needed, another consideration is language. You want to speak *to* your audience, not over their heads or at such a basic level that you sound condescending. We have the following two suggestions that highlight how important it is to analyze your audience's needs:

- **Do not assume that expertise in one area necessarily means expertise in others.** For example, if you are a stockbroker delivering a speech to a group of scientists about investment opportunities, you may have to define the rules that govern even simple stock trades. Although the more educated your audience, the more sophisticated these explanations can be, explanations must still be included for your speech to make sense.
- **Be careful about assuming what your audience knows—and does not know—about technical topics.** Mention a server to people who know nothing about computers, and they may be baffled. Define it for a group of computer experts, and they will wonder why you were asked to speak to them. In both cases, you run the risk of losing your audience; people who are confused or who know much more about a subject may simply stop listening.

5   GROUP AFFILIATION. Listeners may identify themselves as members of formal and informal interest groups. An informal interest group generally doesn't require signing up or paying for membership, or making any type of formal commitment. Examples include YouTube watchers, Starbucks customers, and residents of an inner-city neighborhood. A formal interest group usually requires an official commitment, such as signing a membership form or paying dues. Examples include members of Future Farmers of America, the Chamber of Commerce, or a LISTSERV on alternative treatments for Alzheimer's.

If you are addressing members of the Sierra Club, you can be sure the group has a keen awareness of environmental issues. Similarly, if you are addressing an exercise class at the local Y, you can be sure that physical fitness is a priority of everyone in the room. It is important to know something about the group you are speaking to so you can adapt your message to their interest.

Our main suggestion with regard to group affiliation is to *avoid assuming that all members of a group have similar attitudes.* All members of the International Students group on campus do not share the same set of values or beliefs. They represent different countries with different political and religious practices. Their one shared demographic is that they come from a country outside of the United States. While our two-party system in the United States classifies individuals as either Democratic or Republican, we know that there are conservatives and liberals in both parties. Knowing group affiliation may help us construct our main points and identify appropriate supporting material. We need to take caution, however, and avoid stereotyping the group.

ENGAGING IN COMMUNITY

While giving a motivational speech to Lakeshore Middle School students, John Quinn proudly discussed how he'd spent 20 years in the U.S. Navy. Although his distinguished service record was noteworthy, as was his rank of senior chief petty officer (the second highest rank for enlisted personnel), Quinn had an even more impressive reason for being on that stage. What made his two decades in the armed services so incredible is the fact that Quinn has suffered from cerebral palsy his entire life.

"My brain doesn't send all the signals to my muscles in order for them to function as smoothly as I would like," said Quinn. "I couldn't walk on my own until I was 4 1/2 years old." (Wrege, 2016). Quinn told students how the Navy rejected his first application because he failed the duck walk test. Quinn talked about how he went home and practiced duck walking every day for a year, about how initially he would fall over after about two seconds of practice. By the time he applied for the Navy again, Quinn said he was the best duck walker in the building. After speaking to the entire student body, Quinn spoke to students in a special-needs classroom. He encouraged these students to focus on their abilities, not their disabilities, and never to give up on their dreams (Wrege, 2016). "Just because you do things differently doesn't mean it's wrong," Quinn said. "It's just different."

As you think of ways to engage your audience in ways that help the community, remember John Quinn's struggle. Despite suffering a debilitating neurological disorder, Quinn persevered through sheer effort and will, then shared his experience to help motivate others. Many middle school students are at a point in their life where they are very unsure of themselves, and can be easily discouraged from trying; Quinn's story served as an excellent motivator to that audience.

6 OCCUPATIONAL GROUPS. You may find an occasion that involves speaking to a specific occupational group, such as teachers, students, doctors, lawyers, union representatives, miners, or factory workers.

Occupational information can often tell you a great deal about listeners' attitudes. An audience of physicians may be unwilling to accept proposed legislation that would strengthen a patient's right to choose a personal physician if it also makes it easier for patients to sue for malpractice. A legislative speaker might need to find creative ways to convince the doctors that the new law would be in the best interests of both doctors and patients.

Knowledge of what your listeners do for a living may also tell you the type of vocabulary appropriate for the occasion. If you are addressing a group of newspaper editors, you can use terms common to the newspaper business without bothering to define them. Do not use job-related jargon indiscriminately; rather, use it to your advantage.

When conducting your audience analysis, try to determine what your listeners do for a living. The speaking occasion often makes this clear. You may be invited by a group of home builders to speak about the dangers of radon, or a group of insurance agents may ask you to talk about the weather conditions associated with hurricanes. Knowing the occupations of your audience may lead you to decide not only what type of information to include, but what specific statistics, examples, or illustrations would be most effective for the particular group.

Our suggestion regarding occupational groups is to *avoid too little analysis or too much analysis of the importance of occupational affiliation to your audience members.* When you ask people to describe themselves, what is the first thing they say? It might be "I'm a white female," "I'm a gay activist," "I'm the mother of four young children," or "I'm a lawyer." Some people *define* themselves by their occupation; others view their jobs as a way to feed a family and maintain a reasonable lifestyle. By determining how important the occupational group characteristic is to your audience, you can create an on-target message that meets their needs.

7   Socioeconomic status. Depending on the situation, it may be difficult to determine whether members of your audience earn more than $100,000 a year or less than $30,000. However, this demographic characteristic may influence how you develop your speech and create common ground with your audience.

We suggest you be *mindful of your audience's financial status while framing your message.* Giving a speech linking high credit card debt to filing for bankruptcy would need to be adapted to an audience that has no debt. However, those facing financial ruin do not need to hear a "holier-than-thou" lecture on the dangers of credit card debt.

8   RELIGIOUS BACKGROUND. Speakers seldom intend to offend their audiences. However, when it comes to religion, speakers can offend unwittingly. Please consider that *religious beliefs may also define moral attitudes.* When speaking on issues such as abortion, premarital sex, birth control, gay marriage, and the death penalty, we risk alienating our audience. By no means are we suggesting you avoid such topics. However, failing to acknowledge and address the religious beliefs of your listeners when your speech concerns a sensitive topic sets up barriers to communication that may be difficult to overcome.

So, what do you do if you are religious? What if your comments are framed in that specific moral attitude? Explaining your frame of reference and personal biases is ethical and builds rapport, even with those who don't share your convictions. Audiences expect and respect honesty. One student handled her religious frame of reference directly: "Now I am a Christian, and the in-vitro procedure I received was in a Catholic hospital. I understand there are many other ways to look at the ethics of my decision, but I want to put that aside for now and focus only on the process." Where possible, remove stumbling blocks for your audience by being forthright and truthful about your own religious convictions while also communicating tolerance and open-mindedness to other perspectives.

9   POLITICAL AFFILIATION. In an election year, our interest in political affiliation is heightened. Whether you self-identify as a Libertarian, a mainstream Democrat or Republican, a member of the Tea Party, or an Independent, political affiliation may influence how you respond to a given speaker. If you are fundraising for the homeless, you will probably give a different speech to a group with liberal beliefs than to a group of conservatives.

10 GEOGRAPHIC IDENTIFIERS. We have a variety of ways to discuss geographic identifiers. One is directional differences, such as north/south or east/west. Think how an audience composed largely of people from the Deep South might vary from an audience of individuals from the Northwest. A second geographic identifier is upstate versus downstate. For example, Illinois is divided into two general areas, Chicago and Downstate (everything south of Chicago). This also

alludes to the geographic identifier of urban versus rural. You may have an audience that lives in the same community, or you may have an audience that represents a number of communities. A third geographic identifier relates to terrain, such as living near mountains, lakes, oceans, or, as one of your authors describes herself, living near corn and bean fields and being a "flatlander."

Your authors suggest that understanding geographical identifiers as well as *focusing your message as much as possible on geographical areas of concern will enhance your message's impact and your credibility with your audience.* You may need to adapt your message to accommodate not only differences in language, speech rate, and references, but also specific interests and issues.

ETHICS MATTER

Dave is a public relations liaison for a local politician's office. Recently, Dave's boss has been trying to gain support for a "brighten the streets" initiative. The proposal would use taxpayer money to pay for new streetlights to be placed in the downtown area of the city, in theory to decrease crime and vandalism. However, an article from the local paper published an independent study asserting there would be no statistically relevant decrease in crime from this measure. Also, a rival politician revealed that the work would be contracted to a company that Dave's boss owns.

For damage control, Dave has been instructed to find dirt on the rival politician for his boss to use in his next public appearance. Although the accusations levied against his boss are accurate, Dave is torn between loyalty to his employer and loyalty to his fellow constituents. With days left to decide, Dave ponders the ethical dilemma in front of him.

QUESTIONS TO CONSIDER:
1. Is there a way for Dave to defend the initiative without misleading the public?
2. Would it be ethical for Dave to reframe the initiative in a way that people support, even if his boss still profits from the measure?
3. When adapting your presentation and becoming audience-centered, is it okay to omit critical information if your audience doesn't like it?

Psychographic Analysis

Psychographics refer to the behaviors, attitudes, beliefs, and values of your listeners. Although an analysis of demographic characteristics will give

Psychographics

Refer to the behaviors, attitudes, beliefs, and values of your listeners.

you some clue as to how your listeners are likely to respond to your speech, it will not tell you anything about the speaking occasion, why people have come together as an audience, how they feel about your topic, or about you as a speaker. This information emerges from the second stage of analysis—psychographics—and centers on the speaking situation specifically.

BEHAVIORS. Your lifestyle choices say something about you. Do you walk, bike, drive, or take public transportation to work? Perhaps you avoid driving because walking and biking are "greener" and viewed as healthier. If you choose to be a city dweller who lives in a 22nd-story studio apartment, you probably have less inclination to experience nature than if you opt to live on a 50-acre farm in Vermont. If you put in 12-hour days at the office, your career is probably more important to you than if you choose to work part-time. Behavioral choices are linked to the attitudes, beliefs, and values of your listeners.

Attitudes
Predispositions to act in a particular way that influences our response to objects, events, and situations.

Attitudes, beliefs, and values. Attitudes are predispositions to act in a particular way that influences our response to objects, events, and situations. Attitudes tend to be long lasting, but can change under pressure. They are often, but not always, related to behavior. If I like vegetables, I am likely to bring a vegetable tray to a party. If I don't like big business, I'm less likely to shop at Walmart. Someone who doesn't care about the environment is less likely to recycle.

Green energy such as these solar panels has become an important issue to a large audience in the United States.

© chuyuss/Shutterstock.com

Beliefs represent a mental and emotional acceptance of information. They are judgments about the truth or the probability that a statement is correct. Beliefs are formed from experience and learning; they are based on what we perceive to be accurate. To be an effective speaker, you must analyze the beliefs of your audience in the context of your message. For example, if you are dealing with people who believe that working hard is the only way to get ahead, you will have trouble convincing them to take time off between semesters. Your best hope is to persuade them that time off will make them more productive and goal directed when they return. By citing authorities and providing examples of other students who have successfully followed this course, you have a chance of changing their mind-set.

Values are deep-seated abstract judgments about what is important to us. According to Rokeach's (1968) seminal work, we have both terminal and instrumental values. *Terminal values* are those we would like to achieve within our lifetime. These include national security, family security, equality, and freedom. *Instrumental values* help us achieve the terminal values, such as intellect, ambition, self-control, responsibility, and independence. Values separate the worthwhile from the worthless and determine what we consider moral, desirable, important, beautiful, and worth living or dying for.

An audience of concerned students that values the importance of education might express this value in the belief that "a college education should be available to all qualified students" and the attitude that "the state legislature should pass a tuition reduction plan for every state college." If you address this audience, you can use this attitude as the basis for your plea that students picket the state capitol in support of the tuition reduction plan. Understanding your listeners' attitudes, beliefs, and values helps you put your message in the most effective terms.

Beliefs

Represent a mental and emotional acceptance of information. They are judgments about the truth or the probability that a statement is correct.

Values

Socially shared ideas about what is good, right, and desirable; deep-seated abstract judgments about what is important to us.

Adapting to Different Audiences and Situations

Throughout this chapter and this textbook, you will read the words "it may" or "it might," or "perhaps." We are equivocal because audiences behave differently and have different expectations depending on their characteristics *and* the context or situation. An effective speaker adapts his/her message based on audience characteristics, both demographic and psychographic, and the situation that brings the audience together. A politician may give a speech in New York City, then tweak it before appearing at a gathering in America's heartland. Adapting a speech may be easy or difficult. In your public speaking class, it is important to keep in mind that your teacher is part of the audience. As such, you might need to make a few minor changes to be inclusive.

At a funeral, we know the mood is somber, but depending on the person being remembered and the individuals congregated, there may also be smiles and laughter. The circumstances may call for fond memory of a person's idiosyncrasies, or in case of a tragic death, laughter may be inappropriate. Also, if seven people are giving eulogies, then each one should be relatively brief, but if only two or three are speaking, more time can be allotted to each person. At a political rally, a speech given to an audience that has just seen its candidate soundly defeated would sound different than a speech given by someone on behalf of the winning candidate.

Interest Level and Expectations

Discovering the interest level in your topic and your audience's expectations helps you adapt to your audience. Interest level often determines audience response. High school seniors are more likely than high school freshmen to listen when someone from the financial aid office at the local college discusses scholarships, grants, and financial aid possibilities. People who fly frequently are less likely to pay attention to the flight attendant's description of safety procedures than individuals who fly less often. We tend to pay attention to things that are timely and that we know will affect us.

Presidential campaigners such as Donald Trump rely greatly on experts to supply them with voter information.

© Christopher Halloran/Shutterstock.com

Experienced and successful professionals who speak frequently to audiences around the country collect information that will tell them who their listeners are and what they want and expect from their presentations. Robert Waterman Jr., coauthor of the successful book *In Search of Excellence*, indicates he spends a day or two before a speech observing his corporate audience at work. What he learns helps him address the specific concerns of his listeners (Kiechel, 1987). Waterman achieved success as a professional speaker in part because he assumed little about the characteristics of his prospective audience. To analyze an audience, questionnaires, observation, and interviews are techniques that can be used successfully.

Accessing Audience Information

To adapt our message to a particular audience within a specific situation, we need to gather information. Three ways to access your audience's demographic and psychographic characteristics as well as their interest level and expectations include creating a questionnaire, observing, and interviewing.

Using a Questionnaire

Public opinion polls are an American tradition, especially around election time. Just about anything is up for analysis, from views on candidates to opinions on foreign policy to ice cream preferences and brand recognition.

A questionnaire can determine the specific demographic characteristics of your listeners as well as their perceptions of you and your topic. It can also tell you how much knowledge your listeners have about your topic and the focus they would prefer in your speech.

By surveying all your classmates, sampling every fourth person in your dorm, or emailing selected members of your audience to ask them questions, you can find out information about your audience in advance. These methods are simple and effective. In addition, and depending on the age of your intended audience, online survey creation and response tabulation companies like SurveyMonkey.com now make it easier to poll a group of people via the Internet.

The first step in using a questionnaire is to design specific questions that are likely to get you the information you need. Three basic types of questions are most helpful to public speakers: fixed-alternative questions, scale questions, and open-ended questions (Churchill, 1983).

Fixed-alternative questions limit responses to specific choices, yielding valuable information about such demographic factors as age,

Fixed-alternative questions

Limit responses to several choices, yielding valuable information about such demographic factors as age, education, and income.

education, and income. Fixed-alternative questions can offer many responses, or they can offer only two alternatives, such as yes/no questions. Following is an example of a fixed-alternative question focusing on attitudes:

Do you think all professional athletes should be universally tested for performance-enhancing drugs and steroids? (Choose one)

Professional athletes should be carefully tested for performance-enhancing drugs and steroids.

Professional athletes in selected sports should be tested for performance-enhancing drugs and steroids.

Professional athletes should never be required to be tested for performance-enhancing drugs and steroids.

No opinion.

This type of question is easy to answer, tabulate, and analyze. These questions yield standardized responses. For example, it would be more difficult to ask people, "How many times a week do you eat out?" without supplying possible responses, because you may receive answers like "regularly," "rarely," "every day," and "twice a day." Interpreting these answers is more difficult.

Fixed alternative questions avoid confusion. When asking for marital status, consider providing specific choices. Do not ask marital status if it is irrelevant to your topic.

What is your marital status?
Single
Widowed
Married
Divorced

Scale questions

A type of fixed-alternative question that asks people to respond to questions set up along a continuum.

The disadvantage of using fixed-alternative questions is that it may force people to respond to a question when they are uncertain or have no opinion, especially if you fail to include "no opinion" as a possible response.

Scale questions are a type of fixed-alternative question that asks people to respond to questions set up along a continuum. For example:

How often do you vote?
Always   Regularly   Sometimes   Seldom   Never

If you develop a continuum that can be used repeatedly, several issues can be addressed quickly. For example, you can ask people to use the same scale to tell you how frequently they vote in presidential elections, congressional elections, state elections, and local elections. The disadvantage of the scale question is that it is difficult to get in-depth information about a topic.

In an **open-ended question**, audience members can respond however they wish. For example:

How do you feel about a 12-month school year for K–12 students?

In response to this question about extending the school year, one person may write, "Keep the school year as it is," while another may suggest a workable plan for extending the year. Because the responses to open-ended questions are so different, they can be difficult to analyze. The advantage to these questions is that they allow you to probe for details and you give respondents the opportunity to tell you what is on their minds. Here are some guidelines for constructing usable questions.

Open-ended question
Audience members can respond however they wish

Guidelines for Survey Questions

Avoid leading questions. Try not to lead people to the response you desire through the wording of your question. Here are two examples of leading questions:

> Do you feel stricter handgun legislation would stop the wanton *killing* of innocent people?

> Do you believe able-bodied men who are *too lazy* to work should be eligible for welfare?

These questions should be reworded. For example, "Do you support stricter handgun legislation?" is no longer a leading question.

Avoid ambiguity. When you use words that can be interpreted in different ways, you reduce the value of a question. For example:

How often do you drink alcohol?
Frequently   Occasionally   Sometimes   Never

In this case one person's "sometimes" may be another person's "occasionally." To avoid ambiguity, rephrase the possible responses to more useful fixed-alternatives:

How often do you drink alcohol?
More than once a week
At least once a month
Less than twice every six months
Never

Ask everyone the same questions. Because variations in the wording of questions can change responses, always ask questions in the same way. Do not ask one person, "Under what circumstances would you consider enlisting in the Army?" and another, "If the United States were attacked by a foreign nation, would you consider joining the Army?" Both of these questions relate to enlisting in the military, but the first one is an open question while the second is a closed question. The answers you receive to the first question have much more information value than the second, which could be answered "yes" or "no." If you do not ask people the same questions, your results may be inaccurate.

Be aware of time constraints. Although questionnaires can help you determine interest, attitudes, and knowledge level, they also take time. If your instructor allows you to pass out a questionnaire in class, make sure it takes only a few minutes to complete. Make it brief and clear. Ask only what is necessary and make sure the format fits your purpose. Even if there is no structured time in class for a survey, you can still catch students between classes, during group work in class, and by email. Any time spent getting to know your audience helps ensure you are audience-centered.

Observe and Interview

You may find that the best way to gather information about a prospective audience is to assume the role of an observer. If you want to persuade your classmates to use reusable bottles, you might watch over a few weeks to see how many students in your class have throw-away (or recyclable) bottles, and how many are bringing reusable bottles to class. Then you could ask students who bring reusable bottles to class how long they've been using reusable bottles and why they do it. You could also interview students who bring recyclable bottles to class to ascertain their attitudes.

If you want to persuade your audience to get more involved with issues on campus, you might attend a student government meeting to see how many students attend (other than those *in* student government), and what types of issues are brought forth. Then you could interview members of the group as well as audience members to find their perceptions of student involvement on campus.

The information you gather from observing and interviewing is likely to be richer if you adopt a less formal style than you used in a traditional audience analysis questionnaire to gather information about your speech topic.

Speaking Well with Technology Is an Essential for Excellence

Have you ever been on a social media site and encountered a "bot"? Perhaps you receive a chat message on Facebook from a cute girl or boy, and they ask you several questions before requesting personal information. How long did your interaction last before you realized the person you were speaking to was not another person? Bots are computer programs that generally perform highly repetitive operations, usually to extract some type of information from you (email addresses, passwords, financial information, etc.). However, one communication professional is putting bots to work—to help her find a job.

"She fell into tech because of her love for creating and building," EstherBot says. "That's even how I came to be. Because it's 2016 and bots are everyyywhere!" (Melendez, 2016).

EstherBot is a creation from product marketer Esther Crawford. Crawford says she decided to create the bot to answer questions about her career history, educational background, and other interests. The bot, which can communicate through Facebook Messenger or text messages, crafts its responses with all-caps keywords, which indicate subjects the bot is capable of talking about. Crawford notes that the bot does not understand complete sentences or open-ended questions; it only understands the keywords it provides. According to Crawford, the goal is to have a medium that can automatically answer questions about professional experiences and culture fit that job recruiters often have. It is important to note that Crawford is not a trained software engineer; she was able to build the program with almost no coding using the Smooch bot-crafting platform.

"I wanted to use a bot to tell the story of how I got from having a master's in international relations to being a product marketer for startups," she says. "I've been fascinated by the emerging messaging and, specifically, bot space, and I felt like with my career and what I've done, I could just kind of merge those things together through the bot." (Melendez, 2016).

Creating the Speaker–Audience Connection

It takes only seconds for listeners to tune out your message. Convince your audience your message has value by centering your message on your listeners and adapting your message to that specific audience and situation. The following suggestions will help you build the type of audience connection that leads to the message being understood and well received.

Get to the Point Quickly

First impressions count. What you say in the first few minutes is critical. Tell your listeners how you can help them first, not last. If you save your suggestions to the end, it may be that no one is listening. Experienced speakers try to make connections with their listeners as they open their speeches. For example, here is how one CEO addressed falling sales to his employees, "Good afternoon. Sales are down. Profits are gone. What's next? Jobs. I want to see all of you here again next month, but that may not happen. Let me explain how we got here and what we can do." With an opening like that, you can bet the CEO had the full attention of all employees present.

Have Confidence: They Want to Hear Your Speech

It happens frequently: Speakers with relatively little knowledge about a subject are asked to speak to a group of experts on that subject. An educator may talk to a group of athletes about intercollegiate sports. A lawyer may talk to a group of doctors about the doctor–patient relationship. When you feel your listeners know more than you do about your topic, realize they have invited you for a reason. In most cases, they want your opinion. Despite their knowledge, you have a perspective they find interesting. Athletes may want to learn how the college sports program is viewed by a professor, and doctors want to hear a lawyer's opinion about malpractice. Simply acknowledging your audience's education or intelligence and mentioning your contribution may be a unique approach, and also may help create a bond of mutual respect.

Be of the People, Not Above the People

We do not want to listen to speakers who consider themselves more accomplished, smarter, or more sophisticated than we are. If speakers convey even a hint of superiority, listeners may tune them out.

For example, one of the world's richest men and founder of Facebook, Mark Zuckerberg, demonstrated that he is "of the people" when he gave a speech to a graduating class…of a *middle* school! When Facebook moved its operation to Menlo Park, California in 2011, Zuckerberg reached out to his new neighborhood by speaking to students and parents at Belle Haven Middle School. Wearing jeans and a t-shirt at the outdoor ceremony, Zuckerberg presented informally a message that was clearly developed for that particular audience.

> "…I just want to share with you guys a few things that I've learned today that I think have enabled me and the people I work with to not succumb to the attitude of 'I can't.' And those things are that everything that is worth doing is actually pretty hard and takes a lot of work. That's one. The second is that you should focus on building great friendships and people that you trust because those really matter. And the third is just do what you love."

Billionaire Mark Zuckerberg appears relaxed and informal when presenting to certain audiences.

Rather than focus on his wealth, or brag about his accomplishments, he constructed a message that made him appear to be an ordinary guy with a meaningful message for the graduates.

Use Humor

Humor can help you connect with your audience and help them think of you as approachable rather than remote. Opening your speech with something that makes people smile or laugh can put both you and your listeners at ease. Subject and self-deprecating humor play well; insulting your audience does not. Effective humor should be related in some way to the subject of your speech, your audience, or the occasion. So, starting

© catwalker/Shutterstock.com

with a joke that is wholly unrelated to your topic is inappropriate. Also, remember that some of us have difficulty being funny. Others of us do not gauge the audience well. In either of these cases, attempts at humor may end up falling flat or offending. So be careful: Useless or ineffective humor can damage your credibility and hurt your connection with your audience. Yet, when well executed, humor is a powerful tool in your speaker arsenal.

SPEAKING EXCELLENCE IN YOUR CAREER

Being audience-centered can be challenging for new communication professionals. With hurdles such as speaking anxiety, audience apathy, and general lack of experience, it can be difficult for speakers to connect with their audience in a meaningful way. It has been well established that humor is an effective tool for gaining rapport with an audience, but many students have issues with using humor effectively (and appropriately). Researcher Adam Sharples from the University of Alabama seeks to connect the scholarship of humor to the practice of after-dinner speaking.

Through applying theories of humor to the practice of After-Dinner Speaking (ADS), Sharples examined the effectiveness of scholarly researched humor in crafting well-received speeches. His findings indicated that studies of humor in classical and contemporary scholarship provide useful frameworks for the construction of ADS (Sharples, 2014). Classical theories of rhetoric offered by Cicero, Quintilian, and Aristotle exemplify the use of humor to advance argument in public speeches. Sharples posits that, as individuals with the power of speech, we must challenge ourselves to use the rhetoric of humor to create connections between theory, research, and presentation. As you continue your progress in becoming more audience-centered, remember the connection that reason and humor share in order to create more effective presentations.

Get Personal

Connections can be made by linking yourself directly to the group you are addressing and by referring to your audience with the pronoun "you" rather than the third-person "they." The word "you" inserts your listeners into the middle of your presentation and makes it clear that you are focusing attention on them.

Content is another way to make it personal. Stories, anecdotes, and examples from your own experience are generally appreciated. But keep in mind, there is too much of a good thing where self-disclosure is concerned. Abide by this rule: If you are not comfortable with it being put in the headlines of the local paper, leave it out of your speech.

Encourage Participation

When you invite the listeners to participate in your speech, they become partners in the event. One of the author's friends, a first-degree black belt in karate, gave a motivational speech to a group of college women at a state university in Michigan. At the beginning of her speech, and to the excitement of the crowd, she broke several boards. She talked about her childhood, her lack of self-esteem, and her struggle to become a well-adjusted businesswoman. She used the phrase "I can succeed" several times during her speech and encouraged her audience to join in with her. By the end of her speech, the group, standing, invigorated, and excited, shouted with her, "I can succeed!"

Another way to involve your listeners is to choose a member of your audience to take part in your talk—have the volunteer help you with a demonstration, do some role-playing—and the rest of the group will feel like one of their own is up there at the podium. Involve the entire audience and they will hang on your every word. While adding participation takes time away from your speaking, it is well worth the investment. And, like using humor, you will find it also lightens the mood and sets a favorable tone.

Examine Other Situational Characteristics

When planning your speech, other situational characteristics need to be considered, including time of day, size of audience, and size of room.

Room size is important because it influences how loudly you must speak and determines whether you need a microphone. As a student, you will probably be speaking in a classroom. But in other speaking situations, you may find yourself in a convention hall, a small office, or an outdoor setting where only the lineup of chairs determines the size of the speaking space.

If you are delivering an after-dinner speech in your own dining room to 10 members of your reading group, you do not have to worry about projecting your voice to the back row of a large room. If, on the other hand, you are delivering a commencement address in your college auditorium to a thousand graduates, you will need to use a microphone. And keep in mind, proper microphone technique takes practice, preferably in the auditorium in which you will speak.

Learn as You Go

Discovering what your audience thought of your speech can help you give a better speech next time. Realizing the importance of feedback, some professional speakers hand out post-speech questionnaires designed to find out where they succeeded and where they failed to meet audience needs. At workshops, feedback is often provided through questionnaires that can be turned in at the end or at any time during the event. When you are the speaker, you may choose to interview someone, distribute questionnaires randomly to a dozen people, or even ask the entire audience to provide feedback.

Valuable information often emerges from audience feedback, which enables speakers to adjust their presentation for the next occasion. For example, let's assume you delivered a speech to a civic organization on the increasing problem of drunk boating. You handed out questionnaires to the entire audience after your message. Results indicated that your audience would have preferred fewer statistics and more concrete suggestions for combating the problem. In addition, one listener offered a good way to make current laws more easily understood, a suggestion you may incorporate into your next presentation.

Finding out what your audience thought may be simple. In your public speaking class, your fellow classmates may give you immediate, written feedback. In other situations, especially if you are running a workshop or seminar, you may want to hand out a written questionnaire at the end of your speech and ask listeners to return it at a later time. Online survey tools (e.g., SurveyMonkey) are free and can provide rich feedback for you after your speech. Here are four questions you might ask:

1 Did the speech answer your questions about the topic? If not, what questions remain?
2 How can you apply the information you learned in the presentation to your own situation?
3 What part of the presentation was most helpful? Least helpful?
4 How could the presentation have better met your needs?

To encourage an honest and complete response, indicate in the instructions that people do not have to offer their names in the questionnaire. Remember that the goal of feedback is improvement, not ego gratification. Focus on positive feedback as much as possible and take negative comments as areas for growth.

Your ability to create and maintain a strong connection with your audience is helped by a clear understanding of their demographics and psychographics. Using this information will set you on track for an exceptional experience, for you *and* your audience.

ESSENTIALS FOR EXCELLENCE

In this chapter, you have learned the skills necessary to become more audience-centered. As you use the knowledge gained from this chapter, remember that there is always room to grow as an effective speaker. Dr. Michelle Mazur, CEO of Communication Rebel and author of *Speak Up for Your Business*, offers essential advice for building rapport with your audience.

Delve deep into the audience's psyche.
Many speakers make the mistake of preparing for presentations by getting on the computer, firing up PowerPoint, and typing; the audience is their last concern. Answer three questions to dive into the audience's mind:

1. *What do they already know about the topic?*
2. *What misconceptions do they have about your message?*
3. *What areas of your message will they likely resist?*

Addressing these questions will let the audience know you care about them and that their point of view matters to you (Mazur, 2015).

Activate action.
Many audience members listen to a presentation and think, "Fascinating. But now what?" Even if your content is good and the stories persuasive, you need to tell the audience what to do with all this new information. Every point in your speech should have an action the audience can take that moves them closer to the premise of the presentation.

Invite interaction.
As you create your presentation, think strategically about how to involve your audience (Mazur, 2015). Tell a story they can empathize with, so they feel like a part of the story. The more the audience feels involved with your presentation, the more memorable and valuable the message is.

WHAT YOU'VE LEARNED:

Now that you have studied the chapter, you should be able to:

1. Know how to analyze your audience and tailor your speech to their wants, needs, and interests.
    - Being audience-centered and adapting to the audience's needs are critical factors in creating effective presentations.
    - Demographics include age, gender, race and ethnicity, education/knowledge, group affiliation, occupational group, socioeconomic status, religious background, political affiliation, and geographic identifiers.
    - Psychographics include lifestyle choices, attitudes, beliefs, and values of your listeners. Information that emerges from demographic and psychographic analyses is the raw material for a successful speaker–audience connection.
2. Understand the best practices for obtaining audience information and tailoring your presentation to their expectations.
    - A questionnaire can determine the specific demographic characteristics of your listeners as well as their perceptions of you and your topic. It can also tell you how much knowledge your listeners have about your topic and the focus they would prefer in your speech.
    - The information you gather from observing and interviewing is likely to be richer if you adopt a less formal style than you used in a traditional audience analysis questionnaire to gather information about your speech topic.
    - One of the best ways to gather information about a prospective audience is to assume the role of an observer. Watch the actions and mannerisms of your audience, and learn what their motivations and expectations are.
3. Speak with confidence, use humor effectively (and appropriately), and create a personalized experience for your audience.
    - Humor can help you connect with your audience and help them think of you as approachable rather than remote. Opening your speech with something that makes people smile or laugh can put both you and your listeners at ease.
    - Remember that some of us have difficulty being funny. Others of us do not gauge the audience well. Try to get as much feedback from your peers as possible before giving a presentation.
    - Be careful; useless or ineffective humor can damage your credibility and hurt your connection with your audience.
4. Learn how to adjust your message as you present it, and also encourage participation from your audience.
    - One way to involve your listeners is to choose a member of your audience to take part in your talk—have the volunteer help you with a demonstration, do some role-playing—and the rest of the group will feel like one of their own is up there at the podium. This can help make the presentation a dynamic experience.
    - Your ability to create and maintain a strong connection with your audience is helped by a clear understanding of their demographics and psychographics. Using this information will set you on track for an exceptional experience, for you and your audience.

Key Terms

adapting, 75	demographics, 76	psychographics, 83
attitudes, 84	ethnocentrism, 78	scale questions, 88
audience-centered, 75	fixed-alternative questions, 87	stereotypes, 78
beliefs, 85	open-ended questions, 89	values, 85

Reflect

1   Why will a speech fail in the absence of audience analysis?
2   What underlying principles should you use to conduct an effective audience analysis?
3   What demographic characteristics does this class have in common? Where does this class differ in terms of demographic characteristics?
4   Why are some demographic characteristics important to the success of your speech in one situation but not so important in another situation?
5   How are behaviors, attitudes, beliefs, and values related to your next speech topic in the minds of your prospective audience members?
6   If you wanted to gather information for your topic from members of your class, what do you think would be the most effective way to get responses? How does your answer differ based on the types of questions you want to ask?

Review Questions

1   _____ involves showing your audience you understand their needs and want to help them achieve their goals.

2   _____ is making your speech fit the audience's needs.

3   _____ are the age, gender, race and ethnicity, education/knowledge, group affiliation, occupational group, socioeconomic status, religious background, political affiliation, and geographic identifiers of listeners.

4   _____ are the lifestyle choices, attitudes, beliefs, and values of your listeners.

5   _____ are related to race, ethnicity, or nationality, even if these groups are not present in your audience.

6   _____ is the belief that one's own culture is superior to other cultures.

7   _____ are predispositions to act in a particular way that influences our response to objects, events, and situations.

8   _____ represent a mental and emotional acceptance of information.

9   _____ are socially shared ideas about what is good, right, and desirable; deep-seated abstract judgments about what is important to us.

10 _____ are questions that limit responses to several choices, yielding valuable information about such demographic factors as age, education, and income.

11 _____ are a type of fixed-alternative question that asks people to respond to questions set up along a continuum.

12 _____ are questions that allow audience members to respond however they wish.

100 Gloria Steinem preaches the importance of being good listeners in her pursuit of gender equality.

CHAPTER**FOUR**
LISTENING AND CRITIQUING SPEECHES

▉ OUTLINE

WHAT YOU'LL LEARN

After studying this chapter, you will be able to:

1. Understand the difference between listening and hearing
2. Know and practice the four stages of listening
3. Utilize the five criteria for evaluating speeches
4. Identify the steps needed to become an active listener

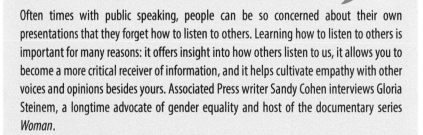

SPEAKING IN CONTEXT

Often times with public speaking, people can be so concerned about their own presentations that they forget how to listen to others. Learning how to listen to others is important for many reasons: it offers insight into how others listen to us, it allows you to become a more critical receiver of information, and it helps cultivate empathy with other voices and opinions besides yours. Associated Press writer Sandy Cohen interviews Gloria Steinem, a longtime advocate of gender equality and host of the documentary series *Woman*.

Woman is a collection of eight short documentaries, all by young female journalists, that each focus on an issue facing women in different regions of the world (Cohen, 2016). The first episode documents the epidemic of rape as a tool of subjugation in the war in Congo. Other episodes look at child brides in Zambia, female guerrilla fighters in Colombia, and mothers in prison in the United States. Cohen asked Ms. Steinem what she hopes her documentaries will accomplish:

"We have to know before we can act," said Steinem, "and the very fact that this is allowing millions of people to have the experience of walking around and talking to people and listening is a step forward in itself." (Steinem, 2016).

As you navigate this chapter and learn the tools needed to become an effective listener, contemplate about your personal experiences in listening closely to others. Many of us are guilty of being so excited to speak our opinions that we block out our communication partners completely. Use the lessons learned in this chapter to train yourself to actively listen to others.

Listening and Public Speaking

Two of the first researchers to study listening, Thomas Lewis and Ralph Nichols (1965), wrote that "effective listening and effective speaking are so closely woven together as to be inseparable" (p. 7). In other words, to discuss speaking without a concurrent discussion of listening is not productive. In Chapter 1, our communication model identifies the Sender/Receiver and the Receiver/Sender elements of the model, noting that sending and receiving are simultaneous activities.

One way to improve your chances of successful public speaking is to approach the process from the listening side—that is, to work at developing better listening skills. These skills are essential for two different but complementary reasons. First, by understanding the needs of your listening audience, you are able to develop and deliver speeches that have the greatest chance of communicating your intended meaning. The earliest Jesuit missionaries made it a point to enter new locations and not speak for six months. Instead, they listened. They recognized the importance of understanding the other person's perspective before attempting to educate.

Second, by understanding the factors affecting listening, you are able to monitor your own listening habits, and more effectively evaluate and criticize the speeches of others, including your classmates. A direct relationship exists between the quality of your listening and the quality of your speaking. *Good speakers use what they hear to analyze and respond to the needs of their audience, and to present information in a way that promotes communication.*

This chapter focuses on listening. First we discuss some basics about listening, including defining it, noting how much time we spend listening, and discussing memory and retention. Then we provide reasons people stop listening, the four stages of listening, and tips for better listening. Next, we discuss evaluating speeches, and provide some guidance to help you critique your classmates' speeches. We end the chapter by considering how you might use technology to provide feedback to your classmates after their speeches.

Listening and Other Communication Activities

Listening and hearing are not synonymous. Hearing is the physical ability to receive sounds. The Hearing Loss Association of America reports

Hearing
The physical ability to receive sounds.

that, according to recent statistics from the National Center for Health, 36 million Americans, or 17 percent, have some hearing loss. This places hearing loss third in a line of public health issues behind heart disease and arthritis (www.hearingloss.org). So, we shouldn't assume our entire audience will hear us.

Listening is an active process that includes hearing. Many definitions of listening exist, but the International Listening Association defines **listening** as "the attending, receiving, interpreting, and responding to messages presented aurally" (ILA White Pages, 2009). This is a complex process with multiple elements, and *responding* is part of the listening process. We discuss the four stages of listening later in the chapter. But before we discuss listening in further depth, it makes sense to see what role listening plays in our everyday communication.

Listening
The attending, receiving, interpreting, and responding to messages presented aurally.

The Importance of Good Listening Skills

We listen for entertainment (watching movies, listening to Spotify, watching YouTube), and we listen to our professors to understand and retain material, and ultimately succeed in class. We listen to friends so we may develop and maintain relationships. Listening impacts our lives in many ways and, specifically, is related to success. Following are a few interesting research results:

- Listening has been identified as one of the top skills employers seek in entry-level employees as well as those being promoted (AICPA, 2005).
- Listening is tied to effective leadership (Johnson & Bechler, 1998).
- Confident individuals listen to message content better than individuals who lack confidence (Clark, 1989).
- Listening and nonverbal communication training significantly influence multicultural sensitivity (Timm & Schroeder, 2000).
- Effective listening is associated with school success (Bommelje, Houston, & Smither, 2003).
- Individual performance in an organization is found to be directly related to listening ability or perceived listening effectiveness (Haas & Arnold, 1995).

These brief research results demonstrate some of the long-term positive effects of listening. Good listening may lead to success in school, help a person get a job, result in positive evaluations at work, help with promotion, and result in successful leadership and being seen as culturally sensitive. A poor listener may suffer several consequences in both the long and short term. Among some short-term effects are:

- Missing a message (not paying attention)
- Not understanding a message
- Taking extra time for repetition or clarification
- Creating a negative impression by appearing disinterested
- Being unable to participate fully in conversations

Each of these short-term effects may not seem terribly problematic, but in the long term damage to personal and professional relationships can occur. For example, when we perceive someone is not listening to us or seems disinterested, it may hurt our feelings or we may feel defensive. We may choose not to communicate with that person again.

On a professional level, we want to make sure the messages we send are interpreted correctly. Having to clarify, repeat, or rephrase takes time away from the task at hand. Poor listeners at the organizational level may get chastised for their ineffective behavior, or colleagues may start to avoid working with someone who does not listen well.

So far, we have shown that listening is an important activity that consumes a large portion of our waking hours. We also know that good listeners are valued in the professional world, and poor listening leads to a variety of negative personal and professional consequences. Next, we provide an opportunity for you to think about your own listening habits.

Reflect on How You Listen

Many people think of listening as a simple task that involves sitting back and giving the speaker your attention. As public speakers, we hope our message and meaning will be understood. As audience members, we may have other things on our minds—distractions, preconceived notions, prejudices, misunderstandings, and stress—and the message we receive may be much different from the message sent. As the interchange in **Table 4.1** suggests, listening is more complicated than it appears. The speaker (left column) is an elderly activist from the 1960s. The listener (right column) is a 24-year-old student.

TABLE 4.1

SPEAKER	LISTENER
Around 40 years ago, at about this time of year, I—and a whole lot of other committed students—spent a solid week—day and night—in the offices of our college president. Needless to say, we hadn't been invited.	*Here I am again—listening to another speaker who says he stormed his college administration building in the 60s. This must be a popular topic on the college speaking circuit. Maybe this guy will be different from the other three middle-aged radicals I heard, but I doubt it . . . The least they could do is turn up the air conditioning. It's so hot I can hardly breathe, let alone listen.*
We were protesters and proud of it. We were there because we believed the Vietnam War was wrong. We were there because we believed racism was wrong. We were there because we believed that women should be given the same opportunities as men.	*These guys keep talking about how they know the way and how we're all wrong . . . I wonder what he does for a living. I'll bet he hasn't saved any lives lately or helped the poor. He probably earns big bucks giving speeches on campus telling us how horrible we are . . . He looks like he spends a lot of time cultivating his hippie look. He must have slept in those clothes for a week. These guys all look the same.*
Were we victorious? For about 10 years, I thought so. Then something happened. The signs were subtle at first. Haircuts got shorter. The preppie look replaced torn jeans. Business became the major of choice.	*He's harping on the same old issues. Doesn't he know the Vietnam War is ancient history; that women have more opportunities than they ever had—I wish I could earn as much as Rachael Ray . . . I guess I'll have a pizza for dinner. I should have eaten before I came. I'm really hungry.*
In a flash—it happened that quickly—these subtle changes became a way of life. Campus life, as I knew it, disappeared. Revolution and concern for the oppressed were out, and conservatism and concern for the self were in.	*Of course we're interested in business. Maybe he had a rich father who paid his tuition, but I don't. I need to earn money when I graduate so I can pay back my student loans.*
From the point of view of someone who has seen both sides—the radical, tumultuous 60s and the calm, money-oriented 80s, 90s, and the new century—students of today are really 40-year-olds in 20-year-old bodies. They are conservative to the core at the only time of life when they can choose to live free. I am here to help you see how wrong you are.	*Who does he think he is—calling us conservatives. I'm not a bigot. When I believe something is wrong, I fight to change it—like when I protested against ethnic cleansing overseas and flag burning right here.* *I wonder when he'll finish. I've got to get back to the dorm to study for my marketing exam. He just goes on and on about the same old things.*

The civil rights movement challenged the United States to listen to the plight of minorities, and remains active today.

© Rena Schild/Shutterstock.com

Reasons Audiences Stop Listening

You may see a bit of yourself in the speaker–listener example. Maybe this internal dialogue does not occur frequently, but most of us experience this occasionally. Based on the listening facts stated earlier, it is clear that listening is important, and research has shown that we do not retain much of what a speaker says. So, the question remains, Why do we stop listening? There is no single answer to this question, but the following six reasons may strike a familiar chord. We stop listening:

1 WHEN OUR ATTENTION DRIFTS. Listeners drift in and out of a speech, thinking about the heat, their next meal, or an impending exam. Studies have shown that few of us are able to pay attention to a single stimulus for more than 20 seconds without focusing, at least momentarily, on something else.

2 WHEN WE ARE DISTRACTED. Our environment determines how well we can listen. In the speaker–listener example, the heat made it difficult to pay attention. Internal stresses—hunger, unresolved conflict, and concern about exams—are also distractions. With people leaving cell phones on, checking messages, and texting or tweeting during a speech, listeners can be distracted, either because they're creating the distraction or they are near the distraction.

3 WHEN WE HAVE PRECONCEIVED NOTIONS. Before the speaker in the example above opened his mouth, the listener had already decided what the speaker stood for based on the speaker's appearance and on a stereotype of what 60s radicals stood for. Although in this case the listener was right—the speaker's views conformed to the listener's preconceived notions—he/she may be wrong about other speakers.

4 WHEN WE DISAGREE. Although the speaker identified continuing social ills, the listener did not share his concerns. From the listener's point of view, much more was right with the world than the speaker admitted—a perspective that reduced the listener's willingness and ability to consider the speaker's message.

5 WHEN WE ARE PREJUDICED OR INFLEXIBLE. Few women earn as much as Rachael Ray. Yet the listener based his/her reaction to the speaker's message on the premise that if one member of a group can succeed, all can. His prejudice prevented him from seeing the truth in the speaker's words.

6 WHEN WE ARE FACED WITH ABSTRACTIONS AND FORM OUR OWN OPINIONS.

The speaker never defined the term "conservative." As a result, the listener brought his/her own meaning to the term, equating it with bigotry. This meaning may or may not have coincided with the speaker's intent.

As audience members, we know our purpose is to listen, think critically, and retain the central idea of the message. But think about what *you* do as you listen and why you stop listening. You may consciously or unconsciously tune the speaker out. You may focus on minor details at the expense of the main point. You may prejudge the speaker based on appearance. You may allow your own emotional needs and responses to distort the message, and so on. Later, we provide specific tips for improving your listening skills, but first, we discuss the four stages of listening.

ENGAGING IN COMMUNITY

Kuwame Kinsel did not begin his multimedia career in the safest of environments. Growing up in Pittsburgh's Hill District at a time when gang activity was surging, Kinsel would find himself attending six funerals before his senior year in high school. However, rather than let his unfortunate experiences bring him down, Kinsel found himself moved towards mentorship to the members of his community.

"It's mentorship that makes a difference in people's lives," Kinsel says. (Aldrich, 2016).

Kinsel engages in many community outreach programs for his neighborhood. He is a head cyclist for Bike Pittsburgh (a program designed to give young people a healthy outlet to explore their city) and a supervising intern at BOOM Concepts, a community arts space where artists and musicians are able to showcase their work. Kinsel acknowledges his skill in listening to others as a crucial part of his work; he admits that being a good listener helped him overcome some of his own misconceptions and prejudices.

"Interacting with various artists has caused me to change my entire perspective about women—my sensitivities are heightened around the prevailing sexism in our culture," Kinsel says. (Aldrich, 2016).

As you continue to hone your active listening skills, reflect over Kinsel's story and how it stands as a testament to the power of having an open mind.

The Four Stages of Listening

Think back to a time when, in an argument with a family member or friend, you responded with "I hear you!" True, you may have *heard* them. It is possible, however, that you did not *listen* to them. Although listening appears to be instinctual and instantaneous, as noted earlier, it consists of four identifiable stages (See Figure 4.1). We move through these stages every time we listen, regardless of the situation. We may be part of a formal audience listening to a paid speaker, we might be engaged in conversation with a friend, or we might be home alone, listening to "things that go bump in the night." Listening can take place on several different levels, which are characterized by different degrees of attention and emotional and intellectual involvement. At times, we only partially listen as we think about or do other things; other times we listen with complete commitment. The following is an elaboration of the four stages of listening.

1. Sensing

Listening starts when you sense information from its source, which requires the ability to hear what is said. For a variety of reasons, sometimes we don't "sense" that someone is talking to us, so we miss part or all of the message. Sight is also a factor with sensing, since the speaker's gestures, facial expressions, and the use of presentational aids communicate intent. Normally, the speaking voice is in the range of 55–80 decibels, a level that comfortably enables us to hear a speaker's words.

Sensing
To become aware of or to perceive.

REACTION:
What is the reaction or response of the receiver(s)? How does it match with the sender's objective?

EVALUATION:
How is the message evaluated or judged by the receiver(s): Acceptance or rejection, liking or disliking, agreement or disagreement, etc. on the part(s) of the receiver(s)?

INTERPRETATION:
How is the message interpreted by the receiver(s)? What meaning is placed on the message? How close (similar) is the interpreted message's meaning to the intended message's meaning?

SENSING:
Is the message received and sensed by the intended receiver(s)? Does the message get into the stream-of-consciousness of the intended receiver(s)?

© Kendall Hunt Publishing Company

FIGURE 4.1 The four-stage communication model.

As anyone who has tried to listen to a speech over the din of a car siren will realize, obstacles can—and often do—interfere with reception. These obstacles are known to communication theorists as "noise," which was discussed in Chapter 1 as part of the communication model. Physical noise, such as sitting next to someone who has a persistent cough, and environmental annoyances, like uncomfortable chairs, stuffy rooms, cell phone and texting-related distractions, or struggling air-conditioning systems, make concentrated listening nearly impossible.

As we noted in Chapter 1, sometimes a remedy for physical noise is possible. The speaker, for example, can ask the audience to move closer to the front, silence their phones, and resist texting. Audience members can find more comfortable seats. When nothing can be done about noise, work hard to tune out the remaining noise so you can listen to the message.

2. Interpreting

Interpreting

Attaching meaning to a speaker's words.

Interpreting messages, which involves attaching meaning to the speaker's words, is also part of listening. As a listener, keep in mind that words have different meanings to different people, and we interpret words based on subjective experiences. Our ability to interpret what we hear is influenced by emotional and intellectual barriers that get in the way of the speaker's intended message.

Sign language, just like vocal language, still requires active listening skills to receive the complete message.

© Anthony Correia/Shutterstock.com

3. Evaluating

Listening involves evaluating the message. **Evaluation** requires that you assess the worth of the speaker's ideas and determine their importance to you. It is a mistake to assume that we judge messages solely on their own merits. Research shows that our assessment is influenced by how the message fits into our value system. According to Friedman (1986), there is a "human preference for maintaining internal consistency among personal beliefs, feelings, and actions" (p. 13). We agree with messages that are consistent with other beliefs we have, and we disagree with messages that conflict with our beliefs.

This tendency to agree with ideas that fit our value system and disagree with those ideas that conflict with our value system was first identified as **cognitive dissonance** by psychologist Leon Festinger (1957). Essentially, the theory argues that we seek internal consistency between attitudes and behaviors. If we do not like a colleague and that person acts badly, we experience consistency between attitude and behavior. If someone we do not like acts in a sincere, friendly manner, we experience inconsistency.

When inconsistency exists, we experience mental stress. To reduce the stress, we are forced to change one or more of our attitudes or behaviors so that the inconsistency is reduced or eliminated. For example, assume you are a school board member who holds a high opinion of the school superintendent, until he angrily tells you to "Shut up!" during a meeting with administrators and other board members. You may experience dissonance because you cannot reconcile your previous esteem for this person with your new feelings of being disrespected.

Dissonance disappears when your overall impression is consistent. In the case mentioned above, you have a choice. You either rationalize the inappropriate behavior and go back to having a high opinion of the school superintendent ("He was under a lot of stress; he didn't mean it") or, you change your opinion of the person ("Someone who behaves this way in a formal meeting should not be leading our district"). Thus, as listeners, we seek information consistent with what we already know; we accept ideas more readily if they are linked to our values and commitments.

To preserve psychological balance, we often reject conflicting ideas and retain our original point of view. This rejection can take many forms, including the following (Friedman, 1986, p. 13):

SHOOT THE MESSENGER. If you are a member of a college fraternity, you may reject the notion that any group found guilty of a hazing

Evaluation

Assessing the worth of the speaker's ideas and determining their importance to you.

Cognitive Dissonance

The tendency to agree with ideas that fit our value system and disagree with those ideas that conflict with our value system.

violation should be banned from campus. You may criticize the speaker as uninformed or as someone who was never in a fraternity like yours himself.

RALLY 'ROUND THE FLAG. Listeners who disagree with a speaker's message may seek the support of others who share their point of view—in this case, other fraternity members. Shared support provides comfort and reassurance. However, it does not necessarily mean you are right.

WHAT THE SPEAKER SAYS IS NOT WHAT YOU HEAR. Although the speaker may focus on hazing violations that put fraternity pledges in physical jeopardy, you hear him say that all violations—even minor infractions—should result in any group being banned.

ETHICS MATTER

Mia is part of her college's debate team. During one of their competitions with a rival campus, the opposing team began their debate on the subject of financial aid. In their argument, the other team asserted that low-income students should be given priority in receiving financial aid. As her team works on their rebuttal, one of Mia's partners suggests they accuse their opponent of wanting to withhold scholarships from middle-class students altogether. A quick glance around the auditorium reveals that many people were not listening during the opponent's speech. Although Mia knows this is clearly not what the other team meant, she is almost certain the insinuation will turn the audience unfairly against her opponents.

QUESTIONS TO CONSIDER:
1. Is there an ethical breach in taking advantage of an audience of passive listeners?
2. Is it immoral to use audience misconceptions to strengthen Mia's arguments?
3. What (if any) ethical obligations does the audience have in a debate scenario such as this one?

CONVINCE YOURSELF THAT THE SPEAKER'S MESSAGE HAS NOTHING TO DO WITH YOU. Even when opinions collide, you may convince yourself that you and the speaker are talking about two different things. You decide that the issue does not really have any bearing on *your* fraternity because the speaker is giving examples of fraternity mishaps at other schools.

DO NOT THINK ABOUT IT AND IT WILL GO AWAY. If, as a fraternity member, you took part in several unpleasant hazing incidents, listening to the speech may force you to question what you have done. To avoid the emotional discomfort that goes with this soul-searching, you may unconsciously block messages with which you disagree.

Although these methods are counterproductive, we all rely on one or more of them at one time or another. It is important to avoid using them excessively, and to recognize the behavior when it happens. Although evaluating does involve judging the speaker's ideas, we need to work on being as objective and open minded as possible. Not all messages are pleasant, nor should we expect to agree with all speakers. However, we should avoid using mechanisms that block out or alter ideas different from ours.

4. Reacting/Responding

Listening involves **reacting/responding** to the speaker's message. Feedback is also part of the listening process. In a conversation, the roles of listener and speaker change regularly. As the listener, you can interrupt the speaker, ask questions, and provide nonverbal cues such as eye contact, touching, or hugging.

At the mass communication level, you may respond positively to a television series by watching it weekly or by purchasing a product advertised during the commercial. Listeners in a public speaking setting provide feedback in a variety of ways: laughing, smiling, nodding in agreement, cheering or booing, clapping, or questioning the speaker after the presentation. Listeners also provide feedback on a less conscious level,

Reacting/responding
Providing feedback to the speaker's message.

The 2016 election challenged political candidates to listen to their constituents and respond in an effective and persuasive manner.

© Joseph Sohm/Shutterstock.com

such as yawning, texting, looking around the room, or whispering to the person next to them.

Effective speakers rely on and encourage feedback from their audience. They watch carefully for messages of approval or disapproval and adjust their presentations accordingly. We discuss audience feedback in our chapter on audience analysis and adaptation.

Eight Steps for Fine-Tuning Your Listening Skills

As a skill, listening is notoriously undervalued. Philosopher Mortimer Adler (1983) uses the following sports analogy to describe why the act of listening is as important as the act of speaking: "Catching is as much an activity as throwing and requires as much skill, though it is a skill of a different kind. Without the complementary efforts of both players, properly attuned to each other, the play cannot be completed." The players involved in the act of communication are speakers and listeners, all of whom have a role in the interaction. In this section, we explain how you can improve your listening skills—and, therefore, the chances of meaningful communication—by becoming conscious of your habits and, when necessary, redirecting your efforts.

1. Get Ready to Listen

Preparation is critical, especially when you have other things on your mind. Plan to make the effort to listen even before the speech begins, deliberately clearing your mind of distractions so you are able to concentrate on the speech. This also means turning off your cell phone. In some cases, it may involve having proper "tools" with you, such as pen and paper.

2. Minimize Personal Barriers to Listening

This step is more difficult than it sounds, for it involves overcoming emotional and intellectual barriers to listening that we identified in preceding passages. Often, we need help in recognizing our listening "blind spots." As you talk with your classmates about each other's speeches, determine whether the message you received from a speaker was the same message they heard. If it was not, think about what the topic means to you and identify reasons for your differences in interpretation. It may be possible that you are the only one who accurately understood the speaker's message. Sometimes an entire audience misses the point. If a question-and-answer period follows the speech, you can question the speaker directly to make sure you have the right meaning.

3. Leave Distractions Behind

Some distractions are more easily dealt with than others. You can change your seat to get away from the smell of perfume but you cannot make a head cold disappear. You can close the door to your classroom, but you cannot stop the speaker from rattling change in his pocket. Although dealing with distractions is never easy, try putting them aside so you can focus on the speaker and the speech. This task becomes easier when you view listening as a responsibility—and as work. By considering listening as more than a casual interaction, you are more likely to hear the message being sent.

© Olga Besnard/Shutterstock.com

Nobel Prize-winning author Toni Morrison uses vivid writing to encourage her audience to listen with empathy to the plight of others.

4. Do Not Rush to Judgment

As noted earlier, evaluation is part of the listening process. However, it is important to resist the temptation to *prejudge* speakers. Listeners have the tendency to prejudge topics as well as speakers. You may yawn at the thought of listening to one of your classmates deliver an informative speech about the "pickling process" or "stage make-up" until you realize that the topic is more interesting than you expected. You may not have an inherent interest in the topic, but that does not mean the speaker cannot be interesting or thought provoking. Some speakers save their best for last. They may start slowly and build a momentum of ideas and language. Your job is to listen and be patient.

We demonstrate prejudgment of a speaker when we find ourselves dismissing someone because "she's old," "he's conservative," or "he always dresses funny." As a listener, you have the responsibility to evaluate the content of the speech and not jump to conclusions based on surface speaker characteristics.

5. Listen First for Content, Second for Delivery

Confronted with poor delivery, it is difficult to separate content from presentation. The natural tendency is simply to stop listening when speakers drone on in a monotone, deliver speeches with their heads in their notes, or sway back and forth. However, delivery often has little to do with the quality of the speaker's ideas. Many of the speakers you will hear over the years will be in the position to address you because of their accomplishments, not their speaking ability. While a Nobel Prize–winning scientist may be able to explain a breakthrough in cancer therapy, he or she may have no idea how to make eye contact with an audience. To avoid missing these speakers' points, look past poor delivery and focus on content. In some situations, it is helpful to outline the main ideas as the speaker presents them so that you focus on the ideas instead of the delivery.

6. Become an Effective Note Taker

Each time a professor lectures or conducts a class discussion, you and your fellow students are expected to take notes. After years of note taking, this activity probably seems as natural as breathing; it is something you do to survive (in this case, college). Ironically, this skill often disappears at graduation. Most people do not pull out a pad and pen when listening to a speech in the world outside the classroom. But note taking is as appropriate and necessary for nonstudents as it is for students.

When you listen to a speech at a public event, a political rally, or on TV, taking notes helps you listen more effectively. For example, if your school district plans a referendum, which means registered voters will have to choose "yes" or "no" to raising taxes, being able to take notes allows you to keep track of the purpose of the referendum, how funds will be distributed, and so on. The following suggestions will help you improve your note-taking—and listening—skills:

- CREATE TWO COLUMNS FOR YOUR NOTES. Write "Facts" at the top of the left column and "Personal reactions/questions" at the top of the right column. If the speaker does not answer your questions during the course of the speech, ask for clarification at the end. This is particularly important when the speaker covers something complex, such as a change in insurance coverage, taxes, or city development.

- USE A KEY-WORD OUTLINE INSTEAD OF FULL SENTENCES TO DOCUMENT THE SPEAKER'S ESSENTIAL POINTS. If you get bogged down trying to write full sentences, you may miss a huge chunk of the message. At the end of the speech, the key-word outline gives you a quick picture of the speaker's main points.
- USE YOUR OWN ABBREVIATIONS OR SHORTHAND SYMBOLS TO SAVE TIME. If you know that "comm" means communication, then use that. If you are not sure whether it means "communication," "communism," or "community," then the abbreviation is not working for you. We have seen students use up and down arrows instead of writing "increase" or "decrease." Develop a system that works for you.
- USE DIAGRAMS, CHARTS, SCALES, AND QUICK-SKETCH IMAGES TO SUMMARIZE THEMATIC CONCEPTS OR THEORIES. Using emoticons may seem trite, but they can express succinctly how you feel about a concept. Drawing a scale may be useful as someone presents the pros and cons of some issue.
- USE A NUMBERING SYSTEM TO GET DOWN PROCEDURAL, DIRECTIONAL, OR STRUCTURAL UNITS OF INFORMATION. Numbering helps organize information, especially if the speaker did not organize the units of information for you.
- ASK THE SPEAKER—VERBALLY OR NONVERBALLY—TO SLOW DOWN, IF, NO MATTER HOW QUICKLY YOU WRITE, YOU CANNOT KEEP UP. Be cautious here. Do not ask the speaker to slow down so you might write full sentences. Instead, ask the speaker to slow down for purposes of general understanding. If you are the only person who is experiencing difficulty, you may want to ask questions at the end instead, or make an appointment to fill in gaps in understanding.

7. Be an Active Listener

As instructors, we have observed that when lecturing to 200 or more students, some appear to believe they cannot be seen. They talk to their neighbors, text friends, slouch low in the seat, put their heads on their desks, or disappear into the hood of their sweatshirt. What these students do not know (surely you are not one of them!) is that we can see you, and we want you to be engaged in the listening process.

As listeners, we can process information at the rate of about 400 words per minute. However, as most people talk at only about 150 words per minute, we have a considerable amount of unused thinking time to spare (Wolf et al., 1983, p. 154). This "extra time" often gets in the way of listening because we tend to take mental excursions away from the speaker's topic. It is natural to take brief trips ("I wonder what's for lunch?") but it can be problematic when they become major vacations ("Wow. Last night when I was talking to Suzy on the phone … and she said … and I thought … and I couldn't believe it when she said … so I said …"). To minimize the potential for taking a lengthy vacation while listening, experts suggest the following techniques:

- Take notes to keep your focus on the speech.
- **Before the speech begins, write down questions you have about the topic.** As the speech progresses, determine whether the speaker has answered them.
- **Apply the speaker's comments to your own experience and knowledge.** This makes the message more memorable.
- **Identify the thesis statement and main supporting points.** This helps you focus on the critical parts of the speech.
- **Decide whether you agree with the speaker's point of view and evaluate the general performance.** This keeps you engaged by focusing on the message and the speaker.

8. Provide Feedback

Let speakers know what you think. You may be able to provide feedback through the use of questions during or after the speech, and there may be an opportunity to give feedback to the speaker later on a personal level.

Even in a large lecture hall, the speaker is aware of the audience and will establish eye-contact with audience members. As a listener, you can provide nonverbal feedback by leaning forward in your chair, nodding your head, smiling, and frowning when the occasion or your emotions call for it. This kind of participation forces you to focus your attention on the speaker and the speech. Providing feedback at the various stages of a speech is hard work that requires total involvement and a commitment to fighting distractions.

Speaking Well with Technology Is an Essential for Excellence

Companies that cater to teenagers and young adults are always challenged to gain and maintain the interest of their audience. As teenagers grow accustomed to the rapid-fire communication of social media, traditional advertising mediums (such as television and radio) find themselves at a disadvantage in reaching the millennial audience. Lauren Johnson, a digital marketing reporter at *Adweek*, admits there is a challenge. "The agencies tend to be a bit older," says Johnson, "so they're trying to understand what millennials talk about with their friends, and how that can be translated into marketing that feels the same way." (Johnson, 2016).

Taco Bell is one such company that is feeling the pressure to get the attention of the elusive teenage demographic. Some marketing experts note that Taco Bell's laid-back approach is one to watch. The company prides itself on engaging with consumers on social media platforms such as Snapchat and Twitter (Cruz, 2016). In November of 2015, Taco Bell took advantage of the new taco emoji, launching a social media campaign called #TacoEmojiEngine. Chief marketing officer Marisa Thalberg explains how it works:

"If you tweet at Taco Bell and type the taco emoji plus any other emoji, you're going to get tweeted back an original piece of content," says Thalberg. For example, one person tweeted a taco and unicorn emoji. Within seconds, the tweeter received a video of a horse eating a taco and turning into a unicorn (Cruz, 2016).

© Toni Genes/Shutterstock.com

Taco Bell hopes that its foray into social media marketing gets the teenage audience to listen.

As you can see, there are many professional applications to listening to your audience. While it remains to be seen how successful Taco Bell's emoji campaign is, this story is a prime example about how technology, communication, and professional excellence go hand-in-hand.

Critiquing Speeches

As an audience member in a public speaking situation, you listen to be informed on some topic, to be persuaded to change an attitude or engage in some specific behavior, or to be entertained. Your overall impression may be "I learned something," or "I was not persuaded," or "That wasn't very funny." Your response is not random; you have some reason for your reaction. If you "learned something," perhaps it was because the speaker provided facts or statistics you did not know. If you "were not persuaded," perhaps the speaker used faulty logic or relied on sources that were not credible.

As an audience member, several options exist for providing feedback on the speech. Clapping, laughing, asking questions at the end of the speech, giving a standing ovation, walking out on the speech, and talking to the speaker afterward are all forms of feedback. At a workshop or seminar, you may be asked to provide written feedback for a speaker, and in a public speaking class, you may be asked to give written and/or oral feedback.

When you evaluate speeches, you are engaging in a feedback process that makes you a speech critic. As you consider the elements included in a speech and note the speaker's strengths and weaknesses, you are taking part in a formal process of analysis and appraisal.

Outside the classroom, chances are slim that you would receive a graded critique. Regardless, the point to keep in mind is that criteria are applied each time someone in an audience thinks about a speech, what it means, and what its value may be. As a participant in a public speaking course, you are expected to criticize constructively your classmate's speeches. It is important that you note the *constructive* nature of this process.

Five Key Criteria for Evaluating Speeches

As you criticize the strengths and weaknesses of speakers, keep in mind that your comments help your classmates develop as speakers. Your remarks help focus their attention on areas that work effectively as well as areas that need improvement. All speakers need this feedback to improve the quality of their performance.

Five general criteria can be applied to a special occasion speech, an informative speech, or a persuasive speech. We present these with guiding

SPEAKING EXCELLENCE IN YOUR CAREER

More and more often, companies are challenged to increase their branding by using social media platforms to better listen to their audience. This is often a difficult task; social media is notorious for changing drastically in a very short period of time. However, investigation into the relationship between social media and advertising is critical for the success of contemporary businesses. Researcher Joseph Rosendale examines the connection between communication technologies in organization communications and branding.

Of all the technologies available for business organizations, social media currently attracts the most attention. Not only is social media a revolutionary tool for communicating and organizing information, but these benefits are also practically free of charge (Rosendale, 2015). However, Rosendale notes that businesses cannot simply send an old message through a new medium and expect results; communication must be two-way in social media. The way that consumers and businesses communicate and engage with one another in a turn-taking format is crucial to create and maintain interest. As marketing officer Tim Leberech notes, an organization's brand quality can be measured by paying attention to what people say when they do not think the company is listening (Leberech, 2012). Social media now allows companies to be listening and active in that conversation at all times. An organization's success, performance, and overall valuation can be tied to its brand-communication strategy (Argenti, 2013). Clearly, social media savvy underscores the importance of social media integration in creating a profitable bottom line for companies in the present and future.

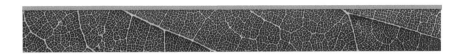

questions that allow the critic to examine both content and delivery. These are *not* presented in order of importance.

1 ORGANIZATION
   - Was the speech effectively organized?
   - Were the general and specific purposes clear and relevant to the assignment?
   - Were the functions of the introduction and conclusion clear (such as gaining attention and previewing)?

- Were main points clear?
- Did the speaker use appropriate transitions and internal summaries?
- Was an organizational pattern clear?

2 RESEARCH/SUPPORTING MATERIAL
- Did the speaker use effective and relevant material to support the thesis statement?
- Was there evidence of sufficient research?
- Was supporting material timely?
- Did the speaker include a variety of supporting material?
- Was supporting material relevant, helpful, and credible?
- Were sources integrated into the speech appropriately and cited correctly?

3 ANALYSIS
- Was the topic appropriate for the assignment/audience?
- Was the structure of the speech consistent with the specific purpose?
- Did the speaker make an effort to analyze the audience and adapt the speech to their needs?
- Was all the evidence presented made relevant and concrete?
- If used, did presentational aids contribute to the effectiveness of the speech?

4 LANGUAGE
- Did the speaker use clear and accurate language?
- Did the speaker use various language techniques to engage the listener?
- Were unfamiliar terms defined?
- Was language appropriate to the situation and the audience?

5 VERBAL AND NONVERBAL DELIVERY
- Did the speaker appear confident and self-controlled?
- Did the speaker establish and maintain appropriate eye contact?
- Were movements and gestures meaningful?
- Was the quality of the speaker's voice acceptable?
- Did the speaker pronounce words correctly and articulate effectively?
- Did the speaker look for and respond to feedback?
- Did the speaker include relevant emphasis and pauses?
- Was the speech relatively free of fillers (such as um, er, like, etc.)?
- Did the speaker use notes effectively?

© Drop of Light/Shutterstock.com

As Secretary of State, John Kerry had his public speeches evaluated not only by the U.S. public, but by the world at large.

Use these five criteria as a guide to evaluate your classmates' speeches. Often instructors ask students to use a speech evaluation form similar to the one provided in **Figure 4.2**. This gives feedback to the speaker on a sliding scale and also gives listeners the opportunity to provide constructive comments.

Using an evaluation form helps you give a speaker constructive criticism. You can change the scale to checks, check minuses, and check pluses; or use letter grades; or avoid using a scale altogether. No matter what criteria are used, the goal of evaluating speeches is to provide each speaker with valuable feedback

FIGURE 4.2 Using a public speaking evaluation form like this one helps you give a speaker constructive and valuable criticism.

Public Speaking Evaluation Form

Speaker:_____ Evaluator: _____ Date: _____

Topic: _____

    5 — excellent   4 — very good   3 — satisfactory   2 — fair   1 — unsatisfactory

Rating Organization
Organization
Was the speech effectively organized? 1 2 3 4 5
(effective introduction and conclusion; clear main points; used transitions and internal summaries; pattern related to specific purpose)
Comments:

Research/Supporting Material
Did the speaker use effective and relevant material to support the thesis statement? 1 2 3 4 5
(Evidence of sufficient research; supporting material timely, varied, relevant, helpful, credible; sufficient sources; integrated appropriately and cited correctly)
Comments:

Analysis
Were the topic and structure appropriate for the assignment/audience? 1 2 3 4 5
(Clear audience analysis, evidence relevant and concrete; presentational aids contributed to effectiveness)
Comments:

Language
Did the speaker use clear and accurate language? 1 2 3 4 5
(Varied language technique; defined unfamiliar terms; appropriate to the situation)
Comments:

Verbal and Nonverbal Delivery
Did verbal and nonverbal delivery enhance the effectiveness of the speech? 1 2 3 4 5
(Appeared confident; effective eye contact; appropriate gestures and movement; relatively free of nonfluencies; solid pronunciation and diction; good vocal quality; responded to feedback)
Comments:

ESSENTIALS FOR EXCELLENCE

In this chapter, you learned what it means to be an active listener as well as how listening can benefit your speaking skills. Remember, being an active listener is crucial to developing a healthy rapport with not only a communication partner, but an audience as well. Dr. John Grohol, researcher and CEO of Psych Central, offers several steps to become a better active listener.

Give feedback.
Let your communication partner(s) know your initial thoughts on the situation at hand. Share relevant information, insights, and experiences. Also, remember to listen and give considerate thought to their response.

Redirect divisive questions.
When another speaker shows signs of agitation, anger, or aggressiveness, try altering the topic to place participants on more common ground. Make others feel you are by their side instead of confronting them.

Offer validation to the speaker.
Acknowledge the speaker's problems, issues, and feelings (Grohol, 2015). Use empathy and respond in an interested way; when others open themselves up to you, make sure they remain the object of your attention.

WHAT YOU'VE LEARNED:

What You've Learned: Now that you have studied the chapter, you should be able to:

1. Understand the difference between listening and hearing.
    *   Listening is defined as the attending, receiving, interpreting, and responding to messages aurally.
    *   Hearing is the physical ability to receive sound.
2. Know and practice the four stages of listening.
    *   Sensing: listening starts when you sense information from its source, which requires the ability to hear what is said.
    *   Interpreting: interpreting involves attaching meaning to a speaker's words
    *   Evaluating: evaluation requires that you assess the worth of the speaker's ideas and determine their importance to you.
    *   Reacting/responding: both reacting and responding ask you to offer feedback, which is a crucial part of the listening process.
3. List the five criteria for evaluating speeches.
    *   Organization
    *   Research/supporting material
    *   Analysis
    *   Language
    *   Verbal and nonverbal delivery
4. Identify the most effective practices for self-evaluation.
    *   We tend to be hypercritical at times and completely unaware of our errors at other times; critiques from your classmates and peers can be extremely helpful
    *   Remember to first reflect on how you *think* you did before analyzing audience feedback. Although feedback from others is important, it is healthy to run through the evaluation process internally at first.

Key Terms

hearing, 103
listening, 104
sensing, 109

interpreting, 110
evaluation, 111

cognitive dissonance, 111
reacting/responding, 113

Reflect

1 Describe a crisis you have experienced or heard about where the direct cause was due to poor listening skills. What lessons from this chapter can you apply to the situation that could have avoided the problem?

2 How can we use active listening techniques to reach people who are inflexible or prejudicial against certain topics? How can these techniques be utilized in public speaking?

3 How do you handle negative feedback? How are some ways you can offer constructive feedback without coming off as negative?

4 What nonverbal codes do you think are important in conveying that you are open-minded and willing to be an active listener?

5 Think about the relationship between speech content and delivery. Can you describe a presentation that had incredible delivery, but the content was either uninformative or prejudicial?

Review Questions

1 _____ is the physical ability to receive sounds.

2 The attending, receiving, interpreting, and responding to messages presented aurally is known as _____.

3 _____ is to become aware of or to perceive.

4 _____ is the practice of attaching meaning to a speaker's words.

5 Assessing the worth of a speaker's ideas and determining their importance is the process of _____.

6 _____ is to provide feedback on a speaker's message.

PART**TWO**

PREPARING AND PRESENTING YOUR SPEECH

Actor Shia LaBeouf has had many accusations of plagiarism leveled against him.

CHAPTER FIVE
RESEARCH AND SUPPORTING MATERIAL

▓ OUTLINE

■ WHAT YOU'LL LEARN

After studying this chapter, you should be able to:

1. Know the steps needed to develop a research strategy.
2. Recall the five web evaluation criteria identifed by Radford, Barnes, and Barr.
3. Identify the five functions of research support.
4. Use best practices when documenting information in your speeches.

SPEAKING IN CONTEXT

On May 18, 2016, Anthony Hamlet became a cautionary tale about the importance of documenting and citing research used in public presentations. Hamlet, who was hired by the Pittsburgh Public Schools board to be their new superintendent, used words that were not his own (and without attribution) on his resume and during his first news conference with the public.

"A successful superintendent has to satisfy many constituencies, keeping high achievers in the system while devoting resources to those who need them the most," Hamlet wrote in his resume (Behrman & Lindstrom, 2016). That sentence first appeared in a February 2015 *Washington Post* editorial describing a superintendent in Maryland. Also, during his first speech with the public, Hamlet described himself as a transformational leader "charged with identifying the needed change and creating a vision to guide the change through inspiration." That sentence is lifted word-for-word for the definition of transformational leadership listed on Wikipedia.

As you learn about the best practices for conducting research and documenting supporting material, keep in mind how plagiarism (intentional or not) can affect your credibility. Hamlet, chosen to be the top administrative official for an entire school district, is expected to maintain the same standards of academic honesty that are applied to his students. In his case, an oversight such as this could cost him his job. Remember, however, that this applies to most professional fields outside of education as well; any instance of plagiarism in the workforce could land you out of a job as well. Use the skills and strategies in this chapter to ensure your research is effective and academically honest.

The Shia LaBeouf and Anthony Hamlet examples emphasize the importance of research and citing appropriate sources in the public speaking process. You may feel relief when your instructor approves the topic you have chosen, but your work has just begun. After choosing a topic and developing the general and specific purposes of your speech, it is time to research your topic and search for appropriate supporting material. Starting with what you know is important, but giving a speech based *only* on what you know is not sufficient. To a large extent, your listeners evaluate your speech on the amount and relevance of information gathered and the types of supporting material used.

We live in an information society that produces far more information than we can use. Print resources such as books, journals, magazines, and newspapers are added to library collections daily. Computers give us access to innumerable websites and voluminous databases. As a result of this galaxy of available information, one of your most important jobs will be to decide what is relevant and what is not, what you should incorporate into your speech and what you should discard. Once you have a topic, you need to stay focused on your specific purpose, keep your audience in mind, and search for reliable, credible information that will provide the most effective support for ideas.

Research provides the foundation for your speech. It enhances knowledge you may already have by giving you the tools to expand your thesis statement into a full-length presentation. Your research may include interviewing experts on your topic and locating print and web-based information, or data you gathered personally. The result of this process is your knowledge of the topic.

Often, research can lead you to deliver a slightly different version of your speech than originally anticipated. As facts emerge you may expand your idea in one place, streamline it in another, or take it apart to accommodate new information. Ultimately, you will piece it together in its final form.

A speech that is well researched is still not complete. You must determine how to use the information gathered most effectively. **Supporting material** is the information used in a particular way to make your case. Supporting material, as we discuss later in this chapter, includes examples, testimony, statistics, facts, and analogies.

For example, if you wanted to inform your class about services available in your community for individuals who are categorized as low income, your research process may lead you to one organization that specializes in debt consolidation, one that offers free or low-cost medical

Supporting material
The information used in a particular way to make your case.

care, another that gives out food for low-income individuals, and yet another that provides children with free school supplies. Having found all of these services, you might decide to include one main point that is stated, "A variety of services are available in our community."

For supporting material, the previously noted agencies provide examples of available services. As the types of supporting material vary, you must determine what is most suited to the topic and to your listeners. In a speech about available community services, facts are important because listeners should know how many individuals qualify for specific services as well as how many individuals use these services. Testimony from those who work in the agencies or from those who use their services would provide excellent support for such a speech.

Examples
Support that illustrates a point or claim.

Develop a Research Strategy

Instructors rarely say, "Go! Prepare an informative speech." Instead, they establish parameters regarding appropriate topics, length of speech, minimum number of sources, and types of sources. Before you begin to research your topic, make sure you know the constraints of the assignment as specified by your instructor. No matter how brilliant your delivery, if you haven't met the constraints of the assignment, your speech grade will reflect that. It is important to answer the following questions. What is the minimum number of sources required? How many sources do you need? If you use three issues of *Newsweek*, do they count as one source or as three? Can you use information that is 30 years old, 20 years old, 10 years old, or did your instructor say all material needs to be no more than five years old? Do you need both print and online sources? Does online access to a magazine count as a print source? Can you use all types of print sources? Do you need different types of print sources? Does your instructor allow you to count an interview as a source? Can you use a family member or yourself as a source? Once you know the answers to these questions, you are ready to start the research process.

Once you leave the college environment, constraints still exist. For any speaking engagement, among other things, you need to know the length of the speech, the audience you'll speak before, the audience's expectations in terms of topic/content, and the most effective types of supporting material for that audience. The best-delivered speech will fall short if it is too long, poorly developed, and insufficiently supported.

Whether you are planning to give an informative or persuasive speech, developing an effective research strategy involves the following:

1 ANALYZE THE AUDIENCE. What are the needs, interests, and knowledge level of my audience?

2 ASSESS YOUR KNOWLEDGE/SKILL. What knowledge or skill do I have in relation to this topic?

3 SEARCH PRINT AND ONLINE RESOURCES. Based on available resources, where and what will I find most useful?

4 INTERVIEW, IF APPROPRIATE. Will interviewing someone with personal knowledge or expertise about this topic strengthen this speech?

Each of these aspects can be viewed as research stages. The following section examines each of these stages in detail.

ENGAGING IN COMMUNITY

As you learn how to become a better researcher and public speaker, it's important to acknowledge those who volunteer to teach these skills free of charge. In Suffolk, Virginia, hundreds of volunteers offer their time at Suffolk public schools helping in classrooms, supporting library staff, and many other educational activites. Regina England, treasurer of a local PTA, has personally logged over 541 hours.

"I love this school," said England. "I love the atmosphere of the school and the teachers and staff." (Agnew, 2016).

Across the city, over 2,000 registered volunteers logged over 10,900 volunteer hours in the school system's VolunteerConnect program. Their assistance eased many of the burdens of the school district's faculty and staff, freeing them to focus on educating their students. In many cases, this amount of volunteer aid drastically increases the quality of education for their students.

Volunteering is one of many ways you can engage in your community. As you earn your college degree and move into the professional world, reflect on the thousands of volunteers in Suffolk. Many of the researching skills you learn from this text can be utilized to better engage and aid in your community.

Start (and End) with an Audience Analysis

Throughout this book we stress the importance of connecting with your audience. Before you determine the general or specific purpose for your speech, consider your audience's needs. As explained in Chapter 3, a careful audience analysis gives you information about who they are, what they know, and what they value. Understanding your audience helps you develop specific questions that can be answered as you follow your search strategy. For example, suppose you are planning an informative speech explaining prenuptial agreements. You may have some general questions about the topic, such as the following:

- At what age do most people get married?
- What are the statistics on the number of marriages and divorces each year?
- Who benefits financially and who suffers financially as a result of a divorce?
- What happens to property in divorce?
- How expensive is an agreement?
- What issues are addressed in a typical agreement? Is there a "typical" agreement?
- Can people draw up the agreement without legal counsel?

To construct an effective speech that achieves its specific purpose, whether it is informative or persuasive, think about your specific audience. So, if you are working on a speech about prenuptial agreements, consider additional questions such as:

- Considering the age of my audience, how much do they know about prenuptial agreements?
- How do most people feel about prenuptial agreements?
- What might be this audience's greatest areas of concern or interest regarding the topic?

Answering the more specific questions related to your audience helps you determine the depth and breadth of information needed to answer your more general questions. Informally, you may ask students a few questions while waiting before class in the hallway or in the classroom. Your instructor may allow you to ask the class to respond briefly during class, or at the end of class. Perhaps you can survey your class online.

Politicians such as former Texas Governor Rick Perry rely heavily on audience analysis when campaigning for office.

By developing questions based on your understanding of the needs of your audience, you can increase the likelihood of establishing an effective speaker–audience connection. Reflect again on your audience *after* you have gathered information to determine whether you have collected enough material and if it is the right type of material to meet your audience's needs and interests.

Assess Your Own Knowledge and Skills

Start your research process by assessing your own knowledge and skills. Most likely, you have direct knowledge or experience related to several topics. Your family may own a bike shop or a restaurant, and you grew up exposed to issues related to these professions. Maybe you were raised in a bilingual family. Perhaps by the time you started college, you held one or more jobs, joined a political club, pursued hobbies like video games, or played sports such as soccer or rugby. You may know more about Jackie Chan movies than anyone on campus, or you may play disc golf. Examining your unique experiences or varied interests is a logical starting point for developing a speech.

Having personal knowledge or experience can impact your audience. A student with Type I diabetes can speak credibly on what it is like to take daily injections and deal with the consequences of both low and high blood sugar. A student who works as a barista at the local coffee shop can demonstrate how to make a good latte. Under no circumstances, however, should your research stop with your own personal knowledge or skills. Someone who knows how to make a good latte needs additional research on topics such as coffee shops and how much money they make, types of coffee beans and where they come from, how beans are processed, brand names of espresso machines for those who are interested in making their own espresso, fair-trade coffee, and so on.

Choosing a topic on which you have no personal knowledge and skills is not forbidden, of course. However, be aware that speaking about something that is new to you may increase your communication apprehension, and *may* lead audiences to view you as less credible.

Search Print and Online Resources

Once you have assessed your own knowledge or skills, it is time to search print and online resources for other supporting material. The Internet provides a rich playing field that also complicates our lives. We have more choices, but we have to work harder to sift through them.

Your search may result in more questions, including the following: What information is most essential to this topic? What will have the greatest impact? How much background do I need to give? Using a variety of sources is advantageous because some sources focus on research whereas others focus on philosophy or current events. Information may be found in regularly published sources or in a onetime publication. Sources target different audiences. We suggest you examine and evaluate materials from a variety of sources to select materials that will benefit you most.

Narrow Your Focus

It is natural to start with a broad topic. But as you search, the information you find helps you move to a more focused topic, enabling you to define— and refine—the approach you take to your speech. Perhaps you are interested in giving an informative speech about the use of performance-enhancing drugs in sports. You must narrow your topic, but you are not quite sure what aspects are most compelling.

Try conducting a key-word search on Google for "drugs in sports." This is very general. For any given topic, you may have more than a million records or "hits" from which to choose. We suggest you look for valid subject headings, and search more deeply than the first three or four records listed.

Google remains one of the most popular search engines in the world.

© The_Pixel/Shutterstock.com

Results of the key-word search lead you to many possibilities, including "anabolic steroids." You can discover what they are, how they work, who uses them, how prevalent they are, the different types, drugs banned by the NCAA, and medical uses. Now you have other areas to pursue. Decide what aspects you want to cover that are relevant to the audience and can be discussed effectively within your time constraints. Perhaps you are interested in who uses them. You type, "Who uses anabolic steroids?" This leads you to a website on uses and abuses of steroids. For your audience, you most likely need to define what anabolic steroids are and how they are used and abused. You can continue your research by examining both print and online resources for these specific aspects of performance enhancement drugs. Next, you can develop a specific purpose statement and search for information to support it.

As you search for information, keep three aspects of research in mind: First, recognize the distinction between primary and secondary sources. Primary sources include firsthand accounts such as diaries, journals, and letters, as well as statistics, speeches, interviews, questionnaires, and studies. They are records of events as they are first described. According to Raimes (2008), the use of primary sources "can bring an original note to your research and new information" to your listeners (p. 101). Primary sources generally are seen as credible sources but may be more difficult to obtain.

Secondary sources generally provide an analysis, an explanation, or a restatement of a primary source. If the U.S. Surgeon General issues a

Primary sources

Firsthand accounts such as diaries, journals, and letters, as well as statistics, speeches, and interviews. They are records of events as they are first described.

Secondary sources

Generally provide an analysis, an explanation, or a restatement of a primary source.

report on the dangers of smoking, the report itself (available from the U.S. Surgeon General's Office) is the primary source; newspaper and magazine articles *about* the report are secondary source material. Secondary sources may contain bias because someone has interpreted information from the primary source. Both, however, are useful in your search process.

Second, there is a relationship between the length of your speech and the amount of time you must spend in research. Many students learn the hard way that five minutes of research will not suffice for a five-minute speech. We recommend that for every one minute of speaking time, you spend an hour in preparation. Whatever the length of the speech, you have to spend time uncovering facts and building a strong foundation of support. If you only spend an hour researching your topic, it is likely you have not met the constraints of the assignment. You may have relied too heavily on one source, or you may not have enough sources.

Third, finding information is not enough; you must also be able to evaluate it, and to use it in the most appropriate way to achieve your specific purpose. For example, your audience analysis may suggest that specific statistics are necessary to convince your audience. On the other hand, perhaps personal or expert testimony will be most persuasive. Evaluating sources and types of supporting material are discussed later in this chapter. Overall, developing a research strategy is one of the most useful things you will learn in college.

Specific Library Resources

In addition to providing access to computers for online searches, each library houses a variety of research materials, including books, reference materials, newspapers, magazines, journals, and government documents. If information is not housed in your library, you can electronically extend your search far beyond your campus or community library through interlibrary loan. It may take two weeks or longer to process requests, so planning is especially important when relying on interlibrary loan. The following identifies various library resources, and includes several suggestions for making your library search most effective.

BOOKS. Historically, libraries have been most noted for their collection of books. Many universities have built several libraries so students can access large general collections, archived collections, and specific collections. Using the library catalog is essential. In addition to identifying what books are available and where to find them, an online catalog indicates whether a particular book is checked out and when it is due back. Keep in mind that libraries group books by subject, so as you look in the stacks for a particular book, it makes sense to peruse surrounding books for additional resources.

GENERAL REFERENCE MATERIALS. At the beginning of your search, it may be helpful to start with one or more general reference resources, including encyclopedias, dictionaries, biographical sources, and statistical sources. Most likely, your time spent with these materials will be short, but these resources can provide you with basic facts and definitions.

Unlike some of our experiences in primary school, seldom does a student's research start and end with the encyclopedia. The *World Book Encyclopedia* is helpful if you are unfamiliar with a topic or concept. It can provide facts that are concise as well as easy to read and understand. General encyclopedias (e.g., *The Encyclopedia Americana* and *Encyclopedia Britannica*) cover a wide range of topics in a broad manner. In contrast, specialized encyclopedias, such as the *Encyclopedia of Religion* and the *International Encyclopedia of the Social Sciences*, focus on particular areas of knowledge in more detail. Articles in both general and specialized encyclopedias often contain bibliographies that lead you to additional sources.

Encyclopedias are helpful as a basic resource, but they generally are not accepted as main sources for class speeches. Use them to lead to other information.

General encyclopedias
Cover a wide range of topics in a broad manner.

Specialized encyclopedias
Focus on particular areas of knowledge in more detail.

Although popular, Wikipedia.com is not a credible resource due to the ability for anybody to edit its articles.

Similarly, most instructors discourage, if not ban, use of Wikipedia. Although teachers don't want students quoting the encyclopedia, librarians will point out that Wikipedia, like *World Book*, is sometimes useful for getting an overview of the topic, especially if you know nothing about the topic, but information should be verified by a different source.

Dictionaries are helpful when you encounter an unfamiliar word or term. They also provide information on pronunciation, spelling, word division, usage, and etymology (the origins and development of words). As with encyclopedias, dictionaries are classified as either general or specialized. The dictionary is also just a click away. You might try *Merriam-Webster Online* (www.m-w.com). Specialized dictionaries cover words associated with a specific subject or discipline, as in the following: *The American Political Dictionary*, *Black's Law Dictionary*, *Harvard Dictionary of Scientific and Technical Terms*, and *Webster's Sports Dictionary*. Many disciplines use their own specialized terminology that is more extensive and focused, and those definitions are found in their journals and books. **Caution:** Check with your instructor before beginning your speech with "According to Webster's dictionary, the word _____ means ..." As Harris (2002) notes in his book on the effective use of sources, "Generally speaking, starting with a dictionary definition not only lacks creativity but it may not be helpful if the definition is too general or vague" (p. 35).

BIOGRAPHICAL SOURCES. Biographical sources, which are international, national, or specialized, provide information on an individual's education, accomplishments, and professional activities. This information is useful when evaluating someone's credibility and reliability. A biographical *index* indicates sources of biographical information in books and journals, whereas a biographical *dictionary* lists and describes the accomplishments of notable people. If you are looking for a brief background of a well-known person, consult the biographical dictionary first. If you need an in-depth profile of a lesser-known person, the biographical index is the better source. Some examples of these sources are *Author Biographies Master Index*, *Biography Index*, *The New York Times Index*, *Dictionary of American Biography*, *European Authors*, *World Authors*, and *Dictionary of American Scholars*. Librarians agree that biography.com is a useful online source for individuals currently famous or infamous.

STATISTICAL SOURCES. When used correctly, statistics provide powerful support. Facts and statistics give authority and credibility to research. Many federal agencies produce and distribute information electronically.

The *American Statistics Index* (ASI) includes both an index and abstracts of statistical information published by the federal government. Try also the *Index to International Statistics* (IIS) and the *Statistical Abstract of the United States* (available online at www.census.gov/compendia/statab/). If your library has it, the online source LexisNexis touts itself as providing "content-enabled workflow solutions designed specifically for professionals in the legal, risk management, corporate, government, law enforcement, accounting, and academic markets" (www.lexisnexis.com).

MAGAZINES, NEWSPAPERS, AND JOURNALS. Magazines (also known as periodicals) and newspapers provide the most recent print information. Once you identify ideas that connect with the needs of your audience, you can look for specific information in magazines and newspapers. General indexes cover such popular magazines and newspapers as *Time*, *Newsweek*, *U.S. News & World Report*, the *New York Times*, and the *Chicago Tribune*. Other popular indexes include *The New York Times Index*, *The Education Index*, *Humanities Index*, *Public Affairs Information Service Bulletin*, *Social Sciences and Humanities Index*, and *Social Sciences Index*.

Journals are serious, scholarly publications that report research conducted by professionals within their fields of study. Newspapers and magazines are differentiated from journals in at least four ways. First, the frequency of distribution is different, with newspapers published daily, magazines published weekly or monthly, and journals published quarterly, monthly, or bimonthly. Second, newspaper and magazine writers are paid, whereas researchers who write journal articles are generally experts in their particular fields and have submitted their work on a competitive, peer-reviewed basis. Third, magazines and newspapers are written for general audiences, whereas journal articles are written for a specific audience. For example, faculty and graduate students in the communication field would be interested in studies conducted on communication apprehension. Fourth, and very importantly, journals focus on original research. Much of the content in a journal is considered to be a primary source because it reports findings from scholarly research.

GOVERNMENT DOCUMENTS. Government documents are prepared by agencies, bureaus, and departments that monitor the affairs and activities of the nation. Documents are issued by the Office of the President, the U.S. Congress, the departments of Commerce, Agriculture, Education, Navy and Army, Indian Affairs, the Veterans' Administration, the Food and Drug Administration, and the FBI.

Through the U.S. Government Printing Office (GPO) one can find unique, authoritative, and timely materials, including detailed census data, vital statistics, congressional papers and reports, presidential documents, military reports, and impact statements on energy, the environment, and pollution. However, it is now archive only, and has been replaced, for the most part, by the Federal Digital System (FDsys).

Overall, a speaker has a wealth of information available at the library. An effective speaker uses a variety of sources, such as books, magazines, and statistics. This requires deep research, more than a quick Google search can uncover. At the library, expert help is on hand to assist you in your search. Also remember, whether you use print or online sources, you need to evaluate the credibility and timeliness of each source.

Online Searches

Consider using online databases such as ProQuest, InfoTrac, and EBSCO. According to InfoTrac College Edition's website (infotrac.thomsonlearning. com), more than 20 million scholarly and popular articles from nearly 6,000 sources are available to you. The advantage of using this resource is that you can access cross-disciplinary, reliable, full-length articles. It is free of advertising and available 24 hours a day. EBSCO (www.ebsco. com) offers a similar service, and claims to be the most widely used online resource, with access to over 100 databases and thousands of e-journals.

Web Evaluation Criteria

Many students start their research online. Although there is nothing inherently wrong with this, we urge you to proceed with caution. Evaluating the credibility of your online resources is critical.

Purdue University's online writing lab warns readers to "never use Web sites where an author cannot be determined, unless the site is associated with a reputable institution such as a respected university, a credible media outlet, government program or department, or well-known non-governmental organizations" (owl.english.purdue.edu). Seek information from competent, qualified sources and avoid information from uninformed individuals with little or no credentials. Ultimately, you are accountable for the quality and credibility of the sources you use.

As you access each website, it is important to evaluate its legitimacy as a source for your speech. In Radford, Barnes, and Barr's book on selecting, evaluating, and citing Web research (2006), five Web evaluation criteria are identified that serve as useful standards for evaluating online information.

Speaking Well with Technology Is an Essential for Excellence

As electronic communication becomes more and more ingrained into our personal and professional lives, we must learn to recognize both the benefits and shortcomings that instant communication has in our lives. In some cases, the electronic messages we receive are so overwhelming and constant that we choose to ignore them. In the medical field, this can have terrible consequences.

Recently, the federal government has been pushing for electronic patient records in an effort to coordinate health care and reduce mistakes. These electronic records often involve automated alert systems attached to patients' health information. However, the sheer number of instant messages doctors receive has led to an issue known as "alert fatigue" (Luthra, 2016). According to some doctors and IT experts, the number of these pop-up messages has become unmanageable. According to Shobha Phansalkar, assistant professor of medicine at Harvard Medical School, between 49 and 96 percent of clinicians ignore safety notifications sent via sms messages. "When providers are bombarded with warnings, they will predictably miss important things," said David Bates, a senior vice president of Brigham and Women's Hospital in Boston (Luthra, 2016).

Throughout this text, the authors will show you many examples of how speaking with technology leads to communication excellence. However, the previous example also teaches another important lesson: there are pitfalls to excessive electronic communication. As you are introduced to new and exciting ways to use electronic communication in your life, remember to use your critical thinking skills and recognize when electronic communication can cause information overload.

1 AUTHORITY. Authority relates to the concept of credibility. As we know, virtually anyone can become a web publisher. A website that passes this first test contains information provided by an individual, group, or organization known to have expertise in the area. Questions to guide evaluation include the following:

- What type of group put up the site? (Educational institution? Government agency? Individual? Commercial business? Organization?)

Authority

An individual cited or considered to be an expert; power to influence or command thought; credible.

- Can you identify the author(s)? (What is the organization or who is the person responsible for the information?)
- What are the credentials of those responsible?

Accurate

Reliable, current, and error-free.

2 **ACCURACY.** An accurate website is reliable and error-free. If the site was last updated two years ago and the site is discussing a bill before the legislature, then it is no longer accurate. Millions of websites are also considered *secondary sources*, so the information has been interpreted by someone else. The information may be less accurate. Also, it is relatively easy to take information out of context when it is put online and can be removed at will. Questions to guide evaluation include the following:
- Is the information correct?
- Does the information confirm or contradict what is found in printed sources?
- Are references given to the sources of information?

Objectivity

Information that is fair and unbiased.

3 **OBJECTIVITY.** The extent to which website material is presented without bias or distortion relates to objectivity. As you examine the material, you want to determine if it is presented as opinion or fact. Questions to guide evaluation include the following:
- What is the age level of the intended audience? (Adults? Teenagers? Children?)
- Is the information on the site factual or an expression of opinion?
- Is the author controversial? A known conservative? A known liberal?
- What are the author's credentials?

Coverage

The depth and breadth of the material.

4 **Coverage.** Coverage refers to the depth and breadth of the material. It may be difficult to determine whom the site is targeting. As a result, material may be too general or too specific. Determine if it meets your needs or if critical information is missing. Questions to guide evaluation include the following:
- What is the intended purpose of the site? (Educational? Informational? Commercial? Recreational?)
- Who is the intended audience? (General public? Scholars? Students? Professionals?)
- Is the information common knowledge? Too basic? Too technical?
- Does the information include multiple aspects of the issue or concern?

5   **Currency.** **Currency** refers to the timeliness of the material. Some websites exist that have never been updated. Information may be no longer valid or useful. If you look for "Most popular books of the year" and find a site from 2003, that information is no longer current or relevant. Looking at birth rates or literacy rates from the past would not produce relevant information if you are looking for the most recent information. Questions to guide evaluation include the following:

   • When was the site created?

   • Is the material recent?

   • Is the website updated?

When using these five criteria to evaluate your online information, remember that all criteria should be met, not just one or two of the above. Accurate and current information must also be objective. If critical information is missing (coverage), no matter how accurate and current the information is, it should be eliminated as a source.

Interview, If Appropriate

Interviews are useful if you want information too new to be found in published sources or if you want to give your listeners the views of an expert. By talking to an expert, you can clarify questions and fill in knowledge gaps, and you may learn more about a subject than you expected. In the process, you also gather opinions based on years of experience. If you decide to interview one or more people, we offer the following four suggestions:

Interviewing experts in their field (such as Stephen Hawking in physics) is invaluable to public speaking research.

© The World in HDR/Shutterstock.com

CONTACT THE PERSON WELL IN ADVANCE. Remember, *you* are the one who needs the information. Do not think that leaving one voice message or one email is the extent of your responsibility. You may have to make several attempts to contact the person. Schedule a date and time to interview that leaves you with ample time to prepare your speech.

Prepare questions in advance. An interview is a conversation between two or more people guided by a predetermined purpose. Know the purpose, and make sure you know what topics need to be covered and what information needs to be clarified.

Develop questions in a logical order. One question should lead naturally to another. Place the most important questions at the top to guarantee that they will be answered before your time is up.

Stay within the agreed time frame. If you promise the interview will take no longer than a half hour, keep your word, if at all possible. Do not say, "It'll just take a minute," when you need at least 15 minutes. Build in a little time to ask questions based on the interviewee's answers or for clarification.

After reading this section on research, we hope you recognize that it involves a significant time commitment. It is never too early to start thinking about your next speech topic and where you might find sources. Explore a variety of resources. Ask for help from your instructor or librarian. Make sure you know the constraints of the assignment.

Supporting Your Speech

Imagine a chef with a piece of steak, some cauliflower, and rice; the main ingredients for a dinner special. What the chef does with these raw materials will influence the response of the consumers. The chef decides whether to grill, broil, bake, steam, or fry. Different spices are used for different results. Numerous possibilities exist.

Research you gathered for your speech can be viewed as the raw material. Now you need to determine how to organize and present your information in the most effective way for your audience. It is important to spend sufficient time making choices about how much and what type of supporting material to include in your speech.

Supporting material gives substance to your assertions. If you say that *Casablanca* is the best movie ever produced in Hollywood, you are stating your opinion. If you cite a film critic's essay that notes it is the best movie ever, then your statement has more weight. You may find data that indicate how well the movie did, and a public opinion poll that ranked it as the top movie. These different resources provide support. Just about anything that affirms a speaker's idea in some way can be considered supporting material.

When developing your speech, you have many decisions to make. Consider the following example:

Your public speaking professor asks your class to develop an informative speech addressing the problem of shoplifting. The two following hypothetical versions are among those presented:

Version 1:

>Shoplifting is an enormous problem for American retailers who lose billions of dollars each year to customer theft. Not unexpectedly, retailers pass the cost of shoplifting onto consumers, which means that people like you and I pay dearly for the crimes of others.
>
>Shoplifting is increasingly becoming a middle-class crime. Experts tell us that many people shoplift just for kicks— for the thrill of defying authority and for the excitement of getting away with something that is against the law. Whatever the reason, 1 in 15 Americans is guilty of this crime.

Version 2:

>Imagine walking up to a store owner once a year and giving that person $300 without getting anything in return. Could you afford that? Would you want to do that? Yet that's what happens. Every year, the average American family of four forks over $300 to make amends for the crimes of shoplifters.
>
>Shoplifting is a big cost to big business. According to recent statistics from the National Association for the Prevention of Shoplifting, people who walk out of stores without first stopping at the cash register take with them more than $13 billion annually. That's more than $25 million per day. Their website claims that 1 out of 11 of us is guilty of this crime. To bring this figure uncomfortably close to home, that's at least two students in each of your classes.
>
>Interestingly, shoplifting is no longer a poor person's crime. Hard as it is to imagine, many shoplifters can well afford to buy what they steal. Actress Lindsay Lohan received media attention in February 2011 when she

was charged with felony grand theft of a necklace from a jewelry store in Venice, California.

Why do middle- and upper-income people steal? According to psychiatrist James Spikes, quoted in *Ms. Magazine*, shoplifters are "defying authority. They're saying, 'The hell with them. I'll do it anyway … I can get away with it …'" Psychologist Stanton Samenow, quoted in *Life* magazine, agrees: "Shoplifters will not accept life as it is; they want to take shortcuts. They do it for kicks."

Although both versions say essentially the same thing, they are not equally effective. The difference is in the supporting materials. Notice, providing supporting material adds depth and breadth to the speech. Listeners are more likely to pay attention when they hear something that relates to their world in some way.

ETHICS MATTER

Jeremy is writing a research paper for his intercultural communication class. While completing his rough draft, Jeremy cited multiple sources from an online database based out of another country. After giving his rough draft to a friend to proofread it, he discovered that most of his citations were not credible, and in some cases patently false. Because the paper was due in a few days, Jeremy began to panic. His friend pointed out, however, that at a glance the sources appeared legitimate, and their professor's workload was so great that she might not have a chance to properly check Jeremy's citations. This left Jeremy with a difficult decision: turn his paper in as it stands and hope for the best, or start over from scratch and risk missing the due date. A poor grade could keep Jeremy from passing his class, but a plagiarism infraction might get him kicked out of school. However, Jeremy also recognized this was an introductory class, and he might be able to feign ignorance of the rules and avoid charges of plagiarism. Jeremy decided to think over his options, sleep on it, and make a decision in the morning.

QUESTIONS TO CONSIDER:
1. How many ethical breaches would Jeremy make by deciding to turn in his original paper with inaccurate citations?
2. Given that this is an introductory class, should strict standards of academic honesty be applied to students with little to no experience?
3. Can you think of any other options available to Jeremy that could help him turn in a competent, academically honest paper?

Five Functions of Support

Support should strengthen your speech in five ways. Comparing Version 1 with Version 2 illustrates the value of supporting material.

1   SUPPORT IS SPECIFIC. Version 2 gives listeners *more details* than Version 1. We learn, for example, how much shoplifting costs each of us as well as the financial burden retailers must carry.

2   SUPPORT HELPS TO CLARIFY IDEAS. We learn more about the reasons for shoplifting from Version 2. This clarification—from the mouths of experts—reduces the risk of misunderstanding.

3   SUPPORT ADDS WEIGHT. The use of credible statistics and expert opinion adds support to the second version's main points. This type of support convinces listeners by building a body of evidence that may be difficult to deny. The testimonies of Drs. Spikes and Samenow are convincing because they are authoritative. We believe what they say far more than we do unattributed facts.

4   SUPPORT IS APPROPRIATE TO YOUR AUDIENCE. Perhaps the most important difference between these two versions is Version 2's determination to gear the supporting material to the audience. It is a rare college student who would not care about a $300 overcharge or who cannot relate to the presence of two possible shoplifters in each class. Also, Hollywood actress Lindsay Lohan's shoplifting is noted in Version 2. Students are familiar with her name, but college students would not be as familiar with an older famous person who has shoplifted, such as Bess Myerson, winner of Miss America in 1945 and actress on several television shows in the 1960s.

5   SUPPORT CREATES INTEREST. Although Version 1 provides information, it arouses little or no interest. Listeners have a hard time caring about the problem or becoming emotionally or intellectually involved. Version 2, on the other hand, creates interest through the use of meaningful statistics, quotations, and an example. When used properly, supporting materials can transform ordinary details into a memorable presentation.

Effective support is used to develop the message you send to your listeners. It is through this message that communication takes place between speaker and audience. In public speaking, you cannot separate the act of speaking from the message the speaker delivers. Supporting your message is one of your most important tasks as you develop your speech.

Forms of Support

Effective speeches generally rely on multiple forms of support. To give your speech greater weight and authority, at least five forms of support can be used. These include facts, statistics, examples, testimony, and analogies.

Facts

Facts

Verifiable and irrefutable pieces of information.

Opinions

Points of view that may or may not be supported in fact.

Nothing undermines a presentation faster than too few facts. Facts are verifiable and irrefutable pieces of evidence. Opinions are points of view that may or may not be supported in fact. Too often, speakers confuse fact and opinion when adding supporting material to a speech. For example, while it is a fact that Leonardo DiCaprio won the 2016 Academy Award for Best Actor, it is opinion to state that he is the best actor in Hollywood.

Facts serve at least three purposes:

1   FACTS CLARIFY YOUR MAIN POINT. Facts remove ambiguity, making it more likely that the message you send is the message your audience will receive.
2   FACTS INDICATE YOUR KNOWLEDGE OF THE SUBJECT. Rather than say, "The League of Women Voters has been around for a long time," report, "The League of Women Voters was founded in 1919." Your audience wants to know that you have researched the topic and can discuss specifics about your topic.
3   FACTS DEFINE. Facts provide needed definitions that may explain new concepts. In Megan's informative speech on "functional illiteracy," she defined the term in the following way:

> While an illiterate adult has no ability to read, write, or compute, relatively few Americans fall into this category. However, some 30 million Americans can't read, write, compute, speak, or listen effectively enough to function in society. They cannot read street signs, write out a check, apply for a job, or ask a government bureaucrat about a Social Security check they never received. Although they may have minimal communications skills, for all intents and purposes, they are isolated from the rest of society. These people are considered functionally illiterate.

Megan anticipated the potential confusion between the terms illiteracy and functional illiteracy, and differentiated between them. While defining this term for your public speaking class is necessary, if the audience comprises literacy coaches, this would not be necessary.

Guidelines for Using Facts

CAREFULLY DETERMINE HOW MANY FACTS TO USE. Too few facts reveal that you spent little time researching, while too many may overwhelm your listeners. Sometimes, students want to impress their audience, or at least their instructor, with the amount of research completed for a particular speech. The desire to include *all* information may result in a "data dump," where facts are given in a steady stream with little or no connection to the speech or to each other. This overload of information is difficult to process.

To be effective, the number and complexity of the facts must be closely tied to the needs of your listeners. A speech to a group of hikers on poison ivy prevention may include practical issues such as identifying the plant and recognizing, treating, and avoiding the rash. However, when delivering a speech on the same subject to a group of medical students, a detailed explanation of the body's biochemical response to the plant is probably more relevant.

DEFINE TERMS WHEN THEY ARE INTRODUCED. The first time you use a term that requires explanation, define it so your meaning is clear. If you talk about the advantages of belonging to a health maintenance organization, define the term the first time it is used.

MAKE SURE YOUR MEANINGS ARE CLEAR. If words or phrases have different meanings to you than they do to members of your audience, the impact of your speech is lessened. Misunderstandings occur when your audience attributes meanings to terms you did not intend. Think about the following words: success, liberal, conservative, patriot, happiness, good, bad, and smart. Collectively, we do not agree on the meanings of these words. One person may define success in terms of material wealth, while another may think of it in terms of family relationships, job satisfaction, and good health. When it is essential that your audience understand the meaning you intend, take the time to clarify terms.

Statistics

Statistics

The collection, analysis, interpretation, and presentation of information in numerical form.

The second form of supporting material is statistics: the collection, analysis, interpretation, and presentation of information in numerical form. Statistics give us the information necessary to understand the magnitude of issues and to compare and contrast different points.

STATISTICS CAN BE MISLEADING. For example, if one were to examine the National League of Baseball (NLB) salaries for 2010, one would find the highest salary went to Alex Rodriguez of the New York Yankees. He earned $33,000,000. However, the average, or mean, salary for the New York Yankees was $8,253,335, and both the mean *and* median salaries were $5,500,000. The lowest salary was just over $400,000 (usatoday.com/sportsdata/baseball). In this case, simply discussing these three statistical measures is not helpful, unless you want to make the point that salaries are not consistent. It might make more sense to discuss the range of salaries or look at a particular group of players' salaries. When using statistics in your speech, it is important to understand what they mean.

The wide range of salaries in Major League Baseball can make it easy to manipulate or misinterpret statistics.

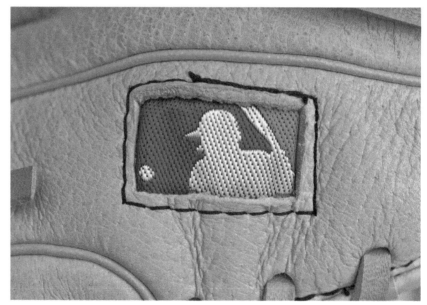

© dean bertoncelj/Shutterstock.com

SPEAKING EXCELLENCE IN YOUR CAREER

Research in the field of Communication (and many others) relies heavily on the ability to draw substantive conclusions from statistics. Effective use of statistics allows us to quantify study results and use that information to create meaningful data. However, statistics can be a double-edged sword; students and professors alike run the risk of misinterpreting data and making incorrect assertions. Researcher Timothy Levine outlines some of the potential problems with statistical research.

Levine argues that because of its simplicity and ubiquity, the use and interpretation of statistics has the potential to invite complacency (Levine, 2012). Statistics can be misleading, and are commonly misused or misinterpreted. In particular, Levine argues that statistics (averages in particular) can provide a distorted picture of findings when no attention is paid to the distribution of scores from which the average is calculated. For a simple example: a professor on campus uses statistics to show that students that complete his class consistently average a B grade, showing effective retention of the course material. However, looking at the actual dispersion of grades shows that although half of his students average an A, the other half consistently fails the class or passes with a low grade. Although the average is technically accurate, the dispersion of scores indicates that many (perhaps even a majority) of students are not effectively learning the course material.

As you immerse yourself in research and learn the importance of statistics, remember not to take them at face value. As the previous example shows, averages in research do not necessarily tell an accurate or complete story.

Guidelines for Using Statistics

BE PRECISE. Make sure you understand the statistics before including them in your speech. Consider the difference between the following statements.

> A 2 percent decrease was shown in the rate of economic growth, as measured by the gross national product, compared to the same period last year.

The gross national product dropped by 2 percent compared to the same period last year.

In the first case, the statistic refers to a drop in the rate of growth—it tells us that the economy is growing at a slower pace but that it is still ahead of last year—while in the second, it refers to an actual drop in the gross national product in comparison to the previous year. These statements say two very different things.

It is critical that you not misinterpret statistics when analyzing the data. If you have questions, refer to a basic statistics text or another source that further explains the data.

AVOID USING TOO MANY STATISTICS. Too many statistics will confuse and bore your audience and blunt the impact of your most important statistical points. Save your statistics for the places in your speech where they will make the most impact.

CITE YOUR SOURCES. Because statistics are rarely remembered for very long, it is easy for speakers to misquote and misuse them—often in a calculated way for their own ends. As an ethical speaker, you need to make sure your statistics are correct and you need to quote your sources.

USE VISUAL AIDS TO EXPRESS STATISTICS. Statistics become especially meaningful to listeners when they are presented in visual form. Visual presentations of statistics free you from the need to repeat a litany of numbers that listeners will probably never remember. Instead, by transforming these numbers into visual presentations, you can highlight only the most important points, allowing your listeners to refer to the remaining statistics at any time.

Examples

Examples enliven speeches in a way that no other form of supporting material can. Grounding material in the specifics of everyday life has the power to create an empathic bond between speaker and audience, a bond strong enough to tie listeners to a speech and the speaker even after the example is complete.

Faculty supply-and-demand projections in the social sciences and humanities

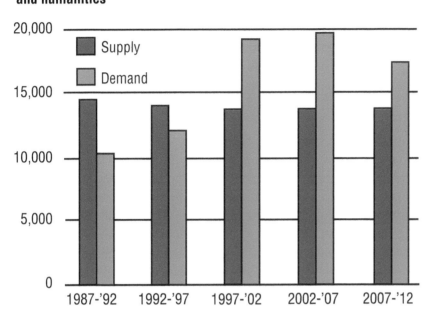

www.payscale.com/best-college/degrees.asp

Examples can be brief or extended, real or hypothetical, and narrative. Although examples differ in length, factual base, and source, their effectiveness lies in the extent to which they support the speaker's core idea.

EXAMPLES ARE BRIEF OR EXTENDED. Brief examples are short illustrations that clarify a general statement. If you made the following assertion: "Americans are more modest than Europeans," you could support it by using brief examples, such as, "If you take a walk on the beach in Italy or France, you should not be surprised to find women sunbathing topless. Also, many European countries, such as Sweden and Germany, have public saunas that are enjoyed by men and women—who are in the same sauna, sitting naked on their towels." Brief examples can be used effectively throughout a speech. Your decision to use them depends on many factors, including the needs of your audience, the nature of your material, and your approach.

Extended examples are longer and richer in detail than brief examples. They are used most effectively to build images and to create a lasting impression on the audience.

Because of their impact, extended examples should not be overused or used at inappropriate points. As with other forms of support, they should be reserved for the points at which they will have the greatest effect: in clarifying the message, persuading listeners to your point of view, or establishing a speaker–audience relationship.

EXAMPLES ARE REAL OR HYPOTHETICAL. Sometimes the best examples are real, and come from your personal experience. By revealing parts of your life that relate to your speech topic, you provide convincing evidence and, at the same time, potentially create a powerful bond between you and your audience. Consider the student who has watched her mother die from lung cancer. The experience of hearing about the diagnosis, discussing treatment possibilities, and making final arrangements while her mother was alive can have a powerful effect on the audience. The words and emotion have great impact because the situation is real, not hypothetical, and the speaker provides a sense of reality to the topic.

Hypothetical examples are useful when you want to exaggerate a point or when you cannot find a factual illustration for your speech. To be effective, they must be tied in some way to the point you are trying to illustrate.

Although these examples are not based on an actual event, the circumstances they describe are often realistic and thus effective. For example, a student might develop the following:

> Courtney, a 27-year-old, arrived at Springfield Emergency department at 10:30 p.m., after her mother found her lying unconscious and choking on her saliva. At the initial evaluation, the nurse noted certain symptoms. Courtney's pupils were dilated, her temperature was high, her blood pressure was extremely high, and her heart rate was extremely fast. Doctors immediately ordered fluids to be given to rehydrate her and worked to stabilize her vital signs. Then, she began to show signs of a heart attack. She received CPR but about two hours later, she suffered another heart attack. This time, doctors were unable to

Hypothetical example

A fictional example; the circumstances a hypothetical example describes are often realistic and thus effective.

PART TWO: PREPARING AND PRESENTING YOUR SPEECH

revive her, and Courtney died. Following a urine analysis, lab technicians discovered she had ingested a lethal dose of methamphetamine.

The hypothetical format of the above example allows us to distance ourselves somewhat from a terrible situation since we aren't personally connected, but, at the same time, we feel the emotional impact because the situation reflects reality.

EXAMPLES CAN BE IN NARRATIVE FORM. Narratives are stories within a speech; anecdotes that create visual images in listeners' minds. In many ways, they take extended examples a step further by involving listeners in a tale that captures attention and makes a point—a story connected to the speaker's core idea. Many listeners love a good story, and when the speech is over, the narrative is what they remember. Narratives should have an opening where the characters and the situation are introduced, the action or complication that is the point of the story, and then some type of conclusion or resolution.

A narrative can be used anywhere in a speech. No matter where it is placed, it assumes great importance to listeners as they become involved with the details. Through the narrative, speakers can establish a connection with the audience that may continue even after the story is over.

Nobel Laureate Malala Yousafzai is regarded for her impactful narratives when giving a public speech.

Guidelines for Using Examples

Examples add interest and impact. They should be representative because examples support your core idea only when they accurately reflect the situation. No matter the type of example you use as supporting material, the following three guidelines will help you choose examples for your speeches:

USE EXAMPLES FREQUENTLY. Examples are often the lifeblood of a speech. Use them to make your points—but only in appropriate places.

When using examples to prove a point, more than one example generally is needed.

USE ONLY THE AMOUNT OF DETAIL NECESSARY. To make your examples work, you want to use only the amount of detail necessary for your audience and no more. The detail you provide in examples should be based on the needs of your audience. If your listeners are familiar with a topic, simply mention what the audience already knows. Interspersing long examples with short ones varies the pace and detail of your discussion.

USE EXAMPLES TO EXPLAIN NEW CONCEPTS. Difficult concepts become easier to handle when you clarify them with examples. Keep in mind that your listeners might be hearing about complex concepts for the first time. The quality of your examples can make the difference between communicating with and losing your audience.

Testimony

The word testimony may conjure a vision of witnesses in a court of law giving sworn statements to a judge and jury, adding credibility to a case. In public speaking, testimony has nothing to do with the law, but it has everything to do with credibility. When you cite the words of others, either directly or through paraphrasing, you are attempting, in effect, to strengthen your position by telling your audience that people with special knowledge support your position or take your side. Testimony can cite either experience or opinion. Also, short quotations are an effective way to provide testimony.

To be effective, however, testimony needs to be used in its proper context. Purposefully distorting testimony to suit the needs of your speech is misleading and unethical. Be honest to your source as well as your audience. Imagine the following (fictitious) statements *with* and *without* the information in parentheses:

> Michael Crane, head of the local disaster preparedness team, indicated, "The tornado will not have a great impact (if you have found an appropriate shelter)."

> Jenny Smith, director of Sexual Assault Counseling and Information Services said that "Jogging late at night is not very risky for women (who are jogging together in well-lit areas)."

The local police chief stated, "Crime seldom happens in this town (when a strong police presence is felt)."

Clearly, the statements without parentheses are vastly different from the full statement. To leave out crucial information when providing testimony as supporting material is unethical, and can be dangerous.

EXPERIENCE AS TESTIMONY. Experience may be the most credible choice in some cases because someone was "on the scene." It is possible to use your own testimony when you are an expert. If you are developing a speech on what it is like to recover from a spinal cord injury, use your own expert testimony if you have suffered this injury. Similarly, if you are a female talking about the advantages and problems of being a female lifeguard, cite your own testimony if you have spent summers saving lives at the beach. When you do not have the background necessary to convince your audience, use the testimony of those who do. Remember that, in any speech, it is not sufficient to use your expertise as the sole supporting material. Your personal testimony is only one source. An effective speech uses multiple sources and various forms of supporting material.

Former president Jimmy Carter is known for his strong testimonials in favor of Habitat for Humanity.

OPINION AS TESTIMONY. In some circumstances, the opinion of a recognized authority may provide the credibility needed to strengthen your argument or prove a point. Jimmy Carter, former president and winner of the Nobel Peace Prize in 2002, was an outspoken critic of the Iraq War. CBS News (February 9, 2011) quoted him as saying, "I thought then, and I think now, that the invasion of Iraq was unnecessary and unjust. And I think the premises on which it was launched were false" (www.cbsnews.com). While he is clearly stating an opinion, Carter carries a certain amount of credibility because of his previous position as president of the United States and as a Nobel Peace Prize winner.

© Nir Levy/Shutterstock.com

SHORT QUOTATIONS. A short quotation is a form of testimony, but its purpose is often different. Frequently, short quotations are used to set the tone of a speech, to provide humor, or to make important points more memorable. If you were receiving the MVP award for football at your high school or college, you might start out with something like this:

> Wow. I'm reminded of John Madden's words when he was inducted into the Pro Football Hall of Fame in 2006, "And right now, I don't have, I got like numb, you know, a tingle from the bottom of my toes to the top of my head." Yep. That's exactly how I feel.

Madden's quote is not the most articulate or insightful comment, but it certainly expressed the emotion the football player was feeling, and this quote would set an engaging tone for an acceptance speech.

Sometimes quotations are too long or too complicated to present verbatim. You can choose to cite the source but paraphrase the message. The following is a relatively long quote by activist Judy Heumann, special advisor on disabilities rights for the U.S. State Department under President Obama, in her speech at the International Forum on Independent Living on how education empowers women with disabilities:

Quote:

> We are here today because disabled women still rank at the bottom of every scale that measures progress. Recent studies show that disabled women are among the least likely people to be employed, the most likely to live in dire poverty, and among the people most likely to die young! Studies have shown that strong networks, both national and international, are needed to enable girls and women with disabilities to support each other in their efforts to live independent, productive lives. (DINF.ne.je)

Based on her background and experience, Judy Heumann qualifies as an expert on disabilities issues. If a speaker believed that this quote was an appropriate length for the audience, that it added support, and time was not a factor, the whole quote could be used. However, paraphrasing might be a better choice. Here is another way to use information from her speech.

Paraphrase:

According to Judy Heumann, the State Department's special advisor on disability rights, disabled women are the most likely people to be unemployed, live in dire poverty, and die young. However, strong support networks can help them lead independent, productive lives.

Paraphrasing is more effective when time is an issue and when getting facts out succinctly is important. Speakers always need to be mindful of the audience and what might have the greatest impact.

Guidelines for Using Testimony

USE ONLY RECOGNIZABLE OR CREDIBLE TESTIMONY AND QUOTATIONS. At a time when media exposure is so pervasive, it is easy to find someone who will support your point of view. Before citing a person as an authoritative source, be sure that he or she is an expert. If you are giving a speech on the greatest movies ever produced, it would make sense to quote Roger Ebert, film critic and author of numerous books on the subject of film. However, he would not be the proper choice for a speech on the joys of collecting and trading baseball cards.

As you review expert testimony, keep in mind that the more research you do, the more opinions you will find. Ultimately, your choice should be guided by the relevance and credibility of the source. The fact that you quote Supreme Court justice Elena Kagan in a speech on affirmative action is as important as the quote itself.

CHOOSE UNBIASED EXPERTS. How effective is the following testimony if its source is the *owner* of the Oakland Athletics?

There is no team in baseball as complete as the Athletics. The team has better pitching, fielding, hitting, and base running than any of its competitors in the National or American League.

If the same quote came from a baseball writer for *Sports Illustrated* you would probably believe it more. Thus, when choosing expert testimony, bear in mind that opinions shaped by self-interest are less valuable, from the point of view of your audience, than those motivated by the merits of the issues.

IDENTIFY THE SOURCE. Not all names of your experts will be recognizable, so it is important to tell your audience why they are qualified to give testimony. If you are cautioning overseas travelers to avoid tourist scams, the following expert testimony provides support:

> According to Rick Steves, travelers should be wary of "The 'helpful' local: Thieves posing as concerned locals will warn you to store your wallet safely—and then steal it after they see where you stash it. Some thieves put out tacks and ambush drivers with their 'assistance' in changing the tire. Others hang out at subway ticket machines eager to 'help' the bewildered tourist buy tickets with a pile of quickly disappearing foreign cash." (www.ricksteves.com)

Without knowing anything about Rick Steves, your readers have no reason to trust this advice. However, if you state his credentials first, you can establish the credibility of your expert. So instead, the speaker could start begin with, "According to Rick Steves, host and producer of the popular public television series *Rick Steves' Europe* and best-selling author of 30 European travel books, travelers should be wary of …"

DEVELOP TECHNIQUES TO SIGNAL THE BEGINNING AND ENDING OF EACH QUOTATION. Your audience may not know when a quote begins or ends. Some speakers prefer to preface quotations with the words "And I quote" and to end quotations with the phrase "end quote." Other speakers indicate the presence of quotations through pauses immediately before and immediately after the quotation or through a slight change of pace or inflection. It may be a good idea to use both techniques in your speech to satisfy your listeners' need for variety. Just do not make quotation signs with your fingers!

Analogies

At times, the most effective form of supporting material is the analogy, which points out similarities between what we know and understand and what we do not know or cannot accept.

Analogies fall into two categories: figurative and literal. Figurative analogies draw comparisons between things that are distinctly different in an attempt to clarify a concept or persuade. Biology professor and

Analogy
Establishes common links between similar and not-so-similar concepts.

Figurative analogy
Drawing comparisons between things that are distinctly different in an attempt to clarify a concept or persuade.

world-renowned environmentalist Paul Ehrlich uses an analogy of a globe holding and draining water to explain the problem of the world population explosion. The following is an excerpt from a speech delivered to the First National Congress on Optimum Population and Environment, June 9, 1970:

> As a model of the world demographic situation, think of the world as a globe, and think of a faucet being turned on into that globe as being the equivalent of the birth rate, the input into the population. Think of that drain at the base of that globe—water pouring out—as being the equivalent to the output, the death rate of the population. At the time of the Agricultural Revolution, the faucet was turned on full blast; there was a very high birth rate. The drain was wide open; there was a high death rate. There was very little water in the globe, very few people in the population—only above five million. When the Agricultural Revolution took place, we began to plug the drain, cut down the death rate, and the globe began to fill up.

This analogy is effective because it helps the audience understand the population explosion. It explains the nature of the problem in a clear, graphic way. Listener understanding comes not from the presentation of new facts (these facts were presented elsewhere in the speech) but from a simple comparison. When dealing with difficult or emotionally charged concepts, listeners benefit from this type of comparative supporting material.

Keep in mind that while figurative analogies may be helpful, they usually do not serve as sufficient proof in a persuasive argument. Ehrlich, for example, must back his analogy with facts, statistics, examples, and quotations to persuade his listeners that his analogy is accurate—that we are indeed in the midst of a population crisis.

A literal analogy compares like things from similar classes, such as a game of professional football with a game of college football. If, for example, you are delivering a speech to inform your classmates about Russia's involvement in the war in Afghanistan, the following literal analogy might be helpful:

Literal analogy
Compares like things from similar classes, such as a game of professional football with a game of college football.

> The war in Afghanistan was the former Soviet Union's Vietnam. Both wars were unwinnable from the start. Neither the Vietnamese nor the Afghans would tolerate foreign domination. Acting with the determination of the

Biblical David, they waged a struggle against the Goliaths of Russia and the United States. In large part, the winning weapon in both wars was the collective might of village peasants who were determined to rid their countries of the superpowers—no matter the odds.

Literal analogies serve as proof when the aspects or concepts compared are similar. When similarities are weak, the proof fails. The analogy, "As Rome fell because of moral decay, so will the United States," is valid only if the United States and Rome have similar economic and social systems, types of governments, and so on. The fewer the similarities between the United States and ancient Rome, the weaker the proof.

Guidelines for Using Analogies

USE ANALOGIES TO BUILD THE POWER OF YOUR ARGUMENT. Analogies convince through comparison to something the audience already knows. It is psychologically comforting to your listeners to hear new ideas expressed in a familiar context. The result is greater understanding and possible acceptance of your point of view.

BE CERTAIN THE ANALOGY IS CLEAR. Even when the concept of your analogy is solid, if the points of comparison are not effectively carried through from beginning to end, the analogy will fail. Your analogy must be as consistent and complete as in the following example:

> In political campaigns, opponents square off against one another in an attempt to land the winning blow. Although after a close and grueling campaign that resembles a 10-round bout, one candidate may succeed by finding a soft spot in his opponent's record, but the fight is hardly over. Even while the downed opponent is flat against the mat, the victor turns to the public and tells yet another distortion of the truth. "My opponent," he says, "never had a chance." Clearly, politicians and prize fighters share one goal in common: to knock their opponents senseless and to make the public believe that they did it with ease.

AVOID USING TOO MANY ANALOGIES. A single effective analogy can communicate your point. Do not diminish its force by including several in a short presentation.

Documenting Information Accurately in Your Speech

Any research included in your speech needs to be cited appropriately to give due credit. A citation is the way you tell your readers that certain material in your work came from another source (plagiarism.org). Some might think that citing sources makes their work seem less original. On the contrary, citing sources helps your listener distinguish your ideas from those of your sources, which will actually emphasize the originality of your own work.

Citing or documenting the sources used in your research serves two purposes. First, it gives proper credit to the authors of the materials used. Second, it allows those who are reading your work to duplicate your research and locate the sources that you have listed as references (www. olinuris.library.cornell.edu).

If you interviewed someone, your audience should know the person's name, credentials, and when and where you spoke with the person. If you use information from a website, the audience should know the name of the website and when you accessed it. For print information, the audience generally needs to know the author, date, and type of publication. Your credibility is connected to your source citation. Expert sources and timely information add to your credibility.

Essentially, all research used in your speech needs to be cited. Otherwise, you have committed an act of plagiarism. According to the *Merriam-Webster Online Dictionary,* to *plagiarize* means:

- To use [another's production] without crediting the source
- To commit literary theft
- To present as new and original an idea or product derived from an existing source
- To steal and pass off [the ideas or words of another] as one's own

Most institutions of higher learning specify what consequences will accrue to the student who plagiarizes. However, not all instances of plagiarism occur within the ivory tower. Following are examples of plagiarism that were considered newsworthy:

- In June 2010, Philip Baker, the University of Alberta's dean of medicine, resigned in the wake of allegations that he plagiarized a speech he gave at a banquet for graduating medical students (www.montrealgazette.com).
- In February 2010, *New York Times* reporter Zachery Kouwe reused language from *The Wall Street Journal*, Reuters, and other sources without attribution or acknowledgment (www.guardian.co.uk).

- An anonymous online poll of more than a thousand students at Britain's Cambridge University found 49 percent admitting that they have passed someone else's work off as their own at some point in their academic career (www.globalethics.org).
- A French writer lost her plagiarism suit against the makers of the George Clooney film *Syriana* with a court in Paris ruling that an author "cannot claim a monopoly on facts of history or current affairs or on political ideas" (www.globalethics.org).

Plagiarism is unethical, and it can result in academic punishment, public embarrassment, or damage to your career. We cannot underscore enough the importance of doing your own work and giving credit to sources. Following are ways to cite sources in your speech. *Consult your instructor*, however, as he or she may have specific concerns.

EXAMPLE 1:
- CORRECT SOURCE CITATION. In their 2016 book on intercultural communication, researchers Samovar, Porter, and McDaniel argue that travel has extended our sources of diversity because we can now be exposed "to cultural idiosyncrasies in the perception of time and space, the treatment of women and the elderly, the ways and means of conducting business, and even the discovery and meaning of truth."
- INCORRECT SOURCE CITATION. Researchers on intercultural communication argue international travel exposes us to many more aspects of culture than it used to, including observing how people treat women and the elderly, and how they conduct business.
- EXPLANATION. We need the date to evaluate the timeliness of the material. We need to know this information was found in a book, as opposed to a TV show, a newspaper, magazine, or other source. We need the authors' names so we know who wrote the information, and so we can find the book. (Remember that if this quote were on your outline, you would need to provide the page number after the quotation marks.)

EXAMPLE 2:
- CORRECT SOURCE CITATION. According to a personal interview last week with Diane Ruyle, principal of Danube High School, fewer students are choosing vocational classes than they were 10 years ago.
- INCORRECT SOURCE CITATION. According to Diane Ruyle, fewer students are choosing vocational classes.

- EXPLANATION. We need to know why the speaker cited Diane Ruyle. As a principal, she ought to be able to provide accurate information regarding course selection. Adding "than they were 10 years ago" gives the listener a comparison basis. Also, we need to know that this interview was timely; it occurred "last week."

EXAMPLE 3:
- CORRECT SOURCE CITATION. According to an Associated Press article published in the *New York Times* on August 9, 2010, "[U]nlike in South Carolina, state laws in Iowa and New Hampshire require officials there to hold the first caucus and primary in the nation, respectively."
- INCORRECT SOURCE CITATION. Unlike in South Carolina, state laws in Iowa and New Hampshire require officials there to hold the first caucus and primary in the nation, respectively.
- EXPLANATION. First, if this is published information, it should be cited. Second, since most of us do not know these facts, a citation is necessary. Otherwise, the listener may believe the speaker is making this up. The date provided allows us to check the source and shows us that the information is timely. No author was identified, and since Associated Press articles can be found in many newspapers, it is important to note this was found in the *New York Times*.

EXAMPLE 4:
- CORRECT SOURCE CITATION. According to the American Diabetes Association website accessed last week, "Cholesterol is carried through the body in two kinds of bundles called lipoproteins—low-density lipoproteins and high-density lipoproteins. It's important to have healthy levels of both."
- INCORRECT SOURCE CITATION. Cholesterol is carried through the body in two kinds of bundles called lipoproteins—low-density lipoproteins and high-density lipoproteins. It's important to have healthy levels of both.
- EXPLANATION. This information is not common knowledge, so it should be cited. Many organizations might include such information on their website, so it is important to note that it came from the American Diabetes Association (ADA). An audience would infer that the ADA is a credible organization regarding this topic. Using the words "last week" suggests current information on the ADA website, which reinforces the timeliness of the material.

In summary, remember that you *do not* need to cite sources when you are reporting your own original ideas or discussing ideas that are commonly held. You *must* cite sources when you are quoting directly or paraphrasing (restating or summarizing a source's ideas in your own words). You must also cite the source of an illustration, diagram, or graph. Providing the date of publication, date of website access, credentials of the source, and/or type of publication where applicable allows the listener to evaluate the credibility of the information. Failing to do so is plagiarism, which is a form of academic dishonesty. Not only may your speech grade suffer, but your instructor is encouraged to report incidents of academic dishonesty to the office on campus that deals with student misconduct.

ESSENTIALS FOR EXCELLENCE

In this chapter, you learned the tools and steps neccessary to find research and supporting materials for your presentations. Although you have learned how to identify credible and accurate research articles, actually *finding* the articles in an online format can still be a daunting task. Researcher Paige Henson offers three simple tips to help you with online research.

Save it all.
Saving information you come across, whether you are sure you will use it or not, is essential to the process. You may find a source that isn't applicable to your current message, but is perfect for a for another section of your research paper. Multiple tabs, bookmarks, and note-taking services like OneNote are useful tools to keep track of multiple information sources.

Use greater browse-power.
Use more than one web browser when conducting online research. Using more than one web browser (and search engine) will yield a greater variety of information than simply sticking with one option.

Primary and secondary sources.
Know the difference between primary and secondary sources. Primary information is directly associated with its producer, such as a personal diary, original government document, or a news broadcast (Henson, 2016). Secondary sources are reproductions or references of primary source material cited by other writers. Both primary and secondary sources have their benefits in a well-researched speech.

■ WHAT YOU'VE LEARNED:

What You've Learned: Now that you have studied the chapter, you should be able to:

1. Know the steps needed to develop a research strategy.
    - Analyze the audience. What are the needs, interests, and knowledge level of my audience?
    - Asses your knowledge/skill. What knowledge or skill do I have in relation to this topic?
    - Search print and online resources. Based on available resources, where and what will I find most useful?
    - Interview, if appropriate. Will interviewing someone with personal knowledge or expertise about this topic strengthen your speech?
2. Recall the five web evaluation criteria identifed by Radford, Barnes, and Barr.
    - Authority. Authority relates to the concept of credibility. A website that passes this first test contains information provided by an individual, group, or organization known to have expertise in the area.
    - Accuracy. An accurate website is reliable and error-free. If the site was last updated two years ago and the site is discussing a bill before the legislature, then it is no longer accurate.
    - Objectivity. The extent to which website material is presented without bias or distortion relates to objectivity. As you examine the material, you want to determine if it is presented as opinion or fact.
    - Coverage. Coverage refers to the depth and breadth of the material. It may be difficult to determine whom the site is targeting. As a result, material may be too general or too specific. Determine if it meets your needs or if critical information is missing.
    - Currency. Currency refers to the timeliness of the material. Some websites exist that have never been updated. Information may be no longer valid or useful.
3. Identify the five functions of research support.
    - Support is specific.
    - Support helps to clarify ideas.
    - Support adds weight.
    - Support is appropriate to your audience.
    - Support creates interest.
4. Use best practices when documenting information in your speeches.
    - If you interviewed someone, your audience should know the person's name, credentials, and when and where you spoke with the person.
    - If you use information from a website, the audience should know the name of the website and when you accessed it.
    - For print information, an audience needs to know the author, date, and type of publication.

Key Terms

accurate, 146
analogy, 164
authority, 145
coverage, 146
currency, 147
examples, 134

facts, 152
figurative analogy, 164
general encyclopedias, 141
hypothetical example, 158
literal analogy, 165
objectivity, 146

opinions, 152
primary sources, 139
secondary sources, 139
specialized encyclopedias, 141
statistics, 154
supporting material, 133

Reflect

1   How important is research in the preparation of most speeches? How can an audience tell if a speech lacks a sound research base?
2   Why is it important that you conduct both an audience analysis and reflect on your own knowledge and skills when it comes to developing your topic?
3   When you are considering information you found on a website, how do you evaluate whether the information you found is appropriate to include as supporting material?
4   How can you best use the services of a librarian?
5   With the idea of a research strategy in mind, how will you determine the types and amount of support you will need to meet the specific purpose of your next speech?
6   Which supporting materials are most effective for clarifying a point and which are most appropriate for proof? Can some forms of support serve both aims? If so, how? If not, why not?
7   In the hands of an unethical speaker, how can statistics and analogies mislead an audience? What is your ethical responsibility in choosing supporting materials?

Review Questions

1   _____ is the information used in a particular way to make your case.

2   _____ involve support that illustrates a point or claim.

3   _____ are firsthand accounts such as diaries, journals, and letters, as well as statistics, speeches, and interviews. They are records of events as they are first described.

4   _____ generally provide an analysis, an explanation, or a restatement of a primary source.

5   _____ cover a wide range of topics in a broad manner.

6 _____ focus on particular areas of knowledge in more detail.

7 _____ is an individual cited or considered to be an expert; power to influence or command thought; credible.

8 _____ information is reliable, current, and error-free.

9 _____ refers to information that is fair and unbiased.

10 _____ refers to the depth and breadth of the material.

11 _____ refers to the timeliness of the material.

12 _____ are verifiable and irrefutable pieces of information.

13 _____ are points of view that may or may not be supported in fact.

14 _____ are the collection, analysis, interpretation, and presentation of information in numerical form.

15 A _____ is a fictional example; the circumstances it describes are often realistic and thus effective.

16 A _____ establishes common links between similar and not-so-similar concepts.

17 A _____ draws comparisons between things that are distinctly different in an attempt to clarify a concept or persuade.

18 A _____ compares like things from similar classes, such as a game of professional football with a game of college football.

Musician Gene Simmons faced significant criticism from fans following his remarks about Prince's death

CHAPTER**SIX**
ORGANIZING AND OUTLINING YOUR IDEAS

OUTLINE

WHAT YOU'LL LEARN

After studying this chapter, you should be able to:

1. Identify the three major aspects contained in the body of your speech.
2. Describe chronological organization, past-present-future organization, spatial organization, cause and effect organization, problem-solution organization, and topical organization.
3. Know the guidelines for constructing speaker's notes.
4. Recognize best practices for utilizing speaker's notes.

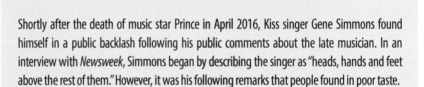

SPEAKING IN CONTEXT

Shortly after the death of music star Prince in April 2016, Kiss singer Gene Simmons found himself in a public backlash following his public comments about the late musician. In an interview with *Newsweek*, Simmons began by describing the singer as "heads, hands and feet above the rest of them." However, it was his following remarks that people found in poor taste.

"But how pathetic that he killed himself," Simmons said. "Don't kid yourself, that's what he did. Slowly, I'll grant you ... but that's what drugs and alcohol is: a slow death." (Respers, 2016).

Simmons' remarks came as authorities were investigating possible opiate use by Prince in the final stages of his life. Many people found the remarks insensitive and untimely, coming so soon after the singer's death. Simmons later apologized for his remarks, admitting that he didn't express himself properly.

As you learn the skills needed to properly organize and outline your ideas, use the previous example as a lesson about what can happen when speaking without clear direction. If Simmons had taken the time to practice and reflect on over his words, he could have realized how callous his remarks would sound to the general public. Although you may not find yourself with an audience as large as Simmons', you will more than likely find yourself giving some sort of presentation in your personal or professional life. A proper outline and organization will give you ample chances to reflect over what type of communication is effective (as well as identify communication that is ineffective or outright insulting).

The Importance of Organizing a Speech

A good speech flows smoothly and consists of a clear introduction, body, and conclusion. Your listeners should be able to identify these parts of your speech. Also, listeners expect your speech to be logical and organized. A speech that is missing a clear introduction or that has main points unrelated to the introduction will confuse, irritate, or simply turn off your listeners. It doesn't matter if you have gathered astounding facts or if you have incredible quotations to support your points if your speech is not structured logically.

Rather than just starting to write your speech, first consider how best to organize it. If you spend time outlining your ideas, you will discover where you have deficiencies in research, where you have too much information, or where you haven't made appropriate connections from one point to the next. This chapter leads you through organizing the body of a speech step-by-step. We begin with selecting and supporting your main points. Next, we present several organizational patterns as well as a template for organizing your main points. You have many decisions to make when organizing, such as the pattern of organization, the number of main points needed, what relevant subpoints to include, and where to put transitions and internal previews. We conclude with a discussion of outlining as a tool to aid you in becoming an organized speaker.

Organization of ideas
The placement of lines of reasoning and supporting materials in a pattern that helps to achieve your specific purpose.

Introduction
Supports the body of your speech and should capture your audience's attention and indicate your intent.

Conclusion
Supports the body of your speech, reinforces your message, and brings your speech to a close.

Body
Includes your main points and supporting material that reinforces your specific purpose and thesis statement.

Organizing the Body of Your Speech

The organization of ideas in public speaking refers to the placement of lines of reasoning and supporting materials in a pattern that achieves your chosen general purpose and specific purpose by supporting your thesis. Following a consistent pattern of organization helps listeners pay attention to your message. An organized speech with connected main points helps you maintain a clear focus that leads listeners to a logical conclusion. An organized speech flows smoothly and clearly, from introduction through body to conclusion.

Your introduction and conclusion support the body of your speech. The introduction should capture your audience's attention and indicate your intent. The conclusion reinforces your message and brings your speech to a close. The body includes your main points and supporting material that bolster your specific purpose and thesis statement. The introduction and conclusion are important, but audiences expect you to spend the most time and effort amplifying your main points.

For the body of your speech to flow in an organized, logical way, reflect first on your general purpose, specific purpose, and thesis statement. Your **general purpose** is either to inform, persuade, or entertain. Since your **specific purpose** is a statement of intent and your **thesis statement** identifies the main ideas of your speech, referring to them as you determine your main points prevents misdirection. For example, consider a speech discussing how family pets help children with psychological problems. You might develop the following:

General purpose

There are three general purposes for speeches: to inform, to persuade, and to entertain or inspire.

Specific purpose

The precise response you want from your audience.

Thesis statement

The core idea; identifies the main ideas of your speech.

> GENERAL PURPOSE: To inform
>
> SPECIFIC PURPOSE: To explain to my class how pets can provide unexpected psychological benefits for children with emotional problems by helping to bolster their self-esteem
>
> THESIS STATEMENT: A close relationship with a family pet can help children with emotional problems feel better about themselves, help therapists build rapport with difficult-to-reach patients, and encourage the development of important social skills.

Your thesis statement indicates your speech will address self-esteem, rapport with therapists, and the development of social skills. This suggests that there are many peripheral topics you will *exclude*, such as the type of pet, pet grooming tips, medical advances in the treatment of feline leukemia, how to choose a kennel when you go on vacation, and so on.

Select Your Main Points

Organizing the body of your speech involves a *four-step process: select the main points, support the main points, choose the best organizational pattern, and create unity throughout the speech.* Before organizing your speech, determine your main points. Main points are the key ideas, or most important issues you want to discuss with your audience. One way to discover your main points is through **brainstorming**. Brainstorming can occur at any stage of a process, but brainstorming for main points should happen *after* you have gathered sufficient information during topic research.

Brainstorming

Generating a list of ideas consistent with the goals of your speech.

A best practice is to arrive at *no fewer than two and not more than five main points*. If you add more, you may confuse your listeners, and you may not have time to provide adequate support. All ideas must relate to your general purpose, specific purpose, and thesis statement. The audience analysis you have done previously should ensure your main points are audience-centered.

For purposes of illustration, consider the following:

> GENERAL PURPOSE: To inform
> SPECIFIC PURPOSE: To describe to my class the causes, symptoms, and treatment of shyness
> THESIS STATEMENT: Shyness, which is an anxiety response in social situations that limits social interactions, may respond to appropriate treatment.

Your brainstorming process for the topic of shyness might result in a list of possible main points that include, but are clearly not limited to, the following: symptoms of shyness, shyness and heredity, shyness as an anxiety response, physical and psychological indications of shyness, number of people affected by shyness, shyness and self-esteem, how to handle a job interview if you are shy, treatment for shyness, and what to do when your date is shy.

On reflection, you may realize that several of these points overlap, and others do not relate as much to your thesis statement and should be discarded. So, you make the following list of six possible important points: symptoms of shyness, causes of shyness, treatment for shyness, number of people affected by shyness, shyness as an anxiety response, and shyness and self-esteem.

With six being too many main points to develop, you decide that "shyness as an anxiety response" describes a symptom of shyness and that "shyness and self-esteem" describes a cause. You decide that a discussion of the number of people affected by shyness belongs in your introduction because it is startlingly widespread. Your final list of main points may look like this: symptoms of shyness, causes of shyness, treatment for shyness.

Through this process, you transformed a random list into a focused set of idea clusters reflecting broad areas of your speech. Your main points should be mutually exclusive; each point should be distinct. In addition, each point must relate to and support your thesis statement. We now turn our attention to supporting your points.

Support Your Main Points

After selecting your main points, use the supporting material you gathered to strengthen each main point. Fitting each piece of research into its appropriate place may seem like completing a complex jigsaw puzzle. Patterns must be matched, rational links must be formed, and common sense must prevail. Each point underneath the main point is called a subpoint (and subsubpoint, and so on). Each subpoint is an extension of the point it supports. If the connection seems forced, reconsider the match. Here, for example, is one way to develop three main points for the speech on shyness. As you sit at your computer, you can expand phrases into sentences. So for now, you can begin to think in terms of the language of your speech. Keep in mind, we are focusing on organization, not the formal outline.

Politicians like Speaker of the House Paul Ryan must use great discretion when framing the main points of their arguments.

I. **MAIN POINT 1:** The symptoms of shyness fall into two categories: those that can be seen and those that are felt.
   A. Objective symptoms (symptoms that can be seen) make it apparent to others that you are suffering from shyness, including blushing, dry mouth, cold clammy hands, trembling hands and knocking knees, excessive sweating, and belligerence.
   B. According to psychologist Philip Zimbardo, many shy people never develop the social skills necessary to deal with difficult situations (symptoms that are felt).
   C. They may experience embarrassment, feelings of inferiority or inadequacy, feelings of self-consciousness, a desire to flee, and generalized anxiety. They overreact by becoming argumentative.
   D. Internal symptoms like an unsettled stomach and dizziness make the experience horrible for the sufferer.
II. **MAIN POINT 2:** Recent research has focused on three potential causes of shyness.
   A. Heredity seems to play a large part.
   B. Psychologists at Yale and Harvard have found that 10 to 15 percent of all children are shy from birth. Dr. Jerome Kagan of Harvard found that shy children are wary and withdrawn even with people they know.

C. Shyness is also the result of faulty learning that lowers self-esteem instead of boosting self-confidence.
   1. When parents criticize a child's ability or appearance or fail to praise the child's success, they plant the seeds of shyness by lowering self-esteem.
   2. Older siblings may destroy a child's self-image through bullying and belittlement.
D. Shyness is also attributable to poor social skills, due to never having learned how to interact with others, which leaves shy people in an uncomfortable position.

III. **MAIN POINT 3:** Shyness is not necessarily a life sentence; treatment is possible and so is change.
   A. In a survey of 10,000 adults, Stanford University researchers found that 40 percent said that they had been shy in the past but no longer suffered from the problem.
   B. People who are extremely shy may benefit from professional therapy offered by psychiatrists and psychologists.

As you weave together your main points and support, your speech should grow in substance and strength. It will be clear to your listeners that you have something to say and that you are saying it in an organized way.

Choose the Best Pattern for Organizing Your Main Points

The way you organize your main points depends on your general purpose, specific purpose and thesis statement, the type of material you are presenting, and the needs of your audience. As you develop your main points, consider what you want to emphasize. Assuming you have established three main points, choose how to weight your main points. Three options are possible. First, you may choose the **equality pattern**, which involves giving equal time to each point. This means that you will spend approximately the same time on each main point as you deliver the body of your speech.

Using the **strongest point pattern** is a second option. In this case, your first point would take about half of the time you devote to the body of your speech, the second point would be given about one-third, and your final point would receive the least. The advantage to this method is in getting the audience to process, retain, and recall your strongest points. When testing memory, psychologists discovered that, when presented with a list

Equality pattern
Giving equal time to each point.

Strongest point pattern
You spend the most time in your speech on the first point, less time on the second point, and even less time on the last point of your speech.

of items, individuals remembered information that was presented either at the beginning of the list *or* at the end. The strongest point pattern, which weighs the first point more heavily than the other points, reflects the phenomenon known as the **primacy effect**. Note there is danger of using this pattern. Our strongest points may also be the most complex and if discussed early in the speech may confuse or turn off the audience.

A third option is to follow a **progressive pattern**. This involves presenting your least important point first and your most important point last. The amount of time given to each is the inverse of the strongest point pattern, so that the last point receives the lion's share of time, the second point receives less, and the first point is the briefest. **Recency effect** suggests people will remember most what they have just processed. Anyone who has heard the phrase "What have you done for me lately?" understands the recency effect. A danger of this pattern is present when we lose our audience by providing weak material first, and in so doing, fail to capture interest.

The pattern for weighting your main points depends on your topic and audience. Based on these three options, keep in mind that your strongest argument does not go in the middle of your main points.

In addition to weighting your main points for emphasis, your information should fit within an overall organizational framework. Many choices exist for any given speech but based on the general purpose, specific purpose, and thesis sentence, one pattern of organization is generally more appropriate than the others. Typically, the right organizational pattern emerges organically as you work with the body of your speech, provided you know in advance what patterns you are seeking. The five effective patterns of organization to look for are chronological, topic, spatial, causal, and problem–solution. To show how different organizational patterns affect the content and emphasis of a speech, we choose a topic, establish different purposes for speaking, and show how the presentation differs when the organizational pattern is changed.

Chronological Organization

In a chronological speech, information is focused *on relationships in time.* Events are presented in the order in which they occur. When developing your speech chronologically, you might choose to organize your ideas by starting at the beginning and moving to the present, then looking to the future, as in a story, or going step-by-step, as you would if following a recipe.

Primacy effect

The belief that it is the first point in your speech that listeners will most likely remember.

Progressive pattern

Progression from least important argument to most important argument.

Recency effect

The belief that it is the last point in your speech that listeners will remember.

Chronological organization is an effective framing technique for discussing the foundation of the European Union.

TOPIC: The development of the European Union

GENERAL PURPOSE: To inform

SPECIFIC PURPOSE: To inform the class about crucial events that occurred over a 40-year span that influenced the development of the European Union (EU)

THESIS STATEMENT: Although the European Union was formed in 1992, the creation of a coal and steel community, establishment of a common market, and direct elections to the European Parliament were critical events that influenced its development.

MAIN POINTS:

I. West Germany, together with France, Italy, and Benelux, signed the Treaty of Paris in 1951 which created the European Coal and Steel Community.

II. In 1957 the Treaty of Rome established the European Economic Community, known as the common market to English-speaking countries.

III. In 1979 the first direct elections to the European Parliament were held.

IV. In 1992, with the signing of the Maastricht Treaty, the European Union was created.

Chronological order can also be used to construct a past-present-future organizational pattern. For example, in a speech addressing the development of the European Union, one could present the same topic with a slightly different specific purpose statement that would lead to a different thesis statement and different focus for the main points. Consider the following:

TOPIC: The development of the European Union
GENERAL PURPOSE: To inform
SPECIFIC PURPOSE: To inform the class how the European Union became a 27-member community that is poised to grow significantly
THESIS STATEMENT: Developed after three important treaties, the 27-member European Union is poised to add another nine countries to its community.
MAIN POINTS:
I. Treaties of Paris, Rome, and Maastricht were crucial to the development of the European Union.
II. Currently, the European Union is a community of 27 member states connected both politically and economically.
III. As an indicator of future growth, at least nine countries are potential candidates for inclusion in the European Union.

Past-Present-Future

Using a past-present-future order allows a speaker to provide perspective for a topic or issue that has relevant history and future direction or potential. Notice that in the regular chronological pattern, the three treaties are the main focus of the speech. In the past-present-future pattern, the three treaties would receive much less coverage.

Step-by-Step

Chronological patterns can be used to describe the steps in a process. Here is a step-by-step description of how college texts are produced. Like the other patterns, the process shows a movement in time:

STEP 1: The author, having gathered permissions for use of copyrighted material, delivers a manuscript to the publisher.

STEP 2: The manuscript is edited, a design and cover are chosen, photos are selected, and illustrations are drawn.

STEP 3: The edited manuscript is sent to a compositor for typesetting and set in galley and page proof form.

STEP 4: The final proof stage is released to the printing plant where the book is printed and bound.

ENGAGING IN COMMUNITY

Mary Stanton is no stranger to the realm of public speaking. Beginning with the 4-H Club in elementary school, Stanton learned the importance of effective speaking long before she became the operations manager for the Waunakee Neighborhood Connection (WNC), a charitable organization in her community. Following the 4-H slogan "learn by doing," Stanton began participating in student exchanges though the organization, leading to a final exchange in Australia. Stanton acknowledged that her openness to learning about other people allowed her to get the most out of her experiences. After working various jobs after her marriage, Stanton decided to give back to her community by starting her own nonprofit called High Expectations.

The goal of High Expectations was to build up their community, mainly though volunteering and youth programs (Harkins, 2016). In addition to her own charity's work, Stanton also subcontracted for other nonprofits in order to help their organizations operate within limited budgets. Stanton's nonprofit ran for 15 years before she decided to take her position at the WNC, an organization of which she is particularly proud.

© Barry Blackburn/Shutterstock.com

Organizations like the 4-H Club give students a head start in learning effective presentation skills.

"I've never seen a nonprofit as comprehensive as WNC when it comes to taking care of people's needs," Stanton said (Harkins, 2016).

As you make the transition from student professional, reflect over Mary's success with her charitable work, as well as her acknowledgement about the role her public speaking skills had on her achievements. You will find that community engagement and professional communication skills often go hand-in-hand.

Spatial Organization

In speeches organized according to a spatial pattern, the sequence of ideas moves from one physical point to another—from London to Istanbul, from basement to attic, from end zone to end zone. To be effective, your speech must follow a consistent directional path. If you are presenting a new marketing strategy to the company sales force, you can arrange your presentation by geographic regions—first the East, then the South, then the Midwest, and finally, the West. So, in a speech on the European Union, one could use a spatial organization pattern to discuss the growth of the EU over time.

I. Six Western European countries joined to establish the European Union.
II. Countries bordering the Eastern Mediterranean are candidates for inclusion in the European Union.
III. As Central and Eastern European countries emerged from dictatorship, they wanted to join the European Union to avoid falling back into the Russian sphere of influence.

Notice the differences between the main points for this speech organized spatially versus chronologically. A speech with the above three points would focus more on the countries involved with the European Union than how the EU came about.

Cause and Effect

With the cause and effect organizational pattern, the speaker can focus specifically on why something happened and what the consequences of the event or action were. The following statements could be developed into a speech that uses a cause and effect pattern:

- Difficult economic times after World War II created the necessity for European countries to work together.
- Alcoholism damages American family life.
- Too much positive feedback in primary school results in young adults being unable to cope with life's problems.
- Fast food is a significant contributor to obesity in America.
- Traveling abroad reduces prejudice.
- Smoking hurts relationships.

Note that in each case, the speaker is trying to show that something caused something to happen. For example, the effect alcoholism has on family life is that it causes harm. The effect traveling has on people is reducing prejudice. Therefore, traveling is seen as a cause. Some topics have direct links that can be made with facts and/or statistics (smoking causes cancer) and others have indirect links that must be proved with facts and other forms of support, such as testimony, examples, or illustrations (smoking hurts relationships).

ETHICS MATTER

June is a member of her university's debate team. For their upcoming competition, June's team has been assigned to debate against the practice of taxpayer-funded food assistance programs. Although most of June's team is in favor of these government programs, they feel it is their obligation to try to win the debate.

While doing research for their position, June and her teammates found that many people are willing to vote against food assistance programs when news stories surface about individuals abusing or defrauding the program. Recently, a news article was released in June's community about a family being treated to an extravagant five-course dinner while participating in the local food stamp program. However, the article notes that the meal was paid for through a privately held fundraiser to recognize the family's work in local community projects. One of June's teammates offered the idea of using the article in their argument, but omitting the details about the fundraiser. June voiced her disapproval, but the team voted in favor of using the doctored article. Torn between helping her team and telling the complete truth, June deliberated over what action she should take.

QUESTIONS TO CONSIDER:
1. What ethical issues are at stake when participating in civil debate?
2. Are there any other strategies that June's team could use that are both ethically responsible and effective?
3. If you were in June's position and a major class grade was on the line, how would you respond to the situation?

Problem–Solution Organization

A common strategy, especially in persuasive speeches, is to present an audience with a problem and then examine one or more likely solutions. For example, in a classroom speech, one student described a serious safety problem for women walking alone on campus after dark. He cited incidents in which women were attacked and robbed, and described unlit areas along campus walkways where the attacks had taken place. Next, he turned to a series of proposals to eliminate, or at least minimize, the problem. His proposals included a new escort service, sponsored and maintained by campus organizations, the installation of halogen lights along dark campus walks, and the trimming of bushes where muggers could hide.

Occasionally, speakers choose to present the solution before the problem. Had this student done so, he would have identified how to provide effective security before he explained why these solutions were necessary. Many audiences have trouble with this type of reversal because they find it hard to accept solutions when they are not familiar with the problems that brought them about.

Later in this chapter is an outline of a speech entitled "Revisiting Standard American English." The topic is developed using a problem–solution pattern.

> PROBLEM: Requiring speakers and writers to use Standard American English only promotes racism and classism.
> SOLUTION: Insist that teachers teach grammar by separating written English and spoken English and study the differences in grammar of both styles in the classroom.

Here the goal is to persuade an audience that a problem still exists and to have listeners agree about how it can be effectively handled.

Topical Organization

The most frequently used organizational system is not tied to time or space, problem or solution, or cause-and-effect, but to the unique needs of your topic. The nature and scope of your topic dictate the pattern of your approach.

If you are delivering an after-dinner humorous speech on the responses of children to their first week of preschool, you can arrange your topics according to their level of humor. For example:

1 The *school supplies* preschoolers think are necessary to survive at school
2 The *behavior of youngsters at school* when they do not get their own way
3 Children's stories of *their lives at home*
4 *The reasons children believe their parents send them to school*

These topics relate to children and their first week at school, but there is no identifiable chronological pattern, so topical order makes sense. When organizing topically, think about how to link and order topics. Transitions can help the audience understand the connections and are discussed in the following section.

Create Unity Through Connections

Without connections, your main points may be difficult to follow. Your audience may wonder what you are trying to say and why you have tried to connect ideas that do not seem to have any relationship with each other. To establish the necessary connections, use transitions, internal previews, and internal summaries.

Transitions

Transitions are the verbal bridges between ideas. They are words, phrases, or sentences that tell your audience how ideas relate. Transitions are critical because they clarify the direction of your speech by giving your audience a means to follow your organization. With only one opportunity to hear your remarks, listeners depend on transitions to make sense of your ideas.

It helps to think of transitions as verbal signposts that signal the organization and structure of your speech. Here are several examples:

"The first proposal I would like to discuss …"

This tells listeners that several more ideas will follow.

"Now that we've finished looking at the past, let's move to the future."

These words indicate a movement in time.

"Next, I'll turn from a discussion of the problems to a discussion of the solution."

Comedians like Kevin Hart rely on effective use of transitions for their comedy segments.

© Jaguar PS/Shutterstock.com

Transitions
Verbal bridges between ideas, words, phrases, or sentences that tell your audience how ideas relate.

This tells your listeners that you are following a problem–solution approach.

"On the other hand, many people believe ..."

Here you signal an opposing viewpoint.

Table 6.1 lists common transitional words that reflect the speaker's purpose in using them.

TABLE 6.1	Suggested Transitional Words
Speaker's Purpose	
1. To define	*that is to say; according to; in other words*
2. To explain	*for example; specifically*
3. To add	*furthermore; also; in addition; likewise*
4. To change direction	*although; on the other hand; conversely*
5. To show both sides	*nevertheless; equally*
6. To contrast	*but; still; on the contrary*
7. To indicate cause	*because; for this reason; since; on account of*
8. To summarize	*recapping; finally; in retrospect; summing up*
9. To conclude	*in conclusion; therefore; and so; finally*

(Makay & Fetzger, 1984, p. 68)

Internal Previews and Summaries

Internal previews

Extended transitions that tell the audience, in general terms, what you will say next.

Internal previews are extended transitions that tell the audience, in general terms, what you will say next. These are frequently used in the body of the speech to outline in advance the details of a main point. Here are two examples:

- I am going to discuss the orientation you can expect to receive during your first few days on the job, including a tour of the plant, a one-on-one meeting with your supervisor, and a second meeting with the personnel director, who will explain the benefits and responsibilities of working for our corporation.
- Now that I've shown you that "junk" is the appropriate word to describe junk bonds, we will turn to an analysis of three secure

financial instruments: bank certificates of deposit, Treasury bonds, and high-quality corporate paper.

While the first example would be found at the end of the introduction, notice that in the second example, the speaker combines a transition linking the material previously examined with the material to come. Previews are especially helpful when your main point is long and complex. Previews give listeners a set of expectations for what they will hear next. Use them whenever it is necessary to set the stage for your ideas (Turner, 1970, pp. 24–39).

Internal summaries follow a main point and act as reminders. Summaries are especially useful if you are trying to clarify or emphasize what you have just said, as is shown in the following two examples:

Internal summaries

Follow a main point and act as reminders; useful to clarify or emphasize what you have just said.

- In short, the American family today is not what it was 40 years ago. As we have seen, with the majority of women working outside the home and with divorce and remarriage bringing stepchildren into the family picture, the traditional family—made up of a working father, a nonworking mother, and 2.3 kids—may be a thing of the past.
- By and large, the job market seems to be easing for health care professionals, including nurses, aides, medical technicians, physical therapists, and hospital administrators.

When summaries are combined with previews, they emphasize your previous point and make connections to the point to follow:

Overall, it is my view that cigarette advertising should not be targeted specifically at minority communities. As we have seen, R. J. Reynolds test-marketed a cigarette for African Americans known as "Uptown," only to see it come under a barrage of criticism. What is fair advertising for cigarette makers? We will discuss that next.

Organization plays an important role in effective communication. Internal previews and summaries help the speaker create meaning with the audience by reinforcing the message and identifying what comes next. Keep in mind that audience members do not have the opportunity to replay or to stop for clarification. Transitions, previews, and internal summaries are tools a speaker can use to facilitate understanding and reduce the potential for misunderstanding (Clarke, 1963, pp. 23–27; Daniels & Whitman, 1981, pp. 147–160).

Speaking Well with Technology Is an Essential for Excellence

Using online mediums to communicate with one another is not a new idea. The ability to reach a massive audience with the click of a button is what makes the Internet such a special communication platform. For many of us, our first thought concerning the Internet is its ability to provide us with entertainment. Given all the wonderful distractions that are available online, it can be easy to forget the educational applications the Internet can provide to others. With this in mind, we look at researchers in India who are using the Internet to teach parents more about speech disorders.

In early 2016, the Indian National Institute of Speech & Hearing (NISH) conducted a series of online seminars to help parents understand speech sound disorder and how to manage it in children. While being available online, the seminars were also streamed to all District Child Protection Units (DCPU) offices. The program focused on educating parents and caregivers who might not be aware about the disability or its implications. Individuals who did not have personal access to broadband were given the opportunity to watch the stream from any DCPU office in their vicinity.

As we discuss speaking well with technology, keep in mind we are not only discussing personal communication skills. The ways you use technology to find your audience is equally important. In the previous example, health officials in India found a relatively inexpensive way to educate a large audience about a public health issue. Whether you are communicating to entertain, work, or educate, remember to think about the myriad ways you can use technology to reach an untapped audience.

Constructing an Outline and Speaker's Notes

Presenting your ideas in an organized way requires a carefully constructed planning outline and a key-word outline to be used as speaker's notes. Both forms are critical to your success as an extemporaneous speaker— one who relies on notes rather than a written manuscript. Your outline is your diagram connecting the information you want to communicate in a rational, consistent way. It enables you to assemble the pieces of the information so that the puzzle makes sense to you and communicates your intended meaning to your audience. Think of outlining as a process of layering ideas on paper so that every statement supports your thesis. It is a time-consuming process, but one that pays off in a skillful, confident presentation.

Be familiar with the criteria for each speech assignment. Each instructor has his/her own requirements. Some may want to see your planning outline and speaker's notes while others may not. Instead of a planning outline, your instructor may ask you to turn in a full-sentence outline that includes points, subpoints, source citations, and reference pages, but excludes statements about transitions or speech flow. The following discussion is designed to help you develop and, by extension, deliver an effective speech. Your instructor will have specific ideas about the outline and note cards.

The Planning Outline

The planning outline, also known as the full-content outline, includes most of the information you will present in your speech. It does not include every word you plan to say, but gives you the flexibility required in extemporaneous speaking. An effective outline has four main components: parallelism, coordination, subordination, and division (Tardiff & Brizee, 2011).

PARALLELISM. On the face of it, parallelism and consistency may sound like the same thing. However, consistency refers to the numbering of sections and points of your outline, whereas parallelism refers to how you construct your sentences. For example, if one point is, "Having a pet gives your children responsibility," another main point *should not* be stated, "When should you *not* have a pet?" Instead, that main point would be phrased something like, "Knowing when not to have a pet is important." Following are a few brief examples:

> POINT 1: Destroyed are the great redwoods that have survived over the centuries.
> POINT 2: Vanished is the small animal life that used to grow in the great forests of our nation.
> POINT 1: Joining the military will provide specific job skills.
> POINT 2: Staying in the military will provide a stable income.

Parallelism goes beyond phrasing sentences, however. True parallel structure means that your introduction and your conclusion are related. For example, let's say that in your introduction to a speech on world harmony, you paint a picture of how life would be if all people on earth lived together without war or international conflict. With parallel structure, you bring back this picture after the body of your speech, so that you can show your audience that if they did what you're asking them to do (travel, communicate with people from other countries, accept differences, or whatever you propose), this is what life would be like. Parallel structure is an effective organizational tool and provides listeners with a sense of closure.

COORDINATION. *Coordinate points* are your main ideas. We suggested earlier that your speech be composed of three to five main points. Generally speaking, each of your coordinate points should have the same significance, even though, for purposes of an informative or persuasive speech, you may find one point to be your strongest argument or one point to be your most valuable piece of information. In a speech, each coordinate point will require supporting material. In the above example about the military, it can be argued that specific job skills and stable income are two equally significant benefits of being in the military. Finding facts and statistics about these two points is part of your research process for such a speech.

SUBORDINATION. *Subordinate points* support your main or coordinate points. Information in your coordinate points is more general, while information in the subordinate points is more specific. Subordinate points provide relevant supporting material, such as facts, statistics, examples, or testimony. Every speech, and therefore every outline, will have both coordinate and subordinate points. For example, if you were trying to convince college students to buy a scooter, you might include the following main, or coordinate, point with the corresponding subordinate points.

I. Buying a scooter saves money
   A. A new scooter costs less than $2,500, which is only a fraction of what a new car costs.
   B. A scooter gets between 80 and 100 miles per gallon, thus saving hundreds of dollars each year.
   C. An on-campus parking sticker for a scooter costs only $5.

Notice that the cost of a scooter, the gas mileage, and the parking sticker costs are all facts that support the idea that buying a scooter saves money.

As you notice in the examples, coordinate and subordinate points are stated as one full sentence that represents one idea. Phrases and incomplete sentences will not state your points fluently, nor will they help you think in terms of the subtle interrelationships among ideas, transitions, and word choice. *Singularity* refers to the notion that each point and subpoint comprises one, separate, but logically connected, idea. A main point should not be "We should all volunteer, and we should require that each person partake in six months of community service before age 21." These are two separate points. A well-constructed planning outline ensures a coherent, well-thought-out speech. Using full sentences defines your ideas and guides your choice of language.

DIVISION. Division refers to the fact that points and subpoints are distinct and identifiable on your outline. Each level has at least two points. So if you have a Roman numeral "I," minimally, you will see a "II." If you have a capital "A," minimally, you will see a "B." You should never have just one point or subpoint. Technically, there is no limit to how many main points or subpoints you include on your outline. If you have a large number of points, however, you may want to see if some of them can be combined, making sure you are still developing one fluid idea.

As you develop your outline, check to see how many subpoints you have under each main point. Perhaps you are providing an information overload in one section but you lack support in another area. If you believe that there isn't more than one subpoint under a main point, then perhaps you do not have an adequate main point, and you need to rethink the general structure of your argument.

Guidelines for Constructing a Planning Outline

In addition to addressing the four components of an effective outline, your outline should follow a consistent pattern. In a traditional outline, Roman numerals label the speech's main ideas. Subordinate points are labeled with letters and numbers.

The proper positioning of the main and subordinate points with reference to the left margin is critical, for it provides a visual picture of the way your speech is organized. Be consistent with your indentation. The main points are along the left margin, and each subpoint is indented. Each subsubpoint is indented under the subpoint. This visual image presents a hierarchy that expresses the internal logic of your ideas.

In summary, as you construct your outline, check to see that you are following the principles of outlining. Doing so identifies strengths and weaknesses in support and logic, and overall, helps you create an effective speech. The following "boilerplate" suggests the format for a speech.

NAME:

SPECIFIC PURPOSE:

THESIS STATEMENT:

TITLE OF SPEECH:

INTRODUCTION

I. Capture attention and focus on topic
II. Set tone and establish credibility
III. Preview main points

BODY

I. First main point
    A. First subordinate (sub-) point to explain first main point
        1. First subpoint/supporting material for first subpoint
            a. Subpoint that provides greater details or explanations
            b. Subpoint that provides more details, examples, or explanations to clarify and explain
        2. Second subpoint/supporting material for first subpoint
    B. Second subordinate (sub-) point to explain first main point
        1. First subpoint/supporting material for second subpoint
        2. Second subpoint/supporting material for second subpoint
            a. Subpoint that provides greater details or explanations
            b. Subpoint that provides more details, examples, or explanations to clarify and explain
II. Second main point
    A. First subordinate (sub-) point to explain second main point
        1. First subpoint/supporting material for first subpoint
            a. Subpoint that provides greater details or explanations
            b. Subpoint that provides more details, examples, or explanations to clarify and explain
        2. Second subpoint/supporting material for first subpoint
    B. Second subordinate (sub-) point to explain second main point

      1. First subpoint/supporting material for second subpoint

      2. Second subpoint/supporting material for second subpoint

III. Third main point

    A. First subordinate (sub-) point to explain third main point

    B. Second subordinate point to explain third main point

      1. First subpoint/supporting material for second subpoint

      2. Second subpoint/supporting material for second subpoint

CONCLUSION

I.   Summary of main points

II.   Relate to audience

III. Provide closure/final thought

REFERENCES **(on separate sheet)**

Notice the particulars:

1   Your name, the specific purpose, thesis statement, and title of your speech are all found at the top of the page.

2   Each section (introduction, body, and conclusion) is labeled.

3   Each section begins with a Roman numeral.

4   Each point is not developed identically. In some cases, there are subpoints and subsubpoints. One point may need more development than another point.

Check with your instructor to see if you should have a regular planning outline or a full-sentence outline. A full-sentence outline requires that each point be written as one full sentence. This means no sentence fragments, and no more than one sentence per point.

Include at the end of your planning outline a reference page listing all the sources used to prepare your speech, including books, magazines, journals, newspaper articles, videos, speeches, and interviews. If you are unfamiliar with documentation requirements, check the style guide preferred by your instructor, such as the *American Psychological Association (APA) Publication Manual* (www.apastyle.apa.org) and the *Modern Literature Association (MLA) Handbook for Writers of Research Papers* (www.mla.org).

Check with your instructor to see how detailed your source citations should be in the outline. They should include last name, credentials, type of book (or magazine, journal, web page, etc.), year/date of publication.

Knowing how to cite your sources correctly is essential to cultivate credibility and audience trust.

© Erce/Shutterstock.com

Transitional sentences are valuable additions to your planning outline. They are needed when you move from the introduction to the body to the conclusion of the speech. They also link main points within the body and serve as internal previews and summaries. Put these sentences in parentheses between the points being linked and use language you actually speak. When appropriate, include internal summaries and previews of material yet to come.

Here is an example of a planning outline that includes transitional sentences.

SPEAKER'S NAME: Corey Schultz

SPECIFIC PURPOSE: To persuade my audience that Standard American English (SAE) should be considered as only one of many acceptable forms of spoken English

THESIS STATEMENT: Since Standard American English (SAE) promotes racism and classism, and is difficult to enforce, it should be only one of many acceptable forms of spoken English.

TITLE OF SPEECH: Revisiting Standard American English

INTRODUCTION

I. It is a common belief shared by almost all Americans that there is only one form of acceptable spoken English, known to linguists as Standard American English (SAE).

A. An enforced standardization of language is a common occurrence within languages across the world, and is created out of the perception that the natural evolution of language is harmful.

B. As a result, most grammar is taught without acknowledging a difference between spoken English and written English.

II. Recent research suggests, however, that SAE's prescriptive grammar instruction is not the most ideal form.

A. Grammar instruction in public education almost exclusively teaches SAE, which has led to the belief that "nonstandard" forms of English like African American Vernacular English, Chicano English, or Southern dialects are somehow incorrect.

B. This stigma encourages the marginalization of several groups.

(Transition): Because most of us have learned that there is actually one form of "correct" grammar, I see a lot of confused faces in the audience. However, the perpetuation of Standard American English only serves to marginalize racial and socioeconomic groups, and should therefore be considered as only one of many acceptable forms of spoken English.

In this speech, I will examine the problems with the standardization of spoken English, such as its promotion of racism and classism. Next, I will discuss its causes, before finally addressing its solutions.

BODY

I. Initially, Standard English promotes racism and classism.

A. According to a recent personal interview with Dr. K. Aaron Smith, author of *The Development of the English Progressive*, mandating the use of Standard English in American classrooms remains the largest, most unapologetic form of racism left in the United States.

B. In the 2010 article "Codeswitching: Tools of Language and Culture Transform the Dialectically Diverse Classroom," authors Wheeler and Swords argue that commenting on the invalidity of a student's language indirectly makes a statement about the invalidity of that student's culture.

II. By not addressing the validity of "nonstandard" English, all students are missing out on unique, important cultural perspectives.

A. Many people do not understand that African American Vernacular English, Chicano English, and all other dialects of the language have structured and complex systems of grammar and phonology.

1. For example, according to the previously cited interview with Dr. Smith, "aks" is one of the most commonly corrected aspects of African American Vernacular English.

2. Aks most likely derived from the Old English verb "acsian," meaning "to ask," and was considered standard English until about 1600.
3. As "aks" is still maintained in African American Vernacular English, Jamaican English, and many dialects of British English, it isn't wrong, it's only different.

B. Failing to open a dialogue with students about differences in dialects and vernaculars teaches students to ignore the important history of language, and teaches students to blindly follow them in assuming that their English is the only "correct" English.

(**Transition**): While we now understand the problems with the enforcement of Standard American English, it is also equally as important to study its causes.

III. First, English speakers hold the belief that speech must be formal to be intelligent.

A. In 1712, Jonathan Swift wrote *A Proposal for Correcting, Improving and Ascertaining the English Tongue*, in which, among other things, he advocated for the creation of an English Academy literally for the purpose of making the language sound fancier.
1. The concept of the double negative, which is something that many students of English struggle with, was instated to reflect the rules of math: Two negatives make a positive.
2. However, if I say, "I ain't gonna do no work," it, in no way, means that I am going to do work.

B. If students learned this history of the rules of grammar, it is possible that the prestige and superiority felt by many speakers of Standard English might be lessened.

IV. Second, many teachers fail to recognize a difference between written English and spoken English.

A. According to Dr. Rai Noguchi in his book *Grammar and the Teaching of Writing*, the growing influence of the oral culture and the accompanying decline of writing complicate grammar instruction.
1. As people read less, they have less exposure to the conventions of writing.
2. Thus, the conventions of writing (as opposed to those of speech) often go unnoticed and must be taught formally in the schools.

B. Similar to how scientists and doctors use specialized language to avoid ambiguity, writing in an academic context should be standardized.

    1. This is the reason for grammar instruction.

    2. When educators fail to recognize the difference between spoken English and written English, they marginalize specific groups within their classroom.

(Transition): Now that we've examined the implications of this phenomenon and looked at the reasons why we enforce standardization, let's look at some solutions to end this problem.

V. Initially, there are several ways in which you can help on a personal level.

    A. Don't correct anyone's spoken English.

    B. According to the Linguistic Society of America's *Language Rights Resolution*, many of the dialects, vernaculars, and indigenous languages of the United States are severely threatened, which means the cultures that speak those languages are also threatened.

        1. Therefore, do not judge speakers (in classrooms or otherwise) based on the way they choose to use language.

        2. Also, stand up for those who are unfairly criticized.

VI. There are several institutional changes that should be made.

    A. Because the U.S. government has never and *will* never create an institution to control and standardize language, I'm not going to ask you to write your senators.

    B. However, it may help to write a letter to your high school principal or English department chair, insisting that teachers teach grammar by separating written English and spoken English, and study the differences in grammar of both styles in the classroom.

Conclusion

I. Today, I have discussed how standardization of the English language is a major problem in society.

II. It's clear that if nothing is done, Standard American English will only continue to marginalize certain cultural and socioeconomic communities.

III. It is important that we, as a society, help end this severely underestimated problem.

REFERENCES

Language rights resolution. Linguistic Society of America. Retrieved from www.lsadc.org/lsa-res-rights.

Noguchi, R. R. (1991). *Grammar and the teaching of writing: Limits and possibilities.* Urbana, IL: National Council of Teachers of English.

Smith, K. A. (2010, September 23). Personal interview at Illinois State University.

Wheeler, R. S., & Swords, R. (2010). Codeswitching: Tools of Language and Culture Transform the Dialectally Diverse Classroom. *Workshop on Developing Writers, Series #5.* Christopher Newport University. Annenberg, 1–19.

A Brief Analysis of the Planning Outline

When applying a real topic to the boilerplate provided earlier, it is easy to see how the process unfolds. Note how transitions work, moving the speaker from the introduction of the speech to the body, from one main point to the next and, finally, from the body of the speech to the conclusion.

Remember, although the word transition appears in the outline, it is not stated in your speech. Transitions help connect listeners in a personal way to the subject being discussed. It also provides the thesis statement and previews the main points of the speech.

Notice that quotes are written word for word in the outline. Also, the preview is found just before the body of the speech. Once stated, the audience will know the main ideas you intend to present. As the outline moves from first- to second- to third-level headings, the specificity of details increases. The planning outline moves from the general to the specific.

Websites with ".gov" at the end of their URL can be considered trustworthy online sources.

© Stefano Garau/Shutterstock.com

SPEAKING EXCELLENCE IN YOUR CAREER

As new technology moves us to a more globalized economy, the ability to speak more than one language can be a significant advantage in advancing your professional career. In relation to speech preparation, many communication researchers have questioned how advance preparation can help professional interpreters. Researchers Stephanie Díaz-Galaz, Presentación Padilla, and María Teresa Bajo offer their research into the role of advance preparation in simultaneous interpreting.

The authors conducted a study with 23 participants: sixteen students about to complete a two-year undergraduate program in English-Spanish conference interpreting, and seven professional interpreters who (at the time of the study) were working regularly in institutional and private markets in Spain (Díaz-Galaz, Padilla, & Bajo, 2015). Both sets of participants were given sets of audio to interpret, and were divided into two groups: one group with a half-hour of preparation, and one group with no prior preparation time. Participants were analyzed based on their accuracy of interpretation and length of ear-voice span (EVS), with EVS being the measure of how long it took between hearing the audio and vocally interpreting the communication. Results indicated that both students and professionals alike benefitted from advance preparation (Díaz-Galaz, Padilla, & Bajo, 2015). Advance preparation resulted in increased accuracy and shorter EVS. As with public speaking, the habit of preparing in advance could also be evidence of deliberate practicing leading to expert performance.

Speaker's Notes

Speaker's notes are an abbreviated key-word outline, lacking much of the detail of the planning outline. They function as a reminder of what you plan to say and the order in which you plan to say it. Speaker's notes follow exactly the pattern of your planning outline, but in a condensed format.

Follow the same indentation pattern you used in your planning outline to indicate your points and subpoints. Include notations for the introduction, body, and conclusion and indicate transitions. It is helpful to include suggestions for an effective delivery. Remind yourself to slow down, gesture, pause, use visual aids, and so on. This is helpful during your speech, especially if you experience public speaking apprehension.

Guidelines for Constructing Speaker's Notes

1 AVOID OVERLOADING YOUR OUTLINE. Some speakers believe that having substantial information with them at the podium will give them confidence and make them more prepared. The opposite is usually true. Speakers who load themselves with too many details are torn between focusing on their audience and focusing on their notes. Too often, as they bob their heads up and down, they lose their place.

2 INCLUDE ONLY NECESSARY INFORMATION. You need just enough information to remind you of your planned points. At times, of course, you must be certain of your facts and your words, such as when you quote an authority or present complex statistical data. In these cases, include all the information you need in your speaker's notes. Long quotes or lists of statistics can be placed on separate index cards or sheets of paper (if allowed in the situation).

3 REDUCE YOUR SENTENCES TO KEY PHRASES. Instead of writing: "The American Medical Association, an interest group for doctors, has lobbied against socialized medicine," write: "The AMA and socialized medicine." Your notes should serve as a stimulus for what you are going to say. If you need only a few words to remind you, then use them. For example, Therese, who had directed several high school musicals, planned to discuss aspects of directing a high school musical. Her speaker's notes could include the following key words:
- Casting
- Blocking
- Choreography
- Singing
- Acting

Little else would be needed, since she can easily define and/or describe these aspects of directing. However, under the key word "casting," she might include "when to cast," and "how to cast." Relevant quotes or perhaps a reference to a dramatic story would be included in the notes as well.

4 INCLUDE TRANSITIONS, BUT IN AN ABBREVIATED FORM. If you included each transition, your notes would be too long, and you would have too much written on them. Look at one of the transitions from the previous speech on the standardization of American English:

(Transition): Because most of us have learned that there is actually one form of "correct" grammar, I see a lot of confused faces in the audience. However, the perpetuation of Standard American English only serves to marginalize racial and socioeconomic groups, and should therefore be considered as only one of many acceptable forms of spoken English.

In this speech, we will examine the problems with the standardization of spoken English, such as its promotion of racism and classism. Next, we will discuss its causes, before finally addressing its solutions.

Instead of these two paragraphs, your speaker's notes might look like this:

- Confused faces
- SAE marginalizes
- Will discuss problems, causes, solutions

If you practice your speech, these words should suffice as notes. Abbreviate in a way that makes sense to you. Each person will have his or her own version of shorthand.

5   NOTES MUST BE LEGIBLE. Your notes are useless if you cannot read them. Because you will be looking up and down at your notes as you speak, you must be able to find your place with ease at any point. Do not reduce your planning outline to eight points and paste them to note cards. If you can type your notes, make sure they are 14-point or larger. If you write your notes, take the time to write legibly. Think about this: You may have spent several hours researching, preparing, and organizing your speech. Why take the chance of reducing the impact of your speech by writing your notes at the last minute?

Following is an example of a set of speaker's notes. The transformation from planning outline to key-word outline is noticeable in terms of length and detail. Transitions, delivery hints, and the parts of the outline are in boldface. Note that the quotes would be written out in full in the notes, to avoid misquotation.

"Revisiting Standard American English," sample speaker's notes.

Introduction	1
I. Belief in form of English	
A. Common throughout the world	
B. Difference between spoken and written	
II. Prescriptive grammar instruction is bad	
A. Belief that "nonstandard" English is wrong	
B. Marginalizes groups	
(Look around room. Make eye contact. Slow down.)	
(Standard English is racist and classist. We will examine the problems, causes, and solutions.)	

Body *(Slow down)*	2
I. Racist and classist	
A. Smith quote on racism	
B. Codeswitching	
II. Students miss cultural perspectives	
A. Other forms are legitimate	
1. "aks"	
2. Not wrong, different	
B. Teaches to ignore history of language	

(Equally important to understand causes)	3
III. Formal speech = Intelligent speech	
A. Jonathan Swift	
1. Concept of the double negative	
2. "I ain't gonna do no work" ≠ "I'm gonna do work"	
B. Don't know history of rules	

IV.	No perceived difference between spoken and written		4
	A.	Dr. Rai Noguchi quote	
		1. Less exposure to conventions	
		2. Must be taught formally	
	B.	Writing should be standardized	
		1. This is the reason for SAE	
		2. Separate written and spoken English	

(Let's look at solutions)			5
V.	Personal solutions		
	A.	Do not correct	
	B.	Threat to dialect	
		1. Do not judge	
		2. Stand up for others	
VI.	Institutional solutions		
	A.	Do not write to Congress	
	B.	Write to school	

Conclusion		6
I.	Discussed problems, causes, and solutions	
II.	No change, SAE will always be bad	
II.	Help	
(Pause. Wait for applause.)		

A Brief Analysis of Speaker's Notes

Including your specific purpose and thesis statement in your speaker's notes is unnecessary. Speaker's notes follow exactly the pattern of the planning outline so you maintain the organizational structure and flow of your speech. The introduction, body, and conclusion are labeled, although

it is possible you might need only the initial letters "I," "B," and "C" to note these divisions. Nonessential words are eliminated, although some facts are included in the speaker's notes to avoid misstatement. Delivery instructions can provide helpful reminders.

Creating effective speaking notes (and rehearsing your speech) will become easier as you gain more experience in public speaking.

ESSENTIALS FOR EXCELLENCE

In this chapter, you have examined the best practices associated with organizing and outlining ideas for your public presentations. However, even with the knowledge gained from this chapter, many of you will probably have significant speaking anxiety when speaking in front of a classroom. For more practical advice on how to organize and outline your speeches, author Cam Barber offers three simple suggestions.

Craft a clear message.

The best speakers use clear messages when passing information to their audience. A vivid message should be short, and shouldn't exceed one or two sentences. Remember, it needs to be catchy and relevant, since many audience members can forget what they hear in a matter of days.

Structure your ideas.

Progressively build a compelling story though clear structure, especially if you're developing a complex argument (Barber, 2016). A good method is to break each idea into two, three, or four chunks. Also, use rhetorical devices to assist your audience in comprehending your argument.

Challenge yourself.

Be prepared to answer tough questions from the audience. Question preparation is too often overlooked when practicing a speech. Create a list of potential difficult questions and draft multiple responses. This will help you plan for the unexpected and reveal any potential weaknesses in your argument.

WHAT YOU'VE LEARNED:

Now that you have studied the chapter, you should be able to:

1. Identify the three major aspects contained in the body of your speech.
   - First, identify a general purpose—to inform, persuade, entertain, or inspire.
   - Offer a specific purpose—a statement of intent detailing the precise response you want from your audience.
   - Craft a thesis statement identifying the main ideas of your speech—the core idea.
2. Describe chronological organization, past-present-future organization, spatial organization, cause and effect organization, problem-solution organization, and topical organization.
   - In a chronological speech, information is focused *on relationships in time.* Events are presented in the order in which they occur.
   - Past-present-future organization allows a speaker to provide perspective for a topic or issue that has relevant history and future direction or potential.
   - In spatial organization, the sequence of ideas moves from one physical point to another (e.g., from London to Istanbul, from basement to attic, etc.)
   - With the cause and effect organizational pattern, the speaker can focus specifically on why something happened and what the consequences of the event or action were.
   - Problem-solution organization asks the speaker to present an audience with a problem and then examine one or more likely solutions. The goal is to persuade an audience that a problem still exists and to have listeners agree about how it can be effectively handled.
   - Topical organization relies on knowing the unique needs of your topic. The nature and scope of your topic dictate the pattern of your approach.
3. Know the guidelines for constructing speaker's notes.
   - Avoid overloading you outline. Speakers who load themselves with too many details are torn between focusing on their audience and focusing on their notes.
   - Include only necessary information. You need just enough information to remind you of your planned points.
   - Reduce your sentences to key phrases. Your notes should serve as a stimulus for what you are going to say. If you only need a few words to remind you, then use them.
   - Include transitions, but in an abbreviated form. Abbreviate in a way that makes sense to you. Each person will have his or her own version of shorthand.
   - Notes must be legible. Because you will be looking up and down at your notes as you speak, you must be able to find your place with ease at any point.
4. Recognize best practices for utilizing speaker's notes.
   - Including your specific purpose and thesis statement in your speaker's notes is unnecessary. Speaker's notes follow exactly the pattern of the planning outline so you maintain the organizational structure and flow of your speech.
   - Label the introduction, body, and conclusion in your speaker's notes. This can be as simple as using the initial letters "I," "B," and "C".
   - Eliminate nonessential words, but make sure that some facts are included in speaker's notes to avoid misstatement.

Key Terms

body, 177
brainstorming, 178
conclusion, 177
equality pattern, 181
general purpose, 178
internal previews, 190

internal summaries, 191
introduction, 177
organization of ideas, 177
primacy effect, 182
progressive pattern, 182
recency effect, 182

specific purpose, 178
strongest point pattern, 181
thesis statement, 178
transitions, 189

Reflect

1. How can you tell an organized speaker from an unorganized one?
2. When do you usually think about how you're going to organize your speech?
3. Why do you think the topical organizational pattern is the most frequently used pattern? Which organizational pattern do you think is used least, and why?
4. If you were going to give an informative speech on "space exploration," think of two organizational patterns that might be appropriate. Now, assume you're going to give a persuasive speech on space exploration. What might be the most appropriate way to organize your ideas? Why?
5. In public speaking, what functions are served by transitions and summaries? Can you think of several effective transitional statements to develop the speech topic from question #4?
6. Review the essential requirements for planning and key-word outlines. Why is it necessary to develop both outline forms, and why are both equally important in extemporaneous speaking?

Review Questions

1. The _____ supports the body of your speech and should capture your audience's attention and indicate your intent.

2. The _____ supports the body of your speech, reinforces your message, and brings your speech to a close.

3. The _____ includes your main points and supporting material that reinforces your specific purpose and thesis statement.

4. There are three _____ for speeches: to inform, to persuade, and to entertain/inspire.

5. The _____ is the precise response you want from your audience.

6   A _____ is the core idea and identifies the main ideas of your speech.

7   _____ involves generating a list of ideas consistent with the goals of your speech.

8   Giving equal time to each point is known as the _____.

9   The _____ believes that it is the first point in your speech that listeners will most likely remember.

10 The _____ involves progression from the least important argument to the most important argument.

11 When using the _____, you spend the most time in your speech on the first point, less time on the second point, and even less time on the last point of your speech.

12 The _____ believes that listeners are most likely to remember the last point of your speech.

13 _____ are verbal bridges between ideas, words, phrases, or sentences that tell your audience how ideas relate.

14 _____ are extended transitions that tell the audience, in general terms, what you will say next.

15 _____ follow a main point and act as reminders; useful to clarify or emphasize what you have just said.

Craig Sager delivers a powerful acceptance speech for the Jimmy V Award for Perseverance.

CHAPTER SEVEN
INTRODUCING AND CONCLUDING YOUR SPEECH

OUTLINE

3. Use a Dramatic Illustration
            4. Conclude with a Quotation
            5. Conclude with a Metaphor that Broadens the Meaning of Your Speech
            6. Conclude with Humor
        C. How to Conclude the Same Speech in Different Ways
        D. Common Pitfalls of Conclusions
III. What You've Learned
IV. Key Terms
V. Reflect
VI. Review Questions

◼ WHAT YOU'LL LEARN

After studying this chapter, you should be able to:

1. Identify the functions of introductions.
2. Describe the five guidelines for introductions.
3. List the functions of conclusions.
4. Recognize common pitfalls of conclusions.

SPEAKING IN CONTEXT

At the Excellence in Sports Performance Yearly Awards (ESPYs) in July 2016, longtime NBA sideline reporter Craig Sager received the Jimmy V Award for Perseverance. Sager was diagnosed with leukemia in April of 2014. Although his cancer went into remission and he returned to reporting for "NBA on TNT" after an 11-month absence, he found out his cancer had returned shortly later. In March 2016, Sager revealed that his cancer was no longer in remission and doctors were only giving him three to six months to live (Flaherty, 2016). After receiving his award, Sager gave a powerfully inspirational speech asserting his will to fight, and his thanks to all the support he has received around the world. Sager concluded his speech with inspiring words about hope.

"I see the beauty in others, and I see the hope for tomorrow. If we don't have hope and faith, we have nothing," Sager said in closing. "I will never give up, and I will never give in. . . . I will live my life full of love and full of fun. It's the only way I know how. Thank you and good night." (Tsuji, 2016).

PART TWO: PREPARING AND PRESENTING YOUR SPEECH

Sager's words serve as a perfect example of how a powerful conclusion can create an impactful speech. Sager stirred the minds of his audience by describing his plight, and his determination to continue fighting no matter what the cost. He encouraged the audience to continue donating to the fight against cancer, and moved many in the audience to tears as he left the stage. As you learn the most effective strategies to introduce and conclude your presentation, remember Craig Sager's exemplary acceptance speech.

This chapter approaches introductions and conclusions in relation to how your speech can make a lasting impression. Two topics are considered: how to engage your audience at the beginning of your speech so they will be motivated to listen to the rest of it, and how to remind your audience at the end of your speech what you said and why it was relevant. For both introducing and concluding your speech, strategies and pitfalls are identified to help you craft your best start and finish.

The primacy/recency effect, explained in the previous chapter, sheds light on the importance of effective speech beginnings and endings. This theory suggests that we tend to recall more vividly the beginning and ending, and less of the middle of an event. When several candidates are interviewing for a job, the first and last candidates have an advantage because the interviewer is most likely to remember more about these two than the others. This theory also holds true for speeches: Your audience will likely recall more of the beginning and ending of your speech than the content in the middle.

The familiar speaker adage, "Tell them what you are going to say, say it, and then tell them what you said," addresses this truth. Beginning and ending a speech well helps your audience remember and, later, use, the ideas you present. Let's begin with a closer look at introductions.

Introductions

If done well, an **introduction** helps your audience make a smooth transition to the main points of your speech, create a positive first impression, and set an appropriate tone and mood for your talk. If done poorly, your audience may prejudge your topic as unimportant or dull and stop listening.

Consider the following example. As part of a conference for a group of business executives, business consultant Edith Weiner was scheduled

Introduction
Supports the body of your speech and should capture your audience's attention and indicate your intent.

to deliver a speech on the unequal distribution of world resources—admittedly, a topic with the potential to put her listeners to sleep. She was experienced enough as a speaker, though, to realize that the last thing her listeners wanted to hear at the beginning was a long list of statistics comparing the bounty of North America to the paucities in other parts of the world. Her speech would never recover from such a dull start. The challenge she faced was to capture the audience's attention at the outset.

Arriving at the auditorium early on the morning of her speech, Weiner marked off different-sized sections of the hall to represent, proportionately, the continents. She allotted coffee, pastries, and chairs according to the availability of food and income in each. Then she assigned audience members to these areas according to actual world population ratios.

What happened was memorable. While 30 people in the area representing Africa had to divide three cups of coffee, two pastries, and two chairs, the 17 people assigned to North America had more coffee and pastries than they could eat in a week, surrounded by 40 chairs. As participants took their seats (with those in Asia and Africa standing), they did so with a new perspective on world hunger and poverty, and with a desire to listen to whatever Weiner had to say. She began:

> I wanted to speak … about a topic most people tire of, but you, being so important to the financial community, cannot ignore. …

> Hunger and poverty aren't comfortable, are they? Neither is bounty when you realize the waste and mismatch of people and resources. …

> (Interview with Edith Weiner, October 10, 1989)

Edith Weiner's risky introduction grabbed the attention of all audience members in a powerful way.

Functions of Introductions

The emphasis on strong opening comments has long been held as important. In the first century Roman philosopher Quintillian noted that for a speech to be effective, an introduction must do four things (Corbett & Connor, 1999). Introductions must:

1. Capture attention and focus
2. Provide a motive for the audience to listen
3. Enhance the credibility of the speaker
4. Preview the message and organization

Edith Weiner's introduction was effective because it accomplished each of these objectives, as we shall see.

Capture Attention and Focus

Every experienced speaker knows that the first few moments are critical to the success of the entire speech. It is within these minutes that your listeners decide whether they care enough to continue listening. You want your listeners to think, "This is interesting," or "I didn't know that," or 'That was really funny." The common denominator in each of these responses is piqued audience interest.

Many introductions contain a personalized greeting. This acknowledges the audience and tells listeners that you see the speech as an opportunity to communicate your point of view. William Kamkwamba (2009) was invited to speak before participants at a TED (technology, entertainment, and design) conference to tell how, at 14 years of age, he invented a windmill from scraps in his poverty-stricken country. He began his message in this way: "Two years ago I stood on the TED stage in Arusha, Tanzania. I spoke very briefly about one of my proudest creations. It was a simple machine that changed my life."

TED talks offer speakers a massive platform to make a powerful

Kamkwamba's first appearance at TED two years earlier was unsuccessful because he was too nervous and overwhelmed. At that first speech, his only words were "I tried, and I made it." In his address two years later, he referenced this failure in his introduction, explaining: "Before that time I had never been away from my home in Malawi. I had never used a computer. I had never seen an Internet. On the stage that day, I was so nervous. My English lost, I wanted to vomit. [(Laughter)] I had never been surrounded by so many azungu, white people. [Laughter)]"

Such self-effacing humor and honest, vulnerable explanation created a bond with his audience and piqued their interest in what he would have said two years earlier. Kamkwamba continued with: "There was a story I wouldn't tell you then. But, well, I'm feeling good right now. I would like to share that story today."

As you capture the attention and focus of your audience, you also need to set the mood and tone of your speech. The **mood** of a speech refers to the overall feeling you hope to engender in your audience. **Tone** is the emotional disposition of the speaker as the speech is being delivered. Tone is created verbally by the words and ideas you select and nonverbally by the emotions you communicate.

Imagine observing the following scenario: Angela stood behind the podium beside the closed casket as she delivered the eulogy to tearful faces. Her sentimental message of grief was appropriate in every way except that she delivered it with a smile. The disconnect between her words and facial expressions was unsettling, to say the least. Angela later confessed that she smiled because she wanted to communicate that she was glad to be there and honored to perform such an important duty. Unfortunately, Angela did not create an appropriate tone and mood in her introduction.

Consider the desired mood and adjust your tone appropriately in the introduction. By setting the tone at the very beginning, you ensure that your tone matches your reason for speaking and that your speech creates the desired mood in your audience.

Provide a Motive to Listen

An effective speaker quickly establishes a reason for audience members to listen. Edith Weiner's introduction helped build that critical relationship with her public speaking audience. She wanted her listeners to care about her message. She wanted them to decide from the outset that what she was saying had meaning and importance. Although the introduction also helped make her point with its physical demonstration of world food problems,

Mood

The overall feeling you hope to engender in your audience.

Tone

The emotional disposition of the speaker as the speech is being delivered.

its primary purpose was to build a psychological bridge that would last throughout the speech. Her well-designed demonstration led her audience to care about her topic because Weiner had effectively related the topic of her speech to something the audience cared about, their own hunger.

The introduction should seek to establish common ground with the audience. By focusing on something you and your audience can share and announcing it early, you help people identify with your topic. When people perceive that your message is meant for them and is relevant to their lives, they will listen attentively.

ENGAGING IN COMMUNITY

While working as a police officer for the Albertville Police Department years ago, Doug McGee received a call from a concerned woman; someone had dropped off six puppies, and she wanted animal control to come get them. Knowing the animal control department would euthanize the animals because of the overpopulation in the area, McGee responded to the call. McGee took the puppies to his house, and eventually found homes for all of them. After fielding numerous other calls about strays (and finding homes for them), McGee decided to take his volunteer work a step further.

McGee retired from the police force in 2008 and opened Second Chance Shelter. The shelter, which is a nonprofit organization, takes in most of its animals from surrounding animal control departments (Hrynkiw, 2016). Before the shelter opened, the city of Albertville euthanized approximately 1100 animals; currently, it is estimated only 200-300 are put down. McGee spoke passionately about his community work, as well as his desire to do even better.

"I'd love to shut my doors," said McGee. "I'd love to do such a great job at the shelter that we have to close because we have no more homeless dogs." (Hrynkiw, 2016).

Organizations that rely on charitable donations, like the Humane Society, require that their representatives make powerful connections with their audience.

When McGee speaks to reporters or the general public, he always reminds his audience how they can help, either by adopting or volunteering. By ending his interviews with a call to action, McGee encourages members of the public to take an active role in their community. When learning how to conclude your speech, remember that motivating your audience can leave a lasting impression and even lasting change.

© ValeStock/Shutterstock.com

Enhance Credibility

Credibility

The extent to which a speaker is perceived as a competent spokesperson.

During your introduction, your listeners make important decisions about you. They decide whether they like you and whether you are credible. Your **credibility** as a speaker is judged, in large part, on the basis of what you say during your introduction, how you say it, and how you carry yourself.

Edith Weiner (1989) became a credible speaker by demonstrating, in a participatory way, that she understood the problems of world food distribution and that she cared enough about her audience—and topic—to come up with a creative way to present her ideas. Credibility also increases as you identify, early on, what qualifies you to speak about a topic. Weiner might have said, "I want to talk to you about world resources because for several years I have studied how your investments overseas can have important impacts on your future economic well-being." Similarly, Angela, the inappropriately smiling mourner, might have mentioned early on that she was close to the deceased, knew her for 30 years, and thought of her as a sister. Offering an explanation linking you to the topic you are covering helps your audience believe in you and trust your ideas.

Audiences may have an initial sense of your credibility even before you speak. Your introduction is an ideal place to enhance that impression. As we discuss later in the text, you can think of your credibility in terms of your perceived competence, concern for your audience, dynamism, and personal ethics. Put another way, if you know your subject, care about your audience, offer an enthusiastic delivery, and communicate a sense of ethical integrity, your audience's impression of your credibility will likely be positive. The content and delivery of your introduction must maximize these four aspects if you want your audience to listen attentively throughout your speech.

Preview Your Message and Organization

Finally, Weiner used her introduction to tell her audience what she would talk about during the rest of her speech. In a sentence, she previewed her focus. ("I intend to explore several options during the rest of my speech.") This simple statement helped her listeners make the intellectual connections they needed to follow her speech. Instead of wondering, "What will she talk about?" or "What is her point of view?" they were ready for her speech to unfold.

As we said in the opening of this chapter, your audience will recall your message more fully if you tell them what you are going to say, say it, and then tell them what you said. Repeating key ideas helps us recall important information. But the first part, telling them what you are going to say, also provides a preview of the organization you intend to use. If your audience knows the main points you intend to develop in your speech, they are less likely to be confused and distracted. So, an effective introduction might offer a preview statement similar to "Today it is important that we better understand the nature of world hunger, explore creative solutions to this problem, and, finally, see if some of these solutions might also be profitable to your business." In this example, the audience learns that there will be three main points to the message.

Here is how Agnes, a student at an international university in Manila, Philippines, started her informative speech on child obesity and junk food at home. The preview statement is italicized:

> In July, 2011, McDonald's announced changes to their well-known "Happy Meals" to offer healthier food. Happy Meals target children. United States First Lady Michelle Obama, who has been campaigning against childhood obesity, has commended McDonald's for their action.
>
> Following suit, the National Restaurant Association in the U. S. announced their Kids Live Well program. This means dozens of restaurant chains, including Burger King and Denny's, committed to offering healthier meals for children, too. Great, right? But what about candy, soda, pizza, and other snacks at home?
>
> Changes have been made and are starting to be made across the globe, but many individuals are not taking action here in Manila. More parents need to get involved in this movement because it will better the lives of many children. *Today, I will more clearly define "junk food," discuss the health issues it creates for our kids, and offer easy alternatives to junk food in your home.*

When Agnes finished this statement, her audience had no doubt what her speech would cover. When you preview your message, your audience will listen and understand with increased clarity and will remember more of your message later.

How to Introduce the Same Speech in Different Ways

Many topics lend themselves to different types of introductions. A startling statement, a dramatic anecdote, a quotation, or a humorous story may each serve as an effective introduction to the same speech. Here, for example, is the same speech introduced three ways:

5 STARTLING STATEMENT.

Microwave cooking can be hazardous to your child's health. Children have been burned by opening bags of microwave-heated popcorn too close to their faces. Their throats have been scalded by jelly donuts that feel cool to the touch, but are hot enough inside to burn the esophagus. These and other hazards can transform your microwave into an oven of destruction in the hands of a child. What I would like to talk about today is how dangerous microwaves can be to young children and how you can safeguard your family from accidents.

6 DRAMATIC STORY.

Nine-year-old Jenny was one of those kids who managed quite well on her own. Every day she got home from school at 3:30 while her parents were still at work and made herself a snack in the microwave. She had been using the microwave since she was five, and her parents never questioned its safety—that is, not until Jenny had her accident.

It began innocently enough. Jenny heated a bag of microwave popcorn in the oven and opened it inches from her face. The bag was cool to the touch, hiding the danger within. Hot vapors blasted Jenny's face, leaving her with second- and third-degree burns.

What I would like to talk about today is how dangerous microwaves can be to young children and how you can safeguard your family from accidents.

7 Quotation.

Three out of every four American homes have microwave ovens and with them a potential for danger. Louis Slesin, editor of *Microwave News,* a health and safety newsletter, explains how this common kitchen appliance can present potential hazards for young children:

"On a rainy day," says Slesin, "a kid could climb up on a stool, put his face to the door and watch something cook for a long time. It's mesmerizing, like watching a fish tank, but his eye will be at the point of maximum microwave leakage. We don't know the threshold for cataract formation—the industry says you need tons of exposure, but some litigation and literature say you don't need much [for damage to occur]. Children younger than 10 or 12 shouldn't use the oven unsupervised. It's not a toy. It's a sophisticated, serious, adult appliance, and it shouldn't be marketed for kids."

I agree with Slesin, and what I want to talk about today is how dangerous the microwave can be to a young child.

The point of providing these three examples is to demonstrate how differently an introduction can be constructed. Avoid "settling" for an introduction; consider how you might create the most impact.

Speaking Well with Technology Is an Essential for Excellence

Many people find public speaking to be one of the most stressful experiences in their professional life. While practicing alone can definitely help communication professionals prepare for a live presentation, many people still dread that first moment of stepping up in front of a live audience. However, modern public speakers have a plethora of new communication technology to assist them. In particular, two communication technology startups are attempting to give speakers the benefit of practicing in front of a virtual audience.

One British startup now offers a program called Virtual Speech, which uses virtual reality that allows speakers to test out their presentation in front of a simulated audience (Gaskell, 2016). Presenters can upload their slides, select a simulated environment (conference hall, classroom, boardroom, etc.), and then deliver their presentation. The software even allows the speaker to select from a number of distractions to practice their delivery in a dynamic setting. Another piece of technology, called Rhema, has been developed by Rochester University. The program provides live feedback on your delivery via augmented reality glasses (Gaskell, 2016). The glasses can provide feedback for aspects like your volume and cadence, giving presenters an outside perspective about how they sound to audience members.

Virtual Speech and Rhema are but a small sampling of communication-enhancement technologies available to public speakers. As the market continues to grow, communication professionals will find countless ways to practice their speech in ultra-realistic settings. As you hone your speaking skills throughout this course, be sure to keep an eye out for presentation technologies that can give you an upper hand during your studies.

Developing Effective Introductions

Following are 10 techniques often used in introductions. You might consider using one or combining several to provide the initial impact you want. This is one area where a little creativity can go a long way. Keep your audience in mind. A few of these techniques may be more appropriate or attention-getting for your specific audience and specific purpose.

Startling Facts/Intriguing Statements

Some introductions seem to force listeners to pay attention. They make it difficult to think of other things because of the impact of what is being said. The effectiveness of these introductions comes in part from the audience's feeling that the speaker's message is directed at them.

Here is how Lady Gaga began her speech at a rally in Portland, Maine in September 2010 to repeal the military's Don't Ask, Don't Tell policy. After noting that the title of her speech was "The Prime Rib of America" she stated:

> I do solemnly swear, or affirm, that I will support and defend the Constitution of the United States, against all enemies foreign and domestic, and I will bear true faith and allegiance to do the same, and I will obey the orders of the president of the United States and the orders of the officers appointed over me, according to regulations and the uniform code of military justice, so help me God.

© Everett Collection/Shutterstock.com

Lady Gaga is known for her powerful introductions in both her performances and public speeches.

> Unless, there's a gay soldier in my unit, sir.

Starting with this oath served as an intriguing statement, since it wasn't clear initially why she would include it in her speech. Her last statement is startling, and quickly gets to the heart of the issue. In this case, she took the familiar and turned it on its side to arouse audience emotions.

Startling statements often challenge the listener. Instead of revealing the expected, the speaker takes a slightly—or perhaps even a radically—different turn.

Dramatic Story/Build Suspense

Closely related to the startling statement is the dramatic story, which involves listeners in a tale from beginning to end. Shortly after returning from a winter vacation break, Shannon delivered a speech to her classmates that began this way:

My friends and I were driving home from a day at the ski slopes when suddenly, without warning, a pair of headlights appeared directly in front of our car. To avoid a collision, I swerved sharply to the right, forcing our car off the road into a snow-filled ditch.

It's funny what comes into your mind at moments like this. All I could think of was how Justin Mentell, who used to be on *Boston Legal,* one of my favorite TV shows, died on icy roads just a month ago. And he was only 27. I thought I was going to die, too, just because of another driver's stupidity and carelessness.

Obviously, I didn't die or even suffer any serious injuries. And my friends are safe, too, although my car was totaled. I'm convinced that we are all here today because we were locked into place by our seat belts. Justin Mentell might have been here, too, had he bothered to buckle up.

Everyone in the audience knew what it was like to be driving home with friends—feeling safe and secure—only to be shocked into the realization that they were vulnerable to tragedy. Audience attention was riveted on the speaker as she launched into her speech on seat belt use.

Quotation and/or Literature Reference

You can capture audience attention by citing the words of others. If you use an appropriate quotation, the words themselves may be compelling enough to engage your listeners. One of the most well-known quotes from Harry Potter was used by a student to introduce the subject of his speech, sarcasm:

> "You know your mother, Malfoy? The expression on her face—like she's got dung under her nose? Is she like that all the time or just because you were with her?"

This passage was selected because it is funny, clever, and sarcastic. He set the stage for a lighter look at the harms of sarcasm with this quotation.

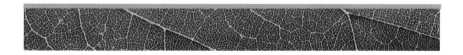

SPEAKING EXCELLENCE IN YOUR CAREER

As we discuss strategies to develop effective introductions, you will find that many experts (this text's authors included) recommend creating an emotional story. The benefits are obvious; sympathetic/empathic audiences are more likely to hold interest in a presentation or story. This strategy is commonly seen in the news media. Most news agencies will routinely publish human-interest stories in order to connect with their audience. With how often this strategy is used, a question arises: can an oversaturation of human-interest stories eventually desensitize listeners to the point of not caring? Researchers Audun Beyer and Tine Figenschou examine the effects that repetitive emotional stories can have on an audience.

Using an explorative survey, the researchers measured the response of a representative sample of the population about a human-interest story as it peaked in traditional media. In relation to the human-interest piece, participants were asked to evaluate the performance of key institutions (government, police, immigration authorities, political opposition, and media). Also, respondents were asked open-ended questions regarding their opinion on how the media covered the issue. Responses indicated that the general population is highly critical of media coverage, especially regarding the scale and scope of the coverage (Beyer & Figenschou, 2014). The researchers posited that oversaturation of human interest stories creates an interesting conundrum: the human-interest frame, which is designed specifically to capture an audience's attention and engage them in the story, can actually make people tired and detached when overused. The authors note that future research in this area should examine other effects of media hype and framing, as well as consider the nature of the human-interest story itself.

Robert Frost, well-known American poet, is frequently quoted from his poem *The Road Not Taken,* particularly, the last three lines:

> Two roads diverged in a wood, and I—
> I took the one less travelled by,
> and that has made all the difference.

The last three lines can be the start of a speech about following your heart, choosing your own path, making your own decisions, not following the crowd.

The two examples above have been used by others to start a speech or make some point. In addition to using the words of a *well-known individual,* you could also cite the words of *a recognized authority* whose reputation enhances your credibility.

Here, for example, is how Toby, a public speaking student, began his speech to capture the attention of his audience. Quoting a knowledgeable public figure, he began:

> "Today, 12.5 million children are overweight in the United States—more than 17 percent. Overweight children are at greater risk for many serious health problems." These are the words of your U.S. Surgeon General, Dr. Regina M. Benjamin (OSG, 2011). Dr. Benjamin continues with the following facts:
>
> Overweight adolescents have a 70 percent chance of becoming overweight or obese adults.
>
> The number of overweight children has more than tripled over the past three decades.
>
> Studies show that nearly 34 percent of children and teens in America are either overweight or at risk of becoming overweight.
>
> Research has shown that parents are often their children's most important role model. If children see their caregivers enjoying healthy foods and being physically active, they are more likely to do the same.

These powerful words from a recognized expert set the stage for Toby to advocate parental involvement in combating the childhood obesity epidemic our nation faces.

In similar fashion, Christopher, another public speaking student, captured his audience's attention when speaking about the nation's health care crisis by stating:

If a criminal has a right to an attorney, don't you have a right to a doctor? President Obama put it like this: "Everybody here understands the desperation that people feel when they're sick. And I think everybody here is profoundly sympathetic and wants to make sure that we have a system that works for all Americans" (msnbc.com, 2011). Obama sent a clear wake-up call to Congress to get serious about health care reform in America.

Christopher introduces the topic of health care by quoting the words of our president. Although these words could have been uttered by anyone, Christopher establishes credibility at the beginning of his speech by using a recognized authority.

Humor

At the beginning of a speech, humor helps break down the psychological barriers that exist between speaker and audience. Here is how Karen used humor at the start of a classroom speech on the problem of divorce in America:

Janet and Lauren had been college roommates, but had not seen each other in the 10 years since graduation. They were thrilled when they ran into each other at a college reunion and had a chance to talk.

"Tell me," asked Janet, "has your husband lived up to the promises he made when he was dating you in college?"

"He certainly has!" said Lauren. "He told me then that he wasn't good enough for me and he's proven it ever since."

The class laughed, Karen waited, then:

I laughed, too, when I heard that story. But the fact remains that about half the marriages in our country end in divorce and one of the major reasons for these failures is that one partner can't live up to the expectations of the other.

Humor works in this introduction for two reasons. First, the story is genuinely funny; we chuckle when we hear the punch line. And, second, the humor is tied directly to the subject of the speech; it is appropriate for the topic and the occasion. It also provides an effective transition into the speech body.

Humor *can* work when it's self-deprecating. Rahm Emanuel, mayor of Chicago, was known for his profanity-laced communication. At a commencement ceremony at George Washington University in 2009, he made reference to that at the beginning of his speech:

> Congratulations. I also want to thank George Washington University for bestowing this honorary degree. This is actually the second honorary degree I've received this year. Just last week I was awarded an honorary degree for my contribution in the field of linguistics, particularly my work in four-letter words.

Again, humor makes the audience snicker, giggle, or cackle, and it can set the right tone for your speech. Make sure you *can* do humor. At the 2011 Academy Awards, the loudest laughter came when Billy Crystal briefly took the stage away from hosts Anne Hathaway and James Franco, who were *trying* to be funny. If you are not comfortable with humor and elect to force it, both you and your listeners will feel awkward.

Comedian Billy Crystal has made a career out of using humor with his audiences.

© drserg/Shutterstock.com

PART TWO: PREPARING AND PRESENTING YOUR SPEECH

Rhetorical Question

When you ask your audience, "How many of you ate breakfast this morning?" you expect to see people raise their hands. When you ask a *rhetorical* question, however, you do not expect an answer. What you hope is that your question will cause your listeners to start thinking about the subject of your speech.

Imagine a speech about the negative effects of snoring. It could start like this:

> Have you ever been told you snore? Have you ever had to sleep in the same room with someone who has a loud snore? Have you been told you have a "cute" little snore?

These are all rhetorical questions. The speaker is not expecting someone to answer these questions aloud. The purpose is to get the audience to start thinking about the topic. Then the speaker continues:

> If you don't snore, be grateful. If you do snore, you need to hear this. If you don't snore, but you marry "a snorer," well, good luck! Studies show that married couples argue about snoring as much as they do money; snoring couples have less sex than nonsnoring couples, and over 20 percent of couples regularly sleep apart due to snoring. Ouch! Oh, and there's more. The nonsnorer faces difficulties from sleep deprivation. In the next few minutes I'm going to describe the economic consequences of being sleep deprived, including increased health care costs, automobile accidents, workplace accidents, and decreased job performance.

The speaker linked the rhetorical questions and startling facts to the audience, and previewed the main points in her speech. The best rhetorical questions are probing in a personal way. They mean something to every listener and encourage active participation throughout your speech.

Illustrations, Examples, and Anecdotes

Speakers often begin with an interesting comment about the immediate surroundings or some recent or historical event. These openings are even more powerful when the speaker carefully plans these comments. Through the skillful use of *illustrations* ("In the short time I will be talking with you, 150 violent crimes will have been committed in our nation"), *examples* ("Lisa was a young woman from our community whose life was forever altered on January 18th"), and *anecdotes* ("Once, while traveling on the subway, I noticed a shifty looking man carefully watching each passenger enter and leave the car"), speakers gather our attention to them and their message.

Physically Involve the Audience

An example of this technique regularly occurs at sales seminars, where the speaker offers a gift, usually money, to the first person in the audience who will simply leave his/her seat and come to the front to get it. Eventually some brave soul approaches, takes the money, and returns to his/her seat. Then everyone else in the audience realizes they could have had the gift themselves if they had only been willing to act instead of sitting passively.

In a speech about the importance of eating a good breakfast, a speaker could start by asking all students who ate breakfast to raise their hands. Then, the speaker could ask how many of those ate fast food, or ate eggs, or fruit. Depending on how the speaker defined a good breakfast, the questions could lead the speaker to comment that "Only a few of you had a good breakfast today. I hope to make a difference for tomorrow."

Some speakers may ask the audience to yell "Good morning" until they've been loud enough. A speaker talking about the need for exercise may ask the audience to jump up and down for a few moments. At a graduation speech in 2003 at the University of Wisconsin, after thanking the administration, director and movie producer Jerry Zucker involved the audience physically when he started his speech with the following:

> Before I start my remarks, I'd like everyone just to do something for me. Very simply—so everyone can kind of just get to know everyone else—on the count of three, I'd like everyone to turn around and shake the hand of the person sitting right behind you. One, two, three—right now, everybody, please do that.

Relate a Personal Experience

Sharing a story or several examples from your past with your listeners can be an effective start. Be sure your personal experiences will not hurt your credibility and that they relate directly to your topic. Recently, a student giving a "speech of presentation" started this way:

> It was the end of my third week of college, and the problem was getting harder and harder to ignore. I, like so many people today, had no idea where to turn, or who to talk to. So, I took to the streets. I walked up 4th, walked around the Courthouse, and then headed due east. Finally, on 9th Street, I found hope again … In the form of Terry's Clip and Chip Barbershop. You see, my hair had started tickling the backs of my ears, and I was getting that abhorrent ring-around-the-collar phenomenon …

The student's speech was to present a Small Business award to the barbershop/golf repair shop. He continued to describe his experience as an illustration of why Terry's Clip and Chip deserved the award. It was a humorous beginning with a personal story that related directly to the topic.

Use a Visual or Media Aid

Before the president of the United States speaks, the broadcast feed from the White House shows the presidential seal. This is no accident; it helps to draw attention to the upcoming speech and also helps reinforce the president's credibility. But you do not have to be the president to use this technique. Beginning your speech with an interesting sound recording, visual, or prop is guaranteed to draw attention to the beginning of your speech, too. Showing the world population clock or the U.S. debt clock grabs attention, as would some funny or startling YouTube video. One student brought a garbage bag filled with one week's worth of used diapers for one child to demonstrate how much waste is produced.

Refer to the Situation

Skilled public speakers often begin with a positive comment related to the occasion, the person who spoke before them, the audience, the date, or even the physical location. Each of these may be more appropriate at one time than at another. For example, a commencement speaker at her alma mater might start, "It's hard for me to believe that 25 years ago I sat in those seats listening to the commencement speaker." Or, if an audience was waiting outside in the rain to hear a Democratic candidate who was late, the candidate might start, "I bet there isn't a more committed group of voters than those of you here who have been standing in the rain waiting for me." When you are planning a speech, ask yourself if referencing the event, a prior speaker, the audience, or the significance of this date in history would create interest and gather attention.

Each of these is an option for opening a speech. Keep in mind that your attention-gaining device must relate in some way to your topic or you run the risk of confusing your audience. Your choice should be guided by several other factors. First, consider the mood you are attempting to create. Second, consider your audience's expectations of you and the occasion. Third, consider how much time and resources each approach will require. Finally, consider your strengths and weaknesses—you may not be as strong at joke telling as recalling a powerful story.

Five Guidelines and Suggestions for Introductions

As you focus on crafting your introduction for your next speech, consider how you can create a strong and effective message. Remember, as in any recipe, no ingredient stands on its own. Attention to each part of the process leads to an excellent final product. After choosing the most appropriate beginning, consider these general guidelines as you prepare and deliver your introduction.

1. Prepare After the Body of the Speech

Your introduction will take form more easily after you have created an outline of the body of your speech. When speakers attempt to create the introduction first, they inevitably rewrite it several times as they continue to change the body of their message. However, some students find that writing the introduction after selecting a thesis and main points helps to "jump start" the rest of the creative process. In either case, the direction and key ideas are in place before the introduction is considered.

2. Make It Creative and Easy to Follow

Whether you are offering a startling statistic or asking a question, keep things simple. When you offer your thesis and even when you preview your main points, look for ways to be concise and straightforward.

Recently, a student beginning his persuasive speech started with his arms open in a pleading gesture, zealously urging the class, "Please! Please I beg of you—stop washing your hands!" He then briefly noted the dangers of too much cleansing and stated his thesis. His enthusiastic approach and startling plea made for a creative introduction that was simple and easy to understand.

Consider your introduction as an invitation to creativity. The more creative your introduction, the more likely your audience will listen to the entire message. One student turned the lectern around on the table so the top sloped toward his audience, climbed up, and perched himself atop with legs dangling, and paused. His audience chuckled at his odd behavior. Then he forcefully announced, "Science has discovered a link between nonconformity and intelligence." His audience roared! His speech about nonconformity and intelligence was well received, but his attention-gaining strategy was risky. Sometimes creativity can backfire. Be sure your strategy suits your occasion and audience expectations of the speaker.

3. Communicate High Energy by Being Well Practiced

The most important part of your speech to practice thoroughly is the introduction, followed by the conclusion, and then the body. The first impression created by a well-practiced introduction lays the foundation for your ultimate success. Rehearse your introduction many times. Your introduction should be delivered enthusiastically. Since introductions are relatively short, put your heart, mind, and energy into it. If you are truly engaged in the introduction, your audience is more likely to become involved in your message.

It is difficult to communicate high energy if you are dependent on notes. Strive to avoid looking at notes during your introduction. Rehearsing your introduction helps you accomplish this.

4. Engage Audience Nonverbally Before You Start

Poise counts! Recall that your speech actually begins as you rise to speak and eyes fall on you. Create a confident, energetic approach to the front. Once there, pause, catch and hold your audience's eye contact for a moment, and take a deep breath. Each of these measures is critical to beginning your speech effectively. You want your audience to know you are interested in the speech and that you want them to be part of the experience. Your nonverbal messages are the first part audiences receive as they form a first impression of you. It may help to picture a favorite speaker or actor whom you admire for their effective posture, poise, and presence. Can you embed these traits in your nonverbal approach?

5. Consider Time Constraints and Mood

When giving a five-minute speech, telling a protracted, dramatic story would be inappropriate. The same is true of showing a one-minute video clip. Alternately, when delivering a 45-minute lecture, such a beginning would be wholly acceptable. The mood you are hoping to create in your audience must be related to the tone you adopt as a speaker. The introduction is your best chance to establish your tone and alter the mood of your audience. Carefully consider what effects different introductions might have on mood. Capture the nonverbal elements of voice and body that reflect the best tone for delivering your message.

Common Pitfalls of Introductions

Excuse the cliché, but as they say, you never get a second chance at a first impression. Here is a list of problematic approaches to avoid during your introduction.

1 BEGINNING WITH AN APOLOGY. Do not use your introduction to apologize for mistakes you are likely to make, for inadequate visual aids, being ill prepared, or even just plain ill. Apologies set a negative tone that is hard to overcome.

2 BEING TOO BRIEF OR TOO LONG. Do not jump into the body of the speech or spend too much time setting up the speech. Your introduction should take between 10 and 20 percent of your total allotted speaking time. Not adhering to this guideline means violating an audience expectation and potentially annoying them.

3 GIVING TOO MUCH AWAY. While the introduction should provide a road map for your speech, you do not want to give the substance of your speech in your preview. Instead, use general terms to tell your audience what you intend to cover.

4 READING. We have advised you to rehearse your introduction thoroughly. Do not read your introductory remarks to your audience. Your script becomes a barrier between you and your audience. Worse yet, you will likely sound more like a reader than a public speaker. Avoid reading extensively in the introduction (or anywhere else).

5 RELYING ON SHOCK TACTICS. Your victory will be short lived if you capture audience attention by screaming at the top of your lungs, pounding the table, telling a bawdy joke, or using material that has nothing to do with your speech. Your audience will trust you less because of the way you manipulated their attention. Using an innovative approach can be effective as long as it is tied directly to the topic of your speech and is not over-the-top.

6 PROMISING TOO MUCH. Some speakers, fearful that their speech says too little, promise more than they can deliver, in the hope that the promise alone will satisfy their listeners. It rarely does. Once you set expectations in the introduction, the body of your speech has to deliver or you lose credibility.

7 USING UNNECESSARY PREFATORY REMARKS. Resist the urge to begin with "I'm so nervous," "I can't believe I have to do this speech," or "Okay, deep breath, here we go." Even if you feel these things, such verbal adaptors are likely to make you even more nervous and hurt your credibility. Instead, begin with your planned opening statement.

8 USING LONG-WINDED POEMS, QUOTATIONS, AND PROSE. We understand that for full effect, an entire piece of prose or poetry should be read. We also know that editing a poem or piece of prose may not be easy. However, it is possible to find an appropriate nugget embedded within the piece that is perfect for your speech. Consider paraphrasing or moving longer passages to the body of your speech.

9 BECOMING SOMEONE ELSE. Because your initial credibility is being established in the introduction, avoid histrionics and melodrama. Being true to yourself will earn the respect of your listeners.

10 OVERUSING SOME TECHNIQUES. Often overused are simple questions, rhetorical questions, and startling, catastrophic stories. This is made worse by relying on trite phrases. Spend some time thinking about how to begin your speech. Think about what might be most effective with your particular audience. Seek originality and creativity.

Conclusions

Think of your conclusion as the pinnacle of your speech—the words you want your listeners to remember as they leave the room. Too often, speakers waste the opportunity with endings like "That's it," "I guess I'm finished now," or "I'm through. Any questions?" Or they simply stop talking, giving the audience no indication that they have finished their speech. Just as an introduction sets a first impression, a well-delivered conclusion leaves a lasting imprint on your audience.

Conclusion

Supports the body of your speech, reinforces your message and brings your speech to a close.

A conclusion should not be viewed as an afterthought. Understand that the conclusion is your last opportunity to have an impact. Just as the introduction should be clear and flow smoothly to the body of the speech, the body should flow smoothly to the conclusion. Following are three functions of conclusions to consider as you think about the transition from the body to the conclusion and determine how to create the greatest effect on your audience.

Functions of Conclusions

Strong endings to speeches summarize important information, motivate listeners, and create a sense of closure. President George W. Bush addressed the nation in the evening following the tragic events in New York City on what has become known simply as 9/11. After talking about the terror that so many Americans experienced, he explained how the rescuers responded, and what the government planned to do to prevent another attack. His conclusion was designed to touch the emotions of all Americans, and he provided closure at the end by stating the following:

President George W. Bush's speech after the 9/11 attacks offered a powerful conclusion to rally U.S. citizens.

© Jason and Bonnie Grower/Shutterstock.com

Tonight, I ask for your prayers for all those who grieve, for the children whose worlds have been shattered, for all whose sense of safety and security has been threatened. And I pray they will be comforted by a Power greater than any of us, spoken through the ages in Psalm 23:

Even though I walk through the valley of the shadow of death, I fear no evil for you are with me.

This is a day when all Americans from every walk of life unite in our resolve for justice and peace. America has stood down enemies before, and we will do so this time. None of us will ever forget this day, yet we go forward to defend freedom and all that is good and just in our world. Thank you. Good night. And God bless America.

Summarizing Important Information

The transition from the body to the conclusion is pivotal in signaling the impending end of your speech. Your instructor and your own personal preference may help you decide how to tell your audience you are ending. Whether you use a formal "In conclusion …" or prefer something less formal, such as "Now, to wrap this up today …," you want your audience to be clear that you are about to finish. Audiences know that when you give them that signal, they are about to get an important recap of your key ideas.

Motivating Listeners

Great speakers do more than summarize in their conclusions; they motivate their audiences. In motivating your audience, you might accomplish three things: relate your topic to your listeners, communicate a feeling, and broaden the message.

1   RELATE YOUR TOPIC TO YOUR LISTENERS. Your speech will achieve the greatest success if your listeners feel you have helped them in some concrete way. Consider making this connection in your conclusion. At the Virginia Statewide Housing Conference in November 2010, U.S. Secretary of Housing and Urban Development Shaun Donovan drew his speech to an end with the following remarks:

> For me, for President Obama, and for Senator Sanders, all this work comes down to a very simple belief: That no matter where you live, when you choose a home, you don't just choose a home. You also choose schools for your children and transportation to work. You choose a community—and the choices available in that community. A belief that our children's futures should never be determined—or their choices limited—by the zip code they grow up in.

> Like our President, I know change is never easy—that revitalizing our nation's communities, rural, urban, and suburban, won't happen overnight. Nor will it happen because of any one policy or the work of any one agency or one party. But working together, in common purpose—

in partnership—we can tackle our toughest challenges. We can push back on this crisis. We can build upon the remarkable change and sense of possibility you're catalyzing in communities across the state.

And most important of all, we can create a geography of opportunity for every American—and every family. Ensuring we do is our goal today. Let us rise to meet it.

In this brief passage, Donovan uses the word *community* four times. His use of the inclusive "we" is yet another way to establish a group identity and a sense of community. Donovan's conclusion clearly serves to motivate listeners to continue to work to improve living conditions in the United States.

2   COMMUNICATE A FEELING. The conclusion sets the psychological mood listeners carry with them from the hall. A student speaking against aspartame noted at the beginning of her speech that she believed aspartame contributed to her previous depression and weight gain. She ended her speech by noting that eliminating aspartame from her diet lifted her depression and led to significant weight loss. Her passion about the topic and the relief she feels were clearly communicated.

3   BROADEN YOUR MESSAGE. Finally, the conclusion can be used to connect your topic to a broader context. If in your speech you talk about the responsibility of every adult to vote on election day, you can use your conclusion to tie the vote to the continuation of our democratic system. If your speech focuses on caring for aging parents, you can conclude with a plea to value rather than discard the wisdom of the elderly.

Creating Closure

Good conclusions create a sense of closure for the speech. The audience feels a sense of satisfaction that you have completed and accomplished something important. If you are having dinner with others, the dessert often completes the dining experience. So, when speaking, it is not enough simply to stop with a comment: "Well, that's it, I guess I can see if anyone has a question," thus leaving the audience without a sense of closure. An effective conclusion tells your listeners your speech has ended. Next we offer four techniques speakers use to create a memorable closing.

Developing Memorable Conclusions

Thanking as Transition

Although saying thank you at the end of the speech indicates you are finished, it is no substitute for a statement that brings your discussion to a close. You can, however, use the "thank you" statement as a **transition** into your concluding remarks. For example, Oprah Winfrey received the first Bob Hope Humanitarian Award at the 54th Emmy Awards in September, 2002.

After saying thank you, Winfrey explained why she was thanking people. Rather than ending by saying thank you to several individuals, she gave the speech more impact by quoting Maya Angelou and leaving the audience with a final thought by asserting that she planned to make herself worthy of the honor by continuing to give to the world.

Transition
Verbal bridges between ideas, words, phrases, or sentences that tell your audience how ideas relate.

Call to Action

As you wrap up your speech, you can make a direct appeal to your listeners by urging them to take a specific action or to change their attitudes. In a persuasive speech, the conclusion is the most forcible and memorable place to position your final appeal.

Living in an age of mass media, Americans hear calls to action almost constantly. We are asked to like, share, or retweet; advertisers plead with us to drop everything and buy their products NOW! Internet sites and service station pumps force us to tune in to the sales pitch of the day. As annoying as these pleas can be, the fact that we are accustomed to calls to action makes them a natural conclusion to a speech.

In a speech designed to persuade her audience that industrial hemp should be grown in the United States, Mary, a public speaking student, ended her speech with a call to action:

© Ovidiu Hrubaru/Shutterstock.com

By thanking her audience at the end of her acceptance speech, Oprah enabled her words to resonate more strongly with her audience.

> It is easy to get excited about this crop. What other plant can give you so many products? Industrial hemp can make

jeans and milk and just about everything in between. And what plant has such a rich and diverse history?

I've only given you a small amount of information, and I'm sure you will be hearing more about industrial hemp in the future. States have stopped waiting for the federal government to legalize it and have begun passing their own bills. Industrial hemp won't save the world, but it will make a big difference. The possibilities are endless, so call your representative today. Tell him or her that the time has come for American to again grow Hemp for Victory.

Mary makes her last persuasive appeal, and then asks the audience to do something about it. Her call could have been stronger and more specific if, for example, she had prepared letters for her colleagues to sign and mail in an addressed, stamped envelope. More letters would be sent because Mary would not be relying on her audience to remember to create and mail their letters later.

Here is how a professor of political science might conclude a lecture:

I have explained my thoughts on the implications of the changes that are now taking place in the Middle East. As you review them, keep this in mind: What we are witnessing is nothing less than a change in world politics. In the days ahead, think about these changes and about how they will affect each and every one of us in the Western democracies.

The call to action, in this case, involves mental activity—reflection, rather than some physical action. This is a perfectly acceptable final statement.

Jane is a volunteer for her local child adoption agency. As part of her service, Jane is often tasked with speaking to reporters about the agency's functions and current needs. Recently, the program has seen a drastic decrease in volunteer hours; although the agency normally needs about 5-7 part-time volunteers on a daily basis, they have only been able to average 2 or 3 volunteers a day. Jane decided to speak at a local town hall meeting about her agency's predicament. Although she made an impassioned speech about the importance and urgent need of the adoption agency, Jane received an apathetic response from members in her audience. In a last-ditch effort, Jane decided to conclude her speech with a rattling statement: if the agency did not receive any additional volunteers in the next week, it would fall below state supervision requirements and be required to remand several foster children to state custody. Jane's conclusion was misleading; although her agency would fall below state supervision standards, the state government would send temporary assistance until volunteer hours picked up. Although Jane succeeded in gaining a temporary boost in volunteers, she wondered if her course of action would come back to haunt her.

QUESTIONS TO CONSIDER:

1. What ethical boundaries did Jane cross by misleading her audience?
2. In this particular situation, do you believe Jane was justified in her actions?
3. What are the possible negative outcomes Jane or her organization could face if her deception went public?

Use a Dramatic Illustration

Ending your speech with a dramatic story connected to your speech's thesis reinforces the theme in your listeners' minds. It is the last message of your speech the audience will hear and, as a story, it is the most likely to be remembered.

German Chancellor Angela Merkel spoke to the U.S. Congress on the 20th anniversary of the falling of the Berlin Wall on November 2009. In her speech, she thanked Americans for their support and for their role in helping to end the Cold War. She also reminded U.S. politicians that the world will be looking to America and Europe for leadership in forging a global climate change agreement. She ended her speech with the following:

> I am convinced that, just as we found the strength in the
> 20th century to tear down a wall made of barbed wire

and concrete, today we have the strength to overcome the walls of the 21st century, walls in our minds, walls of short-sighted self-interest, walls between the present and the future.

Ladies and gentlemen, my confidence is inspired by a very special sound—that of the Freedom Bell in the Schöneberg Town Hall in Berlin. Since 1950 a copy of the original American Liberty Bell has hung there. A gift from American citizens, it is a symbol of the promise of freedom, a promise that has been fulfilled. On October 3, 1990 the Freedom Bell rang to mark the reunification of Germany, the greatest moment of joy for the German people. On September 13, 2001, two days after 9/11, it tolled again, to mark America's darkest hour.

The Freedom Bell in Berlin is, like the Liberty Bell in Philadelphia, a symbol which reminds us that freedom does not come about of itself. It must be struggled for and then defended anew every day of our lives. In this endeavor Germany and Europe will also in future remain strong and dependable partners for America. That I promise you.

Conclude with a Quotation

Closing a speech with the words of others is an effective and memorable way to end your presentation. The Nobel Peace Prize for 2010 was awarded to then-imprisoned Liu Xiaobo of China for his long and nonviolent struggle for human rights in his country. Thorbjorn Jagland, president of the Norwegian Nobel Committee, used a quotation in his concluding remarks.

Isaac Newton once said, "If I have seen further, it is by standing on the shoulders of giants."

When we are able to look ahead today, it is because we are standing on the shoulders of the many men and women who over the years—often at great risk—have stood up for what they believed in and thus made our freedom possible.

Therefore, while others at this time are counting their money, focusing exclusively on their short-term national interests, or remaining indifferent, the Norwegian Nobel Committee has once again chosen to support those who fight—for us all.

We congratulate Liu Xiaobo on the Nobel Peace Prize for 2010. His views will in the long run strengthen China. We extend to him and to China our very best wishes for the years ahead.

© The Nobel Foundation 2010.

The quote serves as a reference point for and transition to the comments that follow. Notice that the quote does not have to be the last words the speaker utters, but the conclusion either leads up to the quote or is structured by the quote.

One of the most famous moments in presidential oratory was the conclusion of President Ronald Reagan's address to the nation from the Oval Office on the *Challenger* disaster, January 29, 1986:

The crew of the space shuttle *Challenger* honored us by the manner in which they lived their lives. We will never forget them, nor the last time we saw them—this morning, as they prepared for their journey, and waved good-bye, and "slipped the surly bonds of earth" to "touch the face of God."

As in this example, quotations can be interwoven into the fabric of the speech without telling your listeners that you are speaking the words of others, in this case *High Flight,* by American poet John Magee. If you use this technique, and you are not the president, we recommend that you use the quotation's words exactly and attribute it to the writer.

Conclude with a Metaphor That Broadens the Meaning of Your Speech

You may want to broaden the meaning of your speech through the use of an appropriate metaphor—a symbol that tells your listeners that you are saying more. Mao Tse-Tung, also known as Chairman Mao and identified by *Time* magazine as one of the 100 most influential individuals of the 20th century, spoke at the opening of the Party School of the Central

Metaphor

A symbol that tells your listeners that you are saying more.

Committee of the Communist Party of China on February 1, 1942. He used a medical metaphor in his closing statement:

> But our aim in exposing errors and criticizing shortcomings, like that of a doctor curing a sickness, is solely to save the patient and not to doctor him to death. A person with appendicitis is saved when the surgeon removes his appendix.

> So long as a person who has made mistakes does not hide his sickness for fear of treatment or persist in his mistakes until he is beyond cure, so long as he honestly and sincerely wishes to be cured and to mend his ways, we should welcome him and cure his sickness so that he can become a good comrade.

> We can never succeed if we just let ourselves go, and lash out at him. In treating an ideological or a political malady, one must never be rough and rash but must adopt the approach of "curing the sickness to save the patient," which is the only correct and effective method.

> I have taken this occasion of the opening of the Party School to speak at length, and I hope comrades will think over what I have said.

Without saying it directly, his use of figurative analogy implied that disagreement with the government is a sickness, a disease, and is separate from the afflicted patient. His conclusion was that government must offer a gentle cure for a willing patient. His speech was not about one person being sick, but about a larger context: how China and its citizens grapple with global politics and ideological dissention. His metaphor helps his audience find a new way to conceive of these broader issues by relating them to something basic and familiar.

Conclude with Humor

If you leave your listeners with a humorous story, you will leave them laughing and with a reservoir of good feelings about you and your speech. To be effective, of course, the humor must be tied to your core idea.

A Hollywood screenwriter, invited to speak to students in a college writing course about the job of transforming a successful novel into a screenplay, concluded her speech with the following story:

> Two goats who often visited the set of a movie company found some discarded film next to where a camera crew was working. One of the goats began munching on the film.
>
> "How's it taste?" asked the other goat, trying to decide whether to start chomping himself.
>
> "Not so great," said the first goat. "I liked the book better."

The audience laughed in appreciation of the humor. When the room settled down, the speaker concluded her speech:

> I hope in my case the goat isn't right and that you've enjoyed the films I've written even more than the books on which they were based.
>
> Thank you for inviting me to speak.

Humor at the end of the speech is especially effective if it corresponds to the introduction. In Colin Firth's acceptance speech for Best Actor in 2011, he started his speech with humor, stating:

> I have a feeling my career has just peaked. My deepest thanks to the Academy. I'm afraid I have to warn you that I'm experiencing stirrings. Somewhere in the upper abdominals which are threatening to form themselves into dance moves. Joyous as they may be for me, it would be extremely problematic if they make it to my legs before I get off stage.

Firth's conclusion related directly to his introduction. The audience laughed when he finished with:

> And to the Anglo-Italian-American-Canadian axis, which makes up my family and Livia for putting up with

When accepting his award for best actor in 2011, Colin Firth's graceful use of humor created a memorable conclusion to his acceptance speech.

my fleeting delusions of royalty and who I hold responsible for this and for really everything that's good that's happened since I met her. Now if you'll all excuse me, I have some impulses I have to tend to backstage. Thank you very much."

Courtesy of Colin Firth and WKT Public Relations.

How to Conclude the Same Speech in Different Ways

Just as many topics lend themselves to different types of introductions, they also lend themselves to various methods of conclusion. Here are three techniques are used to conclude a speech on learning to deal more compassionately with the elderly:

EXAMPLE 1: A quotation that personalizes your message.

In 1878, in a poem entitled *Somebody's Mother,* poet Mary Dow Brine wrote these words:

She's somebody's mother, boys, you know, For all she's aged and poor and slow.

Most of us are likely to be somebody's mother—or father—before we die. And further down the road, we're likely to be grandparents, sitting in lonely places, hoping that our children have figured out a more humane way to treat us than we have treated our elderly relatives.

EXAMPLE 2: A dramatic story that also serves as a metaphor.

Not too long ago, I had a conversation with a doctor who had recently hospitalized an 82-year-old woman with pneumonia. A widow and the mother of three grown children, the woman had spent the last seven years of her life in a nursing home.

The doctor was called three times a day by these children. At first their calls seemed appropriate. They wanted to be sure their mother was getting the best possible medical care.

Then, their tone changed. Their requests became demands; they were pushy and intrusive.

After several days of this, the doctor asked one of the children—a son—when he had last visited his mother before she was admitted to the hospital. He hesitated for a moment and then admitted that he had not seen her for two years.

I'm telling you this story to demonstrate that we can't act like these grown children and throw our elderly away, only to feel guilty about them when they are in crisis.

Somehow we have to achieve a balance between our own needs and the needs of our frail and needy parents—one that places reasonable demands on ourselves and on the system that supports the elderly.

EXAMPLE 3: Rhetorical questions.

Imagine yourself old and sick, worried that your money will run out and that your family will no longer want you. You feel a pain in your chest. What could it be? You ask yourself whether your daughter will be able to leave work to take you to the hospital—whether your grandchildren will visit you there—whether your medical insurance will cover your bills—whether anyone will care if you live or die.

Imagine asking yourself these questions and then imagine the pain of not knowing the answers. We owe our elderly better than that.

By providing these three examples, we note that each has a different feel that surely influences the final mood of the audience. It takes time and effort to create an effective conclusion, just as with an introduction. Both activities are centered on discovering how to best reach your audience.

Common Pitfalls of Conclusions

Knowing what *not* to do is almost as important as knowing what *to* do. Here is a list of approaches to avoid during your conclusion.

1   DON'T USE YOUR CONCLUSION TO INTRODUCE A NEW TOPIC. Develop your main and subordinate points in the body of your speech, not in the conclusion.

2   DON'T APOLOGIZE. Even if you are unhappy with your performance, do not apologize for your shortcomings when you reach the conclusion. Remarks like, "Well, I guess I didn't have that much to say," or "I'm sorry for taking so much of your time" are unnecessary and usually turn off the audience.

3   DON'T END ABRUPTLY. Just because you have made all your points does not mean that your speech is over. Your audience has no way of knowing you are finished unless you provide closure. A one-sentence conclusion is not sufficient closure.

4   DON'T CHANGE THE MOOD OR TONE. If your speech was serious, do not shift moods at the end. A humorous conclusion would be inappropriate and lessen the impact of your speech.

5   DON'T USE THE PHRASES "IN SUMMARY" OR "IN CONCLUSION" EXCEPT WHEN YOU ARE ACTUALLY AT THE END OF YOUR SPEECH. Some speakers use these phrases at various points in their speech, confusing listeners who expect an ending rather than a transition to another point.

6   DON'T ASK FOR QUESTIONS. Never risk asking, "Any questions?" Think about it, if there are no questions, you will be creating an awkward silence—hardly the climactic conclusion you were hoping for. If there is to be a question-and-answer session, consider it as a separate event from the speech. Complete your entire conclusion, receive your well-earned applause, and *then* field any questions.

7   DON'T IGNORE APPLAUSE. Graciously accept the praise of your audience by looking around the room and saying, "thank you."

8   DON'T FORGET TO THANK YOUR AUDIENCE AND HOST. Part of your lasting positive impression will come from a sincere thanks offered to both your audience for their attention and your host for allowing you the opportunity to speak. This is true in many speaking situations, but does not apply to the general public speaking class.

9   DON'T RUN AWAY. Remember to keep your poise as you confidently make your retreat from the speaking platform. Being in too big a rush to sit down gives the appearance that you are glad it is over. You may be ready to leave, but stifle the urge to flee abruptly from the podium.

10   DON'T READ IT. Just as with the introduction, the delivery of the conclusion is important. Practice it enough that you are not dependent on your speaker's notes. Eye contact with your audience as you wrap

up your message will reinforce your perceived credibility as well as your message's importance. Having to rely heavily on notes, or worst of all, reading your conclusion, makes the ending of your message less satisfying to your audience.

ESSENTIALS FOR EXCELLENCE

In this chapter, you have learned the importance of crafting powerful, attention-getting introductions and conclusions. As we conclude this chapter, however, it seems fitting to close with a few more recommendations on how to finish a speech with power and impact. Speechwriter and speaking coach Cam Barber offers several guidelines to finishing your presentation with a bang.

Last words linger. Don't waste them.

The conclusion of your speech is a focal point for the audience. Your last words provide a singular opportunity to embed a message into the mind of your listeners. The end of your presentation is a golden moment to leverage all the words you have said until that point (Barber, 2012).

The door to credibility (don't rush past it).

Weak endings diminish your credibility. The audiences miss out on the structure they crave, and your ideas seem less complete. A strong ending should reinforce the points you made during your speech. Finishing with emphasis boosts your credibility, satisfies your audience, and increases their trust in you.

Just end it!

Learn to observe what a good ending looks like. For example, good comedians often end on a strong joke that receives a great audience reaction—rather than ending at a set point (Barber, 2012). As important as it is to make sure you cover all the appropriate material, know when to disengage from your audience before they grow bored.

WHAT YOU'VE LEARNED:

Now that you have studied the chapter, you should be able to:

1. Identify the functions of introductions.
    *   Capture attention and focus. The first few moments are critical to the success of the entire speech. It is within these minutes that your listeners decide whether they care enough to continue listening.
    *   Provide a motive to listen. The introduction should seek to establish common ground with the audience. By focusing on something you and your audience can share and announcing it early, you help people identify with your topic.
    *   Enhance credibility. During your introduction, your listeners make important decisions about you. They decide whether they like you and whether you are credible. Your credibility as a speaker is judged, in large part, on the basis of what you say during your introduction, how you say it, and how you carry yourself.
    *   Preview your message and organization. Your audience will recall your message more fully if you tell them what you are going to say, say it, and then tell them what you said. Repeating key ideas helps us recall important information.

2. Describe the five guidelines for introductions.
    *   Prepare the introduction after the body of the speech. When speakers attempt to create the introduction first, they inevitably rewrite it several times as they continue to change the body of their message. Writing the introduction after selecting a thesis and main points helps to "jump start" the rest of the creative process.
    *   Make the introduction creative and easy to follow. The more creative your introduction, the more likely your audience will listen to the entire message. Be sure your strategy suits your occasion and audience expectations of the speaker.
    *   Communicate high energy by being well practiced. The most important part of your speech to practice thoroughly is the introduction, followed by the conclusion, and then the body. If you are truly engaged in the introduction, your audience is more likely to become involved in your message.
    *   Engage the audience nonverbally before you start. Recall that your speech actually begins as you rise to speak and eyes fall on you. Create a confident, energetic approach to the front. Your nonverbal messages are the first part audiences receive as they form a first impression of you.
    *   Consider time constraints and mood. When giving a five-minute speech, telling a protracted, dramatic story would be inappropriate. The same is true of showing a one-minute video clip. Also, the mood you are hoping to create in your audience must be related to the tone you adopt as a speaker. The introduction is your best chance to establish your tone and alter the mood of your audience.

3. List the functions of conclusions.
    *   Summarizing important information. The transition from the body to the conclusion is pivotal in signaling the impending end of your speech. In the process of ending, an effective conclusion reinforces the main idea of the speech.
    *   Motivating listeners. In motivating your audience, you might accomplish three things: relate your topic to your listeners, communicate a feeling, and broaden the message.
    *   Creating closure. Good conclusions create a sense of closure for the speech. The audience feels a sense of satisfaction that you have completed and accomplished something important.

4. Recognize common pitfalls of conclusions.
    *   Don't end your conclusion to introduce a new topic. Develop your main and subordinate points in the body of your speech, not in the conclusion.

- Don't ignore applause. Graciously accept the praise of your audience by looking around the room and saying, "thank you."
- Don't run away. Remember to keep your poise as you confidently make your retreat from the speaking platform. Being in too big a rush to sit down gives the appearance that you are glad it is over.

Key Terms

conclusion, 237

credibility, 220

introduction, 215

metaphor, 245

mood, 218

tone, 218

transitions, 241

Reflect

1   What alternatives are available for capturing audience attention in an introduction? What alternatives are available for bringing closure to a speech?
2   What is the relationship between the effectiveness of a speech's introduction and conclusion and speaker credibility?
3   What mistakes do speakers commonly make in preparing the introduction and conclusion of a speech?
4   How do effective introductions and conclusions meet the psychological needs of the audience?
5   What makes some of us funnier than others? Is it genetic or learned? Can it work for you in speeches or is it too dangerous?

Review Questions

1   The _____ supports the body of your speech and should capture your audience's attention and indicate your intent.

2   The overall feeling you hope to engender in your audience is the _____.

3   _____ is the emotional disposition of the speaker as the speech is being delivered.

4   The extent to which a speaker is perceived as a competent spokesperson is measured by _____.

5   The _____ supports the body of your speech, reinforces your message, and brings your speech to a close.

6   _____ are verbal bridges between ideas, words, phrases, or sentences that tell your audience how ideas relate.

7   A(n) _____ is a symbol that tells your listeners that you are saying more.

254

Gwen Stefani's fake pregnancy joke was not well-received by many of her fans.

CHAPTER EIGHT
LANGUAGE

OUTLINE

■ WHAT YOU'LL LEARN

After studying this chapter, you should be able to:

1. Know the differences between denotative and connotative definitions.
2. Give one example each of active and passive voice.
3. Describe the differences between similes and metaphors.
4. Differentiate between slang and jargon.

SPEAKING IN CONTEXT

On April 1st, 2016, Gwen Stefani faced an unexpected public backlash over what she perceived to be an innocent April Fools' Day joke. That day, Stefani posted a picture of a sonogram on Instagram with the caption, "It's a girl," leading people to believe she was pregnant. The joke struck a negative chord with fans; for the many women struggling to conceive and battling infertility issues, the prank came off as insensitive and crass. According to the *Journal of Reproductive Biology and Endocrinology*, approximately 15% of couples globally have difficulty getting pregnant or carrying a pregnancy to term (Agarwal, Mulgund, Hamada, & Chyatte, 2015). Helen Stephens, CEO and president of Diversity Fertility Services LLC, urges pranksters to be mindful of the emotional ramifications of this prank.

"You have to be empathetic that these women, and men in some cases, are trying to understand why is my body not working," she said. "I've had "unprotected" sex for over a year without becoming pregnant, which is the definition of infertility." (McKenzie, 2016).

This chapter discusses many aspects of spoken language, but the preceding story points out an area of particular concern: the use/attempt of humor. As speaking professionals, you have a responsibility to critique your attempts at humor and ensure that they do not offend your audience. As you study this chapter, be mindful of instances where a joke can be in poor taste, and remember always to conduct a proper audience analysis before attempting humor with people.

PART TWO: PREPARING AND PRESENTING YOUR SPEECH

anguage matters. Language provokes us. Language can move us to tears, leave us bewildered, make us laugh, or awkwardly blush. More accurately, speakers *using* language influence our emotions and behavior. Your language will in large part determine the success of your speech. Through words, you create the vivid images that remain in the minds of your audience after your speech is over. Moreover, your choice of words and style of language influence your credibility as a speaker. By choosing language that appeals to your audience—by moving your audience intellectually and emotionally through the images of speech— you create a climate that enhances your credibility, encourages continued listening, and ensures retention of key ideas.

The three Cs for public speaking are: Clear, Concise, and Colorful. In this chapter, we explore tools that help your presentations ring clear, concise, and colorful. First, we identify characteristics of spoken language that differentiate it from written language. Then we provide guidelines for using spoken language more effectively. Finally, we end our discussion of language by considering several common pitfalls that detract from the message.

Characteristics of Spoken Language

If you wrote a paper in a sociology or English class on "Trafficking of Women in Eastern Europe," using it as the basis for an informative speech would be expedient. It would certainly save time and effort, particularly on researching and gathering supporting materials. But be careful. A written report can be used as the foundation for a speech, but it requires major adjustments. The needs of written language and spoken language are different because listeners process information differently than readers. Imagine your instructor speaking for a minute. Then imagine what it would be like if your instructor were reading these comments from a manuscript. It would be remarkably boring. The spoken and written language differ in many ways, including word order, rhythm, and signals. Simply reading a written report would be violating many such spoken language norms.

Speaking Well with Technology Is an Essential for Excellence

As social media has spread across the globe, so has the need for efficient auto-translation software. While auto-translation technology has made significant strides, it still has a long way to go. Poor translations can have major implications for business professions who run the risk of offending customers and losing business, or at least looking unprofessional and amateurish. In one example, photographer Tom Carter was shooting a Skype commercial in China and was using the software to speak in Mandarin. When he attempted to use the software to say "It's nice to talk to you" to a local, Skype translated it into a stream of offensive swear words (Smith, 2016).

Better language translation technology is an essential need for social media platforms.

Currently, most translation programs (including Google Translate) have been built around phrase-based statistical machine translation. This system works by analyzing a back catalogue of texts that have already been translated, including academic papers and glossaries. Its effectiveness depends on the quality of the original language samples, and is often prone to mistakes. Alan Packer, director of engineering language technology at Facebook, is working to create a smarter type of translation technology using neural networks. These networks are structured similarly to the human brain and use complex algorithms to select and use the appropriate translation (Smith, 2016). However, rather than simply translating the words, neural networks can learn metaphors and the meaning behind language. This will allow the technology to select a translation that has the same (or similar) meaning to a different culture, rather than a direct literal translation that can be misunderstood, or even cause offense. Although this communication translation technology is a breakthrough, many experts warn that there is still a great way to go before the tech is perfected.

As the marketplace becomes increasingly globalized, the need for smart and accurate translation technology becomes a greater need than ever before. Once communications professionals like youself move forward in the workforce, you will want to make sure to follow the progress of language translation software. Remember, things like metaphors, colloquiallisms, and idioms are not always recognized across cultures; you will need to rely on your communication expertise to avoid poor or offensive communication.

Word Order

The first characteristic of spoken language is word order, which relates to the order in which ideas should be arranged in a sentence. In general, the last idea presented is the most powerful. Consider this famous line spoken by John F. Kennedy at his inauguration: "Ask not what your country can do for you, ask what you can do for your country." Inverted, the sentence loses its power: "Ask what you can do for your country, ask not what your country can do for you." Because speech is slower than silent reading, individual words take on more importance, especially those appearing at the end of the sentence.

Comedians rely on this technique by making the last word in a punch line the key to the joke. Every "knock knock" joke does the same. Watch for this rule of comedy and see how often the strategy appears and is effective.

Rhythm

The second characteristic of spoken language is rhythm. Rhythm in music and poetry distinguishes these genres from others. The rhythm of a piece of music creates different moods. The rhythm may create a sense of calm and serenity that allows us to listen and reflect, or the rhythm may create the urge to dance like a maniac. Rhythm is important in spoken language, also. It is the speech flow or pattern that is created in many ways, including variations in sentence length, the use of parallel structure, and the expression of images in groups of three.

Read aloud Patrick Henry's famous line, "Give me liberty or give me death," to illustrate the importance of rhythm (Tarver, 1988):

> I know not what course others may take. But as for me,
> give me liberty or death.

Now read the original, and notice the greater impact:

> I know not what course others may take. But as for me,
> give me liberty or give me death.

By taking out one of the repetitive "give me" phrases, the rhythm—and impact—of the sentence changes. As you develop your speech, consider the following ways you can use rhythm to reinforce your ideas and to maintain audience attention.

VARY SENTENCE LENGTH. First, create rhythm by varying sentence length. The rhythm of speech is affected by how well you combine sentences of varying lengths. Long sentences can be confusing and short sentences might be dull and simple, but a combination of long and short sentences adds rhythmic interest.

USE PARALLEL STRUCTURE. Second, create rhythm by using parallel structure. Parallelism involves the arrangement of a series of words, phrases, or sentences in a similar form. Classically, this is done in two ways: anaphora and epistrophe.

Anaphora

The repetition of the same word or phrase at the beginning of successive clauses or sentences.

Anaphora is the repetition of the same word or phrase at the *beginning* of successive clauses or sentences, as in these examples:

> Barack Obama's 2009 inaugural address also made effective use of parallel structure in many places, including anaphora in the memorable: "We will harness the sun and the winds and the soil to fuel our cars and run our factories. And we will transform our schools and colleges and universities to meet the demands of a new age" (Phillips, 2009).

Celebrities like Tina Fey often use parallel structure in their speeches and public appearances.

© Everett Collection/Shutterstock.com

An example of parallel structure can be seen when Tina Fey accepted the Mark Twain Prize for American humor at the Kennedy Center in November 2010. Her repetition of "I am proud" gives rhythm to her speech and allows her to make important points succinctly.

> I'm so proud to represent American humor, I am proud to be an American, and I am proud to make my home in the "'not real'" America. And I am most proud that during trying times, like an orange [terror] alert, a bad economy, or a contentious election that we, as a nation, retain our sense of humor." (Farhi, 2010)

Epistrophe is the repetition of a word or expression at the *end* of phrases, clauses, or sentences. Lincoln used this device in the phrase, "of the people, by the people, for the people." It is an effective technique for emphasis. On January 8, 2008 in his presidential bid, then–Senator Barack Obama delivered an inspired "Yes, We Can" speech. Obama's audience was so captivated by his use of the tag line "Yes, we can" at the end of key sentences that they called back the phrase with him each time he repeated it. Parallel structure emphasizes the rhythm of speech. When used effectively, it adds a harmony and balance to a speech that can verge on the poetic.

Epistrophe

The repetition of a word or expression at the *end* of phrases, clauses, or sentences.

USE THREE AS A MAGIC NUMBER. Third (yes, we intentionally provided three points!), rhythm can be created by referring to ideas in groups of three. Winston Churchill once said, "If you have an important point to make, don't try to be subtle or clever. Use a pile driver. Hit the point once. Then come back and hit it again. Then hit it a third time—a tremendous whack." Experienced speakers know that saying things three times gets their point across in a way that saying it once cannot—not simply because of repetition, but because of the rhythmic effect of the repetition. Many presidents use this device during important speeches. You can hear the emotional impact of Abraham Lincoln's words in his Gettysburg address when he said, "We cannot dedicate, we cannot consecrate, we cannot hallow this ground (Detz, 1984, pp. 68–69).

Re-examine the words quoted above from Barack Obama and Tina Fey, and you will note they freely use the rule of three. Try this in your speeches. For example, in a speech of tribute, you might say, "I am here to honor, to praise, and to congratulate the members of the volunteer fire department."

Signals

A third specific characteristic of spoken language involves using signals. You may reread an important passage in a book to appreciate its meaning, but your audience hears your message only once—a fact that may make it necessary to signal critical passages in your speech. The following signals tell your listeners to pay close attention:

- This cannot be overemphasized …
- Let me get to the heart of the matter …
- I want to summarize …
- My three biggest concerns are …

Although all speakers hope to capture and hold listeners' attention throughout their speech, wise speakers draw people back to their message at critical points. Signals are more necessary in spoken language than in print.

■ Guidelines for Language and Style

Denotative

Literal, objective definition provided by a dictionary.

Connotation

The meaning we ascribe to words as framed by our personal experience.

As you strive to be precise, clear, and understandable, keep in mind the difference between denotative and connotative definitions. A dictionary provides the literal, objective, denotative definition of the word. Connotation is the meaning we ascribe to words as framed by our personal experiences. These often lie in the realm of our subjective, emotional responses. For example, the American flag can be described denotatively by its color and design, but connotatively, its meaning varies around the world. Americans, in general, see the flag as a symbol of freedom and democracy, whereas some from other cultures may view our flag as a symbol of Western imperialism or immorality. Whether the audience favors or disfavors your view, ensure they understand what you mean and what you believe to be the facts that support your ideas. This next section provides six guidelines for effective use of language.

Be Concrete

On a continuum, words range from the most concrete to the most abstract. Concrete language is rooted in real-life experience—things we see, hear, taste, touch, and feel—while abstract language tells us little about what we experience, relying instead on more symbolic references. Compare the following:

TABLE 8.1

Abstract	Concrete
Bad weather	Hail the size of golf balls
Nervousness	Trembling hands; knocking knees
An interesting professor	When she started throwing paper airplanes around the room to teach us how air currents affect lift, I knew she was a winner.

Concrete words and phrases create pictures in listeners' minds and can turn a ho-hum speech into one that captures listener attention. Winston

Churchill understood this premise when he said, during World War II, "We shall fight them on the beaches," instead of "Hostilities will be engaged on the coastal perimeter" (Kleinfeld, 1990). Consider the differences between these two paragraphs:

VERSION 1:

On-the-job accidents take thousands of lives a year. Particularly hard hit are agricultural workers who suffer approximately 1,500 deaths and 140,000 disabling injuries a year. One-fifth of all agricultural fatalities are children. These statistics make us wonder how safe farms are.

VERSION 2:

Farmers who want to get their children interested in agriculture often take them on tractors for a ride. About 150 children are killed each year when they fall off tractors and are crushed underneath. These children represent about half the children killed in farm accidents each year—a statistic that tells us farms can be deadly. About 1,500 people die each year on farms, and an additional 140,000 are injured seriously enough that they can no longer work.

In Version 2 the images and language are more concrete. Instead of wondering "how safe farms are," Version 2 declares that "farms can be deadly." Instead of talking about "disabling injuries," we are told that workers "are injured seriously enough that they can no longer work." Concrete language produces an emotional response in listeners because it paints a more vivid picture, allowing the audience to imagine the situation on a more emotional level.

Use the Active Voice

A direct speaking style involves the use of the active rather than passive voice as often as possible or preferable. The following example demonstrates the difference between the passive and active voice:

VERSION 1: PASSIVE VOICE.

Students in an English class at Long Beach City College were asked by their teacher to stand in line. After a few minutes, the line was broken by a student from Japan who walked a few yards away. The behavior demonstrated by the student shows how cultural differences can affect even the simple act of waiting in line. In this case, the need for greater personal space was felt by the student who considered it impolite to stand so close.

Version 2: Active voice.

An English teacher at Long Beach City College asked the class to stand in line. After a few minutes, a Japanese student broke the line and walked a few yards away. The student's behavior demonstrated how cultural differences affect even the simple act of waiting in line. In this case, the student felt the need for more personal space because the Japanese culture considers it impolite to stand so close.

In the active voice structure, the subject is identified first and it performs the action implied by the verb (Purdue OWL, 2011). Here are two shorter examples: "The cat scratched the girl" is active because the subject (cat) is identified first in the sentence and is performing the action (scratch). "The speaker explored her subject thoroughly before she crafted her speech" is active because the subject (speaker) comes before, and performs the action of the verb (explored). In addition to using fewer words, the active voice is more direct, easier to follow, and more vigorous.

There are times when you may prefer the passive voice because it has the ability to create a shift in the tone of your message and the moods in your audience. For example, in "rules are made to be broken" the rhythm created by a passive structure is so powerful that we would use it over an active version, like "authorities make rules to be broken" (Purdue OWL, 2011). Passive voice is also used when we want the importance of the subject to be deemphasized or omitted. In our "rules are made to be broken" example, the subject (authorities) is left out altogether because the emphasis is really on breaking rules rather than on authorities. To create rhythm or alter emphasis, we sometimes elect to use the passive over the active voice.

Use Language to Create a Theme

A key word or phrase can reappear throughout your speech to reinforce your theme. Each time the image is repeated, it becomes more powerful and is more likely to stay with your listeners. When addressing women's

While helping her husband campaign for the presidency, Michelle Obama emphasized the "Yes, we can!" theme of Barack Obama's platform.

rights in Africa, First Lady Michelle Obama used her husband's now famous "Yes, We Can" speech to conclude her remarks in a powerful way while reinforcing her theme: "And if anyone of you ever doubts that you can build that future, if anyone ever tells you that you shouldn't or you can't, then I want you to say with one voice—the voice of a generation— you tell them, Yes, we can. [Applause] What do you say?" "Yes, we can." [Applause] "What do you say?" "Yes, we can!" (Mooney, 2011).

When something works, the Obamas stick with it! By referring to a key phrase several times in a speech, the message is often more effective and memorable (Berg & Gilman, 1989).

Use Varying Language Techniques to Engage Listeners

A carpenter uses a saw, a hammer, and nails to construct a building. A speaker uses language to construct a speech. Words are literally the tools of a speaker's trade. A speaker has numerous tools to choose from when building a speech.

When constructing your speech, consider using a variety of language techniques to enhance imagery. Imagery involves creating a vivid description through the use of one or more of our five senses. Using imagery can create a great impact and lasting memory. Mental images can be created using many devices, including metaphors, similes, and figures of speech.

Imagery

Creating a vivid description through the use of one or more of our five senses.

Metaphors

Metaphors

State that something is something else.

Metaphors state that something *is* something else. Through metaphors we can understand and experience one idea in terms of another. For example, if you ask a friend how a test went, and the friend responded, "I scored a home run," you would know that your friend thought the test went well for him. In his "Sinews of Peace" speech to Westminster College in Fulton, Missouri, Prime Minister Winston Churchill used the following metaphor on March 5, 1946: "An iron curtain has descended across the continent." During his inaugural address, President Bill Clinton said, "Our democracy must not only be the envy of the world but also the engine of our own renewal." Metaphors create "idea marriages" that bring new insights to listeners.

Similes

Similes

Create images as they compare the characteristics of two different things using words "like" and "as."

Similes create images as they compare the characteristics of two different things using the words "like" or "as." Here are two examples. "Speed reading Charlie Sheen's autobiography would be like a trip through a sewer in a glass-bottom boat." "Watching presentations at this conference is like watching a WNBA playoff game; you are practically the only one there and the rest of the world does not care." Both metaphors and similes rely on concrete images to create meaning and insights, and both invite the imagination out to play. Although these can enliven your speech, guard against using images that are trite, odd, or too familiar.

Figures of Speech

Figures of speech connect sentences by emphasizing the relationship among ideas and repeating key sounds to establish a pleasing rhythm. Among the most popular figures of speech are alliteration, antithesis, asyndeton, and personification.

Alliteration

The repetition of the initial consonant or initial sounds in a series of words.

Alliteration is the repetition of the initial consonant or initial sounds in a series of words. Tongue twisters such as "Peter Piper picked a peck of pickled peppers" are based on alliteration. With "Peter Piper" the P sound is repeated multiple times. Alliteration can be used effectively in speeches, such as in Martin Luther King's 1963 "I have a dream" speech, when he said, "We have come to our nation's capital to cash a check." Alliteration occurs with the repetition of C in "capital to cash a check."

Antithesis is the use of contrast, within a parallel grammatical structure, to make a rhetorical point. Jesse Jackson told an audience of young African Americans: "We cannot be what we ought to be if we push dope in our veins, rather than hope in our brains" (Gustainis 1987, p. 218). During a press conference in November 2008, President Obama used antithesis when he said, "If we are going to make the *investments we need*, we also have to be willing to shed the *spending that we don't need*" (*New York Times*, 2008). Antithesis is powerful because it is interesting; it is the analogy turned on its head to reveal insights by the pairing of two opposite things.

Asyndeton is the deliberate omission of conjunctions between a series of related clauses. Saying "I came, I saw, I conquered" rather than "I came, then I saw, and finally I conquered" is a good choice and excellent use of this figure of speech.

Personification is investing human qualities in abstractions or inanimate objects either through metaphor, simile, or analogy. General Douglas MacArthur, addressing West Point cadets confessed: "In my dreams I hear again the crash of guns, the rattle of musketry, the strange, mournful mutter of the battlefield." The general personifies the inanimate battlefield by ascribing to it human mournful mutters. This personification creates a much stronger emotional appeal.

Many other linguistic and stylistic devices are available to you. Because ancient Greek and Roman rhetoricians delighted in identifying and naming them, a rich heritage of figures of speech is waiting for you to come and explore.

Use Humor with Care

Nothing brings you closer to your audience than well-placed humor. Humor reveals your human side. It relaxes listeners and makes them respond positively. Through a properly placed anecdote, you let your audience know that you are not taking yourself—or your subject—too seriously. Even in a serious speech, humor can be an effective tool to emphasize an important point.

Research has shown the favorable impact humor has on an audience. In particular, humor accomplishes two things. First, when appropriate humor is used in informative speaking, the humor enhances the speaker's image by improving the audience's perception of the speaker's character (Gruner, 1985). Second, humor can make a speech more memorable over a longer time. In a research study, two groups of subjects were asked

---

Antithesis

The use of contrast, within a parallel grammatical structure, to make a rhetorical point.

Asyndeton

The deliberate omission of conjunctions between a series of related clauses.

Personification

Investing human qualities in abstractions or inanimate objects either through metaphor, simile, or analogy.

to recall lectures they heard six weeks earlier. The group who heard the lecture presented humorously had higher recall than the group who heard the same lecture delivered without humor (Kaplan & Pascoe, 1977).

In another experiment, students who took a statistics course given by an instructor who used humor in class lectures scored 15 percent higher on objective exams than did students who were taught the same material by an instructor who did not (Ziv, 1982).

ENGAGING IN COMMUNITY

When asking teenagers about their hobbies, very rarely does "community" top the list. For high school senior Marco Barron, however, community service is his activity of choice. "My community is my hobby," states Barron. As a member of his school's Key Club and International Baccalaureate Club, Barron has been involved in many community service activities, including organizing a 5k run in his local community. However, one of his most interesting community service programs involves improvisational humor.

As a member of the Student Teachers Igniting the Next Generation (STING) program, Barron teaches incoming freshmen improvisational theater (Sanchez, 2016). The goal, according to Barron, is to help ease the transition for middle schoolers entering high school. The use of humor in a public environment helps alleviate much of the anxiety students have about moving to the high school level.

"Improv comedy is more than just being funny," says Barron. "It's about letting freshmen know that high school isn't all serious."

As you learn more about the role language has in public speaking, remember also to reflect on how useful humor can be to a speaker. Use Barron's community service as an example of how humor can relieve tension and anxiety in public settings.

Research has shown that speakers who make themselves the object of their own humor often endear themselves to their listeners. In one study, students heard brief speeches from a "psychologist" and an "economist," both of whom explained the benefits of their professions. While half the speeches were read with mildly self-deprecating humor directed at the profession being discussed, the other half were read without humor. Students rated the speakers with the self-deprecating humor higher on a scale of "wittiness" and "sense of humor," and no damage was done to the perceived character or authoritativeness of the speaker (Chang & Gruner, 1981).

Although comedians like Dane Cook can make aggressive jokes at others, many speakers need to use humor with care.

Jokes at one's own expense can be effective but telling a joke at the expense of others is in poor taste. Racial, ethnic, or sexist jokes are rarely acceptable, nor are jokes that poke fun at the personal characteristics of others. Although stand-up comics like Dane Cook, Jeff Foxworthy, and Chris Rock may get away with such humor, public speakers typically cannot.

Understated Anecdotes Can Be Effective

An economist speaking before a group of peers starts with the following anecdote:

> I am constantly reminded by those who use our services that we often turn out a ton of material on the subject but we do not always give our clients something of value. A balloonist high above the earth found his balloon leaking and managed to land on the edge of a green pasture. He saw a man in a business suit approaching and very happily said: "How good it is to see you. Could you tell me where I am?"
>
> The well-dressed man replied: "You are standing in a wicker basket in the middle of a pasture." "Well," said the balloonist, "You must be an economist." The man was startled. "Yes, I am, but how did you know that?"

"That's easy," said the balloonist, "because the information you gave me was very accurate—and absolutely useless" (Valenti, 1982, pp. 80–81).

This anecdote is funny in an understated way. It works because it is relevant to the audience of fellow economists. Its humor comes from the recognition that the speaker knows—and shares—the foibles of the audience.

Find Humor in Your Own Experiences

The best humor comes from your own experiences. Humor is all around you. You might want to start now to record humorous stories for your speeches so that you will have material when the need arises. If you decide to use someone else's material, you have the ethical responsibility to give the source credit. You might start with, "As Jerry Seinfeld would say …" This gives appropriate source citation and makes clear that line or story is meant as a joke. Usually you will get bigger laughs by citing their names than if you tried to convince your audience that the humor was original.

Sam Aronov/Shutterstock.com

Even comedians like Ricky Gervais must evaluate the context of an event before presenting their material.

Avoid Being *Not* Funny

We chose the double negative to make a point. When humor works and the audience responds with a spontaneous burst of applause or laughter, there is little that will make you feel better—or more relaxed—as a speaker. Its effect is almost magical. However, when the humor is distasteful to the audience or highly inappropriate, a speaker may find no one is laughing.

Ricky Gervais hosted the 2010 Golden Globe awards, and his humor received mixed reviews. Without making specific reference to Mel Gibson's 2006 drunk driving arrest, Gervais quipped, "I like a drink as much as the next man … unless the next man is Mel Gibson" (www.dailymail.co.uk).

Just before introducing Colin Farrell, Gervais remarked, "One stereotype I hate is that all Irishmen are just drunk, swearing hell raisers. Please welcome Colin Farrell" (www.dailymail.co.uk). He also made reference to Paul McCartney's expensive divorce and Hugh

Hefner's marriage to a woman 60 years younger than he. While some jokes were well-received, some felt that he stepped over the line, even for a comedian, because the tone of special occasions should be kept positive.

Often humor is based on direct or implied criticism. We laugh at things people do, what they say, how they react, and so on. In fulfilling our ethical responsibilities, however, while someone or some event is being mocked, the speaker needs to do so with taste and appropriateness.

So, to avoid being *not* funny, audience analysis is vital. As a beginning public speaker, we urge you to err on the side of caution. It is better to avoid humor than to fail at it. While most humor is risky, there are certain things you can be fairly sure your audience will find funny. Stick with those, and try riskier humor as you gain confidence and experience. You might also check with a friend or classmate if you have any question about the humor of a line or story.

Language Pitfalls

Although your speaking style—the distinctive manner in which you speak to produce the effect you desire—like your style of dress, is a personal choice, some aspects of style enhance communication while others detract. You may have a great sense of humor, but it can be used too much and some may be put off by your lack of seriousness. You may be very bright and reflective, but your overly quiet tone may tire many in your audience. You have read several language guidelines for creating an effective speech. Following are five language pitfalls to avoid.

Long and Unnecessary Words

Using long and unnecessary words violates the first principle of language usage, which is to be simple and concrete. When you read, you have the opportunity to reread something or to look up a word you do not understand. In a speech, you do not have the rewind option, and if the audience does not understand, they lose interest.

When Mark Twain wrote popular fiction, he was often paid by the word, a fee schedule that led him to this humorous observation:

> By hard, honest labor, I've dug all the large words out of my vocabulary ... I never write *metropolis* for seven cents because I can get the same price for *city*. I never write *policeman* because I can get the same price for *cop*.

The best speakers realize that attempting to impress an audience by using four- or five-syllable words usually backfires. We prefer "row, row, row your boat" to "maneuver, maneuver, maneuver your craft" most days of the week.

Here are a few multisyllabic words and their simpler alternatives.

TABLE 8.2

Words to Impress	Words to Communicate
Periodical	Magazine
Utilize	Use
Reiterate	Repeat
Commence	Start
Discourse	Talk

Unnecessary words are as problematic as long words. Spoken language requires some redundancy, but when people are forced to listen to strings of unnecessary words, they may find comprehension difficult.

Using Euphemisms: Language That Masks or Muddles

Euphemism

A word or phrase substituted for more direct language.

As a speaker, be clear and provide something meaningful for your audience. Avoid sentences that lack content, mask meaning, or include euphemisms because they can do damage to your credibility. Using a **euphemism** involves substituting a mild, vague, or indirect word or phrase for a more harsh, blunt, or inciting, yet more accurate, word or phrase. Rather than use the word "war" when the U.S. had troops fighting in Vietnam, government officials used the word "conflict" (a term some still maintain is technically correct). Also, "collateral damage" is a euphemism for civilian deaths that occur during a military action. When someone dies, we hear euphemisms such as "passed," "passed away," "gone," as well as "she is no longer with us." A medical procedure may involve "harvesting" an organ instead of "removing" an organ.

While most of us use euphemisms in our everyday speech, we generally do so to avoid offending our listeners or making them uncomfortable. As a speaker, though, it is important that we do not confuse our listeners. Language that masks or muddies rather than clarifies meaning can confuse listeners. An effective speaker avoids using language that is unclear, makes an audience uncomfortable, or confuses the listeners. Using euphemisms is not recommended.

Jargon, Slang, and Profanity

Jargon is the host of technical terms used by special groups. For example, the jargon of the publishing business includes such terms as "specs," "page proofs," "dummy stage," and "halftones." Although these terms are not five syllables long, they may be difficult to understand if you are unfamiliar with publishing.

Jargon
Technical terminology unique to a special activity or group.

A special kind of jargon involves the use of acronyms—the alphabet soup of an organization or profession. Instead of saturating your speech with references to the FDA, PACs, or ACLI on the assumption that everyone knows what the acronyms mean, define these abbreviations the first time they are used. Tell your listeners that the FDA refers to the Food and Drug Administration; PACs, political action committees; and the ACLI, the American Council of Life Insurance.

Jargon can be used effectively when you are *sure* that everyone in your audience understands the reference. Therefore, if you are the editor-in-chief of a publishing company addressing your editorial and production staffs, publishing jargon requires no definition. However, if you deliver a speech about the publishing business to a group of college seniors, definitions are needed.

Slang is the use of informal words and expressions that are not considered standard in the speaker's language. For example, instead of saying "marijuana," one might hear slang terms such as "weed," "dope," "pot," and "ganja" (among others). Some words endure over decades (cool) whereas other words or phrases have a shorter life-span (bee's knees). Slang is generally spoken by the young, but this is not true in all cases. It may be news to you that your parents grew up when "thongs" were the name for "flip-flops," and "pedal-pushers" were what are now known as "capris."

Slang
Use of informal words and expressions that are not considered standard in the speaker's language.

Slang helps individuals identify with their peers, but it is not often appropriate within the formal speaking environment. Grammatical structures such as "ain't" and "you guys" should be used *only* for specific effect. In public discourse, slang used in any way can violate an audience's sense of appropriateness—or propriety.

Profanity is seldom appropriate within the public speaking context. Listeners almost always expect a degree of decorum in a formal speech, requiring that certain language be avoided. Even celebrities are expected to avoid certain profanity in public situations. For example, Melissa Leo

© Denis Makarenko/Shutterstock.com

Actor Robert Pattinson found himself in trouble with television censors after using foul language at an awards show.

dropped the f-bomb during her acceptance speech for Best Supporting Actress at the 2011 Academy Awards ceremony. She quickly apologized for her error during backstage interviews.

Robert Pattinson, while presenting a career achievement award at the MTV Movie Awards in 2011 to actress Reese Witherspoon, his co-star in the film *Water for Elephants*, dropped the f-bomb. This gaffe slipped through the censors. While many individuals use profanity with their peers, when we listen to speakers in a public setting, we have a different set of expectations.

SPEAKING EXCELLENCE IN YOUR CAREER

In a professional environment, communication professionals are expected to use language that does not demean or insult others. However, in many cases the language we have internalized can carry negative connotations, particularly many of the slang terms used to describe gender identity. Researcher Chandrabali Dutta examines how the gendering of language can lead to discrimination and marginalization.

Language often facilitates the construction of social identities, particularly gender identity (Dutta, 2015). In the United States and many other countries, everyday language used about women (by both men and women) is often gendered in such a way as to portray women as less than an individual or substandard to their male counterparts. Although many may argue that many slang words used to describe women are harmless (chicks, doll, broad, etc.), Dutta asserts that this language serves to dehumanize women in a way that makes it easier to marginalize or stigmatize them. To drive home her point, Dutta asserted that similar slang terms used to describe men are almost nonexistant in comparison, or are often seen as categories that also apply to women (calling a male a sissy, for example). Since women generally encounter this type of slang more often than men, they are more likely to accept such language as habitual or natural (Dutta, 2015). Dutta concludes her research by highlighting the societal nature of language, as well as the need for communicators to be wary about how their language can marginalize others when it is not scrutinized properly.

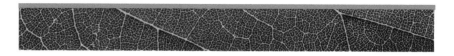

Exaggeration and Clichés

Exaggerations are statements made to impress at the expense of accuracy. Instead of telling your classmates that you "always" exercise an hour a day, tell them that you exercise an hour a day "as often" as you can. Some of your classmates may know you well enough to realize that "always" is stretching the truth. Instead of saying that you would "never" consider double parking, tell your listeners that you would consider it "only as a last resort in an emergency." Obvious exaggerations diminish your credibility as a speaker.

Clichés, according to communication professors Eugene Ehrlich and Gene R. Hawes (1984), are the "enemies of lively speech." They explain:

Cliché
A trite phrase.

> They are deadwood: the shiny suits of your word wardrobe, the torn sandals, the frayed collars, the scuffed shoes, the bobby socks, the fur pieces, the Nehru jackets, the miniskirts—yesterday's chewing gum (p. 48).

Clichés can lull your listeners into a state of boredom because they suggest that both your vocabulary and imagination are limited. Here is a section of a speech purposefully altered with slang and clichés:

> Two years ago, the real estate market was weak. *At that point in time* I would *guesstimate* that there were 400 more houses on the market than there are today. For us, it was time to *put our noses to the grindstone. We toughed it out and kept our eyes on the prize.* The winning *game plan* we should follow from now on is to convince potential buyers that we *have a good thing going* in this community—good schools, good libraries, a good transportation system. We should also convince them that we're a *community with a heart.* We're here to help each other when we're *down and out.* It's a *win-win* relationship we're after today, as…

Imagine listening to this entire speech. Even if the speaker has something valuable to say, it is virtually impossible to hear it through the clichés. Clichés are unimaginative and add unnecessary words to your speech.

ETHICS MATTER

Luis is a writer for his university's school newspaper. For many of his articles, Luis likes to discuss the activities of student organizations on campus. For this week's online issue, Luis decides to write about the university Movie Club's monthly get-together. When interviewing the club president, Luis finds out that the movie theme for this month is "B-movie....horror?!?". For this event, the club will screen three "horror" films from the 70s and 80s—none of which feature excessive violence—and are generally light-hearted in nature. Luis, worried that his article won't receive much attention online, decides to spice up the article by exaggerating the types of movie being shown. The article headline Luis chooses reads, "Students ready for cinematic bloodbath at Movie Club Night." The article succeeded only in getting the attention of university administators, who promptly canceled the event. After Luis was exposed for misleading his readers, he was removed from the school newspaper indefinitely.

QUESTIONS TO CONSIDER:

1. What ethical breach did Luis commit by exaggerating the subject matter of the films?
2. How could Luis have made the article more interesting while still being accurate about the event?
3. Since Luis holds the position of student-journalist, should he be held to a higher standard of honesty than the general public?

Phrases That Communicate Uncertainty

Speakers should avoid phrases that communicate uncertainty. Language can communicate a sense of mastery of your subject or it can communicate uncertainty. Compare the following paragraphs:

> **VERSION 1:**
> Sometimes I think that too many students choose a career solely on the basis of how much they are likely to earn. It seems to me, they forget that they also have to somewhat enjoy what they are probably going to spend the rest of their work lives doing, in my estimation.

> **Version 2:**
> Too many students choose a career based solely on how much they would earn. They forget that enjoying what they spend the rest of their work lives doing is important, too.

Version 1 contains weakening phrases: "sometimes I think," "likely," "it seems to me," "somewhat," "probably," and "in my estimation," adding nothing but uncertainty to the speaker's message. At least it is phrased in an active voice, which does communicate confidence. If you have a position, state it directly without crutch words that signal your timidity to the audience.

ESSENTIALS FOR EXCELLENCE

In this chapter, you have learned the importance of using language carefully and effectively in public speaking. As you continue to practice the art of effective language use, remember to help yourself to all the sound advice you can find. Organizational leadership and management instructor Kat Kadian-Baumeyer offers several tips regarding effective language use.

Use clarity to attract the audience.
Use clear language so the audience knows what you mean. Use concrete words that help your audience visualize the person, place, or thing that you're going to talk about. Also, make sure you use words the audience is familiar with; you may think complicated words make you sound more intelligent, but make sure you do not confuse your audience.

Use vividness as a way to get attention.
Choose descriptive words that generate interest and employ imagery and figures of speech (Kadian-Baumeyer, 2016). Help your audience create a mental visual to complement your presentation.

Ask rhetorical questions.
Rhetorical questions are questions that require no real response, but help make the audience think about your point. Rhetorical questions make great attention-getters for the introduction of a presentation, while also allowing your audience to become personally invested in your speech.

WHAT YOU'VE LEARNED:

Now that you have studied the chapter, you should be able to:

1. Know the difference between denotative and connotative definitions.
   - Denotative definitions provide the literal, objective definition of a word.
   - Connotative definitions refer to the meaning we ascribe to words as they are framed by our personal experiences.
2. Differentiate between active and passive voice.
   - In the active voice structure, the subject is identified first and performs the action implied by the verb ("The cat scratched the girl").
   - In passive voice structure, the action (verb) and object of a sentence are emphasized instead of the subject ("The girl was scratched by the cat").
3. Describe the differences between similes and metaphors.
   - Similes create images as they compare the characteristics of two different things using words "like" and "as."
   - Metaphors state that something is something else; a metaphor is a figure of speech where a word is applied to an object or action in an abstract way.
4. Differentiate between slang and jargon.
   - Jargon is a host of technical terms used by special groups that are generally not understood by people outside their organization.
   - Slang involves the informal use of words and expressions that are not considered appropriate in formal speaking.

Key Terms

alliteration, 266
anaphora, 260
antithesis, 267
asyndeton, 267
cliché, 275

connotation, 262
denotative, 262
epistrophe, 261
euphemism, 272
imagery, 265

jargon, 273
metaphors, 266
personification, 267
similes, 266
slang, 273

Reflect

1   In your opinion, is spoken language significantly different from written language? How can language contribute to or detract from the effectiveness of your speech?

2   Why must language fit the needs of the speaker, audience, occasion, and message? What do you need to consider when choosing proper language in a speech?

3 What are some of the language pitfalls that you have witnessed while watching a speech? What effect did these have on the overall message for you?

4 How does humor affect the speaker–audience relationship? What impact might it have on speaker ethos? Generally, do you believe humor is correlated with higher intelligence? If so, when might this generalization not hold true?

Review Questions

1 _____ is the repetition of the same word or phrase at the beginning of succcessive clauses or sentences.

2 _____ is the repitition of a word or expression at the end of phrases and clauses.

3 _____ definitions are literal, objective definitions provided by a dictionary.

4 _____ definitions refer to the meaning we ascribe to words as framed by our personal experience.

5 Creating vivid descriptions through the use of one or more of the five senses involves the use of _____.

6 _____ create images as they compare the characteristics of two different things using words "like" or "as."

7 _____ is the repetition of the intitial consonant or initial sounds in a series of words.

8 _____ involves the use of contrast, within a parallel grammatical structure, to make a rhetorical point.

9 _____ is the deliberate omission of conjunctions between a series of related clauses.

10 Investing human qualities in abstractions or inanimate objects either through metaphor, simile, or analogy is known as _____.

11 A _____ is a word or phrase substituted for more direct language.

12 _____ is technical terminology unique to a special activity or group.

13 _____ is the use of informal words and expressions that are not considered standard in the speaker's language.

14 Trite phrases are known as _____.

280 CEO of Tesla Elon Musk owes much of his success to revolutionary ideas and confident public speaking.

CHAPTER NINE
CONFIDENTLY DELIVERING YOUR MESSAGE

OUTLINE

◼ WHAT YOU'LL LEARN

After studying this chapter, you should be able to:

1. Know how to choose the right delivery method to confidently project your message.
2. Understand the different tools available when using your voice.
3. Explain the most effective strategies when using your body to accentuate message delivery.
4. Know the strategies for dealing with communication and public speaking apprehension.

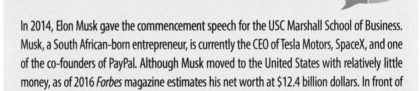

SPEAKING IN CONTEXT

In 2014, Elon Musk gave the commencement speech for the USC Marshall School of Business. Musk, a South African-born entrepreneur, is currently the CEO of Tesla Motors, SpaceX, and one of the co-founders of PayPal. Although Musk moved to the United States with relatively little money, as of 2016 *Forbes* magazine estimates his net worth at $12.4 billion dollars. In front of many future entrepreneurs, Musk outlined his five secrets of success:

Work super hard.
Elon's advice to graduates is that if you want to succeed, especially in your own endeavor, you need to work. And work more than anyone else is working. If you're putting in twice the hours that the other guy is, you'll get double the work done.

Attract great people.
Your success is dependent upon the people who are working with you. It is of utmost importance to seek out those people who are talented and willing to work. They need to be committed to drive the company in the right direction. So set your sights on finding the best people.

Focus solely on the product or service.
Stop and take a look at the results you're getting. Are the results worth the effort? Is the end product improving? Do we need to continue as we are or do we need to make changes?

Don't follow trends.
"...it's good to think in terms of the physics approach of first principles. Which is, rather than reasoning by analogy, you boil things down to the most fundamental truths you can imagine and you reason up from there." (Musk, 2014)

Take risks.

Elon ended his speech by encouraging the graduates to use this time in their lives to take risks... now, before other responsibilities in life that may come along later make it more difficult to take chances.

As you learn how to deliver your message during public presentations, use Musk's commencement speech as an effective example of speaking confidently, coherently, and efficiently. Remember, a good speech is much more than the words you choose; your delivery method, voice, body gestures, and appearance all influence how the audience receives your message. In this chapter, you will learn many of the intangibles needed to become a more confident speaker.

(note: a YouTube video link to Musk's commencement speech can be found at https://www.youtube.com/watch?v=e7Qh-vwpYH8)

Choosing the Right Delivery Method

Speeches can be delivered in one of four ways. Each of the four methods is appropriate in certain situations. Considering your audience, purpose, and the occasion will help you choose the most appropriate and effective delivery method.

Impromptu Speaking

This involves little to no preparation time. Sometimes we are asked to speak briefly without any advance notice. For example, in an employee meeting you may be asked to comment on an innovation at work. During other occasions, you may be asked to "say a few words" at a wedding, funeral, or other special occasion. Impromptu speaking forces you to think on your feet. With no opportunity to prepare, you must rely on what you know.

In a public speaking class, many instructors include impromptu speaking opportunities throughout the semester to help students practice this skill. You may have an activity in class where you introduce yourself or someone in the class or you may asked to give an impromptu speech on "my proudest moment," or "my favorite vacation spot." The more opportunities you have to present, the more comfortable you will feel. Keep in mind that as an impromptu speaker, you are not expected to make a polished,

Impromptu speaking

Speaking with little or no preparation time; using no notes or just a few.

professional speech—everyone knows you have not prepared. But you are expected to deliver your remarks in a clear, cogent manner. Following are several suggestions to help you create an effective impromptu speech.

BEGIN WITH THE AUDIENCE AND OCCASION. Remind your listeners of the occasion or purpose of the meeting. For example, "We have assembled to protest the rise in parking fines from $10 to $25." When unexpectedly called to speak, talk about the people who are present and the accomplishments of the group. You can praise the group leader ("Michelle's done so much to solve the campus parking problem"), the preceding speaker, or the group as a whole. You may want to refer to something a previous speaker said, whether you agree or disagree. This gives you a beginning point, and a brief moment to think about and organize your comments.

KEEP IT SIMPLE. Every speech needs an introduction, body, and conclusion. Create a brief introduction that is tied to the other parts of speech. For example, if you are giving a toast to the bride and groom, consider mentioning them in the introduction ("I am so honored to be able to toast Allison and Adam, two of my favorite people …"), and in the conclusion ("So raise your glasses high, and join with me in congratulating Allison and Adam, a couple who define happiness and commitment"). The body of your speech should include one or two main points and each point should be explained and supported.

BE COLORFUL. Be as concrete as possible, and stay focused on your central idea, but provide listeners with something colorful and memorable too, if possible. Typically the most memorable material comes from you memory. Offering brief examples and anecdotes or sharing your own experiences and stories personalize your message and keep the interest of the audience. In our example of the toast above, you might tell the first time Allison mentioned Adam to you, and how she was so taken as she described him that she overfilled her glass of milk, spilling milk onto the table and in her lap.

BE UNAPOLOGETICALLY FOCUSED. Instead of jumping from point to point vaguely, focus on your specific purpose. When you complete the mission of your speech, turn the platform over to another speaker. Never apologize. Your audience is already aware it is an impromptu moment; apologizing for the informality of your address is unnecessary. You do not need to say anything that will lessen your audience's expectations of your speech. Instead, be bold, be brief, and be gone!

Having notes on a laptop can help keep track of your main talking points, but remember to make eye contact with your audience.

© Matej Kastelic/Shutterstock.com

Extemporaneous Speaking

Extemporaneous speaking

A method of delivery that involves using carefully prepared notes to guide the presentation.

Extemporaneous speaking is a method of delivery that involves using carefully prepared notes to guide the presentation, but this mode of speaking provides flexibility too. Speakers can maintain a personal connection with their listeners and respond to their feedback. This creates more targeted interaction with your audience as you adjust your choice of words and decide what to include—or exclude—in your speech based on the response you are receiving. Speaking extemporaneously also means that your word choice is *fresh*. Although you practice your speech so that key words or phrases remain with you, you choose your exact words as you are delivering your speech. The result is a spontaneous, conversational tone that puts you and your audience at ease. Consider the following guidelines as you prepare your extemporaneous speech:

PREPARE CAREFULLY. Don't treat this as an impromptu speech! Use the same care you would use when preparing a written report. Choose your purpose, develop your core idea, research your topic, organize your ideas, and select the language and presentation style that are most appropriate for your audience. In your speech class if someone delivers an impromptu speech, perhaps having overlooked the assignment and not given it enough prep time, the results are glaringly obvious and sub-par. Everyone in the room can differentiate extemporaneous from impromptu speaking, no matter how smooth the speaker appears to be.

CRAFT FULL CONTENT AND KEY-WORD OUTLINES. Develop an outline containing main points and subpoints, then create a key-word outline that can be transferred to index cards of the appropriate size. The full content outline is *not* your speech written out; it represents the major ideas of your speech and supporting material. The key-word outline is brief enough to be transferred to note cards.

Note cards, which can be held or placed on a lectern, should be large enough to accommodate information from your key-word outline, yet small enough to be unobtrusive. You may include delivery cues, such as using "//" to symbolize where you should pause and look up if you feel cues about eye contact would be helpful.

CAPTURE AND CITE DETAILED INFORMATION ON NOTE CARDS. Facts, figures, and quotations may be written on note cards for easy reference. It is a good idea to be sure you say these things with precision. Rather than take the chance of misquoting people or facts, it may help to have such information written on your cards. Remember to include and orally cite the source for these items.

WRITE LEGIBLY. Your notes are useless if you cannot read them, so be sure the words are large enough and consider highlighting critical ideas. Also remember that your visual aids can serve as prompts to some extent too, reducing the number of words on your cards.

YOUR NOTES ARE PROMPTS, *NOT A SCRIPT*. Notes enable you to keep the speech you rehearsed in mind without committing every word to memory. Notes also make it possible to maintain eye contact with your listeners. You can glance around the room, looking occasionally at your note cards, without giving anyone the impression that you are reading your speech. But this is possible only when you have a few key words on your cards. The more words on your note cards, the longer you must look at them to find the right key words, and the less effective your delivery becomes. With extemporaneous speaker notes, less is more.

Using a Manuscript

Manuscript reading involves writing your speech out word for word and then reading it. A manuscript speech may be necessary in formal occasions when the speech is distributed beforehand, if it is to be archived, translated, or printed after it is given. Having a manuscript speech minimizes the temptation to add remarks during the speech but also loses the benefit of flexibility.

If an issue or occasion is controversial or sensitive, a speaker may choose to rely on a manuscript. Having a carefully crafted statement may help avoid misstating a position. But for those who are not professional speakers, a manuscript may be troublesome. If the font size is too small, it may be difficult to read. It is possible to lose your place in the manuscript because you must look up and then back down. Untrained people tend to sound as though they are reading rather than speaking when working from a manuscript. If you find you must use a manuscript, we offer four performance guidelines.

PAY SPECIAL ATTENTION TO PREPARING THE WRITTEN TEXT. Avoid using a handwritten manuscript. Choose a large font to see without squinting, and have the lines widely spaced. Use larger margins and number your pages. Print the script on one side of the paper only so that you can slide, rather than flip, the pages as you work your way through the message. You will notice that podiums and lecterns have a ridge nearest you that allows you to place loose papers on a stack on the right side and then slide sheets one by one to the left side. If done right, your audience will never even see your script.

PRACTICE. The key to successful manuscript speaking is practice. Practice enough that you are not dependent on the manuscript, and you do not need to look down for each sentence. Try practicing your speech first in sections—introduction, then body, then conclusion. You might find one or more parts of your speech needs more work, or more delivery preparation. Consider inviting friends, roommates, or relatives to listen to your speech and provide constructive feedback. Ask them if you sound like you are reading or speaking to them. Record your rehearsal yourself to ensure you are making eye contact and sound natural.

EXPRESS YOURSELF NATURALLY AND COMMUNICATE YOUR PERSONALITY. Think of the speaking occasion as a way to converse with your audience. You want them to have a peek into your personality. If you're an upbeat, energetic individual, work to convey those traits through movement, meaningful gestures, and solid eye contact.

Keep a somewhat conversational tone with your audience. Think about what you want to emphasize and vary the pitch of your voice to avoid being monotone. Pronounce words as you would in normal speech and be conscious of speaking too quickly or too slowly.

Memorization

Committing your speech to memory may be useful when you know you will be making a toast, proposing marriage, or receiving an award or recognition and you must make sure you thank the right people and express appropriate appreciation. Memorization enables you to write the exact words you will speak without being forced to read them. It also makes it easier to establish eye contact with your audience and deliver your speech skillfully. Memorization begins with a carefully crafted manuscript but requires much more time to get right.

Memorization is risky for a public speaker. In the middle of a 10-minute speech, you may find you cannot remember the next word. Because you memorized the speech (or so you thought), you have no note cards to help you through the crisis. If you find yourself in a situation where memorization is necessary, consider the following five performance guidelines.

1 **START SOON.** You do not want to delay the process so that you are under a severe time constraint. The night before does *not* work! Make sure you have ample time to work on the memorization aspect of your delivery. Even experienced professional speakers have to work hard to remember their lines.

2 **MEMORIZE SMALL SECTIONS OF YOUR SPEECH AT A TIME.** Do not allow yourself to become overwhelmed with the task. Memorizing small sections of your speech minimizes the chance that you will forget your speech during the delivery. Remember that some people can memorize speeches more easily than others, so work at your own pace and do not compare yourself to others.

3 **PRACTICE USING PAUSES, EMPHASIS, AND VOCAL VARIETY.** You want to convey the appropriate tone by emphasizing certain words, speaking faster or more slowly, and increasing or lowering your volume and/or pitch. More about vocal aspects of delivery is discussed shortly.

4   USE EYE CONTACT EFFECTIVELY. Avoid looking like you are trying to remember the speech. This takes away from the effectiveness of the message. A memorized speech is a great time to use eye contact and engage the audience. Sustained eye contact can enhance a speaker's credibility, increase the persuasive effect of the speech, and maintain audience interest.

5   BE CALM IF YOU FORGET. Things go wrong. It is the nature of the universe. Plan on it and handle it with serenity. One teacher told of being in the audience when the speaker kept backing up two sentences each time the audience applauded. Everyone recognized this was because it was a memorized speech. If you lose your place, pause and silently review what you just covered. Remember, your job is not to be perfect, it is to communicate something important to your audience. No need to laugh or curse. And please do not apologize. As a last resort, you can smile and humorously admit the lapse: "I seem to have forgotten the next important and extremely memorable thing I was going to share." Such self-effacing humor buys you time, allows you to show you are a good sport, and creates positive rapport with the audience.

Did you notice that the four modes of delivery we discussed are arranged in an order? They are in order of time commitment, with impromptu requiring the least and memorized the most advance preparation. Now that we have a clearer idea of what delivery option will best serve your message, let's turn to maximizing your voice.

Using Your Voice

How do you think others would picture you if they could only hear your voice? Our voices make an impression. On the phone, the radio, and recordings where the physical image is absent, listeners imagine the person behind the voice. It is no surprise that pleasant, resonant, harmonious voices are attributed to attractive people. Your voice is part of the impression you make. Additionally, poor verbal delivery makes the listeners work hard, and can distract them. You have control over your voice and it is one of the easiest things about you to improve. Consider whether you maximize the following aspects of vocal delivery: articulation, pronunciation, volume, rate, pitch, pauses, and emphasis.

© Featureflash Photo Agency/Shutterstock.com

Former Apple CEO Steve Jobs used articulate, well-presented presentations to unveil many of Apple's new products.

Articulation

The verbalization of distinct sounds and how precisely words are formed.

Pronunciation

Knowing how to say a word and saying it correctly.

Volume

The loudness of your voice, controlled by how forcefully air is expelled through the trachea onto the vocal folds.

Articulation

A person who articulates well is someone who speaks clearly and intelligibly. **Articulation** refers to the production of sound and how precisely we form our words. The more formal the situation, the more precise our articulation needs to be. The more casual the situation, the more likely we are to relax our speech. In front of most audiences, sloppy or careless pronunciation patterns should be avoided.

Pronunciation

Pronunciation is related to articulation, but it involves saying a word correctly as opposed to how you form sounds. Sometimes speakers simply do not know the word and mispronounce it; other times, a word is mispronounced because of dialect differences among speakers. Mispronunciations may hurt your credibility because listeners may perceive you to be less educated or less culturally aware. You want to know how to pronounce all words, including the names of people, places, and foreign terms. Not knowing can convey laziness, lack of concern, or lack of respect. And some words will just be difficult for you to say correctly without practice. Just like learning a foreign language, it may take several efforts to pronounce a word correctly. So practice the word several times over a span of time.

Volume

Volume is controlled by how forcefully contraction of the diaphragm propels air through the trachea and across the vocal folds. The more forcefully you use abdominal muscles to exhale, the greater the force of the air, and the louder your voice. Consider the following suggestions when working on your volume.

PROJECTION. Shouting involves forcing the voice from the vocal folds, which is irritating to the folds, instead of projecting the sound from the abdominal area. Straining your voice will only make you hoarse. Instead, work on your posture and breathing from the diaphragm. Also, some cultures value a lower volume. Speakers need to understand possible cultural differences.

LOOK UP. Do not talk to the podium. If you have your notes on the podium and your head is bent, the audience will not be able to hear. Look up, and speak to your audience. Remember also, if you turn to look at your PowerPoint, you will not be heard as well. Avoid giving your speech to the wall behind you.

USE VOLUME TO ADD VARIETY. Maybe you want to add a bit of humor to your introduction of a speaker. Using a "stage whisper," you could say something like, "And if we all clap very loudly, we can coax him on to the stage." Increasing volume at certain times during your speech draws attention to your point, and having variety, in general, maintains interest.

ADAPT. Adapt your volume to the size of the room as well as to distractions that may be occurring within the room or outside the room. If you use a microphone, conduct a volume check before the speech, or if that's not possible, check your volume as you begin your speech. A microphone is not necessary in a small room but may be vital in a larger room.

Rate

On the average, Americans' rate of speech is between 120 and 160 words per minute. Nervousness may affect your normal pattern. Under the pressure of giving a speech, you may find yourself speeding up ("The faster I talk, the faster I'll finish") or slowing down. Here are two goals to strive for:

Rate
The pace at which you speak.

CHOOSE AN APPROPRIATE RATE. Knowing your audience also influences the rate of your speech. Your rate should be consistent with the ideas being expressed, whether English is your audience's first language, and for the cultural context. For example, it makes sense that a sportscaster announcing a basketball game speaks faster than a sportscaster at a golf match.

VARY YOUR RATE OF SPEECH. By changing your rate of speech, you can express different thoughts and feelings. You may want to speak slowly to emphasize an important point or to communicate a serious or somber mood. A faster pace is appropriate to express surprise, happiness, or fear. But variety in rate is easier on the ears.

Pitch

Pitch

Vocal range or key, the highness or lowness of your voice produced by the tightening and loosening of your vocal folds.

Pitch refers to your vocal range. Your voice produces a high or low pitch by the tightening and loosening of your vocal folds. The range of most people's voices is less than two octaves.

VARY YOUR PITCH. Variety adds interest to your presentation. Avoid a monotone. When you do not vary the pitch of your voice, you risk putting your listeners to sleep. Giving an illustration, telling a story, or providing startling information are openings to raise your pitch to convey a sense of excitement or urgency.

USE YOUR VOICE POTENTIAL. Take advantage of the fact that our voices have incredible range. To add a sense of amazement, disgust, or to share a moment of seriousness with your audience, you can lower the pitch of a word or phrase you want to emphasize or to contrast thoughts or characters.

Pauses

Pauses add color, expression, and feeling to a speech. They should be used deliberately to achieve a desired effect. But they are often misused or absent. Some speakers run thoughts together until they run out of breath. Others pause every three or four words in a kind of nervous verbal chop. Still others, particularly those who read their speeches, pause at the wrong times— perhaps in the middle of an important idea—making it difficult for their listeners to follow.

When done well, pauses serve multiple purposes. First, they communicate self-confidence. Pauses deliver the nonverbal message that you are relaxed enough to stop talking for a moment. Second, they help listeners digest what you are saying and anticipate what you will say next. Third, a significant pause helps you move from one topic to the next without actually telling your listeners what you are doing. Fourth, a pause signals *pay attention*. This is especially true for long pauses lasting two or three seconds.

TIE YOUR PAUSES TO VERBAL PHRASING. To a speaker, a phrase has a different meaning than it does to a writer. It is a unit you speak in one breath to express a single idea. Each pause tells your listeners you are moving from one thought to the next. Pausing when you introduce a new idea or term gives your listeners time to absorb what you are saying.

USE PAUSES TO CHANGE THE PACE AND ADD VERBAL VARIETY. Pauses can be an effective tool speakers use to keep attention or to draw attention to a particular thought or emotion. Pause just before you speed up or pause just before you slow down. In both cases, the pause indicates to the audience that something is going to happen.

EXTEND PAUSES WHEN DISPLAYING A VISUAL. This tactic enables your audience to read the information on the visual without missing your next thought. It is important to pause after the display, not before it. Try pausing for two or three seconds.

Emphasis

A speaker uses emphasis to draw attention to a specific word or phrase. It involves stressing certain words or phrases. It can add weight to what you say, and make a particular word or phrase more noticeable or prominent. An emotion can be highlighted through the use of emphasis. Emphasis is a nonverbal way of saying, "Listen to this!"

Read the following sentences out loud and emphasize the word indicated.

I didn't say she stole the money.

I **didn't** say she stole the money.

I didn't say **she** stole the money.

I didn't say she **stole** the money.

I didn't say she stole the **money**.

Notice how a simple change of emphasis gives different meaning to a word or phrase. By singling out a few words for special attention, you add color to your speech and avoid monotony. When you vary the pitch of your voice, you let everyone know that what you are saying is important. Oftentimes emphasis comes naturally when you speak from the heart. When you have deep feelings about a subject—animal abuse, for example, or the need to protect the environment from pollution—you express your feelings emphatically.

> **Emphasis**
> Stressing certain words or phrases to draw attention.

Politicians like President Barack Obama rely on strong emphasis when appealing to the public.

© Joseph Sohm/Shutterstock.com

ENGAGING IN COMMUNITY

Learning to speak confidently has many applications outside of the classroom. Being a confident speaker allows you to communicate effectively with members of the community, especially those who otherwise would have no one to converse with. One such example is the nationwide organization Meals on Wheels, which promotes health and quality of life for the nation's most vulnerable seniors. Besides offering healthy meals for elders (who would otherwise be unable to afford them), Meals on Wheels also combats the issues of loneliness and isolation that many senior citizens face.

Sunny Davis began her volunteer service with the organization by joining her grandfather on his deliveries. After her grandfather passed away, Davis decided to make the Meals on Wheels service a family tradition. "I felt led to take over his route," said Davis, ".....he loved it so much that I wanted to carry on what he loved." (Hardesty, 2016). The clients of Davis—sometimes up to 20 on a single route—are now longtime friends of her family. The connections she made with clients on her drive emphasize the value that even simple communication can have for those people who have nobody else. Said Davis of one client: "He didn't have any family in the area, and he loved it when we'd stop and talk for a few minutes."

When evaluating the benefits of becoming a confident speaker, try not to think only in terms of how speaking can benefit only your school or career. Look at Sunny Davis as a prime example of using confident speaking to make a difference in her community. What may seem a short, insignificant amount of small talk to you can mean the world to someone who has nobody else to chat with.

Eliminating Nonfluencies

Nonfluencies, also known as verbalized pauses or vocal fillers, are meaningless words and sounds we make that interrupt the flow of our speech. We use nonfluencies for a variety of reasons. They may be used to keep someone else from speaking until we have finished, they may come from nervousness, or they may just be habits.

Nonfluencies can include "like," "you know," "uh," "um," "so," and "okay." These interrupt the flow of speech and may also distract or annoy the audience. If your economics professor says "okay" after every concept presented, you may be distracted and lose focus. Other types of nonfluencies include giggling, throat clearing, lip smacking, and sighing. As you give speeches in class, think about habits you have that may distract your audience. To listeners, a few nonfluencies are excusable, but too many are distracting.

To reduce nonfluencies, if you are videotaped, listen for these verbal fillers as you watch your speech. Once you become aware of a pattern of nonfluency use, you can learn to use pauses instead. Try this: Pause for a second or so after completing a phrase or other unit of thought. Because fillers indicate, in part, a discomfort with silence, this approach will help you realize that pauses are an acceptable part of communication. Over time and with practice you can learn to substitute an ear-refreshing pause for an agonizing 'Um.'"

We hope you noticed two central themes throughout this discussion of vocal delivery. The first is to *practice* so it flows smoothly. Practice pronouncing unfamiliar words so they come easily to you when you give your speech. The second theme is *vocal variety*. Vary pitch, rate, and volume to keep the audience's attention, create interest in your speech, and stress key words, phrases, and thoughts. You have something relevant to share with your audience. You want to make it easy for them to understand you, and you want to keep them interested from start to finish. Your powerful voice, coupled with your confident body, makes for a strong delivery. We now consider aspects of nonverbal behavior related to public speaking.

Nonfluencies

Meaningless words that interrupt the flow of our speech; also known as vocalized pauses or vocal fillers.

A public speech by German Chancellor Angela Merkel would have significant cultural differences when compared to public forums in the United States.

© 360b/Shutterstock.com

◼ Using Your Body

Your physical delivery may convey self-confidence or nervousness, enthusiasm or relative boredom. Your gestures, movement, eye contact, and dress say a great deal about you. More importantly, these elements leave a lasting impression that affects the speaker–audience connection.

Gestures

Gestures

Using your arms and hands to illustrate, emphasize, or provide a visual experience that accompanies your thoughts.

Gestures involve using your arms and hands to illustrate, emphasize, or provide a visual experience that accompanies your thoughts. Gestures tell an audience that you are comfortable and self-confident. As an outlet for nervous energy, they can help you feel more at ease too. They are part of an enthusiastic presentation. Gestures also have a positive effect on breathing, helping you relax the muscles that affect the quality of the voice. Gestures are especially important when you are speaking to a large audience where it may be difficult for some to see your facial expressions. Think about the following three guidelines as you practice using gestures.

1   USE NATURAL GESTURES. Your gestures should reinforce both the ideas in the message and your own personality. Stand straight, with your arms bent at the waist and your hands relaxed, so you are ready to gesture.

2   GESTURE PURPOSEFULLY. Gestures should not appear random but should be meaningful and enhance your message. For example, if you were trying to persuade people to donate blood, you might want to give your audience three reasons for doing so. When you say, "three reasons," you can hold up three fingers. When you say, "First," hold up one finger, and then when you say, "Second," hold up two fingers, and so on. These gestures serve as a guide. If you were giving an after-dinner speech in which you tried to convince your audience to stop complaining, you could put up one hand in the "stop" position when you say, "Stop complaining," to your audience.

3   GESTURE APPROPRIATELY. Gestures should be timely. You do not want to hold up three fingers before or after you say "three reasons," but *as* you are saying it. You do not want arms flailing around as you speak; they should match what you are saying. Appropriate gestures are timely, and they should make sense within the context of your message. If you are speaking before a large audience, gestures are bigger and, generally, more dramatic.

Various actions may communicate uncertainty, nervousness, and may hurt your delivery. As you deliver your speech, try to avoid the actions listed in Table 9.1:

TABLE 9.1	Actions That Inhibit Gesturing
Action	**Why it is problematic**
Clasping your hands together	It makes gesturing impossible.
Hugging your body	It makes you look as though you are trying to protect yourself from assault.
Clasping your hands in the "fig leaf" stance	Holding your hands together at your crotch is another protective position, and it may be distracting.
Locking your hands behind your back	This may encourage you to rock back and forth. The "at ease" military stance looks stiff and reserved.
Hands on hips	This is a position of power that may distance you from your audience, and it restricts gestures.
Arms folded in front of you	This communicates defensiveness and a need for control; creates a barrier.
Putting your hands in your pockets	This restricts movement and may encourage you to play with change in your pocket or something else that will make a sound and distract your audience.
Grasping and leaning into the lectern	Restricts movement and causes white knuckles.

For your next speech, work to gesture more naturally. Being aware of your gestures or lack thereof is the first step. Ask a friend or colleague to comment on your movement and gestures. Gestures should *not* draw attention to themselves and away from your ideas. Start your speech with your hands at your side, near your waist, ready to gesture. If you find yourself engaging in one of the above inhibiting gestures, release yourself from the position and put your hands back at your side or waist.

Using Note Cards

If you work with note cards, it is important to use them effectively. Many instructors restrict the number and size of the note cards you may use during your speech. Stick to their instructions, and consider the following:

- View your note cards as an extension of your arm, gesturing as you would without the note cards.
- Cards should fit into your hand comfortably.
- Generally, 4"x6" cards are easier to work with than 3"x5" cards.
- Avoid distracting note cards.
- Number your note cards. If you drop them, you can get them back in order quickly.
- Check their sequence before speaking.

Common Problems Using Note Cards

Using note cards effectively is not as easy as it seems. Do not wait until the last moment to create note cards. As with every other aspect of speaking, you should practice using note cards and avoid the following:

Playing with note cards. This is a manifestation of your nervousness. Avoid bending them back and forth. Do not fold them. Do not use them as a fan. Do not hit your head with them. Whatever you do, do not shuffle them mindlessly, or you will (a) lose your place, or (b) drop them, which will lead you to, well, (a).

Holding note cards with both hands. Holding onto note cards with both hands may be distracting to the audience because cards are relatively small pieces of paper that do not need the support of both hands. Holding on with both hands also restricts your physical movement (gestures).

Including too much on the note cards. You only need enough information on your note cards to trigger your thoughts. With enough practice, only a few note cards are necessary. Also, if you have most of your speech on note cards, you may end up sounding like you are reading to the audience.

Having too many note cards. Teachers sometimes swap stories about how many note cards a particular student used. The assignment may call for three note cards, and a student has a quarter-inch pile of note cards—sometimes as many as twenty for a four to six-minute speech. This is not necessary if you have practiced your speech!

Writing on both sides of the card. Sometimes students misinterpret the "three cards rule" and use three note cards, but write on both sides. It is easy to lose your place when you have written on both sides, and it can be distracting to the audience ("Hey! She used bright pink ink for her notes!"), and it usually means that you are relying too heavily on your notes. Practice instead!

Using a Legal Pad, Outline, or Electronic Tools

Traditionally, public speaking instructors wince at the notion of allowing students to use something other than note cards. This is because note cards are stiff and sturdy and do not rattle or shake when you hold them. Loose paper does. If you are nervous and have a shaky hand, the tremor is amplified by loose paper in your hand. In reality, not every occasion calls for small note cards. But every occasion calls for some medium that does not broadcast to everyone that you are nervous as loose paper does.

You may find yourself in a speaking situation outside of class where having a pad of paper makes sense. It is certainly not uncommon to see speakers using note pads or smart phones, notebooks, or tablets in the corporate world. Once you have your notes on something larger than your hand, it may be more distracting when you gesture. You do not want a pad of paper waving around in the air. Hold the pad in one hand, at a distance from your eyes that allows you to see your notes but not covering your face. Gesture with your free hand.

If you find yourself in a room where a podium is used, you may find it helpful to use a brief speech outline on one or two pieces of paper. Having notecards on a podium may result in your squinting to see what is written, but if you have a brief outline on regular paper, you can increase the font size. You may also find yourself in a situation where it makes sense to have your notes available on a computer, tablet or smart phone, or embedded in a PowerPoint presentation. If you go PowerPoint, remember that when speakers read slides word for word, audiences become annoyed.

Physical Movements

An active speaker can encourage an active response from an audience, but an immobile speaker can leave listeners listless. When you move from one place to another while you speak, your listeners are more likely to keep their eyes on you. Movement has an additional advantage of helping to release nervous energy. It can work against you, however, if you look like a moving target or if your movement has no purpose. Think about the following three guidelines.

1   MOVE NATURALLY. Relax and use movement reasonably. Do not pace back and forth like a caged lion or make small darting movements that return you to the safety of the lectern.

2   TIE YOUR MOVEMENTS TO YOUR USE OF VISUAL AIDS. Walk over to the visual as you are presenting it and point to its relevant parts. Walk back to the lectern when finished. Aim for fluid movement.

3   BE PREPARED. Your instructor and the speaking environment will influence the opportunities for physical movement. Your instructor may allow or prohibit you from speaking behind a lectern or podium. In informal situations, it may be appropriate to walk through the aisles as you talk. In a small room, you can walk around without a microphone and still be heard. In a large room, you may need the help of a wireless microphone. Be prepared to adapt to your instructor's rules and the speaking environment.

Remember that movement is a way to connect with the audience, get them involved, and keep their attention.

Facial Expressions

Our face not only provides information about our identity, age, and gender, it is the primary source of emotions. As we speak, our facial expressions change continually and are constantly monitored and interpreted by our listeners (Ivy & Wahl, 2014).

Japanese politicians such as Prime Minister Shinzō Abe use more somber, serious expressions in their speeches when compared to Western countries.

© Drop of Light/Shutterstock.com

MATCH FACIAL EXPRESSIONS WITH YOUR TONE. Admittedly, there is much to consider when giving a speech, but sometimes we do not think about facial expressions. Your facial expression, however, should match the tone or emotion present in your speech. A serious tone in your voice should be accompanied by facial expressions that contribute to the serious tone.

SMILE, WHEN APPROPRIATE. Listeners also feel engaged when speakers smile. Even if you are nervous, work to demonstrate enthusiasm not only through your vocal qualities but also through facial expressions.

Eye Contact

No other aspect of nonverbal behavior is as important as eye contact, which is the connection you form with listeners through your gaze (Ivy & Wahl, 2014). Sustained eye contact can communicate confidence, openness, and honesty. It suggests you are a person of conviction, you care what your listeners are thinking, and you are eager for their feedback. When your eye contact is poor, you may be sending unintentional messages that the audience interprets as nervousness, hostility, being uncomfortable, or lack of interest. The audience may think you have something to hide or that you are not prepared.

Eye contact
The connection you form with listeners through your gaze.

Sometimes students only look at the instructor during their speeches. Also, some student speakers ignore half the class by looking at one side of the class only. When a speaker lacks eye contact, we sense that something is wrong. We offer the following three performance guidelines for reflection.

1   DISTRIBUTE YOUR GAZE EVENLY. Work on sustained eye contact with different members in the audience. Avoid darting your eyes around or sweeping the room with your eyes. Instead, maintain eye contact with a single person for a single thought. This may be measured in a phrase or a sentence. It may help to think of your audience as divided into several physical sectors. Focus on a person in each sector, rotating your gaze among the people and the sectors as you speak.

2   GLANCE ONLY BRIEFLY AND OCCASIONALLY AT YOUR NOTES. You may know your speech well, but when you are nervous, it may feel safer to keep looking at your notes. This is counterproductive. Do not keep your eyes glued to your notes.

3   DO NOT LOOK JUST ABOVE THE HEADS OF YOUR LISTENERS. Although this advice is often given to speakers who are nervous, it will be obvious to everyone that you are gazing into the air.

Appearance

Standards for appearance are influenced by culture and context (Ivy & Wahl, 2014; Wahl & Scholl, 2014). Americans visiting the Vatican will find that shoulders and knees should be covered in order to gain entry. It is okay to wear baseball caps outside, but in some contexts, it may be offensive to keep one on inside.

We do not have to move from one country to another to experience differences in perspectives on appearance. Some businesses allow more casual attire; others expect trendy, tailored clothing. As rhetorical theorist Kenneth Burke (1969, p. 119) reminds us, your clothes make a rhetorical statement of their own by contributing to your spoken message.

Your choice of shoes, suits, dresses, jewelry, tattoos, hairstyle, and body piercings should not isolate you from your listeners. If that occurs, the intent of your speech is lost. We offer the following guidelines for appearance, but the bottom line is, *do nothing to distract from the message.*

SPEAKING EXCELLENCE IN YOUR CAREER

While speaking confidently is essential in both school and the workplace, it is also critical to be aware of what your appearance says about you. Indeed, it is crucial to "dress confidently" as well. In a recent study, researchers Rodrigo Praino, Daniel Stockemer, and James Ratis examined the link between physical appearance and electoral success in the 2008 congressional elections. Their findings indicated that attractiveness had an effect on candidates' electoral success, while also having an important effect in intra-gender election races (Praino, Stockemer, & Ratis, 2014).

Reflect on your most recent speech presentation; did you dress appropriately given the subject matter? It can be particularly tempting to dress informally for presentations, especially in the classroom. However, research has consistently indicated that dressing beneath the solemnity of your topic can cause your audience to perceive you as incompetent or uninformed. As you move into the professional field, these perceptions only increase. Always remember to research and dress appropriately for your topic.

Celebrities and public figures must pay special attention to physical appearance and clothing when in the public spotlight.

© Joe Seer/Shutterstock.com

ETHICS MATTER

Trey is a real estate agent for one of the largest firms in his city. Recently, his company has been accused of misleading potential home buyers by failing to disclose negative information about the properties until after the sale. The public relations fallout eventually led to the calling of a town hall meeting, with Trey's company fielding questions from the general public. To prepare for this, Trey's boss asked him and other agents to "pose" as private citizens, in order to ask pre-scripted questions for which the company has ready answers. In essence, the town hall meeting would be altered in a dishonest way that would benefit the company. Although two of Trey's coworkers agreed to the charade, Trey found himself ethically opposed to the plan.

QUESTIONS TO CONSIDER:

1. What are the key ethical issues facing both Trey and his company?
2. Is it possible for Trey to speak with confidence knowing that his role in the meeting is ethically uncertain?
3. In what ways could Trey's company use confident public speaking techniques to answer questions from the public in an honest manner?

Communication and Public Speaking Apprehension

You understand how important effective organization, language, and delivery are, but that doesn't stop one from being nervous in front of an audience (Quintanilla & Wahl, 2016). Some people do not seem to experience much anxiety before or during the speech, but others are overwhelmed. Decades ago comedic entertainer George Jessel quipped, "The human brain is a wonderful organ. It starts to work the moment you are born, and does not stop until you get up to deliver a speech" (brainyquote.com). Maybe you can relate to this. When confronted with an audience ready to listen, you may find yourself lost in a fog.

With a bit of preparation and a few pointers, your nervousness can actually propel you toward a confident, energized delivery style. We take a closer look now at fear responses. Our goal is to help you learn how to listen closely to your body and then regain control.

Speaking Well with Technology Is an Essential for Excellence

As many of you move on to professional careers after school, you will find that there are many methods available to apply for jobs, and also interview for them. Especially for job opportunities that are many states (or even countries) away, video streaming services serve as a useful tool for conducting interviews. Although many classes will teach you about interview tips in the traditional face-to-face setting, it can be unclear what strategies are effective in an online format. Writer Amy Levin-Epstein offers several tips for online interviews.

Look into the camera.
In many Skype interviews, people tend to fixate on themselves on the computer screen. To people on the other end, this gives the impression of not making eye contact. Make sure your eyes stay focused on the camera, not your appearance.

Put your hands where they can see them.
Remember, a good portion of understanding comes from body language and other nonverbal cues (Levin-Epstein, 2011). Make sure that the upper part of your body is visible to the interviewers.

Lean in.

Sitting forward and leaning into the camera is a strategy many newscasters use to appear more intimate and personal with their television audience. This serves as an excellent way for employers to read your facial expression.

Get a "handle" on it.

Regardless of what videoconferencing application you use, make sure that your user name, or "handle," has a professional touch. A user name like PartyGirl247 or NewAgeCasanova may be ok for social interactions, but never in a job interview. Try using a combination of your first and last name, or your name combined with the industry in which you wish to work.

The Nature of Apprehension

For some, speaking in public can be an exciting, adrenalin-producing activity, but for others, it is an experience to be feared (Quintanilla & Wahl, 2016). If you are fearful of public speaking, you are not alone. Research has found that "public speaking is the single most commonly feared situation reported in both community and university samples" (Bottella et al., 2010, p. 407). A Gallup poll found that 40 percent of Americans are terrified at the *thought* of talking to an audience (Naistadt, 2004, p. 1), and approximately 70 percent of the people in the United States report experiencing communication apprehension when they have to give a public speech (McCroskey, 2009, p. 164).

Communication apprehension, as defined by McCroskey (1984), the leading researcher in this area, is "an individual's level of fear or anxiety associated with either real or anticipated communication with another person or persons" (p. 13). The intensity of discomfort most feel when giving a speech varies widely, but we can identify symptoms as falling into three categories: physiological, psychological, and behavioral.

Physical manifestations include a rapid pulse, dry mouth, increased sweating, shallow breathing, shaky hands and knees, stammering, throat constriction, quivering voice, "butterflies" in the stomach, gastrointestinal dysfunction, flushing and heat flashes, dizziness, and loss of concentration. Most of us experience at least one of these symptoms during a public speaking situation. The good news is that a degree of tension is positive

Communication apprehension

An individual's level of fear or anxiety associated with either real or anticipated communication with another person or persons.

because it keeps us alert and energized. Too much, however, can debilitate us, and make it difficult or impossible to continue.

Psychological manifestations of communication apprehension are more difficult to treat, because they are not observable, and they speak to our fears. As we know, whether our fears are real or imagined, they are still a part of us. Naistadt (2004) identifies six obstacles to effective speaking (pp. 52–60):

1   Fear of criticism or being judged negatively
2   Fear of forgetting
3   Fear of embarrassment or humiliation
4   Fear of failure
5   Fear of the unknown
6   Fear of bad (emotional) past experiences

The anxious speaker may need to address one or more of these fears in order to take control from a psychological perspective. Our fears may be the result of negative messages from our parents, siblings, or peers. Or they may be the result of low self-esteem, lack of self-confidence, poor coping strategies, or other psychological barriers. Regardless, as we know, a negative mind-set will most likely yield a negative result.

The *behavioral manifestation* of speech anxiety is defined as "the degree of assumed speaker anxiety perceived by observers on the basis of manifest speaker behavior" (Mulac & Sherman, 1975, p. 276). Unlike physiological and psychological aspects of anxiety, behavioral manifestations are observed by audience members. Audiences receive information from and make judgments about paralanguage (i.e., volume, pitch, rate, pauses, vocal variety, etc.) and physical actions (i.e., eye contact, gestures, body movement, etc.). These observations influence audience members' perceptions of the speaker, including the speaker's anxiety level.

Communication apprehension has been found to exist in virtually every culture in which it has been investigated (Pryor et al., 2005, p. 247). However, while American culture views communication apprehension in a negative light, other cultures—Japanese culture, for example—do not see communication apprehension as having negative implications. Because of its collectivist culture (focus on the group, not on the individual), less value is placed on individual assertiveness (p. 250).

On a related note, speaking English as a second language (as well as living in a different culture with different norms) can cause communication apprehension. Some research has shown that speaking a second language increases apprehension but other results show that, compared to situational factors like years of speaking English or living in the United States, communication apprehension in a first language has a greater impact on communication apprehension in a second language (Jung & McCroskey, 2004). So, while communication apprehension may be found in other cultures, it is not necessarily interpreted the same as it is in the United States.

Personal Report of Communication Apprehension (PRCA-24)

The PRCA-24 is the instrument most widely used to measure communication apprehension. The measure permits one to obtain subscores on the contexts of public speaking, dyadic interaction, small groups, and large groups.

This instrument is composed of 24 statements concerning feelings about communicating with others. Please indicate the degree to which each statement applies to you by marking whether you strongly disagree = 1; disagree = 2; are neutral = 3; agree = 4; or strongly agree = 5.

_____1. I dislike participating in group discussions.

_____2. Generally, I am comfortable while participating in group discussions.

_____3. I am tense and nervous while participating in group discussions.

_____4. I like to get involved in group discussions.

_____5. Engaging in a group discussion with new people makes me tense and nervous.

_____6. I am calm and relaxed while participating in group discussions.

_____7. Generally, I am nervous when I have to participate in a meeting.

_____8. Usually, I am comfortable when I have to participate in a meeting.

_____9. I am very calm and relaxed when I am called on to express an opinion at a meeting.

_____10. I am afraid to express myself at meetings.

_____11. Communicating at meetings usually makes me uncomfortable.

_____12. I am very relaxed when answering questions at a meeting.

_____13. While participating in a conversation with a new acquaintance, I feel very nervous.

_____14. I have no fear of speaking up in conversations.

_____15. Ordinarily, I am very tense and nervous in conversations.

_____16. Ordinarily, I am very calm and relaxed in conversations.

_____17. While conversing with a new acquaintance, I feel very relaxed.

_____18. I'm afraid to speak up in conversations.

_____19. I have no fear of giving a speech.

_____20. Certain parts of my body feel very tense and rigid while giving a speech.

_____21. I feel relaxed while giving a speech.

_____22. My thoughts become confused and jumbled when I am giving a speech.

_____23. I face the prospect of giving a speech with confidence.

_____24. While giving a speech, I get so nervous I forget facts I really know.

SCORING:

Group discussion: 18 − (scores for Items 2, 4, and 6) + (scores for Items 1, 3, and 5)

Meetings: 18 − (scores for Items 8, 9, and 12) + (scores for Items 7, 10, and 11)

Interpersonal: 18 − (scores for Items 14, 16, and 17) + (scores for Items 13, 15, and 18)

Public speaking: 18 − (scores for Items 19, 21, and 23) + (scores for Items 20, 22, and 24)

Group discussion score: _____

Interpersonal score: _____

Meetings score: _____

Public speaking score: _____

To obtain your total score for the PRCA, simply add your subscores together. _____

Scores can range from 24 to 120. Scores below 51 represent people who have very low communication apprehension. Scores between 51 and 80 represent people with average communication apprehension. Scores above 80 represent people who have high levels of trait communication apprehension. **Courtesy of Dr. James C. McCroskey, Department of Communications Studies, University of Alabama-Birmingham**

McCroskey (2009) summarized effects of high communication apprehension:

- People with high communication apprehension (CA) prefer occupations that have low oral communication demands.
- People with high CA are less likely to be turned to as opinion leaders or to be selected as friends than other people.
- College students with high CA prefer classes where they may sit on the sides or back of the room.
- College graduates with high CA are more likely to marry immediately upon graduation.
- Job candidates with high CA have less likelihood of being successful in the job applicant screening process (pp. 167–168).

Overall, the effects of communication apprehension are numerous and varied. Since we value oral communication skills and agree that effective public speaking is a goal, we will turn to strategies one might use to control apprehension.

Strategies for Controlling Public Speaking Apprehension

Coping strategies are numerous and work for some better than others. One study found some instructors treat apprehensive students during their regular class time by concentrating on a skills-training approach to teach the necessary speaking skills. They create a supportive and positive classroom environment by recognizing students' CA as normal and by teaching techniques that help students handle feelings of apprehension (Robinson, 1989). We agree with this strategy. By this point in your class and in the text, you have begun to pick up valuable skills for presenting, feel safe in class because the climate is supportive and positive, and understand that some CA is normal.

Anxiety and coping processes may start with anticipation of a stressful event, may continue through the stressful event itself, and may extend into the period after the event as individuals await feedback or deal with the consequences of their performance (Sawyer & Behnke, 1999).

The chances of completely escaping communication apprehension are slim. However, we can provide some help to reduce its effects. Recognize that your physiological symptoms actually consist of four stages.

> STAGE 1: The *anticipatory stage* takes place in the minutes before the speech—heart rates zoom from a normal rate of about 70 beats per minute to between 95 and 140.
>
> STAGE 2: The *confrontational stage* is typically at the beginning of the speech, when heart rates jump to between 110 and 190 beats per minute. This stage usually lasts no more than 30 seconds.
>
> STAGE 3: *Adaptation stage* is when you begin to calm down, typically after you have been speaking for over 30 seconds to a minute
>
> STAGE 4: The *release stage* is the final stage and is characterized by the pulse returning to anticipation levels or lower.

The confrontational stage is strong, and speakers may not perceive the increase in pulse rate. Also, as a nervous speaker, you may stop feeling nervous without realizing it (Motley, 1988). For this reason, make sure you have planned and rehearsed a strong beginning for your message. Research on psychological and physiological anxiety claims that anxiety is highest during the minute prior to confrontation with an audience and during the first minute of speaking (Behnke & Sawyer, 2004). So, once you have made it through the first minute, you should feel more relaxed.

You may recall other people's advice about your fear. Suggestions such as imagining your audience in their underwear (guaranteed to make you blush), looking above their heads (guaranteed to make you aloof), and drinking plenty of water (guaranteed to make you wet) don't work, as you have no doubt already discovered. That's because they don't treat the problem, your fear, itself. But researchers have found and refined new strategies and interventions to reduce public speaking apprehension (Dwyer, 2000). We present nine strategies as follows:

1   COMPLETE A PUBLIC SPEAKING COURSE. You are probably not surprised that we included this as a strategy. However, data are consistent with the explanation that "completing a public speaking class systematically reduces speaking anxiety" (Duff et al., 2007, p. 85). A public speaking course gives you the opportunity to learn and practice basic skills. As with anything that is skills based, the more opportunity you have to practice, the less anxiety-producing it should be. Research has also shown that watching a video on coping with the fear of public speaking helped to reduce CA and negative thoughts about public speaking (Ayers et al., 1993).

2   FOCUS ON YOUR AUDIENCE, NOT YOURSELF. Sometimes we get caught up in thinking about our performance ("What if I forget?" "What if I don't wear the right thing?" "What if they don't like me?"). Research shows that students who reported experiencing lower levels of communication apprehension were those who focused on the *audience*, not the message (Ayers, 1996, p. 229). Create a message with the audience in mind, and decide how best to convey it to that particular audience. Think of your audience as being on your side.

3   REFRAME YOUR MESSAGE. Another technique to help you reduce your anxiety levels is to reframe the way you view the speaking situation. Turn negative thoughts into positive ones. Researchers discovered that, because some of us think of a speech as a "performance," we become obsessed with trying to deliver speeches as a famous speaker or trained actor might. This added pressure increases our anxiety levels even more.

If we can change our ideas about the speaking situation, we can work toward a positive experience. For example, instead of thinking "I don't want to lose my place," which is negative, replace it with "I want to look confident and poised." Then, reframe that even further with the thought "I am confident and poised speaking in front of groups" (Naistadt, 2004, pp. 81–82).

4   PREPARE! Preparation sharpens your presentation and builds confidence. Interestingly, how you prepare is important. Research has indicated that individuals with high CA spend more time preparing their speeches but get less return for their efforts than low CAs (Ayers, 1996, p. 234).

Evidently, people who are anxious about speaking in public spend a great deal of time *developing* their speech, but they avoid *practicing* it. So, start with a sound speech plan and then rehearse the speech aloud by yourself. Then practice in front of others to get the feel and response of an audience. You will get a sense for how the words sound and how the material flows when you speak before an audience.

5   TAKE SEVERAL DEEP BREATHS. What happens when we get nervous as speakers is that we restrict our breathing capacity, which impacts our ability to speak effectively (Naistadt, 2004, p. 152). Deep breathing has a calming effect on the body and mind. Learning to breathe properly improves the sound of our voice and protects the health of our vocal instrument. You can work on breathing as you are waiting to speak. It also helps to take a final deep breath after you get in front of the audience and just before you speak.

6   REALIZE THAT YOU MAY BE YOUR OWN WORST CRITIC. Studies have shown that the amount of tension a speaker reports has little relationship to the amount of nervousness an audience detects. Even listeners trained to detect tension often fail to perceive it (Motley, 1988, p. 47). Audience members are relatively forgiving, and do not expect perfection.

7   GAIN SKILL AND CONFIDENCE BY CHOOSING TO SPEAK. Find opportunities to speak. Give "minispeeches" at meetings or speak out in classes when discussion is invited. A colleague of ours conquered his considerable fear of public speaking before an audience and became a successful speaker in large lecture classes by volunteering to speak whenever a situation was convenient and available.

Systematic desensitization is based on the premise that people have learned to associate anxious states with public speaking. To reduce the fear of public speaking, one simply learns to associate relaxed states with public speaking (Ayers et al., 1993, p. 133). By doing so, a person with high CA learns to see public speaking as "nonthreatening" rather than "threatening" (Ayers et al., 2000, p. 24). We suggest you find opportunities to speak before an audience so you can reduce anxiety and create a more relaxed state.

Systematic desensitization

A premise that people have learned to associate anxious states with public speaking.

Positive visualization

Creating powerful mental images of skillful performances and winning competitions.

8   VISUALIZE YOUR SUCCESS AS A SPEAKER. Creating powerful mental images of yourself performing well is a technique that is used successfully by both public speakers and athletes. The athlete may visualize winning a medal, throwing a curveball, making lay-ups, and so on. When applied to public speaking, such **positive visualization** has been shown to improve performance and reduce fear levels over time (Ayers et al., 1997).

Using visualization takes you through the day on which you are to speak, with an emphasis on imagining a positive outcome (Ayers & Hopf, 1992). Visualize yourself speaking with confidence and self-assurance and imagine the sound of applause after your presentation. You might visualize yourself approaching the podium with confidence, speaking clearly, engaging in effective eye contact with audience members, noticing that they are attentive and friendly, stating your main points and providing relevant support, then concluding your speech effectively and on time. And there is a bonus side effect: research has found that students who practice performance visualization display fewer nonfluencies, less rigidity, and less inhibition.

James Earl Jones is one of several noted celebrities who overcame a fear of public speaking.

9   RELEASE TENSION THROUGH ASSERTIVE AND ANIMATED DELIVERY. Being nervous can inhibit your delivery, but assertive and animated delivery can actually help you release pent-up tension. So, if you are prepared to speak, you have practiced speaking out loud, and you focus on your audience, you will be able to gesture, use eye contact, and be more animated and forceful. You will be giving a better performance and releasing nervous energy.

Having some level of apprehension before speaking is normal, since most of us have fears about speaking before an audience. Ultimately, your goal is to channel this nervous energy into public speaking with self-confidence.

© Featureflash Photo Agency/Shutterstock.com

▓ Managing Questions

As a presenter you are most vulnerable during a question and answer (Q&A) session. Oftentimes a Q&A session is expected following a speech. This may be the case in your speech class too. Here we take a look at how to manage the session without losing control or allowing for disaster.

Transitioning into a Q&A session does not alter your planned conclusion. You simply add an invitation to your audience to ask questions. Cue your audience when you are nearly out of time for questions ("we have time for one more question"), and when you must stop ("I'm afraid that is all the time I have for questions."). The experienced presenter is not finished yet though. They know the impact of having a second closing comment. This is a second way to end the speech. The second closing reinforces the message and creates a sense of closure and completeness.

Here is an example of a student's informative speech on nutrition that uses this format: "So remember to live right means to eat right! (first closing) I have a few moments for questions. (transition to Q&A session). We just have time for one more question. (signal end of session) That's all the time for questions, and I thank you for the ones we discussed. (concluding the session) But as you walk away today, I want you to remember, you are what you eat! (second closing)."

Consider planting a question or two in your audience in advance. Give a question you have prepared in advance to several people in your audience. Instruct them that they can help you kick off the session with a question to help get things rolling and that you have made up a question for them. Tell them that they may ask it or something different, but you need their help to get people started. Alternatively, you can begin the session with offering several questions and answers yourself. This allows audiences time to think of more questions and also shows you really are interested in answering questions.

The scariest part of these sessions is not knowing who is going to speak up and what their motives and intentions are. Are they asking a question because they are genuinely curious, or is their goal to show how smart they are, disrupt the meeting, or hurt you? Experienced speakers know how to remain in control. They use two strategies: rephrasing and keep moving. Rephrasing means that the speaker listens carefully to the question and then reflects back to the questioner what the question was. But instead of using the original words, the speaker paraphrases the question. This allows the speaker to take ownership of the conversation. It also allows the speaker to steer the question in a more desirable direction.

Q&A sessions can be brisk and invigorating when a speaker knows how to manage them. Remember to plan your transition into and out of the session, deliver a second closing, answer questions truthfully, rephrase potentially problematic questions, and move on when you are not sure of someone's motives. After you master these simple techniques, you may come to really love the Q&A session for all its exciting uncertainty.

ESSENTIALS FOR EXCELLENCE

In this chapter, you learned the strategies necessary to confidently deliver your message to the audience. However, there is always room for improvement, especially when strong speaking skills are required in your occupation. Public speaking teacher Christine Clapp offers several tips to increase your confidence while delivering a speech.

Stance.

Stand firm and tall. Keep your feet planted on the ground around hip distance apart, with your weight equally distributed. Remember, purposeless movement distracts listeners from your message and is a sign of nervousness (Clapp, 2016).

Sound.

Project your voice by speaking from the diaphragm, not the throat. Also, speak louder than you think you should; not very often do people complain that a speaker was too loud.

Smile.

Smiling not only makes your voice more pleasant to listen to, but it also conveys confidence (Clapp, 2016). Don't worry about looking too cheesy; a smile makes you appear friendly, approachable, and composed.

Silence.

Use long pauses when necessary. When losing your train of thought, it can be tempting to use fillers such as "um," "uhh," or "so...." However, these habits make a speaker look unpolished, unprepared, and unprofessional.

Sight.

Make lasting eye contact. Lingering eye contact can build rapport with the audience by giving them the feeling that they are engaged in an intimate one-on-one conversation. Remember, audiences want you to speak to them, not at them.

WHAT YOU'VE LEARNED:

Now that you have studied this chapter, you will be able to:

1. Know how to choose the right delivery method to project your message with confidence.
    -   Every speech needs an introduction, body, and conclusion. Create a brief introduction that is tied to the other parts of the speech.
    -   Be as concrete as possible, and stay focused on your central idea, but provide listeners with something colorful and memorable too, if possible. Typically the most memorable material comes from your memory. Offering brief examples and anecdotes or sharing you own experiences and stories personalize your message and keep the interest of the audience.
    -   Keep a somewhat conversational tone with your audience. Think about what you want to emphasize and vary the pitch of your voice to avoid being monotone.
2. Understand the different tools available when using your voice.
    -   Articulation refers to the production of sound and how precisely we form our words. The more formal the situation, the more precise your articulation needs to be.
    -   Know how to pronounce all the words in your talk, including the names of people, places, and foreign terms. Not knowing can convey laziness, lack of concern, or lack of respect.
    -   Knowing your audience also influences the rate of your speech. Your rate should be consistent with the ideas being expressed and for the cultural context.
3. Explain the most effective strategies when using your body to accentuate message delivery.
    -   Relax and use movement reasonably. Do not pace back and forth like a caged lion or make small darting movements that return you to the safety of the lectern.
    -   Your facial expression should match the tone or emotion present in your speech. A serious tone in your voice should be accompanied by facial expressions that contribute to the serious tone.
    -   Work on sustained eye contact with different members in the audience. Avoid darting your eyes around or sweeping the room with your eyes. Instead, maintain eye contact with a single person for a single thought.
4. Know the strategies for dealing with communication and public speaking apprehension.
    -   Preparation sharpens your presentation and builds confidence. Start with a sound speech plan and then rehearse the speech aloud by yourself. Then practice in front of others to get the feel and response of an audience. You will get a sense for how the words sound and how the material flows when you speak before an audience.
    -   Find opportunities to speak. Give "minispeeches" at meetings or speak out in classes when discussion is invited.
    -   Create powerful mental images of yourself making skillful performances. Positive visualization can improve your speaking engagements and reduce your fear levels.

Key Terms

Extemporaneous speaking, 285
Articulation, 290
Pronunciation, 290
Volume, 290

Rate, 291
Pitch, 292
Emphasis, 293
Nonfluencies, 295

Gestures, 296
Eye contact, 301
Communication apprehension, 305

Reflect

1   Given the different delivery methods available to you (impromptu speaking, extemporaneous speaking, manuscript, memorization), which delivery method do you find most effective in gaining your attention? Is it effective to apply a blend of these styles when speaking?

2   Think back to the last time you had a conversation outside of a speech. How often do you use nonfluencies during regular conversation? Do you think trying to eliminate nonfluencies in regular conversation can help you remove them in public presentations?

3   How often do you think about your own culture when speaking in public? How essential is researching different cultural norms when presenting in a new environment?

4   How much do you rely on written notes or manuscripts when giving a presentation? What are some exercises you could employ to alleviate the need for lengthy notes?

5   What methods have you practiced to manage public speaking anxiety? Is there an approach you would prefer compared to the strategies offered in this text?

Review Questions

1   _____ involves speaking with little or no preparation time; using no notes or just a few.

2   _____ is a method of delivery that involves using carefully prepared notes to guide the presentation.

3   _____ is the verbalization of distinct sounds and how precisely words are formed.

4   _____ involves knowing how to say a word and saying it correctly.

5   _____ is the pace at which you speak.

6   _____ is the vocal range or key, the highness or lowness of your voice produced by the tightening and loosening of your vocal folds.

7 _____ are meaningless words that interrupt the flow of our speech; also known as vocalized pauses or vocal fillers.

8 _____ is the connection you form with listeners through your gaze.

9 _____ is an individual's level of fear or anxiety associated with either real or anticipated communication with another person or persons.

Oklahoma Senator Jim Inhofe used a clear (but misleading) visual aid when discussing climate change before the Senate.

U.S. SENA
JIM INHO

CHAPTER TEN
PRESENTATIONAL AIDS AND TECHNOLOGY

OUTLINE

WHAT YOU'LL LEARN

After studying this chapter, you should be able to:

1. Understand the functions of presentational aids.
2. Know the different types of technology-based presentational aids.
3. Evaluate the effectiveness of presentational aids.
4. Identify the principles for using presentational aids.

SPEAKING IN CONTEXT

In February of 2015, Oklahoma Senator Jim Inhofe brought a snowball to the Senate floor during a debate about global climate change. Inhofe, who (at the time) was the chairman of the Senate Environment and Public Works Committee, used the snowball as a visual aid to support his argument that global warming is a hoax. "...we keep hearing that 2014 has been the warmest year on record," said Inhofe. "I ask the chair, you know what this is? It's a snowball. And that's just from outside here. So it's very, very cold out." (Mirsky, 2015).

In his term as Senator, Inhofe has been a vocal critic of the Obama administration's plans to reduce carbon emissions, which the majority of the scientific community claims leads to climate change. After hearing about numerous scientific studies asserting that the year 2014 was the hottest year on record, Inhofe used the snowball as a visual example of how the dangers of global warming are overblown. NASA actually did determine that 2014 was the warmest year since modern recording began in 1880, but many people still sided with Senator Inhofe following his presentation to the Senate. Accurate or not, Inhofe's snowball gave many people a visual cue to disregard claims of global warming.

As you learn how to use presentational aids effectively in your professional career, it is important to acknowledge the impact (or lack thereof) such aids can have when appealing to your audience. Inhofe's snowball has been roundly criticized as a flawed example with no scientific bearing on the issue of climate change, but it was effective in generating support and visibility for his political position. In this chapter, you will learn how aids like this one can help, hinder, or even ruin your public speaking effectiveness.

In the age of PowerPoint, being tech savvy is clearly an advantage to the public speaker today. Although the tools may have changed, the bottom line has not: Any presentational aids you create must communicate a clear, relevant, direct, and interesting message.

This chapter examines how technology relates to public speaking in general and presentational aids in particular. First, we consider the nature and types of technology and presentational aids available to speakers today. Then, we identify ways to include them in your presentations. We end this chapter by offering guidelines for using presentational aids effectively in your speeches.

The Nature of Presentational Aids Today

"We cannot *not* communicate" is a communication axiom developed by Paul Watzlawick (1967). This suggests that in face-to-face communication, even when we choose to *not* speak, we are still communicating a message through our silence and our nonverbal communication (Ivy & Wahl, 2014). A similar case can be made for communicating through our presentational aids. We cannot not communicate here as well. What message does a poorly designed or displayed aid communicate to an audience about the speaker? Some might draw conclusions regarding

Technology-based presentational aids like Microsoft PowerPoint are used in almost all professional contexts.

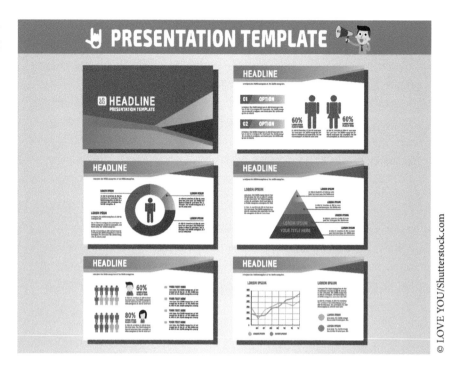

the speaker's commitment to the speech, his/her credibility to speak on the subject, or his/her ability to deliver a captivating, well-thought-out message. Worse yet, what might an audience think of a speech that has no accompanying presentational aids at all? We have come to expect the bells, whistles, and pizzazz presentational aids can bring to a speech.

Functions of Presentational Aids

Presentational aids operate in a variety of ways. They can satisfy an ever-escalating thirst for information and entertainment. They promise to enhance, or hinder, our presentations. They are more than afterthoughts, add-ons, or speech class requirements. Your instructor may require you to use presentational aids not only to enhance the effectiveness of your speech, but also to help you learn how to use them comfortably as you speak. But the main reason you may be required to use them is because nearly *everyone else is using them*!

Did you know greater numbers of us have been exposed to PowerPoint than any other presentation software? Today, more people use PowerPoint to accompany presentations than any other type of technology, including YouTube, video clips, and websites. However, poorly conceived or executed visuals like PowerPoint can bring trouble. Paying attention to how a visual message is received by an audience is essential. We must keep the needs of our audience in mind. The speaker–audience connection is strengthened when the speaker judiciously considers potential advantages and disadvantages of each presentational aid before placing them in a speech.

Advantages of Presentational Aids

Available

As long as one has access to the Internet, a nearly infinite amount of presentational material is available, often without cost. As you prepare for your speech, you can create everything online and transfer it to a flash drive when you're ready. Millions of videoclips, photos and images, and clip art are available, too. Adding music, special effects, timed sequencing, and flash video, for example, may be a little trickier for the novice, but it is being used increasingly in professional and student presentations.

Engaging

Have you ever seen a lotto billboard alongside an interstate? As you approach it, you can see the jackpot amount increasing as the digital numbers change constantly. When a presentational aid is well prepared, little can compete with it to capture—and hold—audience interest. We live in a visual age. Images that surround us in the mass media make us more receptive, on conscious and unconscious levels, to visual presentations of all kinds. We are attuned to these presentations simply because they are visual—a phenomenon you can use to your advantage during a speech.

One student wanted to emphasize how fast the world's population is growing. During her speech, she accessed a website (worldometers. info) that keeps a digital tally of births, and kept the digital counter on the screen for about a minute. Then she made reference to the number of births that had occurred during that minute. This helped keep the interest of the class. A well-placed, professional-looking presentational aid draws attention to the point you are trying to make or to statistics you want your audience to process.

Persuasive

Seeing the devastation a tornado creates is more persuasive than having someone simply talk about it. Watching a video of animals being euthanized

Former U.S. Vice President Al Gore used numerous presentational aids for his documentary film *An Inconvenient Truth*.

© Jayakumar/Shutterstock.com

is more powerful than talking about the process. Looking at statistics that have been organized in a clear manner through graphs or charts is more persuasive than simply hearing the numbers. Presentation software adds impact to your argument.

One of the most well-known examples of presentation software images being used to strengthen and elucidate arguments can be seen in former U.S. Vice President Al Gore's 2006 documentary film *An Inconvenient Truth*. Gore's narration is accompanied by graphs, animation, video clips, and other images derived from presentation software (Wright, 2009). An analysis of that film reveals that slides containing text alone are used only 11 times, and bullet points are used only once. Gore links his main points to events with which Americans can relate, and provides a frame of reference for understanding and comparing his statistics. His presentational aids help to create a powerful message that was persuasive to many.

Entertaining

If you are in the mood, it takes only a few minutes to surf for video that makes you laugh. Comedy abounds on the Internet and funny clips are uploaded to countless video-sharing sites continually. Notice that both appropriate, professional clips exist as well as plenty of, well, unsavory ones. If you searched the term "stupid human tricks," you will find all sorts of hijinks, some guaranteed to make you blush. In other words, speakers have a plethora of options when seeking something entertaining to support their point, but not all are appropriate.

Presentational software offers animation and sound effects, so speakers can add entertainment value to their slides. Even something simple like creating a graphic that uses stacked hamburgers to talk about the number of hamburgers sold, or stacked oranges, apples, and pears to talk about the amount of fruit sold will add visual impact and enhance meaning. With a little forethought, technology can enhance the entertainment value of your message.

ENGAGING IN COMMUNITY

When speaking to elementary school children, finding unique ways to hold their attention can be quite a challenge. Kevin West, a coordinator for the National Society for the Prevention of Cruelty to Children (NSPCC), decided a memorable visual aid might be his best option to get the attention of his young audience. In order to better educate children about personal safety, West introduced "Buddy", a big green soft toy with a smiling face, to help children remember his lesson. Through Buddy, children learned different strategies about how to stay safe on the Internet and in everyday social situations (Haworth, 2016).

"We try to make it fun but it's important that we still get the message across," says NSPCC volunteer Jenny Woodman. "The balance has to be found between making it fun and educational because what we're trying to teach them is important."

Since its founding in 1884, the NSPCC charity has focused on child protection and education. As the organization has grown through the years, NSPCC leaders have learned to rely on the effectiveness of public presentations. Although the organization's grassroots work takes place at schools and regional events, the NSPCC also lobbies the government on issues relating to child welfare. The organization also runs ChildLine, a free 24-hour counseling service for children and young people under the age of 18.

If volunteering in your community appeals to you, use NSPCC's "Buddy" as an example of how visual aids can assist people in engaging with and remembering your message. Remember, stories and presentations that people find entertaining are more likely to stick in their mind, leading to greater understanding and acceptance.

Memorable

Did you read the newspaper this morning? What do you remember from it? Chances are, if you read the paper, a photo comes to mind—the picture of a fireman rescuing a child from a burning building or the president of your university getting a pie in the face at the end of a fundraiser. You may have read the articles that accompanied these pictures, but the images are likely to have had the greatest impact.

Technology gives you the power to etch permanent images into the minds of attendees. Do you recall a TV commercial asking you to assist starving children or neglected pets? These pitches are persuasive and memorable because of the tragic and compelling pictures they offer us. Using pictures, you can create lasting mental images in the minds of your audience. Moving graphics and sound effects can be catchy and add an entertainment effect so long as they are not overdone. Through video-sharing websites like YouTube, you can easily find footage of a variety of current and past events. Such video clips are available, tend to be vivid, and may be unforgettable.

Increase Clarity

A good visual design can make information clearer and more interesting (Cyphert, 2007). It also helps to emphasize key points (Kraus, 2008). Some speeches rely on many facts and statistics, which may be difficult for an audience to process. Using visuals like bar graphs, line graphs, or tables may help. Sometimes technology can lead an audience through complex material by using simple slides that highlight key points. Similarly, if you're talking about a process, such as brewing beer, for example, creating slides that identify the different steps by pairing each with photos will clarify the process.

Presentational aids have the power to clarify complex ideas. They are invaluable tools when explaining mechanical functions such as how a hot air balloon rises or how a computer stores information. They can clarify complex interrelationships involving people, groups, and institutions. They can show, for example, the stages a bill must go through before it becomes a law, and the role Congress and the president play in this process. Visuals may reduce but do not eliminate the need to explain complex details.

Presentational aids take the place of many words, and, therefore, may shorten the length of a speech. They do not replace words, and one or two statements are insufficient verbal support for a series of visual displays. But presentational aids and words *in combination* reduce the amount of time you spend creating word pictures.

The environmental impact of the *Deepwater Horizon* oil spill was conveyed powerfully by clear images of contamination and destruction.

Make Abstract Ideas Concrete

Abstract language can hurt your message clarity. If you are delivering a speech on the effects of the estimated 17–39-million-gallon oil spill from the BP *Deepwater Horizon* explosion in the Gulf of Mexico in the spring and summer of 2010, it may not be enough to tell your audience that the explosion killed 11 people and injured 17 more. But you can add something specific: Actual pictures of the clean-up effort of oil-saturated, sick animals. The image of the spill's devastating effect on wildlife provides us with specific visual pictures that make the situation more relevant, personal, and easily grasped. We need to see something concrete to process abstract ideas such as large catastrophes.

Help Organize Ideas

As with every other aspect of your speech, presentational aids should be audience-centered. They may be eye-catching and visually stimulating, but they serve a more practical purpose. The flow and connection of a speaker's ideas are not always apparent to an audience, especially if the topic is complicated or involves many steps. Pictures, flow charts, diagrams, graphs, tables, and video clips help listeners follow a speaker's ideas. Additionally, presentational aids help keep the speaker on his/her organizational track. This benefit, however, is only realized when a speaker has rehearsed a number of times with the aids.

Disadvantages of Presentational Aids

What about when technology turns ugly? Poorly conceived or executed visuals can bring trouble. Paying attention to how a visual message is received by an audience is essential. Careful consideration of drawbacks, pitfalls, and caveats ensures the technology you use actually serves you, rather than serves to hurt you.

Access

Consider first, technology may not be available. While many colleges have computers in all classrooms, others may have them available in designated classrooms or by request only. Internet access via LAN (Local Area Network) may be out of service temporarily. What if your flash drive elects to self-destruct moments before your speech begins or you used newer, incompatible software, and the dinosaur computer you are now trying to use does not recognize your materials? Murphy's Law for the speaker who relies on technology is "If anything can go wrong, it will go wrong, during your presentation, in the worst possible way!"

Impersonal

When a speaker uses no presentational aids, the audience must focus on the speaker. One of the speaker's tasks is to create a connection with the audience through content, personality, language, and movement. When technology is used, focus often shifts. A problem exists when slides become the message rather than a means to enrich the message. When this happens we "forego an important opportunity to connect with the audience as human beings" (Alley & Neeley, 2005, p. 418). We risk losing our human connection to our audience by overusing technology. Often, technology adds impact and clarity but can also create psychological distance and a perception of rigidity that some audience members will not appreciate.

Time Consuming

Creating slides with a standard background is fairly easy. However, finding the right video clip, creating graphs, incorporating video clips, and synchronizing music are all activities that take time and effort, and may distract you from your primary goal, which is to develop and support your ideas. Surely you have witnessed a presentation that had great visual appeal but little substance.

The speaker may have spent too much time with the "bells and whistles" at the expense of developing sound arguments with ample support.

In addition to expending effort to create the slide show, setting up might take too much time before the speech. Once the computer is on and the projection equipment is warmed up (no guarantee of this actually happening when you need it to), the speaker must control volume, launch and operate software, etc. Speech classes sometimes endure lengthy gaps of dullness while an unprepared speaker bumbles with their set-up. The considerate speaker will find ways to minimize this waste of audience time.

Death by PowerPoint

Speakers (and lecturers) who use slides for the purpose of providing the outline to their talk may find themselves less motivated or excited about the presentation. Knowing they don't have to worry about losing their place, they may spend less time practicing their speech. According to Carey (1999), "PowerPoint's reliability has lulled more than a few presenters and planners into creative complacency, resulting in audiovisual presentations that too often are monotonous, static, even boring" (pg. 47). Death by PowerPoint, as it is termed, is a painful way to go. Strike a balance by not overusing slides. One or two per minute you speak is acceptable; twenty in a five-minute speech will surely power us to the point of unconsciousness.

PowerPointless

Comedian Don McMillan's YouTube video "Life After Death by PowerPoint" is both informative and entertaining (www.youtube.com/watch?v=lpvgfmEU2Ck). What problems do you relate to? What advice can you give someone who uses too much PowerPoint assistance? What are the software's strengths? Weaknesses?

It is possible to be upstaged by your video clip. Your visual presentation—rather than your speech—may hold center stage. To avoid this, carefully prepare an introduction to support the video clip. Point your listeners to specific parts so they focus on what you want rather than on what happens to catch their interest. After the visual, continue your speech, and build on its content with the impact of your own delivery.

When thinking about using any of the above projected images, allow for sufficient set-up time. Check the equipment to make sure you can operate it and that it is in good working order. Remember also, a darkened room can disrupt your presentation if you need to refer to detailed notes, and if you want people to take notes, the room may be too dark.

ETHICS MATTER

Karen works as a public relations director for her city's no-kill animal shelter. In recent months, Karen's organization has seen massive decreases in charitable donations and shelter volunteers. To combat this, Karen decides to initiate a local public relations campaign to increase public awareness and support.

When creating a slide show to highlight the services her shelter offers, Karen comes across several photos of animals that were adopted from her shelter a few years ago. To increase the views and shares her slide show would get on social media, Karen placed these animals' pictures online with the caption "The ones that couldn't afford to wait," insinuating that the animals had been euthanized. Although Karen's presentation was successful in generating public assistance, several of the animals' owners posted on her organization's Twitter feed, showing that their animals were alive and well. Karen and her animal shelter faced severe public backlash over this deception. Karen was dismissed from her job, and the animal shelter faces closure as public funds and trust faded away.

QUESTIONS TO CONSIDER:

1. Although Karen misled the public, was her deception ethically justified since it aimed to help the animals in her shelter?
2. How does Karen's story illustrate the importance of maintaining public trust for professional communicators?
3. What would you have done differently in Karen's situation in order to help the animal shelter?

Potential for Reductionism

Some claim that design defaults in presentation software create the potential for reductionism because they oversimplify and fragment the subject matter (Alley & Neeley, 2005, p. 418). Only a limited amount of information can be presented on any one slide or group of slides. Abstract connections may be difficult to make, and sometimes critical assumptions are left out or relationships are not specified. Research indicates that people often begin to prepare presentations by thinking about what should appear on screen, slide by slide, and then constructing their presentations accordingly, rather than by considering what they want to say or how they can make the audience's experience better (Wright, 2009). When we reduce issues to slides of text and little pictures, we risk our audience not getting the big picture.

Relying too heavily on bullet points may reduce the richness of your ideas by limiting the information your audience focuses on, thereby fostering misinformation, misinterpretation, and mistakes in judgment.

Types of Presentational Aids

Presentational aids fall into four classifications: actual objects, three-dimensional models, two-dimensional reproductions, and technology-based aids.

Actual Objects

Actual objects are real objects. Your authors quickly generated this list of inappropriate objects brought to their speech classes: snakes, guns, grenades, margaritas, M-80 firecrackers, marijuana, and so on. Of course, these were all bad choices. Yet good options abound. One student who had been stricken with bone cancer as a child, a condition that required the amputation of her leg, demonstrated to her classmates how her prosthetic leg functioned and how she wore it. Not one of her listeners lost interest in her demonstration.

Another student, concerned about the volume of disposable diapers lingering in our landfills, brought to class a (heavy) week's worth of dirty diapers from one infant. In addition to visual and olfactory shock value, it left a powerfully strong image to accompany her statistics about the slow decomposition of dirty, disposable diapers.

As these examples demonstrate, objects can be effective visual aids. Because you are showing your audience exactly what you are talking about, objects have the power to inform or convince unlike any other presentational aid.

When bringing an object to class, be concerned with safety. Clear any questionable objects with your instructor. Objects you intend to use must not pose a safety risk to you or your audience. Animals, chemicals, and weapons certainly fall into this category. For example, you may think your pet Madagascar hissing cockroaches are snuggly adorable, but to your instructor and some of your classmates, they may elicit terror and panic.

Three-Dimensional Models

If you decide that an actual object is **too risky**, a three-dimensional model may be your best choice. Models are commonly used to show the structure of a complex object. For example, a student who watched his father almost die of a heart attack used a model of the heart to demonstrate what physically happened during the attack. Using a three-dimensional replica about five times the size of a human heart, he showed how the major blood vessels leading to his father's heart became clogged and how this blockage precipitated the attack.

Models are useful when explaining steps in a sequence. A scale model of the space shuttle, its booster rockets, and the launch pad would help you describe what happens during the first few minutes after blast-off.

When considering a three-dimensional model, take into account construction time and availability. It is possible you already have the model or you know where you can borrow one, so no construction time is needed. If you need to create the three-dimensional model from a kit or your own imagination, consider how much time it will take to put it together. Here is a general rule: You do not want your presentational aid construction time to take longer than your speech preparation time.

Some replicas are easier to find, build, or buy than others. If you are delivering a speech on antique cars, inexpensive plastic models are available. For a talk on how proper city planning can untangle the daily downtown traffic snarl, you would have to build your own scaled-down version of downtown roads as they are now, and as you would like them to be. That would be too time consuming and expensive to be feasible. But a two-dimensional representation (like a map or diagram), as we see next, would be effective and affordable.

Two-Dimensional Reproductions

Two-dimensional reproductions are the most common visual aids used by speakers. Among these are photographs, diagrams and drawings, maps, tables, and graphs. Computer-projected presentations, such as PowerPoint and Prezi, are also two-dimensional reproductions but are discussed as a separate type because of their reliance on newer, higher technologies.

Speaking Well with Technology Is an Essential for Excellence

The year 2016 saw virtual reality (VR) machines spike in popularity and development. Although virtual reality has been tried before, many experts believe that advances in media technology have advanced enough to create a product that can thrive in the marketplace. YouTube, one of the most popular video streaming services in the world, decided to toss its hat in the ring with 360 video.

YouTube's move into the virtual reality market goes hand in hand with Google Cardboard, a virtual reality platform developed for use with a head mount for a smartphone. Using the VR platform, YouTube plans to offer 360 video content, allowing users to view their streaming videos in an interactive way. The company also outlined the advertising capabilities of the brand, included TrueView, masthead sponsorship, and other organic content (Deighton, 2016).

"You can actually find more [people from] 18 to 34 years [old] on YouTube on mobile devices alone than on a TV network," says Debbie Weinstein, YouTube director of brand innovation. "So when it comes to reach, I think we're in a good place."

As we discuss the use of visual aid technology in public speaking, it is important to stay alert for new directions for visual communication. Although a niche market right now, YouTube's foray into VR could become a mainstay in popular culture in a few years. As communication professionals, you help yourself immensely by learning how to use cutting edge tools like these for yourself.

© Melpomene/Shutterstock.com

In conjunction with YouTube, Google introduced Google Cardboard, a virtual reality headset that works with common smartphones.

Photographs

Photographs are realistic two-dimensional choices. They can have great impact. For a speech on animal rights, a photo of a fox struggling to free his leg from a trap will deliver your message more effectively than words. If you are speaking about forest fire prevention, a photo of a forest destroyed by fire is your most persuasive evidence.

Photos must be large enough for your audience to see. If a photo is important to your presentation, consider enlarging it so that the entire audience can see it. Typically, using magazine or newspaper pictures is as clear as photos.

Although photographs are effective aids, overly graphic pictures can yield negative results. If a photograph offends or disgusts your audience, some may tune you out.

Drawings and Diagrams

When you cannot illustrate your point with a photograph—or would rather not use one—a drawing is an alternative. A drawing is your own representation of what you are describing. If you are demonstrating the difference between a kettledrum and a snare drum, a simple drawing may be all you need. If you want to extend your explanation to show how musicians are able to control the pitch of the sound made by a drum, your drawing must include more detail. The location of the screws used to tighten the skin of the drum must be shown as well as the relationship between the size of the drum and the pitch of the sound.

A detailed drawing showing the arrangement and relationship of the parts to the whole is considered a diagram. **Figure 10.1** is a simple diagram of a kettledrum. Labels are often used to pinpoint critical parts.

Do not attempt a complex drawing or diagram if you have little or no artistic ability. Neither should you attempt to produce drawings while your audience is watching. Prepare sketches in advance. Keep your audience's needs and limitations in mind when choosing diagrams. Imagine the audience's eyes as they listen to someone using **Figure 10.2** to discuss every dimension of a complex floor design. Too much detail will frustrate your audience as they strain to see the tiniest parts and labels. And when people are frustrated, they often stop listening.

FIGURE 10.1 A simple diagram can show how the parts of objects such as this drum interact.

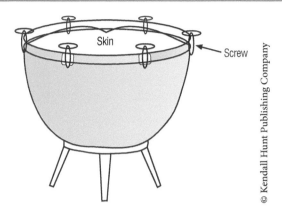

Skin

Screw

© Kendall Hunt Publishing Company

FIGURE 10.2 An intricate line drawing may frustrate your audience. Keep illustrations simple.

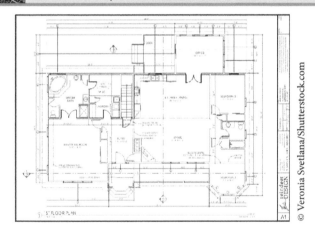

© Veronia Svetlana/Shutterstock.com

Maps

Weather reports on TV news have made maps a familiar visual aid. Instead of merely talking about the weather, reporters show us the shifting patterns that turn sunshine into storms. The next time you watch a weather report, note the kind of map being used. Notice that details have been omitted because they distract viewers from what the reporter is explaining.

Too much detail will confuse your audience. For example, when talking about Europe's shrinking population, do not include the location of the Acropolis or the Eiffel Tower. Because you must focus on your specific purpose, you may have to draw a map yourself. Start with a broad outline of the geographic area and add to it only those details necessary for your presentation.

On election night, many news programs show a map of the United States divided into "blue states" and "red states." Blue states may be those where the majority of voters voted Democratic, and red states voted Republican. Such a map (see **Figure 10.3**) gives a quick visual of where election results stand. Making a visual distinction between Republicans and Democrats began with the 2004 presidential election between John Kerry and George W. Bush, and has been so successful that the concept of "blue states" and "red states" has become part of our political vernacular.

FIGURE 10.3 This map shows "blue states" and "red states," clarifying where election results stand.

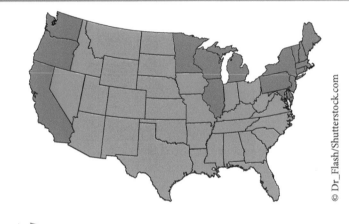

© Dr_Flash/Shutterstock.com

This map from the 2012 presidential election offers an easily comprehensible image of which political party was most popular in each state.

© Dr_Flash/Shutterstock.com

PART TWO: PREPARING AND PRESENTING YOUR SPEECH

Tables

Tables focus on words and numbers presented in columns and rows. Tables are used most frequently to display statistical data. If you were delivering a speech on the fat content of food and you note the types and percentage of fat in nuts, you could refer to a table similar to that shown in **Figure 10.4**. However, this single table should be divided into two parts because it contains too much information to present in one visual. Keep in mind the audience's *information absorption threshold*—the point at which a visual will cease to be useful because it says too much.

Charts

Charts help the speaker display detailed information quickly and effectively. Charts can summarize data in an easy-to-read format, illustrate a process, and show relationships among parts.

    Flow charts are used to display the steps, or stages, in a process. Each step is illustrated by an image or label. If you are an amateur cartoonist, you might give a talk on the steps involved in producing an animated cartoon. **Figure 10.5** displays a simple flowchart of the process a golfer goes through when deciding whether to golf on a particular day. This humorous visual reveals the specific decision-making sequence.

    A flow chart can make use of pictures. You might draw the pictures yourself or, if your artistic ability is limited, use selected photographs available online. Flow charts that depend on words alone should use short, simple labels that move the audience through the stages of the process.

    Organizational charts reflect our highly structured world. Corporations, government institutions, schools, associations, and religious organizations are organized according to official hierarchies that determine the relationships of people as they work. You may refer to an organizational chart if you are trying to show the positions of people involved in a project. By looking at a chart like that shown in **Figure 10.6**, your audience will know who reports to whom.

Flow chart
Used to display the steps, or stages, in a process.

Organizational chart
Organized according to official hierarchies that determine the relationships of people as they work.

FIGURE 10.4 The fat content of food is measured in a single table.

	Saturated	Monounsaturated	Polyunsaturated	Other
Chestnuts	18%	35%	40%	7%
Brazil Nuts	15%	35%	36%	14%
Cashews	13	59	17	11
Pine Nuts	13	37	41	9
Peanuts	12	49	38	6
Pistachios	12	68	15	5
Walnuts	8	23	63	6
Almonds	8	65	21	6
Pecans	6	62	25	7
Hazelnuts	6	79	9	6

Graphs

When referring to statistics or when presenting complex statistical information, a visual representation can be effective because it has the ability to simplify and clarify. Statistics may be presented in numerous ways, including bar graphs, pictographs, line graphs, and pie graphs.

FIGURE 10.5 A simple flow chart of the golfer's decision-making process.

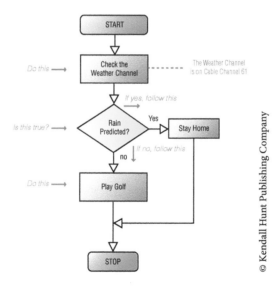

© Kendall Hunt Publishing Company

FIGURE 10.6 Almost every large group or company has an organizational chart to illustrate the official hierarchy and lines of access.

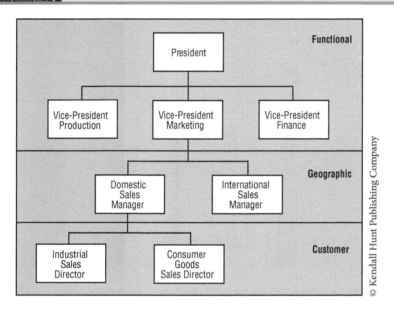

© Kendall Hunt Publishing Company

In a speech urging today's college students to consider teaching social sciences or humanities in college, you want to show, graphically, that our universities will face a serious shortfall of liberal arts professors well into the future. As part of your speech, you tell your audience:

> There were days back in the 1980s when having a Ph.D. in history, sociology, English literature, or philosophy garnered few professional and monetary opportunities. Indeed, many people who aspired to teach the humanities and social sciences were forced into menial jobs just to survive. So great was the supply of potential faculty over the demand that a new phenomenon was created: the taxi-driving Ph.D. Today, the story is different.

The visual referred to is shown in **Figure 10.7**, a bar graph displaying the history of supply and demand for faculty members. The graph compares figures for five-year periods and measures these figures in thousands. This type of graph is especially helpful when you are comparing two or more items. In this case, one bar represents the supply of faculty while the other represents demand. To make the trend even clearer, you may want to color code the bars.

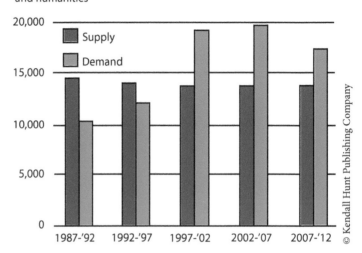

Faculty supply-and-demand projections in the social sciences and humanities

© Kendall Hunt Publishing Company

Pictograph

Most commonly used as a variation of the bar graph. Instead of showing bars of various lengths, comparing items on the graph, the bars are replaced by pictorial representations of the graph's subject.

Line graph

Used to show a trend over time.

Pie graph

Also known as a circle graph, shows how the parts of an item relate to the whole.

Pictographs are most commonly used as a variation of the bar graph. Instead of showing bars of various lengths comparing items on the graph, the bars are replaced by pictorial representations of the graph's subject. For example, if you are giving a speech on the popularity of ice cream bars, you can use a pictograph like that shown in **Figure 10.8** to demonstrate when the most bars were sold. The pictograph must include a legend explaining what each symbol means. In this case, each ice cream bar represents 100 sold.

When you want to show a trend over time, the **line graph** may be your best choice. When two or more lines are used in one graph, comparisons are possible. **Figure 10.9** is a visual representation of the number of Irish immigrants entering the United States between 1820 and 1990. The tall peak in the graph represents the period of time when the potato famine was affecting the majority of Ireland. This simple graph could be used in a speech about Irish immigration trends.

Pie graphs show your audience how the parts of an item relate to the whole. It is one of the most popular and effective ways to show how something is divided. The most simple and direct way to demonstrate percentages graphically is with a pie graph. In a budget presentation to the local school board, the chief financial officer might display a series of pie graphs. She might explain that revenue comes from three levels: federal, state, and local. **Figure 10.10** shows that taxes from local communities provide approximately half the revenue generated for the district. The federal government provides only 10 percent, thus illustrating how dependent the school district is on local funding.

 FIGURE 10.8 Pictographs provide a twist on the traditional bar graph by using pictures of the items discussed to illustrate the "bar." The pictograph should include a scale that explains what each symbol means, such as 100 ice cream bars sold.

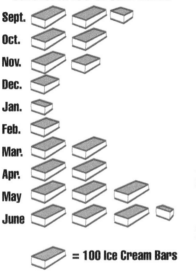

Cafeteria Ice Cream Sales

= 100 Ice Cream Bars

© Kendall Hunt Publishing Company

FIGURE 10.9 This is a graph of the number of Irish immigrants who entered the U.S. from 1820 to 1990. The climax of the migration was in 1851 when 221,253 immigrants entered the U.S. This was around the time when the potato famine seized the majority of Ireland.

Irish Immigration to the United States (1820–1990)

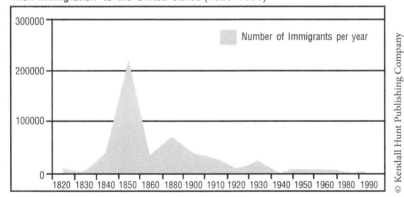

© Kendall Hunt Publishing Company

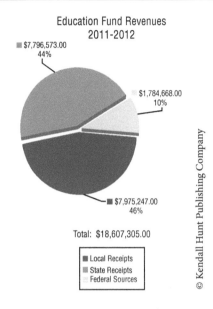

No matter what type of two-dimensional aid you choose, clarity is essential. It may happen that you create a two-dimensional aid that makes your audience think, "What does that *mean*?" Any presentational aid you use must clarify rather than confuse. If the aid contains too much information, your audience will be unable to process it easily, and you may lose their attention. If you use graphs, pie charts, maps, or tables, information must be understandable. For example, if you have an x-axis and a y-axis, they should be clearly labeled so your audience quickly and easily understands what you are referencing.

Displaying Two-Dimensional Presentational Aids

When you decide to use a line graph to illustrate the volatility of the marketplace, your next decision involves how to display the graph. Speakers have numerous options for displaying two-dimensional presentational aids. Time and cost alone are not good predictors of the effectiveness of a presentational aid. Sometimes emphasizing important points on a flip chart or using prepared overhead transparencies are acceptable. This next section focuses on how to display two-dimensional aids. In particular, we discuss the benefits and disadvantages of using erasable boards, large Post-its', posters, and flip charts.

Chalk or Dry Erase Board

It is a rare classroom that does not have some type of erasable board, be it black, green, or white. These serve as the universal presentational aid. Advantages include: It is already in the classroom, you cannot lose or damage it, and it requires no preparation time (other than the day of presentation). Boards are the easiest visual aid to use and involve the least amount of preparation time.

Using a board requires neat, legible handwriting. Seldom is it acceptable to write on the blackboard *during the speech*, but if you must, write as little as possible. Use key terms only. If possible, arrive early and prepare the board in advance. If the board has a screen above it, you might pull the screen down to hide your work until time for your presentation.

In terms of disadvantages, the blackboard is generally viewed as less professional than other presentational aids. We suggest that chalk or eraser boards should serve as your back-up plan. If your poster is ruined, you cannot find an easel for your flip chart, or the computer is unavailable or malfunctioning, then the blackboard is your backup plan.

Your audience may interpret your use of it as lack of preparation. Also, writing on the blackboard requires a speaker to turn away from the audience. Turning your back on your audience is never a good idea, and writing on the board cuts into your valuable speaking time.

Poster Board

A generation ago, the clarity of a poster depended on the art skills of the students since posters were "designed" by hand. If your college has an instructional materials office of some kind, you can make your own posters using die-cuts (generally, Ellison die-cuts). These allow you to cut out letters and shapes to make the poster look more professional. Even better, a computer lab on campus or a photocopying facility will allow access to poster-sized computer-generated graphics. Another option is to use poster-sized foam board in different colors.

Advantages to using a poster board include its low cost and familiarity, and potential use in classrooms where computer-generated technology is not available or difficult to access. Disadvantages include some speakers' lack of time, talent, or patience to create a professional-looking poster; the potential difficulty displaying the poster if there is no easel or the chalkboard lacks a chalk tray; and the possibility that posters may get damaged during transportation.

Flip Chart

Flip charts are still a popular way to display two-dimensional information. There are several advantages to using flip charts. The main advantage is that they allow for spontaneity. The speaker may add words or lines based on audience response. A flip chart can be prepared in advance *or* during your speech. Other advantages are that they do not require electricity, they are economical, and one can add color to them easily (Laskowski, 2006).

Disadvantages to using flip charts are they may difficult to read and they may be distracting. Laskowski (2006) suggests avoiding yellow, pink, or orange markers that are difficult to see, and sticking to one dark color and one lighter color for highlighting. Also, less expensive paper may lead to the marker bleeding through to the following page. Test your markers and paper ahead of time.

Repositional Note Pad

The large repositional note pad, most commonly known as a poster-sized Post-it, is a type of flip chart. These large sticky notes have useful applications in group meetings where members brainstorm and then display the results on multiple pages around the walls. For your speech, you may have some pre-designed Post-its that you stick on the board at different intervals for emphasis. Like posters, these are most useful in rooms lacking more advanced technology.

Two advantages to using poster-sized sticky notes are that you do not have to worry about chalk, tape, push-pins, or staples, and you have tremendous flexibility. In addition to being able to stick them just about anywhere, the speaker can write on them before or during the speech. The main disadvantage is that, as they are most likely handwritten, they may not look as professional as some other display techniques. One way to work around this limitation is to use pencil on the pages in advance so the writing is neat and, at the same time, so light that only you can see it. Then, during your presentation, go over your work with a marker.

Technology-Based Presentational Aids

Often speakers must clearly communicate statistics, trends, and abstract information. As funds become available and technology costs decrease, more classrooms will be technology-enhanced. This does not mean, however, that older options are now useless. Instances still exist where an audio recording or actual object may make more sense than a computer-generated slide presentation. This next section discusses audio and projected images.

Audio and Projected Images

Rarely is the eraser board your only option for a presentational aid. Depending on the needs of your audience, the content of your speech, the speaking situation, and your own abilities, you may choose a presentational aid requiring the use of other equipment.

Audiotape/CD/iPod

Not all presentational aids are visual, and incorporating an audio clip into your speech is a simple task. If you are trying to describe the messages babies send through their different cries, it would be appropriate and helpful to play an audiotape, CD, or a smartphone recording of different cries as you explain each. Of course, in a technology-enhanced room, students can access music and many sounds on the computer.

Take care when using an audio clip. Time is an issue, and the clip can overshadow the oral presentation if it consumes too much time. The inexperienced speaker may not have the sound bite or audio clip set up at the right spot or the right volume, and recording quality may be an issue. Getting set up on the computer may take too much time. As always, check the equipment to make sure it is working, the volume is set correctly, and that it is properly queued before the presentation.

Using an overhead projector, object projector, document cameras (for example, ELMO), or smart board allows you to face your listeners and talk as you project images onto a surface. They may be used in normal lighting, which is an important advantage to the speaker. You may face your listeners and use a pointer, just as you would if you were using any other visual. If you choose to remain near the projector instead, you run the risk of talking down to the material you are projecting rather than looking up at your audience. PowerPoint and Prezi are popular software applications that create visuals to accompany presentations. Both have unique features and common ones (templates, samples, editing, etc.). Using these products as a speech aid is expedient and the finished product looks good and is easy to use, too.

For many communication professionals, the New Media age has been an immeasurable gift. Besides being able to reach a much larger audience more quickly, communicators now have countless different platforms available to interact with their publics. Currently, one of the most popular audio presentations online is the podcast. Podcasts are highly versatile, they are relatively easy and cheap to produce, and they can be released to an enormous audience instantaneously via the Internet. However, given how distracted most podcast listeners are, holding your audience's attention can be difficult. Researcher Kyle Wrather examines how one podcast network keeps their listeners engaged.

For his case study, Wrather observed Maximum Fun, a relatively small podcast network that grew from the variety radio comedy show *The Sound of Young America*. The network now produces over twenty podcasts that are largely funded through listener pledges and donations (Wrather, 2016). One podcast (*Jordan, Jesse, Go!*) gives listeners an active role in their show by encouraging them to call in and record voicemail messages, to which the hosts then respond. Another podcast runs as a loosely structured advice show where the hosts draw their questions from listeners' email, phone, Twitter, and other online spaces. In a third example (*Judge John Hodgman*), listeners are asked not only to submit questions, but also to participate in the show itself. The "judge" John Hodgman (a comedian) listens to submissions from listeners, sometimes inviting them to call in via a Skype interview, then gives his rulings to the participants. In all three examples, the podcasts offer different forms of audience acknowledgment and participation, generally by means of social media. Wrather asserts that this combination of digital technologies, spaces, and tools allow both producers and listeners to expand their connections (Wrather, 2016). This convergence of new media services now enables the podcast medium to formulate nuanced relationships between content generators and their audiences.

Video, DVD, and Online Media Sharing Sites

In certain situations, the most effective way to communicate your message is with a video, DVD, or an online host, such as YouTube. In a speech on tornadoes, showing a video of the damage done by a tornado is likely to be impressive. Showing snippets of a press conference or a movie clip to illustrate or emphasize a particular point can also be interesting and effective.

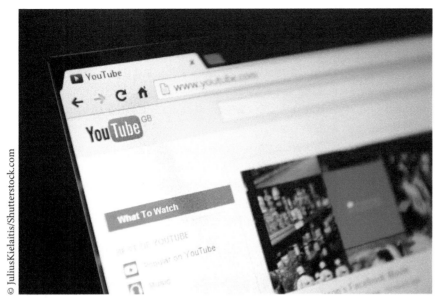

Although video clips from online media sharing sites like YouTube can enhance a presentation, speakers must be careful to avoid copyright infringement.

© JuliusKielaitis/Shutterstock.com

The novice speaker giving a five-minute speech may not edit the video carefully enough, however. The result may be four minutes of video and one minute of speech. If you choose an audio or video clip, practice with it, plan how to use it, and know how to operate the equipment. Plan for what you will do if the equipment fails.

Considerations for Technology-Mediated Communication

Speeches have been broadcast via radio and TV for generations. However, these events were coordinated and executed with a team of individuals connected to radio and TV stations. Now, individuals can create and disseminate their own videos over the Internet, and some self-produced work goes viral on YouTube.

While most speeches you give will involve a live audience, at times you may be required to record your speech. Technology in this respect is the medium, or the channel through which your speech is presented. In this next section, we provide some suggestions for those specific technology-mediated occasions.

Speaking on Camera

You may find yourself facing traditional cameras, including professional cameras associated with TV stations, video cameras, or less traditional cameras, such as built-in or remote webcams, phone cams, or digital cameras with video capabilities. With an audience present, you still need to follow the basic tenets of public speaking and adapt your speech to the particular audience and situation. Without a live audience, your primary focus becomes creating a message that is conveyed effectively to your intended audience through the camera. Adaptation becomes paramount if you are to succeed.

If you have an audience present, give the speech to them and assume those who record you will do a good job. If you do not have a live audience, you should not "play" to the camera unless directed to do so. Treat the camera as another audience member. President Obama has many positive traits as a speaker, but on occasion, he turns his head to audience members on the left and right, and avoids looking forward toward the camera. The result is the at-home viewer may not feel as connected to Obama's message. Eye contact should be direct and sustained, and strong speakers avoid moving their head, eyes, and hands too quickly.

Posture is important, and the camera may not be as forgiving of imperfections as a live audience. Keep your posture erect. Whether your speech is before a live audience or not, do not forget to gesture naturally. Be sincere and conversational. A recorded speech should be similar to a live audience, but those who are not part of the live audience do not share the same context.

When you know your speech will be recorded, consider how your clothes will look on camera. Professional speaker and speaking coach Tom Antion suggests the following and more on his informative web page (www.publicspeaking.org).

- Pastels are the best colors to wear (this applies to men, too!).
- Good clothing colors include beige, gray, green, brown, and blue.
- Avoid white, red, and orange clothing.
- Black, or dark browns and blues are fine alone or combined with pastel colors.
- Avoid fine checks, stripes, herringbone, and similar patterns.
- Avoid very glossy, sequined, or metallic clothing. Also avoid clinging attire, or low-cut necklines.

Radio

A speech on radio may be live or taped, and you may have the option to edit your speech. If it is in front of an audience, you cannot rewind and start again. Audience analysis is a critical element of public speaking. Unlike national and international politicians and dignitaries who may be heard on most radio stations, most speeches you give will be heard locally or regionally. Therefore, it is important to have a basic profile of the listeners within that particular programming market. Establishing common ground is important no matter what the medium.

Once on air, focus on speaking clearly and passionately. Being alone in a room with a microphone may be difficult, but work to energize yourself and deliver your speech enthusiastically. Be aware that pauses are powerful tools, although they may seem longer when the listener can't see you. Since your audience is not present, their awareness of your pacing, articulation, and pronunciation becomes even keener. Work to use pauses strategically and avoid nonfluencies such as um, er, uh, well uh, and so on.

As you craft your message for the radio audience, paying special attention to your main points, transitions, and supporting materials helps ensure effectiveness. Generally, radio also requires us to make key points in shorter sentences. Use effective transitions that help your audience track where you are in your message. Phrases like "Now I will turn to my third point" or "To wrap this talk up" help your listeners understand where you are and where you are headed. Further, anticipate audience questions, and structure your support material in a way that addresses these concerns. For example, if you anticipate many listeners might pose an objection to an idea you present, address the objection yourself and then overcome it with additional support. Often your audience will not have the opportunity to ask for clarification, and lingering questions work against you.

Videoconferencing/Skype/Webinars

Videoconferencing can be set up in three ways: computer-based system, desktop system, and studio-based system. A computer-based system is often the least expensive method, but its drawback is a lower degree of quality. In essence, computer-based systems often include a webcam and software like GoToMeeting. A desktop system has dedicated software installed on the computer and can improve the audio and video quality. The studio-based system offers the best quality, but is also the most expensive and difficult for most to access.

Videoconferencing is a "green" technology. By communicating over video, organizations substantially reduce their carbon footprint. With tools that provide a powerful way to enable conferences and other video content to be streamed live or on demand around the world, we

Computer-based system

Includes a webcam and free software.

Desktop system

Dedicated software improves the audio and video quality.

Studio-based system

Offers the best quality, but also is most expensive.

can communicate, engage, and interact with others across distances at any time, from wherever they are. The need to hop in a car or jet in, in many cases is now circumvented through these technologies. The effects of videoconferencing are evident within the airline industry. Hewlett Packard, for example, has reduced its global travel by 43 percent (*Travel Weekly*, 2008). Travel management companies predict this trend toward videoconferencing to continue over the next several years.

Yet, because these mediated interactions can be awkward and have the potential for technical problems, sometimes live face-to-face meetings are worth the extra effort, cost, and time. However, *Travel Weekly* notes, "[T]he technology for video and web conferencing has got its act together—no longer does it freeze or crash as soon as you overload the data line, as it did in the early 1990s." Even when all works correctly, as is usually the case, the loss of intimacy, comfort, and ease of communicating as well as the somewhat limited access to immediate nonverbal feedback of those not on camera can impact the effectiveness of the conference.

While videoconferencing is often used for group meetings, the medium is used for public speaking, too. In a videoconference speech, we encourage you to look into the camera to create eye contact. Avoid sudden abrupt or sweeping movements to prevent ghosting (motion blur), and in general, move a little more slowly and deliberately than normal to compensate for audio delays.

You may have an occasion to present at a webinar. Generally, a webinar is announced in advance, and people register for it. A date and time for attending via the web is provided. Depending on the situation, those who miss the webinar may be able to access a recording of it later. The audience participating in the webinar may have the opportunity to speak or type questions or comments for the speaker. These questions can be monitored by a third person or by the speaker. This allows the speaker to clarify points, discuss related information, or respond to the audience in some directed manner.

Using Skype

Skype is one of the fastest-growing Voice over IP (VoIP), instant messaging, and video call applications available today. It promotes the creation of many hardware and software add-on products.

Skype runs on Windows, Mac, Linux, Pocket PC, and many cell phones. In addition there are Wi-Fi phones that do not require a computer at all.

- Did you know you can use Skype without sitting at your computer?
- Did you know you can use Skype with the same telephone you use for regular telephone calls?
- Did you know you can have an answering machine with Skype?
- Did you know Skype can call almost any cell or telephone in the world?
- Did you know you can use your cell phone to send messages to a Skype user?

Using Skype is similar to the computer-based system one would use in video conferencing, but the major benefit is, it is free! While many people use Skype to communicate interpersonally, it has a clear public speaking application, and the system provides videoconferencing support. For more information, visit SkypeTips.com.

Podcasts and Streaming Audio

Podcasts most generally are audio presentations. Individuals who produce their own podcasts may not edit their speeches. This leads to mixed success. Podcasts connected to organizations are more likely to have equipment and personnel to create a more polished end result. Podcasts such as "Jimmy's No-Lose Sports Picks of the Week," broadcast live from his parent's garage, on the other hand, can be quite low in production value.

Podcasts are cheap to produce and can reach massive audiences, making them a popular form of technological presentation.

As a speaker, remember that your audience may include people who are listening on their favorite devices while working out, sitting at their desk, or driving to work. Listeners may be multitasking. They may choose to skim the podcast, and not catch the whole speech. Since they are not listening in real time, listeners may allow for distractions. Keeping in mind your listeners' attention span limitations, it makes sense to remind listeners who you are and what your central idea is more frequently in your podcast than in a traditional speech.

Suppose your speech topic is "College Athletes Don't Graduate." You attend a college that graduates a low percentage of its athletes—a guarded scandal gripping your school. Recent articles in the student newspaper have criticized your school's athletic department for emphasizing winning over education. An editorial in last week's paper asked, "How can student-athletes practice 40 hours a week and still go to class, study, and complete their assignments? The answer is they cannot."

As you collect supporting material for your speech, you find statistics about how much money athletes bring to your university, and you discover that not only do they not get a part of the money, they may not be equipped to go professional or be prepared for anything more than menial work. Making things worse yet, great disparity exists between graduation rates of African American student athletes and their white team members. Here is part of the speech your classmates hear:

> According to a 2010 study by the Institute for Diversity and Ethics (TIDES) at the University of Central Florida, of the 64 colleges and universities with Division 1-A basketball programs, 44 teams, or 69 percent of the total, graduated at least 50 percent of their basketball student-athletes, 37 teams (58 percent) graduated at least 60 percent, and 29 teams (45 percent) graduated at least 70 percent. Only 12 teams (19 percent) graduated less than 40 percent. In terms of equity in graduation rates, 13 of the 67 Division 1-A schools graduated less than 40 percent of their African American players, whereas only four schools graduated less than 60 percent of their white counterparts. Also, eight schools graduated 80 to 100 percent of their African American players, but 39 Division 1-A schools graduated 100 percent of their white basketball players.

> The graduation rates for football players of Division 1-A teams is similar. Of the 67 of the 68 teams providing data, 61, or 91 percent, of the total graduated at least 50 percent of their football student athletes, 43 teams (64 percent) graduated at least 60 percent, and 24 teams (36 percent) graduated at least 70 percent. In terms of equity

in graduation rates, seven of the 67 Division 1-A schools graduated less than 40 percent of their African American players, whereas no schools graduated less than 40 percent of their white football players. Also, one school graduated 90 percent of its African American players, but 10 schools graduated 90 percent or more of their white counterparts.

Instead of startling your listeners, these statistics numb them. You may see several people yawning, doodling, whispering, and looking out the window. You have no idea why until your classmates comment during the post-speech evaluation. The complaints are all the same: Your "can't miss" speech was boring and difficult to follow. Instead of stimulating your listeners, your long list of statistics put them to sleep.

In this example, an appropriately constructed visual aid could have helped you avoid saying so much in words. Despite the interest your listeners had in your topic before your speech began, the number and complexity of your statistics made it difficult for them to pay attention. By presenting some of your data in visual form, you would communicate the same message more effectively. Consider the difference when the following speech text is substituted for the text above and combined with **Figure 10.11**.

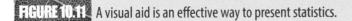

FIGURE 10.11 A visual aid is an effective way to present statistics.

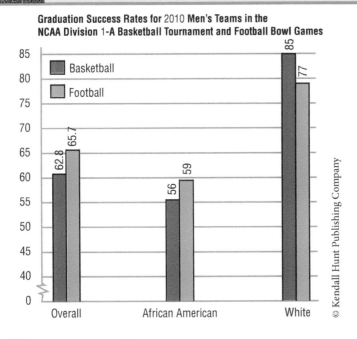

According to a 2010 study by the Institute for Diversity and Ethics (TIDES) at the University of Central Florida, graduation rates for Division 1-A football and basketball players have increased somewhat over previous years. For example, less than half of the basketball teams graduate at least 60 percent of their athletes, and almost two-thirds of the football teams graduate at least 60 percent of their athletes.

The study discovered a disturbing gap between white and African American student-athletes, however. Eight schools graduated 80–100 percent of their African American basketball players, while 39 schools graduated 100 percent of their white counterparts. In football, one school graduated 90 percent of their African American players whereas 10 schools graduated 100 percent of their white football players. But the worst news is some schools only graduate about a third of their athletes—and our college is one of them.

Numbers are still used, but not as many. With the presentational aid, the audience gets a visual feel for the information and they can process the information awhile longer than if you just stated the numbers.

Criteria for Presentational Aids

Your decision to include an aid should be based on the extent to which it enhances your audience's interest and understanding. The type of aid you choose should relate directly to the specific purpose of your speech and information you intend to convey. As you consider using a presentational aid, consider the following four general criteria.

1   VALUE TO PRESENTATION. Your instructor may require you to use a presentational aid for one or more of your speeches, but it does not mean that *any* aid is better than no aid. First and foremost, the aid must add value to your presentation. If you are considering a presentational aid just to meet assignment requirements, make sure you select something that adds meaning or impact.

2   ITEM SAFETY. If the item is precious to you, think twice about bringing it to class. It may rain or snow. You might drop it. In the afterglow of

your stunning speech, you might leave it behind. Also consider the possible implications of the item not being returned to you if someone in your audience "borrows" it. One of your authors, Mark, passed around a pill bottle containing a homeopathic remedy purported to help reduce nervousness called Gelsemium Sempervirens. The occasion was a corporate presentational skills training session and each member was soon going to be delivering their final presentations. By the time the bottle had made its way around the room and was returned, it was empty. All 30 pills were gone! Fortunately, no one had any ill effects, although the remainder of the workshop had taken a decidedly more laid back tone. Mark should have considered carefully what might happen if someone in his workshop had taken the entire amount.

3   EASE OF TRANSPORTATION. Think about what may happen to your object during transportation. Is it a large poster you are trying to carry on a bus or subway? Does it weigh 40 pounds? Do you have to carry it with you all day? Is it bigger than a breadbox? Is it alive? You want to consider how difficult your aid will be to transport, as well as what you are going to do with it before and after your speech.

4   SIZE OF OBJECT AND AUDIENCE. Consider both object and audience size. Bringing a rare coin, say the 1944 steel penny, to show the class is not helpful because it is too small. And, even if you bring in enough coins for everyone, you take the risk of losing their attention as they examine the penny, drop it, make friendly wagers, or otherwise play with it during your speech. Students are better served by viewing an enlarged picture of the coin on a slide or poster. Showing an 8"x10" picture of the penny would be appropriate in a small class but not in an auditorium where it would need to be projected onto a large screen. Next we examine principles for *using* aids.

Principles for Using Presentational Aids

1   DO NOT LET YOUR PRESENTATIONAL AID DISTRACT YOUR AUDIENCE. When you pass things around the room, you compete with them as you speak. Your listeners read your handouts, play with foreign coins, eat cookies you baked, and analyze your models instead of listening to you. If handouts are necessary, distribute them at the end of the speech. When appropriate, invite people to take a close look at your displays after your speech. This first suggestion is provided as a general rule, and as noted earlier, exceptions do exist.

2   BE AWARE OF TIMING AND PAUSES. Timing is important. Display each visual only as you talk about it. Do not force people to choose between paying attention to you and paying attention to your aid. If you prepare your flip chart in advance, leave a blank sheet between each page and turn the page when you are finished with the specific point. Cover your models with a sheet. Turn the projector off. Erase your diagram from the blackboard. Turn your poster board around. These actions tell your audience you want them to look at you again.

Display your presentational aid and then pause two or three seconds before talking. This moment of silence gives your audience time to look at the display. You do not want to compete with your own visual aid. Conversely, try to avoid excessively long pauses as you demonstrate the steps in a process.

3   MAKE SURE THE EQUIPMENT IS WORKING BUT BE PREPARED FOR FAILURE. Set up in advance. Make sure equipment is working *before* class, and know how to operate it. This includes CDs, DVDs, portable music, white board, and the computer/projector. Instructors are frustrated when time is lost, and students become bored when a speaker wastes valuable class time trying to discover how the equipment works. Similarly, find out in advance if the classroom computer is equipped for the Internet, a jump drive or DropBox, and specific programs you are counting on using.

Be prepared for equipment failure. What is Plan B? Having multiple ways to get the visuals across may seem redundant until that one really bad day when Plans A, B, and C do not work and you have to go to Plan D.

4   USE MULTIMEDIA PRESENTATIONS ONLY WITH CAREFUL PLANNING AND PRACTICE. Multimedia presentations are effective, but they can be challenging. Gracefully moving from a flip chart, to the computer, to a tabletop model requires skill that comes from practice and experience. Mixing media increases your chance that something will go wrong. You can mix media successfully, but careful planning and preparation are essential. Can speakers act with the listener in mind when developing multimedia presentations, just as they do when developing their speeches? Is it possible to have audience-centered advanced technologies accompany a presentation? We believe so, and the following section presents guidelines to help you get there.

Making and Using Computer-Generated Images

You probably learned how to create PowerPoint presentations well before you reached college. By now, you have probably seen hundreds, if not thousands, of PowerPoint presentations. This rise in use is surely because effective computer-generated graphics can have a great impact on listeners. But not always. Many of you can relate to the cartoon shown in **Figure 10.12**. Too many slides, coupled with a dry, monotonous delivery, spells disaster. "Some of the world's most satisfying naps, deepest day dreams, and most elaborate notebook doodles are inspired by the following phrase, 'I'll just queue up this PowerPoint presentation,'" states Josh Shaffer (2006), staff writer for the Raleigh, North Carolina *News & Observer*.

Some scholars are concerned that when students give speeches with "poorly designed and poorly performed multimedia," they create ineffective presentations; therefore, students must learn to "distinguish ineptitude from eloquence" in accompanying multimedia (Cyphert, 2007, p. 187). In other words, beginning speakers typically lack skill in public speaking *and* creating presentational aids. For this reason, we include guidance for using presentational software. Although aimed primarily at computer-generated graphics, much of the following applies to all presentational aids.

1   Choose a presentational aid that fits your purpose, the occasion, and your audience. Develop a clear, specific purpose early in the creative process. If you begin with a specific purpose in mind that fits your goals, the audience's needs, and the requirements of the occasion, you are more likely to find and use relevant technology. Katherine Murray, author of more than 40 computer books, offers the suggestion, "Start with the end in mind" (www.microsoft.com). Knowing what you are trying to accomplish should guide you in designing accompanying multimedia presentations.

Choose aids appropriate for the occasion. Certain situations are more serious, professional, intimate, or formal than others. Displaying a cartoon during a congressional hearing, for example, may diminish the credibility of the speaker.

Consider whether the visual support is right for your listeners, analyzing their ages, socioeconomic backgrounds, knowledge, and attitudes toward your subject. Remember that some listeners are offended by visuals that are too graphic. Pictures of abused children, for example, can be offensive to an audience not prepared for what they will see. If you have doubts about the appropriateness of a visual, leave it out of your presentation.

Presentation specialist Dave Parodi (2004) urges people to "awaken themselves to the power of a well-designed, well-structured, well-delivered presentation, and work as hard as they can to make it happen." These words have great instructional value.

2   EMPHASIZE ONLY RELEVANT POINTS. In your desire to create an attractive, professional slide presentation, do not forget the message. It is easy to find tips on general design, the number of words per slide, number of slides, images, transitions, color, and so on. After you select the presentational aid that meets your purpose most effectively, decide what information needs to be on each slide. Link only the most important points in your speech with a presentational aid. Focus on your thesis statement and main points, and decide what words or concepts need to be highlighted graphically.

   Our suggestion: Keep your visuals simple: Convey one idea. You may want to use a second visual rather than include more information than your listeners can process. Animations, sound, and visual effects tend to be overused, distracting, and time consuming both in creation and display. Eliminate extraneous material.

3   IMPLEMENT THE "RULE OF SIX." Use no more than six words per line, and no more than six lines per slide. Avoid using full sentences. This is an outline, not an essay. Make the text easy to read. Words need to be large enough, and do not think that using CAPITALIZED words will help. In addition to being a symbol for yelling when instant messaging, it actually takes more effort to read words that are all

capitalized. Try using 24-point type or larger. If the audience cannot read your slide, the message is lost.

Compare **Figure 10.13A** with **Figure 10.13B**. Similarities include the title, points covered, and organization. However, Figure 10.13A violates many rules of effective PowerPoints, including too many icons (too busy), full sentences, and small font size. Figure 10.13B is clear, simple, and professional. The template used would be appropriate for all slides used for a presentation on traveling abroad.

 FIGURE 10.13A   What features make this an ineffective PowerPoint slide?

© Kendall Hunt Publishing Company

FIGURE 10.13B   What features make this an effective PowerPoint slide?

Tips on Traveling Abroad:
Before you go

- Apply for passport
- Copy important documents
- Visit pharmacy
- Email itinerary
- Contact neighbor
- Pack; Re-pack

© Kendall Hunt Publishing Company

FIGURE 10.14 Colors opposite each other on this wheel provide the most striking contrast for visual displays.

Color Wheel

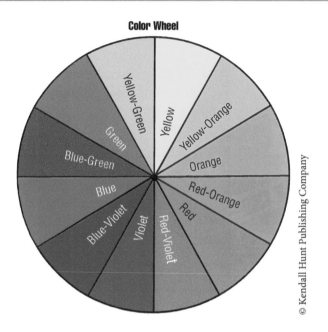

© Kendall Hunt Publishing Company

4   SELECT APPROPRIATE DESIGN FEATURES. Decisions need to be made regarding template, type of font, and color. The template, which provides color, style, and decorative accents, may be distracting to your audience if you change it regularly. Use one template consistently. In general, select a simple font. While unusual font types may look fun, cute, or dramatic, they may be hard to read and distracting. Keep your audience focused on the message; they may be distracted from the text if you have moving animation and slides filled with special effects.

Make sure the font type and font color complement the template. Rely on strong, bold colors that make your message stand out even in a large auditorium. The words you place on the slide should not melt into the background color. Aim for contrast but keep in mind that the contrast you see on your computer screen may not exist on the projected screen.

Research on college students shows that color aids students' ability to organize and recall information and to solve problems (Kraus, 2008). The color wheel in **Figure 10.14** will help you choose contrasting colors. You will achieve the strongest contrasts by using colors opposite one another. Blue and orange make an effective visual combination, as do red and green, and so on.

5   AVOID ALLOWING YOUR PRESENTATIONAL AID TO UPSTAGE YOU. Keep in mind that your audience has come to hear you, not to see your presentational aids. If you create a situation in which the visual support is more important than the speaker or the purpose of the speech, you will have defeated your purpose and disappointed your audience.

Be protective of the beginning and end of your presentation. It is usually prudent to avoid using any presentational aid for the first few moments. After you set the tone of your speech and introduce your main idea, turn to your first aid. Likewise, do not use a presentational aid to end your speech. Doing this risks the person-to-person contact you have built to that point by shifting the focus away from you. These are merely guidelines. Some speakers have both begun and ended speeches effectively with well-selected media.

6   PREVIEW AND PRACTICE. An inability to navigate smoothly through your slides limits your effectiveness (Howell, 2008). After creating your slides, run through them. Make sure slides are in the correct order, and that font type, font color, and font size are consistent. Proofread and run spell check. Make printouts of your slides. Then practice the speech using your slides. According to a 2009 survey, the most annoying aspect of the PowerPoint presentation is "the speaker read the slides to us" (Paradi, 2009).

One way to avoid sounding as though you are reading to the audience is through practice. Adding some type of presentational aid makes practicing even more important because you do not want to disrupt the flow of your speech. A reflective pause after displaying a slide can be powerful (Howell, 2008).

During your practice session, focus on your audience, not your presentational aid. Many speakers turn their backs on the audience. They talk to the projection screen or poster instead of looking at the audience. To avoid this tendency, become familiar with your aid so that you have little need to look at it during your talk. Use a remote control, if possible, so you can move more freely.

ESSENTIALS FOR EXCELLENCE

In this chapter, you have learned about the different types and functions of presentational aids. As a communication professional in today's marketplace, you will be challenged to utilize technology-based presentational aids more often than ever before. For many people, this can include YouTube video clips, online news articles, and other forms of user-generated content. Using these aids, however, can get presenters into trouble if they do not follow "fair use" principles. Attorney at law Rich Stim offers several guidelines to follow when using online material in your presentations.

Assume it's protected.

Operate under the assumption that all works are protected by either copyright or trademark law unless conclusive information tells you otherwise. Works are not public domain simply because they are posted on the Internet or because a copyright notice is not apparent.

Read click-wrap agreements.

Don't assume that clip art, shareware, freeware, or any other materials labeled "royalty-free" or "copyright free" can be used or distributed without authorization (Stim, n.d.). Always read the terms and conditions or "Read Me" files accompanying such materials to be sure that your intended use is permitted.

When in doubt, seek permission.

Copyright protection extends to any original work regardless of who created it. If you are in doubt, seek written permission, even if the material comes from a friend or relative. Although oral consents are valid, they can be difficult to prove.

WHAT YOU'VE LEARNED:

Now that you have studied the chapter, you should be able to:

1. Understand the functions of presentational aids.
   - Presentational aids can enhance (or hinder) presentations. The speaker-audience connection is strengthened when the speaker implements presentational aids effectively.
   - Presentational aids complement the information you are communicating to the audience. Visual aids can give the audience a clear picture that words might not be able to convey.
2. Know the different types of technology-based presentational aids.
   - Audio presentational aids include audiotapes, compact discs (CDs), and iPods.
   - Visual presentational aids include DVDs, streaming video, and other material found on media sharing sites like YouTube or Reddit.
   - Computer programs like PowerPoint and Prezi are designed to complement almost all types of public presentations.
3. Evaluate the effectiveness of presentational aids.
   - When supporting material can become hard to follow or runs the risk of boring your audience, use a visual representation of the data to maintain the interest of listeners.
   - After a presentation, be sure to ask for feedback from audience members to get firsthand accounts of how effective your presentational aids were.
4. Identify the principles for using presentational aids.
   - Don't let your presentational aids distract the audience. Remember, you are competing with your audio/visual aids as you speak. Use aids that complement (instead of overtaking) your speech.
   - Be aware of timing and pauses. Display your presentational aid and then pause for two or three seconds before talking. This gives your audience a few moments to look at your display before needing to focus on your words.
   - Make sure your equipment is working, but be prepared for failure. You should still be able to complete your presentation even if your audio/visual aids are not working. Also, make sure to have multiple backups of your electronic presentational aids.

Key Terms

computer-based system, 349

desktop system, 349

flow chart, 337

line graph, 340

organizational chart, 337

pictograph, 340

pie graph, 340

studio-based system, 349

Reflect

1   Do you think technology is inherently persuasive? When does it add impact beyond the power of the content of a message? When does it distract from the content of a message?

2   What criteria for using presentational aids would you add to the list? If you were Ruler of the World and you had the power, what decrees would you make? Can you provide three laws of the land that you would enforce on all presenters in your world?

3   How might technology augment ethos, pathos, and logos?

4   Is the speaker who uses more technology in a speech more credible than one who uses less or no technology?

5   Has increased technology made people more or less connected? Why?

6   Do students generally rehearse the use of their presentational aids for classroom reports? How about professional speakers; do you think they rehearse? If more students understood the potential payoff for rehearsing with their aids, do you think more would do dress rehearsals, or do you think most already understand this but don't make time for it anyway? Why would that be the case, even for some?

7   What should you keep in mind as you design and develop a PowerPoint presentation? What is death-by-PowerPoint? How can you avoid this epidemic? What is the appropriate level of "PowerPointedness"?

Review Questions

1   _____ are used to display the steps, or stages, in a process.

2   _____ are organized according to official hierarchies that determine the relationships of people as they work.

3   A(n) _____ is used most commonly as a variation of the bar graph. Instead of showing bars of various lengths (comparing items on the graph), the bars are replaced by pictorial representations of the graph's subject.

4   A(n) _____ is used to show a trend over time.

5   Also known as a circle graph, a _____ shows how the parts of an item relate to the whole.

6   In videoconferencing, a _____ system includes a webcam and free software.

7   In videoconferencing, a _____ system has dedicated software that improves the audio and video quality on a computer.

8   In videoconferencing, a _____ system offers the best audio and visual quality, but is also the most expensive and difficult to access.

PART THREE

TYPES OF PUBLIC SPEAKING

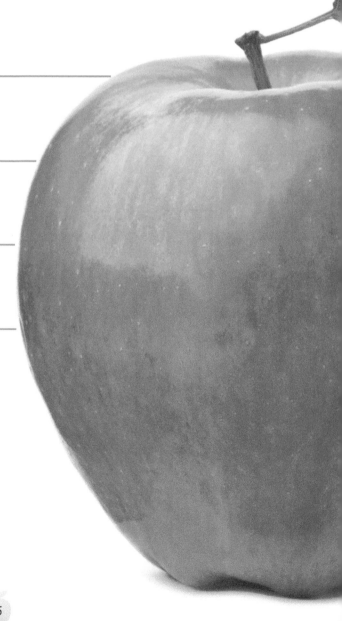

Scientist Bill Nye frequently utilizes informative presentations when discussing climate change.

Mathew Imaging/Contributor/Getty Images

CHAPTER ELEVEN
INFORMATIVE SPEAKING

OUTLINE

WHAT YOU'LL LEARN

After studying this chapter, you should be able to:

1. Know the different types of informative speaking.
2. Identify the five goals of informative speaking.
3. Cite oral sources accurately and effectively.
4. Understand the ethics of informative speaking.

SPEAKING IN CONTEXT

In December of 2015, scientist Bill Nye explained the dangers of climate change in an interview with *National Geographic* magazine. Nye, most known for his television series *Bill Nye the Science Guy*, has been a leading voice in the climate change debate. During his interview, Nye cited scientific studies that observed a 1.2–1.4% increase in the Earth's temperature over the past century. Nye also noted that 10 of the last 13 years have been the warmest on record.

"When it comes to climate change, the main takeaway is it's real," said Nye. "And although we are part of the problem, we can also be part of the solution." (Howard, 2015).

To support his position, Nye discussed the relationship between human activity and the production of greenhouse gases. Nye posits that human activities such as burning fossil fuels, increasing cattle production, and using non-recyclable products all lead to an increase in greenhouse gases. These gases keep more of the sun's heat trapped near Earth's surface, resulting in higher temperatures, warming oceans, rising sea levels, and more natural disasters. Nye concluded his speech by offering potential solutions to the issues raised during his presentation.

Nye's interview with *National Geographic* serves as a good example of how to deliver an informative speech. However, the authors of this book would recommend to always offer a verbal citation when offering statistical information as Nye did in the previous interview. As you read through this chapter, you will learn more about citations and other tools needed to be an effective informative speaker.

Whether you are a nurse conducting CPR training for new parents at the local community center, a museum curator delivering a speech on Impressionist art, or an auto repair shop manager lecturing to workers about the implications of a recent manufacturer's recall notice, your informative speech goal is to communicate information and ideas in a way that your audience will understand and remember. In your job, community activities, and in this public speaking class, remember that the audience should hear new knowledge, not facts they already know. For example, the nurse conducting CPR training for new parents would approach the topic differently if the audience comprised individuals from various fields working on their yearly recertification. New parents most likely are also new to CPR training, whereas professionals receive training at least once a year.

Informative speech

Communicates information and ideas in a way that your audience will understand and remember.

In this chapter, we first distinguish informative speaking from persuasive or commemorative speaking. We identify different types of informative speeches, and present guidelines for informative speaking. Last, the issue of ethics and informative speaking is examined.

Differentiating Informative, Persuasive, and Entertainment Purposes

The situation or context often suggests what type of speech is expected. Commencement speeches are motivational, as are keynote speeches at conventions. Speakers deliver commemorative speeches on Veterans Day, presidents' birthdays, and other occasions that recognize individuals or groups of individuals. Speeches can be classified into three major categories—informative, persuasive, and entertaining (commemorative or inspirational). The next few paragraphs distinguish among these categories.

When you deliver an informative speech, your intent is to enlighten your audience—to increase understanding or awareness and, perhaps, to create a new perspective. In contrast, when you deliver a persuasive speech, your intent is to influence your audience to agree with your point of view—to change attitudes or beliefs or to bring about a specific, desired action. And when you deliver a speech as part of some special occasion, your intent is to entertain, commemorate, inspire, or amuse your listeners. In theory, these three forms are different. In practice, these distinctions are much less obvious.

The key to informative speaking is *intent*. If your goal is to expand understanding, your speech is informational. If, in the process, you want your audience to share or agree with your point of view, you may also be persuasive. And if you want them to pay attention and recall key points later, a little humor and entertaining storytelling always help. After a speech describing the types of assault rifles available to criminals, some of your audience may be moved to write to Congress in support of stricter gun control while others may send contributions to lobbying organizations that promote stricter gun control legislation. Although your speech brought about these actions, it is still informational because your intent was educational. Objective facts can be persuasive even when presented with an informational intent.

A critical place where we often see the intent lines blur is in the conclusion of an informative speech. Take care to avoid providing them with an action plan. Avoid ending a speech with something like "So now that I've explained the history and sociopsychological benefits and drawbacks of tattoos, I hope that you will consider getting one." This final "tag" line changes the nature of the speech from informative to persuasive.

To make sure your speech is informational rather than persuasive or entertaining, start with a clear, specific purpose signifying your intent. Compare the following specific purpose statements:

SPECIFIC PURPOSE STATEMENT #1 (SPS#1). To inform my listeners how the military has historically responded to minorities in the military, including Japanese Americans, African Americans, women, and gays, bisexuals, transgendered individuals, and lesbians

SPECIFIC PURPOSE STATEMENT #2 (SPS#2). To inform my listeners how the military has responded poorly and in an untimely fashion to minorities in the military, including Japanese Americans, African Americans, women, and gays, bisexuals, transgendered individuals, and lesbians

SPECIFIC PURPOSE STATEMENT #3 (SPS#3). To pay tribute to my listeners from minority groups who have suffered under Don't Ask, Don't Tell policies simply to provide invaluable service to our country

While the intent of the first statement is informational, the intent of the second is persuasive, and the third, entertaining. The speaker in SPS#1 is likely to discuss how and where Japanese Americans and African Americans served during WWII, the evolution of women from support

Secretary of State John Kerry was tasked with giving informative speeches to the nation on a regular basis.

positions to combat positions, and the development of the Don't Ask, Don't Tell policy. The speaker in SPS#2 uses subjective words such as "poorly and in an untimely fashion." Most likely this speech would focus more on the negative impact military policy had on minority groups, including being victims of segregation, being placed in high-risk combat situations, and allowing the harassment of women and homosexuals. SPS#3 clearly sets out to commemorate a group of people at a special event, perhaps honoring fallen minority soldiers at a Memorial Day celebration.

Types of Informative Speaking

Although all informative speeches seek to help audiences understand, there are three distinct types of informative speeches. A **speech of description** helps an audience understand *what* something is. When the speaker wants to help us understand *why* something is so, they are offering a **speech of explanation**. Finally, when the focus is on *how* something is done, it is a **speech of demonstration**. Each of these is discussed in detail.

Speeches of Description

Describing the safety features of a typical nuclear power plant, describing the effects of an earthquake, and describing the buying habits of teenagers

Speech of description
Helps an audience understand what something is.

Speech of explanation
Helps an audience understand why something is so.

Speech of demonstration
When the focus is on how something is done.

are all examples of informative speeches of description. These speeches paint a clear picture of an event, person, object, place, situation, or concept. The goal is to create images in the minds of listeners about your topic or to describe a concept in concrete detail. Here, for example, is a section of a speech describing a poetry slam. We begin with a brief, specific purpose and thesis statement:

GENERAL PURPOSE: To inform
SPECIFIC PURPOSE: To describe to my audience how poetry slams moved the performance of poetry to a competitive event
THESIS STATEMENT: To understand the poetry slam, one must understand its history, the performance, and the judging process.

Here is a short list of some possible speech topics for the informative speech of description:

- To describe the important aspects of the Cinco de Mayo celebration
- To describe the life and philosophy of Franz Kafka
- To describe the causes and symptoms of Chronic Fatigue Syndrome (CFS)

Speeches of Explanation

Abstract topics

Ideas, theories, principles, and beliefs.

Speeches of explanation deal with more **abstract topics** (ideas, theories, principles, and beliefs) than speeches of description or demonstration. They also involve attempts to simplify complex topics. The goal of these speeches is audience understanding, such as a psychologist addressing parents about the moral development of children or a cabinet official explaining U.S. farm policy.

To be effective, speeches of explanation must be designed specifically to achieve audience understanding of the theory or principle. Avoid abstractions, too much jargon, or technical terms by using verbal pictures that define and explain. Here, for example, a speaker demonstrates the error of using unfamiliar terms to define Spiritualism:

GENERAL PURPOSE: To inform
SPECIFIC PURPOSE: To explain to my audience how the connection between physical and spiritual elements is a basic foundation of Spiritualism
THESIS STATEMENT: Spiritualism is a belief system grounded in the idea that each being has both physical and spiritual elements.

Speeches of explanation may involve policies, statements of intent or purpose that guide or drive future decisions. The president may announce a new arms control policy. A school superintendent may implement a new inclusion policy. The director of human resources of a major corporation may discuss the firm's new flextime policy.

A speech that explains a policy should focus on the questions likely to arise from an audience. For example, prior to a speech to teachers and parents before school starts, the superintendent of a school district implementing a new inclusion policy should anticipate what the listeners will probably want to know—when the policy change will be implemented, to what extent it will be implemented, when it will be evaluated, and how problems will be monitored, among other issues. When organized logically, these and other questions form the basis of the presentation. As in all informative speeches, your purpose is not to persuade your listeners to support the policy, but to inform them about the policy.

To reiterate, strive to keep focused on the informative intent. For example, a group of university employees gathered to hear about the changes in insurance benefits. One particular insurance plan would cost the state less but cost employees more. The speaker, who represented the state, described each option, but made several references to the plan that cost employees more and the state less. After several such references, audience members started making side comments about how the speaker was trying to persuade individuals into the state's preferred plan. The intent was advertised as an informative one, but the speaker's message had strong persuasive undertones.

Explaining the use of Japanese internment camps, while controversial, requires a speech of explanation.

Following are some sample topics that could be developed into speeches of explanation:

- To explain the five principles of Hinduism
- To explain the effect of colonization on African cultures
- To explain popular superstitions in American culture
- To explain how different cultures perceive beauty
- To explain why Japanese internment occurred in the United States during World War II

© Everett Historical/Shutterstock.com

Speeches of Demonstration

Speeches of demonstration focus on a process by describing the gradual changes that lead to a particular result. These speeches often involve two approaches, one is "how" and the other is a "how to" approach. Here are examples of specific purposes for speeches of demonstration:

- To inform my audience *how* college admissions committees choose the most qualified applicants
- To inform my audience *how* diabetes threatens health
- To inform my audience *how to* sell an item on eBay
- To inform my audience *how to* play the Facebook game FarmVille by Zygna

Speeches that take a "how" approach have audience understanding as their goal. They create understanding by explaining how a process functions without teaching the specific skills needed to complete a task. After listening to a speech on college admissions, for example, you may understand the process but may not be prepared to take a seat on an admissions committee.

One clear difference between the speech of demonstration and speeches of presentation and explanation is that the *speech of demonstration benefits from presentational aids*. When your goal is to demonstrate a process, you may choose to complete the entire process—or a part of it—in front of your audience. The nature of your demonstration and time constraints determine your choice. If you are giving CPR training, a partial demonstration will not give your listeners the information they need to save a life. If you are demonstrating how to cook a stew, however, your audience does not need to watch you chop onions; prepare in advance to maintain audience interest and save time.

Following are several topics that could be developed into demonstration speeches:

- How to make flower arrangements
- How grapes are processed into wine
- How to pick a bottle of wine
- How to swing a golf club
- How to make a website
- How to organize a closet
- How to find cheap airline tickets
- How to determine if you have sleep apnea

ENGAGING IN COMMUNITY

When thinking about the applications of speeches of demonstration, it's important to recognize their usefulness in the field of community service. Speeches of demonstration can educate people about valuable resources that can improve the quality of their life. One group of mothers decided to tap into the informative aspect of demonstrative speeches to educate their community about living healthier lifestyles.

Members of the Episcopal Community Services organization in Philadelphia teamed up with Aramark and the American Heart Association to develop a health engagement program for the community (Jones, 2016). The program, called Healthy for Life, sought to teach simple strategies that could change attitudes about food and health by equipping individuals with new skills for healthy living. During the 12-week program, volunteers taught participants about their health numbers, cooking and shopping skills, proper nutrition, and different strategies to change their current eating patterns and behaviors. The educational presentations were led by Ingrid Perez-Martin, a consultant for Episcopal Community Services.

"I think the purpose of the program was to increase the education and knowledge and to hopefully help change behaviors," Perez-Martin said. "I think everyone left gaining a lot more." (Jones, 2016).

The Healthy for Life program is one of many programs that use demonstrative speeches to assist their communities. As the previous example illustrates, demonstrative speeches have the power to create life-altering changes when performed correctly. As your presentational skills mature, try to brainstorm other uses that these types of presentations can have at the community level.

© Shutterstock.com

The American Heart Association routinely informs the public about new health information.

Five Goals of Informative Speaking

Although the overarching goal of an informative speech is to communicate information and ideas so the audience will understand, there are other goals as well. Whether you are giving a speech to explain, describe, or demonstrate, the following five goals are relevant: be accurate, objective, clear, meaningful, and memorable. After each goal, we present two specific strategies for achieving that goal.

1. Accurate

Informative speakers strive to present the truth. They understand the importance of careful research for verifying information they present. Facts must be correct and current. Research is crucial. Do not rely solely on your own opinion; find support from other sources.

Question the source of information. Is the source a nationally recognized magazine or reputable newspaper, or is it from someone's post on a random blog? Source verification is important. Virtually anyone can post to the Internet. Check to see if your source has appropriate credentials, such as education, work experience, or verifiable personal experience. For example, how valid do you think information is from the Huffington Post?

Consider the timeliness of the information. Information becomes dated. If you want to inform the class about the heart transplant process, relying on sources more than a few years old would mislead your audience because science and technology change rapidly. Your instructor may require sources within a five- or 10-year span. If not, check the date your source was published (online or print), and determine whether it will be helpful or harmful to the overall effectiveness of your speech.

2. Objective

Present information fairly and in an unbiased manner. Purposely leaving out critical information or "stacking the facts" to create a misleading picture violates the rule of objectivity. The following two strategies should help you maintain objectivity.

Take into account all perspectives. Combining perspectives creates a more complete picture. Avoiding other perspectives creates bias, and may turn an informative speech into a persuasive one. The chief negotiator for a union may have a completely different perspective than the administration's chief negotiator on how current contract negotiations are proceeding. They may use the same facts and statistics, but interpret them differently. An impartial third party trying to determine how the process is progressing needs to speak with both sides and attempt to remove obvious bias.

Show trends. Trends put individual facts in perspective as they clarify ideas within a larger context. The whole—the connection among ideas—gives each detail greater meaning. If a speaker tries to explain how the stock market works, it makes sense to talk about the stock market in relation to what it was a year ago, five years ago, 10 years ago, or even longer, rather than focus on today or last week. Trends also suggest what the future will look like.

3. Clear

To be successful, your informative speech must communicate your ideas without confusion. When a message is not organized clearly, audiences become frustrated and confused and, ultimately, they miss your ideas. Conducting careful audience analysis helps you understand what your audience already knows about your topic and allows you to offer a distinct, targeted message at their level of understanding. Choosing the best organizational pattern will also help your listeners understand your message. The following two strategies are designed to increase the clarity of your speech.

DEFINE UNFAMILIAR WORDS AND CONCEPTS. Unfamiliar words, especially technical jargon, can defeat your informative purpose. When introducing a new word, define it in a way your listeners can understand. Because you are so close to your material, knowing what to define can be one of your hardest tasks. Put yourself in the position of a listener who knows less about your topic than you do or ask a friend or colleague's opinion.

In addition to explaining the dictionary definition of a concept or term, a speaker may rely on two common forms of definitions: operational and through example.

Operational definitions specify procedures for observing and measuring concepts. For example, in the United States an IQ test (Intelligence Quotient) is used to define how "smart" we are. According to Gregory (2004), someone who scores 95–100 is of average intelligence, a score of 120 or higher is above average, and a score of 155 or higher is considered "genius." The government tells us who is "poor" based on a specified income level, and communication researchers can determine if a person has high communication apprehension based on his or her score on McCroskey's Personal Report of Communication Apprehension.

Definition through example helps the audience understand a complex concept by giving the audience a "for instance." In an effort to explain what is meant by the term "white-collar criminal," a speaker could provide several examples, such as Jeff Skilling (former Enron executive convicted on federal felony charges relating to the company's financial collapse), Rod Blagojevich (former Illinois governor found guilty of several charges related to his trying to sell President Obama's Illinois Senate seat), and Wesley Snipes (actor convicted of tax evasion and jailed for three years in December 2010).

CAREFULLY ORGANIZE YOUR MESSAGE. Find an organizational pattern that makes the most sense for your specific purpose. Descriptive speeches, speeches of demonstration, and speeches of explanation have different goals. Therefore, you must consider the most effective way to organize your message. *Descriptive speeches* are often arranged in spatial, topical, and chronological patterns. For example, if a speaker chose to talk about Oktoberfest in Munich, a topical speech might talk about the beer tents, food possibilities, entertainment, and tourist activities. A speech following a chronological pattern might talk about when to start planning for the festival, when the festival begins, and what events occur on particular days. The topic is still Oktoberfest, but based on the organizational pattern, the speech focuses differently and contains different information.

Speeches of demonstration often use spatial, chronological, and cause-and-effect or problem–solution patterns. For example, in a speech on how to buy a home, a few organizational patterns are possible, depending on what aspect of the topic you chose as your focus. It would make sense to organize spatially if your focus is on what to examine as you search for homes. You might want to start with the roof and work down toward the basement (or vice versa) or you might look at the lot and outside features and then move inside. The lot could be divided into small parts, such as how big the lot is, how close neighbors are, what the view is all around the house, how much maintenance is needed on the lot, and so on. As you move inside, you could talk about the number of rooms, electricity, plumbing, access (stairs, attic, or crawl space), and so on.

A chronological pattern for how to buy a house would be more appropriate when talking about getting a real estate agent, finding a house, setting up financing, getting an appraisal, making an offer, getting the house appraised, and accepting a counter-offer. As you can see, the speech that is set up to follow a spatial pattern is significantly different than the speech that uses a chronological pattern.

Speeches of explanation are frequently arranged chronologically, or topically, or according to cause-and-effect or problem–solution. For example, for several years, the Asian carp has made headlines in the Great Lakes area because of its potential to harm the habitat of the Great Lakes. Using the Asian carp as a topic, a speech arranged chronologically could discuss how this threat has developed over the last decade, and what the future projection is. A problem–solution speech, on the other hand, could talk about the dangers related to the fish invasion of the Great Lakes and possible solutions to the problem. Important with the second organizational pattern is that the speech be kept as informative as possible, and not identify the "best" solution.

SPEAKING EXCELLENCE IN YOUR CAREER

In many of your communication and public speaking courses, you will be required to complete a self-evaluation form following your classroom presentations. These evaluation forms are useful for helping students better assess their personal performance while also assisting teachers in making adjustments to improve the quality of their courses. For this reason, it is worthwhile to research students' perception of their own performance compared to that of their instructors. Researchers Joseph Mazer, Cheri Simonds, and Stephen Hunt offer their research in assessing evaluation fidelity.

The researchers formulated this study in response to the significant gap in communication literature on the topic of training students to use standard criteria as a method of self-evaluation. Samples were gathered from approximately 180 students in a general education communication course at a large Midwestern state university. Participants were tasked with filling our both informative and persuasive speech self-evaluation forms that mirrored instructor evaluation forms. Results indicated that students tend to provide critical (i.e., negative) comments to open-ended questions from the self-evaluation form after viewing a video of their presentation (Mazer, Simonds, & Hunt, 2013). Also, students provided more positive comments on their persuasive speech self-evaluations in comparison to their informative speech self-evaluations. Other findings suggested that teachers should focus more on training students on how to apply the grading criteria associated with the evaluation forms. The researchers suggest that more training on student assessment will allow students to provide more thorough, descriptive, and critical comments on their evaluations, leading to a more comprehensive understanding of the course material.

4. Meaningful

A meaningful, informative message focuses on what matters to the audience as well as to the speaker. Relate your material to the interests, needs, and concerns of your audience. A speech explaining the differences between public and private schools delivered to the parents of students in elementary and secondary schools would not be as meaningful in a small town where no choice exists. Here are two strategies to help you develop a meaningful speech:

CONSIDER THE SETTING. The setting may tell you about audience goals. Informative speeches are given in many places, including classrooms, community seminars, and business forums. Audiences may attend these speeches because of an interest in the topic or because attendance is required. Settings tell you the specific reasons your audience has gathered.

AVOID INFORMATION OVERLOAD. Information overload can be frustrating and annoying because the listener experiences difficulty in processing so much information. Your job as an informative speaker is to know how much to say and, just as important, what to say. Long lists of statistics are mind-numbing. Be conscious of the relationship among time, purpose, and your audience's ability to absorb information. Tie key points to stories, examples, anecdotes, and humor. Your goal is not to get it all in but to communicate your message as effectively as possible.

5. Memorable

Speakers who are enthusiastic, genuine, and creative and who can communicate their excitement to their listeners deliver memorable speeches. Engaging examples, dramatic stories, and tasteful humor applied to your key ideas in a genuine manner will make a long-lasting impact.

USE EXAMPLES AND HUMOR. Nothing elicits interest more than a good example, and humorous stories are effective in helping the audience remember the material. When Sarah Weddington, winning attorney in the Roe v. Wade Supreme Court case, talks about the history of discriminatory practices in this country, she provides a personal example of how a bank required her husband's signature on a loan even though she was working and he was in school. She also mentions playing "girls" basketball in school and being limited to three dribbles (boys could dribble the ball as many times as they wanted).

Physically involve your audience. Many occasions lend themselves to some type of audience participation. Consider asking for audience response to an observation: "Raise your hand if you have ever seen a tornado." Seek help with your demonstration. If you are demonstrating how to make a cake, for example, you could ask someone to stir the batter. Ask some audience members to take part in an experiment that you conduct to prove a point. For example, hand out several headsets to volunteers and ask them to set the volume level where they usually listen to music. Then show how volume can affect hearing.

Guidelines for Effective Informative Speeches

Regardless of the type of informative speech you plan to give, characteristics of effective informative speeches cross all categories. As you research, develop, and present your speech, keep the following 10 guidelines in mind.

Consider Your Audience's Needs and Goals

Concern for your audience is the theme of the book and applies here. The best informative speakers know what their listeners want to learn from their speech. A group of Weight Watchers members may be motivated to attend a lecture on dieting to learn how to lose weight, while nutritionists drawn to the same speech may need the

© Ken Wolter/Shutterstock.com

information to help clients. Audience goals are also linked to knowledge. Those who lack knowledge about a topic may be more motivated to listen and learn than those who feel they already know the topic. However, it is possible that technology has changed, new information has surfaced, or new ways to think about or do something have emerged. The speaker needs to find a way to engage those who are less motivated.

The Weight Watchers organization must be constantly tuned to the needs and goals of their members.

Make connections between your subject and your audience's daily needs, desires, and interests. For example, some audience members might have no interest in a speech on the effectiveness of halfway houses until you tell them how much money is being spent on prisons locally, or better yet, how much each listener is spending per year. Now the topic is more relevant. People care about money, safety, prestige, family and friends, community, and their own growth and progress, among other things. Show how your topic influences one or more of these and you will have an audience motivated to listen.

Consider Your Audience's Knowledge Level

If you want to describe how to use eSnipe when participating in eBay auctions, you may be speaking to students who have never heard of it. To be safe, however, you might develop a brief pre-speech questionnaire to pass out to your class. Or you can select several individuals at random and ask what they know. You do not want to bore the class with mundane minutiae, but you do not want to confuse them with information that is too advanced for their knowledge level. Consider this golf example:

> As the golf champion of your district, you decide to give your informative speech on the game. You begin by holding up a golf club and saying, "This is a golf club. They come in many sizes and styles." Then you hold up a golf ball. "This is a golf ball. Golf balls are all the same size, but they come in many colors. Most golf balls are white. When you first start playing golf, you need a lot of golf balls. So, you need a golf club and a golf ball to play golf."

Expect your listeners to yawn in this situation. They do not want to hear what they already know. Although your presentation may be effective for an audience of children who have never seen a golf club or ball, your presentation is too simplistic for adults.

Capture Attention and Interest Immediately

As an informative speaker, your goal is to communicate information about a specific topic in a way that is understandable to your listeners. In your introduction, you must first convince your audience that your topic is interesting and relevant. For example, if you are delivering a speech on white-collar crime, you might begin like this:

Imagine taking part of your paycheck and handing it to a criminal. In an indirect way, that's what we all do to pay for white-collar crime. Part of the tax dollars you give the federal government goes into the hands of unscrupulous business executives who pad their expenses and overcharge the government by millions of dollars. For example, General Dynamics, the third-largest military supplier, tacked on at least $75 million to the government's bill for such "overhead" expenses as country-club fees and personal travel for corporate executives.

This approach is more likely to capture audience attention than a list of white-collar crimes or criminals.

Sustain Audience Attention and Interest by Being Creative, Vivid, and Enthusiastic

Try something different. Change your pace to bring attention or emphasis to a point. Aloud, say the following phrase at a regular rate, and then slow down and emphasize each word: "We must work together!" Slowing down to emphasize each word gives the sentence greater impact. Varying rate of speech is an effective way to sustain audience attention.

Show some excitement! Talking about accounting principles, water filters, or changes in planet designations with spirit and energy may keep people listening. Delivery can make a difference. Enthusiasm is infectious, even to those who have no particular interest in your subject. It is no accident that advertising campaigns are built around slogans, jingles, and other memorable language that people are likely to remember after a commercial is over. We are more likely to remember vivid language than dull language.

Cite Your Oral Sources Accurately

Citing sources accurately means putting in the work ahead of time to understand the source. Any time you offer facts, statistics, opinions, and ideas that you found in research, you should provide your audience with the source. In doing this, you enhance your own credibility. Your audience appreciates your depth of research on the topic, and you avoid accusations of plagiarism.

Accurate source representation comes from having a well-rounded understanding of the source. Critical thinking is necessary when assessing the source you intend to use. Among other information, it makes sense to check out who the author is or what the source is, what bias, if any, exists, what the intention of the author or source is, and what its intended use was.

ETHICS MATTER

Grisyan is a communication major at her university. For her final project in Public Speaking, Grisyan is assigned an informative speech on a topic of her choosing. Because of her interest in local government, Grisyan decides to give her presentation on a public works project currently being voted on by her community. The project involves a massive restructuring of the city's public water system, with a city-wide vote occurring the following week.

Shortly after finishing the rough draft of her presentation, Grisyan discovered that the majority of her statistics and facts came from a biased source. The website Grisyan used was hosted by a construction company trying to win the bid for her city's public works project. Most of the data Grisyan planned to use in her presentation was flawed, unreliable, or completely false. Faced with the prospect of starting over from the beginning, Grisyan debated if she should keep her original sources and hope the bias was not discovered by her teacher.

QUESTIONS TO CONSIDER:
1. From an ethical perspective, what is the importance of presenting unbiased sources to your audience?
2. What ethical breach is committed by the construction company by publishing biased information as fact on a public website?
3. What steps should Grisyan have taken early in the research process to avoid accumulating inaccurate sources?

Signpost Main Ideas

Your audience may need help keeping track of the information in your speech. Separating one idea from another may be difficult for listeners who are trying to learn all the information at once. You can help your audience understand the structure of your speech by creating oral lists. Simple "First, second, third, fourth . . ." or "one, two, three, four . . ." helps the audience focus on your sequence of points. Here is an example of signposting:

Having a motorized scooter in college instead of a car is preferred for two reasons. The first reason is financial. A scooter gets at least 80 miles per gallon. Over a period of four years, significant savings occur. The second reason a scooter is preferred in college is convenience. Parking problems are virtually eliminated. No longer do you have to worry about being late to class, because you can park in the motorcycle parking areas. They're all around us.

Signposting at the beginning of a speech tells the audience how many points you have or how many ideas you intend to support. Signposting during the speech acts as a transition because it keeps the audience informed as to where you are in the speech.

Relate the New with the Familiar

Informative speeches should introduce new information in terms of what the audience already knows. Using metaphors, analogies, similes, and other forms of speech is useful. Here is an example of an analogy:

A cooling-off period in labor–management negotiations is like a parentally imposed time-out. When we were children, our parents would send us to our rooms to think over what we had done. We were forbidden to come out for some time in the hope that by the time we were released, our tempers had cooled. Similarly, by law, the President can impose an 80-day cooling-off period if a strike threatens to imperil the nation's health or safety.

Most of us can relate to the "time-out" concept referred to in this example, so providing the analogy helps us understand the cooling-off period if a strike is possible. References to the familiar help listeners assimilate new information. Following is a metaphor for the recent economic crisis.

The economy is a train wreck. The conductor saw the other train coming toward it, and thought the switchman would send the oncoming train onto the sidetrack and save the day. It didn't happen. The train completely derailed, leaving total destruction in its path.

This metaphor is a way to express visually the idea that banks hoped the regulators would cover their losses and stabilize the economy. Everyone is familiar with the concept of a train wreck, but understanding an economic crisis is not so easy. Using various language devices can help with the explanation.

Use Repetition

Repetition is important when presenting new facts and ideas. You help your listeners by reinforcing your main points through summaries and paraphrasing. For example, if you were trying to persuade your classmates to purchase a scooter instead of a car, you might have three points: (1) a scooter is cheaper than a car; (2) a scooter gets better gas mileage than a car; and (3) you can always find a nearby parking spot for your scooter. For your first point, you mention purchase price, insurance, and maintenance costs. As you finish your first point, you could say, "So a scooter is cheaper than a car in at least three ways, purchase price, insurance, and maintenance." You have already mentioned these three subpoints, but noting them as an internal summary before your second main point helps reinforce the idea that scooters are cheaper than cars.

Offer Interesting Visuals

Your audience expects you to put effort into your presentation. This means more than practicing. Using pictures, charts, models, PowerPoint

When discussing data-heavy topics like climate change, it is recommended to offer visual aids like charts, models, and pictures.

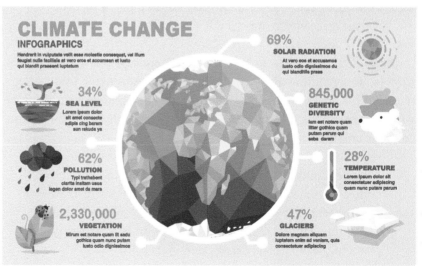

© Cube29/Shutterstock.com

PART THREE: TYPES OF PUBLIC SPEAKING

slides, and other presentational aids helps maintain audience interest. Use humorous visuals to display statistics, if appropriate. Demonstrate the physics of air travel by throwing paper airplanes across the room.

Speaking Well with Technology Is an Essential for Excellence

When creating an informative speech, communication professionals are challenged to gain (and then maintain) audience interest. PowerPoint, while being the most popular technology-based presentation aid, has been criticized for being unoriginal and boring. Given how often PowerPoint is used in both academic and professional environments, audiences are susceptible to "PowerPoint fatigue," which decreases the impact and staying power of your presentation. With this in mind, many professional speakers are using Focusky, an alternative to PowerPoint.

Focusky is an HTML5 PowerPoint alternative that helps presenters create attractive and interactive presentations. Recently, an update to the company's software enables communication professionals to publish their presentations as HTML5 web pages, allowing for a greater audience reach than ever before (Rocket, 2016). This new technology also allows publishers to make their presentations into a mobile-friendly version, allowing people to open presentations on their iPads, iPhones, Android devices, and other mobile gadgets. Given the flexibility Focusky offers, presenters are now able to access their work much more quickly and efficiently.

As a professional speaker, you must constantly assess the effectiveness of your presentational aids. Gauge your audience: are they exposed to PowerPoint presentations on a constant basis? Is there any presentation software that can do a better job holding your audience's interest? Although Focusky may never overtake PowerPoint or Prezi in popularity, it (and other software similar to Focusky) can be effective in breaking the monotony associated with slide-based presentations.

Consider How to Respond to Audience Questions and Distractions

In an informative speech, your audience may have the opportunity to ask questions. Before you give your speech, decide whether you want questions during your presentation or at the end. If you prefer they wait, tell your audience early in your speech or at the first hand raised. Perhaps try, "I ask that you hold all questions to the end of this presentation, where I have built in some time for them."

When fielding questions, develop the habit of doing four things in this order: *thank* the questioner, *paraphrase* the question (put it in your own words), *answer* the question briefly, and then *ask* the questioner if you answered his/her question. Paraphrasing allows the speaker to stay in control of the situation by pointing questions in desirable directions or away from areas you are not willing to address.

For any question, you have five options: (1) answer it (Remember, "I do not know" is an answer), (2) bounce it back to the questioner ("Well, that is interesting. How might you answer that question?"), (3) bounce it to the audience ("I see, does anyone have any helpful thoughts about this?"), (4) defer the question until later ("Now you and I would find this interesting, but it is outside the scope of my message today. I'd love to chat with you individually about this in a moment"), and (5) promise more answers later ("I would really like to look further into that. May I get back to you later?"). Effective speakers know and use all five as strategies to keep their question-and-answer period productive and on track.

While questions may be expected, distractions are not. When random interruptions occur, do not ignore them. Call attention to the distraction. This allows your audience to get it out and then return their attention to you. One speaker was interrupted when a window washer suspended outside the building dropped into view, ropes and all. The speaker paused, looked at the dangling distraction and announced, "Spiderman!" Everyone laughed, and he then returned to his speech. At a banquet, a speaker was interrupted by the crash of shattering dishes from the direction of the kitchen. She quipped, "Sounds like someone lost a contact lens." Whether humorous or not, calling attention to distractions is key to maintaining control.

Ethics of Informative Speaking

Think about the advertising you see on TV and the warning labels on certain products you purchase. After listening to a commercial about a new weight-loss tablet, you believe you have found a solution to get rid of those extra 20 pounds you carry with you. Several happy people testify about how wonderful the drug is, and how it worked miracles for them. At the end of the commercial, you hear a speaker say, "This drug is not for children under 16. It may cause diarrhea, restlessness, sleeplessness, nausea, and stomach cramps. It can lead to strokes and heart attacks. Those with high blood pressure, epilepsy, diabetes, or heart disease should not take this medicine . . ." After listening to the warnings, the drug may not sound so miraculous. We have government regulations to make sure consumers make informed choices.

As an individual speaker, *you regulate yourself*. A speaker has ethical responsibilities, no matter what type of speech he or she prepares and delivers. The informative speeches you deliver in class and those you listen to on campus are not nearly as likely to affect the course of history as those delivered by high-ranking public officials in a time of war or national political campaigns. Even so, *the principles of ethical responsibility are similar for every speaker*.

The president of the United States, the president of your school, and the president of any organization to which you belong all have an obligation to inform their constituencies (audiences) in nonmanipulative ways and to provide them with information they need and have a right to know. Professors, doctors, police officers, and others engaged in informative speaking ought to tell the truth as they know it, and not withhold information to serve personal gain. You, like others, should always rely on credible sources and avoid what political scientists label as "calculated ambiguity." Calculated ambiguity is a speaker's planned effort to be vague, sketchy, and considerably abstract.

Calculated ambiguity
A speaker's planned effort to be vague, sketchy, and considerably abstract.

You have many choices to make as you prepare for an informative speech. Applying reasonable ethical standards will help with your decision-making. An informative speech requires you to assemble accurate, sound, and pertinent information that will enable you to tell your audience what you believe to be the truth. Relying on outdated information, not giving the audience enough information about your sources, omitting relevant information, being vague intentionally, and taking information out of context are all violations of ethical principles.

ESSENTIALS FOR EXCELLENCE

In this chapter, you have learned about the different types of informative speaking, as well as the ethics and guidelines associated with them. While you have gained valuable insight into the academic aspect of informative speaking, this chapter cannot be complete without the observations of a real-world practitioner of informative public speaking. Veteran speechwriter Ian Griffin offers four essentials to informing an audience.

Don't be a foreign policeman.

The goal of delivering a public speech is to communicate as clearly as possible. Imagine being a tourist in a foreign country and hearing a short command from a policeman in a language you don't understand. Although the amount of information is minimal, the failure to understand could be fatal. Always spell out the information in your speech for the audience.

Use road signs.

Even long speeches can be broken down into concise nuggets of information (Griffin, 2013). Your intonation, cadence, and gestures all serve as road signs to your audience. When used effectively, they help reinforce your message.

Be a subject matter expert, but don't overdo it.

Although you should be knowledgeable in the subject you are presenting, be careful to use facts and sources in moderation. You don't want to end up confusing your audience because you buried them in a mass of data. When possible, offer your audience some type of visual aid to convey analytical data.

Be a good storyteller.

The audience can only remember so many facts; what will be remembered are the stories you tell. Creating stories out of raw information helps the audience visualize a situation more effectively. By taking the time to develop stories, you will be able to communicate more complex information and move your audience to action.

■ WHAT YOU'VE LEARNED:

Now that you have studied the chapter, you should be able to:

1. Know the different types of informative speaking.
    *   Speeches of description paint a clear picture of an event, person, object, place, or concept. The goal is to create images in the minds of listeners about your topic or to describe a concept in concrete detail.
    *   Speeches of explanation deal with more abstract topics (ideas, theories, principles, and beliefs) than do speeches of description or demonstration. They involve attempts to simplify complex topics.
    *   Speeches of demonstration focus on a process by describing the gradual changes that lead to a particular result. Speeches of demonstration especially benefit from presentational aids.
2. Identify the five goals of informative speaking.
    *   Accuracy. Informative speakers strive to present the truth. Research is crucial for this goal.
    *   Objectivity. Information must be presented in a fair and unbiased manner. Leaving out critical information or creating a misleading picture violates the principles of objectivity.
    *   Clear, concise explanation. Your informative speech must communicate your ideas without confusion. This goal requires careful audience analysis and an effective organizational pattern.
    *   Meaningfulness. Relate your material to the interests, needs, and concerns of your audience. Consider your setting and avoid information overload.
    *   Memorability. Speakers who are enthusiastic, genuine, and creative can communicate their excitement to their listeners. Use examples and humor, and involve your audience in your presentation whenever possible.
3. Cite oral sources accurately and effectively.
    *   Citing sources accurately means putting in the work ahead of time to understand the source. Your audience will appreciate your depth of research on the topic, and you avoid charges of plagiarism.
4. Understand the ethics of informative speaking.
    *   A speaker has ethical responsibilities, no matter what type of speech they prepare. An informative speech requires accurate, sound, and pertinent information that enables your audience to believe what you say is the truth.

Key Terms

abstract topics, 372

calculated ambiguity, 389

informative speech, 369

speech of demonstration, 371

speech of description, 371

speech of explanation, 371

Reflect

1   How does speaker intent differentiate informative, persuasive, and special-occasion speaking?
2   How do the three types of informative speeches differ?
3   What are the characteristics of an effective informative speech?
4   How can effective visuals enhance an informative speech?
5   What role does ethics play in informative speaking?

Review Questions

1   A(n) _____ communicates information and ideas in a way that your audience will understand and remember.

2   A speech of _____ helps an audience understand what something is.

3   A speech of _____ helps an audience understand why something is.

4   A speech of _____ focuses on how something is done.

5   Ideas, theories, principles, and beliefs are known as _____.

6   A speaker's planned effort to be vague, sketchy, and considerably abstract is referred to as _____.

394   Conservative Party leader Boris Johnson successfully persuaded a
majority of British voters to leave the European Union.

CHAPTER TWELVE
PERSUASIVE SPEAKING

OUTLINE

WHAT YOU'LL LEARN

After studying this chapter, you should be able to:

1. Identify the three different levels on which persuasive communication takes place.
2. Define the five levels of Maslow's Hierarchy of Needs.
3. Recognize the different types of argument fallacies.
4. Organize a persuasive speech using Monroe's Motivated Sequence.

SPEAKING IN CONTEXT

On June 23, 2016, the United Kingdom (UK) voted to leave the European Union (EU), becoming the first nation to leave the EU since its creation in 1993. Known as "Brexit," the move was heavily divisive; more than 30 million British citizens (71.8% of voters) voted in the referendum, with the leave position winning 52%–48% of the vote. Although the referendum was passed, many questions and issues were presented to both the UK and the EU. Would British citizens still be able to move and work freely in European Union countries? What will happen to EU nationals currently working in the UK? While many of these questions await answers, many individuals expressed surprise that the measure passed in the first place. Writers for the British Broadcasting organization examined the persuasive tactics of Boris Johnson, one of the leaders of the Vote Leave campaign.

Boris Johnson, a senior member of the Conservative Party, often argued that the EU was holding Great Britain back by imposing too many rules on British businesses and charging billions of pounds a year in membership fees (Wheeler & Hunt, 2016). Johnson also criticized the "free movement" of EU members, which allowed many non-British citizens to enter and work freely in the United Kingdom. Johnson appealed to citizens to take back full control of their borders and reduce the number of foreigners coming to live and work in the UK. In the end, Johnson was successful in persuading a majority of British voters to end the economic partnership with the European Union.

As you learn the skills needed to become a successful persuasive speaker, remember the importance of appealing to your audience's needs. Many voters in the UK were initially skeptical of the plan to leave the EU, but Johnson and his fellow Vote Leave supporters succeeded in changing public opinion by catering to the concerns and needs of their audience. Whether you agree or disagree with the Brexit vote, analyzing the persuasive tactics employed by both sides can help you become a more effective persuader.

The Audience in Persuasive Speaking

Imagine the following situations:

- You talk to a student group on campus about the benefits of spending a semester with the Disney College Program in Orlando, Florida.
- You speak before your city council, urging them to implement a curbside recycling program.
- You speak before a group of parents of the high school musical cast to get them to volunteer to help make tickets, sell tickets, sell concessions, monitor students during rehearsal, work on the set, work backstage, sell advertisements, work with costume rental, and design and sell T-shirts.

Your success or failure to get your audience to act in the situations above is determined by a number of factors. Knowing who your listeners are is important, as we discussed in Chapter 3. But, in a persuasive speech, knowing *the attitude of your audience* is crucial, and trying to *determine the needs* of the audience is important to your success.

In general, we can classify audience attitudes into three categories: (1) they agree, (2) they don't agree, (3) they are undecided. When you are clear on which category your audience rests in, you will be able to craft a more targeted, effective message. Here is a closer examination of each category.

The **supportive audience**, the audience that agrees with you, poses the least difficulty. This type of audience is friendly; its members like you, and they are interested in hearing what you have to say. Your main objective is to reinforce what they already accept. You want to strengthen their resolve or use it to encourage behavioral change. You also want to keep them enthused about your point of view or action plan. A candidate for state's attorney who has invited a group of friends and colleagues to an ice cream social will use that time to restate his/her strengths and urge attendees to help him/her with the campaign.

Supportive audience
An audience that agrees with you.

The audience that agrees with you will welcome *new* information, but does not need a re-hashing of information already known and accepted. The speaker should work to strengthen the audience's resistance to counterpersuasion. For example, the candidate for state's attorney who is running against an incumbent can talk about how change is necessary, and how his/her experience or background will bring a fresh perspective to the office.

With the opposed audience, the speaker runs the risk of having members in the audience who may be hostile. This audience does not agree with you, it is not friendly or sympathetic, and most likely, will search for flaws in your argument. Your objective in this case is to get a fair hearing. A persuasive speaker facing a group that does not agree with him/her needs to set reasonable goals. Also, developing arguments carefully by using fair and respected evidence may help persuade an audience that disagrees with you.

One thing to consider when facing an audience opposed to you is the nature of their opposition. Is it to you? Your cause? A specific statement you made or information made available to them? If you can determine why they are opposed, your effort can be spent on addressing the nature of the opposition.

Seeking common ground is a good strategy when people do not agree with you. Find a place where you and your audience can stand without disagreeing. For example, hospital employees who smoke may not be willing to quit, but they may recognize the need to have smoking banned on hospital property, so they may still smoke on break if they go off-site.

Acknowledging differences is also a helpful strategy for the opposed audience. Making sure you do not set your attitudes, beliefs, or values to be "right" and the audience's to be "wrong" is essential if any movement toward your point of view is likely. Avoid needless confrontation.

Speaking before an uncommitted audience can be difficult because you don't know whether they are uninformed, indifferent, or are adamantly neutral. This audience is neither friendly nor hostile, but most likely, they are not sympathetic.

The uninformed audience is the easiest to persuade, because they need information. A scholarship committee trying to determine which of the five candidates will receive $2,000 needs sufficient information about the candidates to make an informed choice.

The indifferent audience member doesn't really care about the issue or topic. These audience members can be found in most "mandatory" meetings held at work, school, and sometimes training. In this case, it is important that the speaker gets the attention of the audience members and gives them a reason to care. Making the message relate to their lives is important, and providing audience members with relevant, persuasive material helps move audience members out of the uncommitted category. However, it may be difficult to sway most or all audience members.

Maslow's Hierarchy of Needs

Knowing the audience's disposition toward you helps you structure a more effective persuasive speech. Speakers should also consider the needs of the audience. The persuader can develop lines of reasoning that relate to pertinent needs. Human needs can be described in terms of logic or what makes sense to a listener, but needs are immersed in emotions of the individual as well.

Psychologist Abraham Maslow (1943) classified human needs according to the hierarchy pictured in **Figure 12.1**. Maslow believed that our most basic needs—those at the foundation of the hierarchy—must be satisfied before we can consider those on the next levels. In effect, these higher-level needs are put on "hold," and have little effect on our actions, until the lower-level needs are met. Maslow's hierarchy provides a catalog of targets for emotional appeals, including:

PHYSIOLOGICAL NEEDS. At the foundation of the hierarchy are our biological needs for food, water, oxygen, procreation, and rest. If you were delivering a speech in favor of a proposed new reservoir to a community experiencing problems with its water supply, it would be appropriate to appeal to our very basic need for safe and abundant water, without which our lives would be in danger.

SAFETY NEEDS. Safety needs include the need for security, freedom from fear and attack, a home that offers tranquility and comfort, and a means of earning a living. If you are delivering the same speech to a group of unemployed construction workers, you might link the reservoir project to safe, well-paying jobs.

BELONGINGNESS AND LOVE NEEDS. These needs refer to our drive for affiliation, friendship, and love. When appealing to the need for social belonging, you may choose to emphasize the unity and cohesiveness that will emerge from the community effort to bring the reservoir to completion.

ESTEEM NEEDS. Esteem needs include the need to be seen as worthy and competent and to have the respect of others. In this case, an effective approach would be to praise community members for their initiative in helping to make the reservoir project a reality.

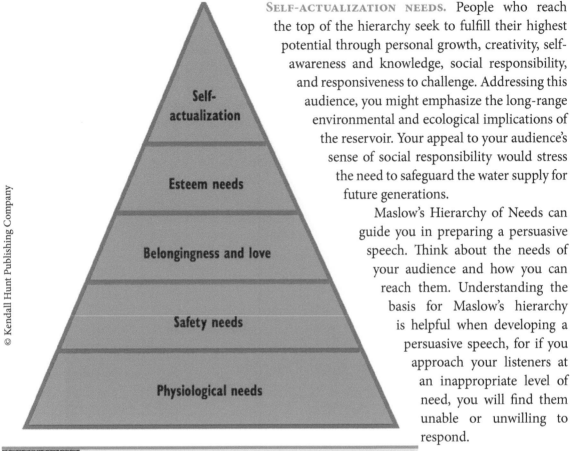

SELF-ACTUALIZATION NEEDS. People who reach the top of the hierarchy seek to fulfill their highest potential through personal growth, creativity, self-awareness and knowledge, social responsibility, and responsiveness to challenge. Addressing this audience, you might emphasize the long-range environmental and ecological implications of the reservoir. Your appeal to your audience's sense of social responsibility would stress the need to safeguard the water supply for future generations.

Maslow's Hierarchy of Needs can guide you in preparing a persuasive speech. Think about the needs of your audience and how you can reach them. Understanding the basis for Maslow's hierarchy is helpful when developing a persuasive speech, for if you approach your listeners at an inappropriate level of need, you will find them unable or unwilling to respond.

FIGURE 12.1 Maslow's Hierarchy of Needs

Elements of Persuasion

We define persuasion as attempting to influence others through communication. Critical building blocks of persuasion have been studied by generations of rhetorical scholars, starting with Aristotle. Persuasion is intended to influence choice through what Aristotle termed *ethos*, *pathos*, and *logos*. More recent scholarly work has provided the addition of *mythos*. These four elements provide the underpinnings of our modern study of persuasion.

To illustrate these, let's consider the speech given days after the deadly earthquake, tsunami, and nuclear disaster struck Japan. Here is how Emperor Akihito addressed a stunned nation on March 16, 2011:

The 9.0 earthquake that struck the Tohoku-Pacific region was an extraordinarily large earthquake. I have been deeply hurt by the miserable situation in the affected areas. The number of deaths from earthquakes and tsunamis has increased day by day, and we do not know yet how many victims we will eventually have. I pray for the survival of as many people as possible.

Emperor Akihito relied heavily on ethos in his speech, as we will see later with other excerpts.

Ethos and the Power of the Speaker's Credibility

As speaker, you must decide not only what to tell your audience, but also what you should avoid saying. In a persuasive speech, you ask listeners to think or act in ways needed to achieve a desired response. Aristotle believed that **ethos**, which refers to speaker credibility, makes speakers worthy of belief. Audiences trust speakers they perceive as honest. Ethics provide standards for conduct that guide us. Persuasive speaking requires asking others to accept and act on ideas we believe to be accurate and true.

We see the Japanese emperor standing on the firm ground of the credibility of his office. In Japanese culture, the emperor has typically been recognized as both statesman-ruler and messenger from God. When the emperor spoke, everyone listened, due in large part to his inherent credibility. Let's take a closer look at what makes up an impression of ethos or speaker credibility.

© thelefty/Shutterstock.com

In Western society, Aristotle is considered one of the founders of persuasive rhetoric.

Ethos

Speaker credibility.

Dimensions of Speaker Credibility

What your audience knows about you before you speak and what they learn about your position during your speech may influence your ability to persuade them. Credibility can be measured according to three dimensions: competence, trustworthiness, and dynamism.

COMPETENCE. In many cases, your audience will decide your message's value based on perceived speaker competence. Your listeners will first

In his position as Emperor, Akihito wields enormous persuasive power.

ask themselves whether you have the background to speak. If the topic is crime, an audience is more likely to be persuaded by the Atlanta chief of police than by a postal worker delivering her personal opinions. Second, your audience will consider whether the content of your speech has firm support. When it is clear that speakers have not researched their topic, their ability to persuade diminishes. Finally, audiences will determine whether you communicate confidence and control of your subject matter through your delivery.

In our example above, Emperor Akihito makes clear that he is abreast of all the relevant information. He relays the strength of the earthquake, the results of the tsunami, and the seriousness of the nuclear disaster. Listeners quickly understood that he was well informed in this emergency. His display of competence by demonstrating an understanding of the facts increases his credibility even further.

TRUSTWORTHINESS. When someone is trying to persuade us to think or act a certain way, trusting that person is important. And although competence is important, research has shown that the trustworthy communicator is more influential than the untrustworthy one, regardless of his/her level of expertise (Wahl, 2013; Wahl & Maresh-Fuehrer, 2016).

Audience perceptions of trustworthiness are based largely on your perceived respect for them, your ethical standards, and your ability to establish common ground. Audiences gauge a speaker's *respect* for them by analyzing the actions a speaker has taken before the speech. If a group is listening to a political candidate running for office in their community, they will have more respect for someone who has demonstrated concern for their community through past actions.

Trustworthiness is also influenced by the audience's perception of your *ethical standards*. Telling the truth is paramount for the persuasive speaker. If your message is biased and you make little attempt to be fair or to concede the strength of your opponent's point of view, your listeners may question your integrity.

Your credibility and your ability to persuade increase if you convince your audience that you share "common ground." In the popular movie *300*, Queen Gorgo addresses a reluctant Spartan Council, pleading with them to send the Spartan army into battle. Rather than appealing to the council as queen, she appeals to common ground in the opening: "Councilmen, I stand before you today not only as your Queen: I come to you as a mother; I come to you as a wife; I come to you as a Spartan woman; I come to you with great humility" (www.americanrhetoric.com).

While few can identify with being a queen, most feel a sense of identification with a humble mother, wife, woman, or citizen. With this common ground appeal in place, the stage is set for the queen to persuade the council to side with her. In this instance, Queen Gorgo establishes common ground by identifying with her audience and provoking them to identify with her.

DYNAMISM. Your credibility and, therefore, your ability to persuade are influenced by the audience's perception of you as a dynamic spokesperson. Dynamic speakers tend to be vibrant, confident, vigorous, attractive, and skilled in public speaking. Your listeners will make critical decisions about how dynamic you are as they form a first impression. This impression will be reinforced or altered as they listen for an energetic style that communicates commitment to your point of view, and for ideas that build on one another in a convincing, logical way. While charisma plays a part in being dynamic, it is not enough. Dynamic public speakers tend to be well-practiced presenters.

Does credibility make a difference in your ability to persuade? Pornitakpan (2004), who examined five decades of research on the persuasiveness of speaker credibility, found that "a high-credibility source is more persuasive than is a low-credibility source in both changing attitudes and gaining behavioral compliance" (p. 266). Lifelong learning in the art of persuasion involves building and enhancing your speaker competence, trustworthiness, and dynamism.

Pathos and the Power of Emotion

Aristotle argued that **pathos**, which is the "consideration of the emotions of people in the audience" is an integral part of persuasion (Kennedy, 2007, p. 15). Aristotle explained:

> The emotions are those things through which, by undergoing change, people come to differ in their judgments and which are accompanied by pain and pleasure, for example, anger, pity, fear, and other such things and their opposites" (Aristotle, 2007).

Emperor Akihito makes use of emotion in his message. Although stoic by American standards, he acknowledges the suffering of victims:

> [U]nder the severe cold weather, many evacuees have been placed in an unavoidable situation where they are subject to extreme suffering due to the lack of food, drinking water, fuel, and so on. I truly hope that, by making the greatest effort possible to rescue the victims promptly, we can improve their lives as much as possible" (www.americanrhetoric.com).

Akihito's reference to extreme suffering adds an emotional appeal to support the need for continued rescue efforts.

Emotional appeals have the power to elicit happiness, joy, pride, patriotism, fear, hate, anger, guilt, despair, hope, hopelessness, bitterness, and other feelings. Some subjects are more emotionally powerful than others and lend themselves to emotional appeals. Look at the list of topics that follow:

- The homeless
- Abused children
- Cruelty to animals
- Death penalty
- Sex education in school
- Teaching evolution in school
- Gun control
- Terrorist attacks

Many of these topics cause listeners to have emotional responses. Emotional appeals are often the most persuasive type of appeal because they provide the motivation listeners need to change their minds or take action. For example, instead of simply listing the reasons sugary foods are unhealthy, a more effective approach is to tie these foods to frightening consequences:

> Jim thought nothing could ever happen to him. He was healthy as an ox—or so he thought. His world fell apart one sunny May morning when he suffered a massive heart attack. He survived, but his doctors told him that his coronary arteries were blocked and that he needed bypass surgery. "Why me?" he asked. "I'm only 42 years old." The answer, he was told, had a lot to do with the sugar-heavy diet he had eaten since childhood.

This illustration appeals to the listener's emotional state, and is ultimately more persuasive than a list of facts.

We must not forget that emotional appeals are powerful, and as such, can be tools of manipulation in the hands of unscrupulous speakers who attempt to arouse audiences through emotion rather than logic. For example, in an effort to lose weight, individuals may buy pills or exercise equipment that may be useless, or worse, a true health risk. Those selling the products accept the emotional message ("lose weight, look beautiful, gain friends, have a great life").

The speaker has an ethical responsibility when using emotional appeals. The ethically responsible speaker does not distort, delete, or exaggerate information for the sole purpose of emotionally charging an audience to manipulate their feelings for self-centered ends.

ENGAGING IN COMMUNITY

For Colonel Christopher Holshek, the value of community service can be defined quite simply: when people serve their community, they help create a better country. Holshek, who has been active in the community spanning a 30-year career in the army, plans to bring home the principles he learned from an unusual career he describes as working "the many spaces in between" a citizen and soldier (Shen, 2016). By participating in a cross-country motorcycle ride, Holshek plans to share his message of community service and citizenship.

The cross-country motorcycle journey will be known as the National Service Ride. Holshek's goal is to generate a more positive narrative about community service by stopping at schools and community events to teach the value of "service learning," the idea that valuable skills can be gained by volunteering at a local level. Anyone is allowed to join in his motorcycle journey, which Holshek believes links the motorcycle's appeal for personal freedom and mobility with the idea of connecting people around the country. The Ride has support from several advocacy organizations, including the Service Year Alliance, United Nations Association, Alliance for Peacebuilding, and several others (Shen, 2016). For anyone else who wants to help, Holshek encourages them to spread the word through social media links and by serving in their own communities.

"Too many of us are looking around and blaming the government or someone other than ourselves for what we think is wrong today," said Holshek. "But if you want to see things get better, start by looking in the mirror and asking yourself, 'how can I contribute?' The more you do that the more you see what's right and good in people and things."

Logos and the Power of Logical Appeals and Arguments

Logos

An appeal that is rational and reasonable based on evidence provided.

Logos, or logical appeals and arguments, refers to the "rational, factual basis that supports the speaker's position" (Walker, 2005, p. 3). For example, if a friend tried to convince you *not* to buy a new car by pointing out that you are in college, have no savings account, and are currently unemployed, that friend would be making a logical argument.

Anatomy of an Argument: Claim, Data, Warrant

Logical, critical thinking increases your ability to *assess*, *analyze*, and *advocate* ideas. Decades ago, Stephen Toulmin (1958), a British philosopher, developed a model of practical reasoning that consists of three basic elements: claim, data, and warrant. To construct a sound, reasonable argument, you need to use three essential parts:

1   The **claim** is a statement or contention the audience is urged to accept. The claim answers the question, "So what is your point?
    Example: It's your turn to do the dishes; I did them last time.
    Example: You need to call your sister this week; she called you last week.

2   The **data** are evidence in support of an idea you advocate. Data provide the answer to "So what is your proof?" or "Why?"
    Example: It looks like rain. Dark clouds are forming.
    Example: When I stop at McDonald's on the road, they seem to have clean bathrooms.

3   The **warrant** is an inference that links the evidence with the claim. It answers the question, "Why does that data mean your claim is true?"
    Example: Augie is running a fever. I bet he has an ear infection.
    Example: Sarah will be on time. There isn't any traffic right now.

Claim

A statement or contention the audience is urged to accept.

Data

Evidence in support of an idea you advocate.

Warrant

An inference that links the evidence with the claim.

To put the three elements of an argument together, let's consider another example. At a restaurant, you take a bite of a steak sandwich and say, "This is the worst sandwich I have ever tried." With this announcement you are making a *claim* that you *infer* from tasting the meat.

The evidence (*data*) is the food before you. The *warrant* is the link between data and claim and is the inference, which may be an *unstated belief* that the food is spoiled, old, or poorly prepared, and will taste bad.

When you reason with your audience it is important to craft claims, warrants, and data your audience will understand and accept. Sound reasoning is especially important when your audience is skeptical. Faced with the task of trying to convince people to change their minds or do something they might not otherwise be inclined to do, your arguments must be impressive.

We persuade others that a claim or conclusion is highly probable by **inductive** and **deductive reasoning**. Strong evidence shows that you have carefully analyzed the support of your points. Only when strong probability is established can you ask your listeners to make *the inductive leap* from specific cases to a general conclusion, or to take the *deductive* move from statements as premises to a conclusion you want them to accept. We now look more closely at inductive and deductive reasoning.

Inductive reasoning

Generalizing from specific examples and drawing conclusions from what we observe.

Deductive reasoning

Drawing conclusions based on the connections between statements that serve as premises.

Inductive Reasoning

Through inductive reasoning, we generalize from specific examples to draw conclusions from what we observe. Inductive reasoning moves us from the specific to the general in an orderly, logical fashion. The inference step in the argument holds that what is true of specific cases can be generalized to other cases of the same class, or of the class as a whole. Suppose you are trying to persuade your audience that the decline of downtown merchants in your town is a problem that can be solved with an effective plan you are about to present. You may infer that what has worked to solve a similar problem in a number of similar towns is likely to work in this case as well.

One problem with inductive reasoning is that individual cases do not always add up to a correct conclusion. Sometimes a speaker's list of examples is too small, leading to an incorrect conclusion based on limited information. With inductive reasoning, you can never be sure that your conclusions are absolutely accurate. Because you are only looking at a sample of all the possible cases, you must persuade your audience to accept a conclusion that is probable, or maybe even just possible. The three most common strategies for inductive reasoning involve analogy, cause, and sign.

Reasoning by Analogy

Analogies establish common links between similar and not-so-similar concepts. They are effective tools of persuasion when your audience is convinced that the characteristics of one case are similar enough to the characteristics of the second case that your argument about the first also applies to the second.

As noted in the chapter on language, a *figurative analogy* draws a comparison between things that are distinctly different, such as "Eating fresh marshmallows is like floating on a cloud." Figurative analogies can be used to persuade, but they must be supported with relevant facts, statistics, and testimony that link the dissimilar concepts you are comparing.

Whereas a figurative analogy compares things that are distinctly different and supplies useful illustrations, a *literal analogy* compares things with similar characteristics and, therefore, requires less explanatory support. One speaker compared the addictive power of tobacco products, especially cigarettes, with the power of alcoholic beverages consumed on a regular basis. His line of reasoning was that both are consumed for pleasure, relaxation, and often as relief for stress. While his use of logical argument was obvious, the listener ultimately assesses whether or not these two things—alcohol and tobacco—are sufficiently similar.

The distinction between literal and figurative analogies is important because only literal analogies are sufficient to establish logical proof. Your analogy should meet the following characteristics:

- There are significant points of similarity.
- Similarities are tied to critical points of the comparison.
- Differences need to be relatively small.
- You have a better chance of convincing people if you can point to other successful cases (Freely, 1993, pp. 119–120).

Reasoning from Cause

When you reason from cause, you infer that an event of one kind contributes to or brings about an event of another kind. The presence of a cat in a room when you are allergic to cats is likely to bring about a series of sneezes until the cat is removed. As the following example demonstrates, causal reasoning focuses on the cause-and-effect relationship between ideas.

> CAUSE: An inaccurate and low census count of the homeless in Detroit
> EFFECT: Fewer federal dollars will be sent to Detroit to aid the homeless

An advocate for the homeless delivered the following message to a group of supporters:

> We all know that money is allocated by the federal government, in part, according to the numbers of people in need. The census, conducted every 10 years, is supposed to tell us how many farmers we have, how many urban dwellers, and how many homeless.
>
> Unfortunately, in the 2010 census, many of the homeless were not counted in Detroit. The government told us census takers would go into the streets, into bus and train station waiting rooms, and into the shelters to count every homeless person. As advocates for the homeless, people in my organization know this was not done. Shelters were never visited. Hundreds and maybe thousands of homeless were ignored in this city alone. A serious undercount is inevitable. This undercount will cause fewer federal dollars to be spent in Detroit aiding those who need our help the most.

When used correctly, causal reasoning can be an effective persuasive tool. You must be sure that the cause-and-effect relationship is sound enough to stand up to scrutiny and criticism. To be valid, your reasoning should exhibit the following characteristics:

- The cause and effect you describe should be connected.
- The cause should be acting alone.
- The effect should not be the effect of another cause.
- The claim and evidence must be accurate (Sprague & Stuart, 1988, pp. 165–166).

To be effective, causal reasoning should never overstate. By using phrases like "This is one of several causes" or "The evidence suggests there is a cause-and-effect link," you are giving your audience a reasonable picture of a complex situation. More often than not, researchers indicate that cause-and-effect relationships are not always clear, and links may not be as simple as they seem.

Reasoning from Sign

With the argument from sign, the inference step is that the presence of an attribute can be taken as the presence of some larger condition or situation of which the attribute is a part. As you step outside in the early morning to begin jogging, the gray clouds and moist air can be interpreted as signs that the weather conditions are likely to result in a rainy day.

The public speaker who reasons from sign must do so with caution. Certainly there are signs all around us to interpret in making sense of the world, but signs are easy to misinterpret. For example, saying, "Where there's fire, there's smoke" is a strong sign relationship, but saying, "Where there's smoke, there's fire," is not so strong. Therefore, the responsible speaker must carefully test an argument before using it to persuade an audience.

Deductive Reasoning

Through deductive reasoning, we draw conclusions based on the connections between statements that serve as premises. Rather than introducing new facts, deductions enable us to rearrange the facts we already know, putting them in a form that will make our point. Deductive reasoning is the basis of police work and scientific research, enabling investigators to draw relationships between seemingly unrelated pieces of information.

At the heart of deductive reasoning is the *syllogism*, a pattern of reasoning involving a major premise, a minor premise, and a conclusion. When deductive reasoning is explicitly stated as a complete syllogism, it leads us down an inescapable logical path. The interrelationships in a syllogism can be established in a series of deductive steps:

1   STEP 1: Define the relationship between two terms.
    Major premise: Plagiarism is a form of ethical abuse.
2   STEP 2: Define a condition or special characteristic of one of the terms.
    Minor premise: Plagiarism involves using the words of another without quotations or footnotes as well as improper footnoting.
3   STEP 3: Show how a conclusion about the other term necessarily follows.
    Conclusion: Students who use the words of another, but fail to use quotations or footnotes to indicate this or who intentionally use incorrect footnotes, are guilty of an ethical abuse.

Your ability to convince your listeners depends on their acceptance of your original premises and the conclusion you draw from them. The burden of proof rests with your evidence. You must convince listeners through the strength of your supporting material to accept your premises and, by extension, your conclusion.

Sound and reasonable statements that employ inductive and deductive reasoning are the foundation for effective persuasion. More recently, scholars have recognized the story or narrative as a powerful persuasive appeal they call *mythos*.

Mythos and the Power of Narratives

Humans are storytellers by nature. Long before the written word people used narratives to capture, preserve, and pass on their cultural identity. Within the last several decades, scholars have begun to recognize the power of stories, folklore, anecdotes, legends, and myths to persuade (Wahl, 2013). Mythos is the term given when content supports a claim by reminding an audience how the claim is consistent with cultural identity.

The strength of the mythos depends on how accurately it ties into preexisting attitudes, values, histories, norms, and behaviors for a cultural, national, familial, or other collective. For example, when you were a child, you may have been told stories of the boy who cried wolf. Every culture has similar

> **Mythos**
> A term given when content supports a claim by reminding an audience how the claim is consistent with cultural identity.

Comedians like Jim Jeffries rely on narrative storytelling and mythos to create material that is relatable for their audiences.

© s_bukley/Shutterstock.com

myths and stories that define what is unique and important to that culture. In the case of the boy who cried wolf, the cultural value is honesty and the intent is to teach children that bad things happen when we lie.

When speakers use mythos effectively, they create common ground with their listeners. If you were addressing an American audience and chided them to not listen to "that little boy who cries wolf" when refuting claims of an impending economic crises, your audience will likely be receptive to your position because of the common ground you invoked through their understanding of the myth.

Mythos may not work as well when the argument is inconsistent with other, stronger cultural myths, however. So, if you offered the same retort of the boy crying wolf in response to allegations that you have engaged in illegal, illicit activities, including collusion, embezzlement, and racketeering, the audience will be less likely to agree with your claim of innocence. They are more likely instead to reject the comparison you are drawing to the myth of the boy crying wolf, and instead decide "sometimes cries are warranted, you crook."

Recall the example of Japan's emperor addressing his people following their calamity. Notice how mythos is employed in the following statement that ties the perceived virtues of a disciplined, collectivist orientation to the need for order and calm solidarity:

> I have been informed that there are many people abroad discussing how calm the Japanese have remained— helping one another, and showing disciplined conduct, even though they are in deep grief. I hope from the bottom of my heart that we can continue getting together and helping and being considerate of one another to overcome this unfortunate time.

The extent to which Emperor Akihito's audience embraces these collectivist ideals reflects a cultural value that becomes a reason for pride in their actions that are consistent with these values.

Aristotle offers the advice of employing all available means when crafting persuasive messages. Availing yourself of ethos, pathos, logos, and mythos brings a balanced, well-received message much of the time. Critical thinking is essential for both persuasive speakers and effective listeners if strong, reasonable arguments are the goal. Recognizing fallacies is an important aspect of critical thinking and can prevent poor arguments from leading us astray.

Argument Fallacies

Sometimes speakers develop arguments either intentionally or unintentionally that contain faulty logic of some kind. A *fallacy* is traditionally regarded as an argument that seems plausible but turns out on close examination to be misleading (Wahl, 2013). So whether the speaker intended to misuse evidence or reasoning to complete his/her persuasive goal, the result is that the audience is led to believe something that is not true. Following are six oft-used fallacies.

Attacking the person. Also known as *ad hominem* ("to the man"), this occurs when a speaker attacks the person rather than the substance of the person's argument. A personal attack is often a cover-up for lack of evidence or solid reasoning. Name calling and labeling are common with this fallacy, and the public is exposed to the ad hominem fallacy regularly through political shenanigans. While fallacies do not meet ethical standards, politicians have been elected based on attacks on their opponents rather than refuting stances on issues.

RED HERRING. A **red herring** occurs when a speaker attempts to divert the attention of the audience from the matter at hand. Going off on a tangent, changing the focus of the argument, engaging in personal attacks, or appealing to popular prejudice are all examples of the red herring fallacy.

The red herring fallacy appears regularly in interpersonal communication. A son might be told to "take your shoes off the table," and retort with, "these are boots, not shoes," thus changing the focus of the argument from the issue to the object. In a public speaking environment, red herrings are relatively common. For example, suppose an audience member asks a candidate at a political debate the following: "Do you realize your proposal to bring in a new megastore will result in the loss of livelihood for owners of smaller businesses in town who are active, contributing members to this community? A red herring response might be: "I think everyone likes to shop for bargains!"

HASTY GENERALIZATION. A **hasty generalization** is a fallacy based on quantity of data. A faulty argument occurs because the sample chosen is too small or is in some way not representative. Therefore, any conclusion based on this information is flawed. Stereotypes about people are common examples of this fallacy. Imagine getting a B on a test, then and asking the students on your right and left what grade they received. Finding out they also received a B on the test, you tell your roommates that "everybody received a B on the test."

Attacking

Occurs when a speaker attacks the person rather than the substance of the person's argument.

Red herring

Occurs when a speaker attempts to divert the attention of the audience from the matter at hand.

Hasty generalization

A fallacy based on quantity of data.

False cause

When a speaker uses a fallacy to point out that because one event happened before another event, the first event caused the second event.

False analogy

Compares two things that are not really comparable.

Slippery slope

This fallacy claims there will be a chain reaction that will end in some dire consequence.

FALSE CAUSE. A false cause is also known as *post hoc ergo propter hoc* ("after this, therefore, because of this"). The speaker using this fallacy points out that because one event happened before another event, the first event caused the second event. For example, a speaker might say that, "Germs are more likely to spread outside of the work environment, because more people call in sick on Mondays than on any other day of the week."

FALSE ANALOGY. A false analogy compares two things that are not really comparable. You may have heard someone say, "You're comparing apples and oranges," or worse, "You're comparing apples to footballs." In the first case, you may be making a faulty comparison because apples and oranges, while both fruits, are different. In the second case, the listener believes you are comparing two things with nothing in common.

SLIPPERY SLOPE. A speaker using this fallacy claims that if we take even one step onto the slippery slope, we will end up sliding all the way to the bottom; that we can't stop. In other words, there will be a chain reaction that will end in some dire consequence.

Focusing Persuasive Messages: Goals, Aims, and Claims

Since Aristotle, some researchers have emphasized the outcomes or the results of persuasion. The definition of persuasion we prefer emphasizes the process of attempting to change or reinforce attitudes, values, beliefs, or behavior (Wahl, 2013). We are not talking about coercion, bribes, or pressure to conform. Persuasion is accomplished through ethical communication. Careful consideration of the goals of persuasion, the aims of your speech, and the type of proposition you are making helps focus your persuasive message.

Goals of Persuasion

Critical to the success of any persuasive effort is a clear sense of what you are trying to accomplish. As a speaker, you must define for yourself your overall persuasive goal and the narrower persuasive aim. The two overall goals of persuasion are *to address attitudes* and *to move an audience to action*.

President Obama successfully persuaded lawmakers to bail out the failing U.S. automotive industry.

© Joseph Sohm/Shutterstock.com

SPEECHES THAT FOCUS ON ATTITUDES. In this type of speech, your goal is to convince an audience to share your views on a topic (e.g., "The tuition at this college is too high" or "Too few Americans bother to vote"). The way you approach your goal depends on the nature of your audience.

When dealing with a negative audience, you face the challenge of trying to change your listeners' opinions. The more change you hope to achieve, the harder your persuasive task. In other words, asking listeners to agree that U.S. automakers need the support of U.S. consumers to survive in the world market is easier than asking the same audience to agree that every American who buys a foreign car should be penalized through a special tax.

By contrast, when you address an audience that shares your point of view, your job is to reinforce existing attitudes (e.g., "U.S. automakers deserve our support"). When your audience has not yet formed an opinion, your message must be geared to presenting persuasive evidence. You may want to explain to your audience, for example, the economic necessity of buying U.S. products.

Speaking Well with Technology Is an Essential for Excellence

In deeply historical cities like Florence, Italy, officials are heavily challenged to keep graffiti off the many national landmarks, especially those from the Italian Renaissance period. Both locals and tourists alike seem motivated to leave their own mark on invaluable monuments. To combat this trend, many institutions in Florence are trying a new persuasive tactic to discourage graffiti: smartphone apps that allow anyone to create and share "digital" graffiti.

"It's actually working beyond our wildest expectations," says Pietro Polsinelli, a member of the technical team at the Opera di Santa Maria del Fiore (Leveille, 2016). The new app, called Autography, gives visitors to monuments the ability to post graffiti online instead of the centuries-old marble walls. Users of the app can snap a picture of any monument and create personalized digital graffiti to superimpose over the image. Polsinelli notes that the number of graffiti on the monument walls has been decreasing dramatically as of late. The desire to "leave a mark" permanently is satisfied by the app's ability to publish users' graffiti in an online gallery (barring ones that contain insults or inappropriate material). According to Polsinelli, the context of the technology is what makes it so effective.

Although this chapter generally focuses on the speaking dimensions of persuasive techniques, you should be aware of the ways technology can persuade us to certain actions or ways of thinking. How often have you used your smartphone to "check in" to events, businesses, or landmarks? As the global community continues to adapt and expand upon communication technology, it falls on communication professionals like yourself to apply traditional persuasive techniques to a new medium.

SPEECHES THAT REQUIRE ACTION. Here your goal is to bring about actual change. You ask your listeners to make a purchase, sign a petition, attend a rally, write to Congress, attend a lecture, and so on. The effectiveness of your message is defined by the actions your audience takes.

Motivating your listeners to act is perhaps the hardest goal you face as a speaker, since it requires attention to the connection between attitudes and behavior. Studies have shown that what people feel is not necessarily what they do. Ahmad may be favorably inclined to purchase a BMW, but still not buy it. Jill may have a negative attitude toward birth control pills, but still use them.

Once you establish your overall persuasive goals you must then decide on your persuasive aim.

Persuasive Aims

Determining your persuasive goal is a critical first step. Next, you must define the narrower persuasive aim or the type and direction of the change you seek. Four persuasive aims define the nature of your overall persuasive goal.

ADOPTION. When you want your audience to start doing something, your persuasive aim is to urge the audience to adopt a particular idea or plan. As a spokesperson for the American Cancer Society, you may deliver the following message: "I urge every woman over the age of 40 to get a regular mammogram."

Adoption
When you want your audience to start doing something.

CONTINUANCE. Sometimes your listeners are already doing the thing you want them to do. In this case, your goal is to reinforce this action. For example, the same spokesperson might say:

Continuance
When your listeners are already doing the thing you want them to do.

> I am delighted to be speaking to this organization because of the commitment of every member to stop smoking. I urge all of you to maintain your commitment to be smoke free for the rest of your life.

Speeches that urge continuance are necessary when the group is under pressure to change. In this case, the spokesperson realized that many reformed smokers constantly fight the urge to begin smoking again.

DISCONTINUANCE. You attempt to persuade your listeners to stop doing something you disagree with.

Discontinuance
An attempt to persuade your listeners to stop doing something.

> I can tell by looking around that many people in this room spend hours sitting in the sun. I want to share with you a grim fact. The evidence is unmistakable that there is a direct connection between exposure to the sun and the deadliest of all skin cancers—malignant melanoma.

Deterrence

Your goal is to convince your listeners not to start something.

DETERRENCE. In this case, your goal is avoidance. You want to convince your listeners not to start something, as in the following example:

> We have found that exposure to asbestos can cause cancer 20 or 30 years later. If you have flaking asbestos insulation in your home, don't remove it yourself. Call in experts who have the knowledge and equipment to remove the insulation, protecting themselves as well as you and your family. Be sure you are not going to deal with an unscrupulous contractor who will probably send in unqualified and unprotected workers likely to do a shoddy job.

Speeches that focus on deterrence respond to problems that can be avoided. These messages are delivered when a persuasive speaker determines something is highly threatening or likely to result in disaster. The speaker may try to bring about some sort of effective block or barrier to minimize, if not eliminate, the threat or danger. New homeowners, for example, may find themselves listening to persuasive presentations about the purchase of a home security system. The thrust of such a persuasive speech is the need to prevent burglary through use of an effective and economical security system.

Types of Persuasive Claims

Within the context of these persuasive goals and aims, you must decide the type of persuasive message you want to deliver. Are you dealing with an issue of fact, value, or policy? To decide, look at your thesis statement. In persuasive speeches, the thesis statement is phrased as a proposition that must be proved.

For example, if your thesis statement was "All college students should be required to take a one-credit physical education course each year," you would be working with a proposition of policy. If instead, your thesis statement was "Taking a physical education course each year will improve the college experience," this would be a proposition of value.

Propositions are necessary because persuasion always involves more than one point of view. If yours were the only way of thinking, persuasion would be unnecessary. Because your audience is faced with differing opinions, your goal is to present your opinion in the most effective way. The three major types of propositions are those of *fact*, *value*, and *policy*.

PROPOSITION OF FACT. A proposition of fact suggests the existence of something. You try to prove or disprove some statement. Because facts, like beauty, are often in the eye of the beholder, you may have to persuade your listeners that your interpretation of a situation, event, or concept is accurate. Like a lawyer in a courtroom, you have to convince people to accept your version of the truth. Here are four examples of facts that would require proof:

1 Water fluoridation can lead to health problems.
2 College is not the place for all students.
3 Hunting is a way to control the deer population.
4 American corporations are not paying enough in income taxes.

When dealing with propositions of fact, you must convince your audience that your evaluation is based on widely accepted standards. For example, if you are trying to prove that water fluoridation leads to health problems, you might point to a research article that cites the Environmental Protection Agency (EPA) warning that long-term exposure to excessive fluoridation can lead to joint stiffness, pain, and weak bones. You may also support your proposition by citing another research study that reports that children who are exposed to too much fluoridation may end up having teeth that are pitted and/or permanently stained.

Informative speakers become persuasive speakers when they cross the line from presenting facts to presenting facts within the context of a point of view. The informative speaker lets listeners decide on a position based on their own analysis of the facts. By contrast, the persuasive speaker draws the conclusion for them.

PROPOSITION OF VALUE. Values are deep-seated ideals that determine what we consider good or bad, moral or immoral, satisfying or unsatisfying, proper or improper, wise or foolish, valuable or invaluable, and so on. Persuasive speeches that deal with propositions of value are assertions rooted in judgments based on these ideals. The speaker's goal is to prove the worth of an evaluative statement, as in the following examples:

1 It is *wrong* to criminalize recreational or medicinal use of marijuana.
2 Violence in professional sports is *unjustified*.
3 Plagiarizing to complete an assignment is *dishonest*.

When you use words that can be considered judgments or evaluations, such as those italicized above, you are making a proposition of value. When designing a persuasive speech based on a proposition of value, it is

Proposition of fact

Persuading your listeners that your interpretation of a situation, event, or concept is accurate.

Proposition of value

Assertions rooted in judgments based on ideals.

important to present facts, statistics, or examples to support your points. Also, using expert opinion and testimony will provide credible support.

Proposition of policy

Easily recognizable by their use of the word "should."

PROPOSITION OF POLICY. Propositions of policy propose a course of action. Usually, the speaker is arguing that something should or should not be done. Propositions of policy are easily recognizable by their use of "should," "ought to," "have to," or "must":

1 Campus safety should be reevaluated by the college administration.
2 The same general student academic standards ought to apply to student-athletes, too.
3 Collegiate athletes should be paid.
4 Animals must not be used for product testing in scientific laboratories.

In a policy speech, speakers convince listeners of both the need for change and what that change should be. They also give people reasons to continue listening and, in the end, to agree with their position and, sometimes, to take action.

Propositions of policy have both fact and value aspects to them. Facts need to support the need for the course of action, and values are inherently part of the policy statement. For example, in a speech about using animals for product testing, the person giving the speech against it most likely values animals, and believes in the humane and ethical treatment of animals.

Presidential candidates like Bernie Sanders are tasked with persuading voters to vote for them based on their positions on government policy.

© Juli Hansen/Shutterstock.com

A speaker's persuasive appeal, in summary, derives from the audience's sense of the speaker's credibility as well as from appeals to an audience's emotion and logic. At times, one persuasive element may be more important to one audience than others. Many speakers try to convince audiences based on logical appeals, emotional appeals, myth appeals, and their image and credibility as a speaker. The most effective speakers consider their audience's expectations and intended outcomes. Now we turn our attention to common techniques used to organize persuasive messages.

SPEAKING EXCELLENCE IN YOUR CAREER

In the field of marketing, the primary goal can be defined as persuading consumers to buy an organization's products or services. Traditional marketing philosophy has encouraged marketers to minimize or eliminate interruptions when they deliver persuasive messages. Eliminating distractions is thought to increase consumers' attention and processing of persuasive messages. However, several studies conducted across different experimental contexts have revealed that interruptions that temporarily disrupt a persuasive message can increase consumers' processing of that message (Kupor & Tormala, 2015). Researchers Daniella Kupor and Zakary Tormala analyze the validity of these findings.

Across five studies, Kupor and Tormala found that interruptions increased message processing by heightening consumer curiosity. They found these effects to be consistent despite significantly different contexts (and materials presented to consumers) in all five research articles. In two studies the distraction took place while a video was loading, one involved a human interruption, and two others involved a combination of both. The persuasive message in four of the studies involved a consumer product, while the fifth involved a public policy issue. Since both the type of interruption and the nature of the persuasive message differed so significantly, the researchers posit that a generalization can be drawn that indicates message interruption can enhance the persuasive effects (Kupor & Tormala, 2015). However, the researchers caution that more experimental studies are needed to measure the possible negative consequences of interrupted persuasive messages.

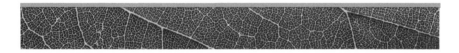

▣ Organizing Persuasive Speeches

Problem–solution pattern

Presenting an audience with a problem and then examining one or more likely solutions.

Cause-and-effect pattern

Arranging main points into causes and effects.

Earlier in this text, we presented different ways to organize your speech. Certain organizational patterns are unique to the persuasive speech pattern. In the chapter on organizing and outlining, we presented the **problem–solution pattern**, which involves presenting an audience with a problem and then examining one or more likely solutions. For a persuasive speech, the speaker persuades the audience to accept one particular solution. We also noted the **cause-and-effect pattern**, which entails arranging main points into causes and effects. The persuasive speaker constructs a case for the audience that persuades them to accept the cause–effect connection.

In the following we present three more possible organizational patterns: comparative advantage, criteria satisfaction, and Monroe's Motivated Sequence. Our primary focus is on the latter, since this pattern follows the normal process of human reasoning as it presents a clear way to move through the problem-solving process.

Comparative Advantages

Comparative-advantages organizational pattern

Place alternative solutions to a problem side-by-side and discuss the advantages and disadvantages of each.

A **comparative-advantages organizational pattern** is useful when the audience already agrees there is a problem that needs a solution. The problem may not be grave, but it is one that may have several potentially acceptable solutions. As a speaker using this pattern, you try to convince the audience that your plan is the best. You place alternative solutions or plans side-by-side and discuss the advantages and disadvantages of each. To some extent, this organizational pattern can be viewed as a structured process of elimination.

For example, Lauren, a high school senior, is trying to decide which college to attend. She has prior approval from her parents to look at both in-state and out-of-state schools. Lauren, a minority student who wants to pursue international study and work possibilities, decides that she wants to attend an out-of-state school, and chooses the comparative-advantages approach when persuading her parents to accept her choice.

COLLEGE 1: INSTATE U

Advantages: Less expensive, close to home, friends are also attending, small to medium-sized college

Disadvantages: Too close to home (might go home too often), school's reputation is OK, but not great, might not make new friends, lack of diversity

Advantages: Within four hours of home, diverse population, large university that offers wide range of diverse majors (can major in Folklore), large study abroad program; ability to live in international dorm, many cultural and entertainment possibilities; good scholarship possibilities

Disadvantages: Significantly more expensive, campus is large, possible safety concern

Since Lauren's parents are prepared to pay out-of-state tuition, Lauren can construct a persuasive argument making the comparison between these schools. Although this example is an interpersonal one (persuading her parents, not a large audience), if we switched the scenario to Lauren being a college student at Outstate U speaking to a group of students at her high school, the same pattern could be applied.

Using a comparative-advantages pattern, you can compare two possibilities, or you can compare several possibilities. For example, if you were talking about how to solve the energy crisis, you could compare solar, wind, and nuclear power to convince your audience that one method is superior to the others.

Criteria-Satisfaction

When using the **criteria-satisfaction pattern**, you demonstrate how your idea has the features your audience needs. It is a clear pattern that is useful when you have an audience opposed to your idea. You can help elicit a "yes" response from your audience through identification of criteria they find acceptable. You indicate the necessary criteria and show how your solution meets or exceeds the criteria.

Consider a "calendar committee" trying to convince the local school board to change the dates for beginning and ending the school year. The committee might argue that any solution should meet the following criteria:

- Acceptable to teachers
- Acceptable to parents
- Cost effective (not have to turn on air conditioning too soon)
- Enhances education or at least does not interfere with learning environment
- Includes appropriate start and ending dates for each term
- Balances mandatory and optional vacation and teacher institute dates

Criteria-satisfaction pattern
Demonstrating how your idea has the features your audience needs.

Based on these criteria, the committee could present the solution to the school board that meets all these criteria. With the criteria-solution pattern, it is important that you find criteria your audience will accept. For example, if the committee identified one of the criteria as "starts as late as possible and ends as early as possible," that might not have been viewed as an acceptable criterion by the school board. Similarly, criteria may differ, depending on circumstances. In a small college town, having spring break and holiday breaks at the same time the college has them may be an appropriate criterion, but in a large city that has several colleges and universities, this may not be as important.

Monroe's Motivated Sequence

As emphasized throughout this text, effective communication requires connecting with your audience. Audience awareness is particularly important in speeches to persuade, for without taking into account the mental stages your audience passes through, your persuasion may not succeed. The *motivated sequence*, a widely used method for organizing persuasive speeches developed by Monroe (1965), is rooted in traditional rhetoric and shaped by modern psychology.

Monroe's motivated sequence focuses on five steps to motivate your audience that follow the normal pattern of human thought from attention to action. If you want only to persuade your audience that a problem exists, then only the first two steps are necessary. If your audience is keenly aware of a problem, then you may focus only on the last three steps. Most of the time, however, all five steps are necessary, and they should be followed in order.

Step 1: Attention. Persuasion is impossible without attention. Your first step is to capture the minds of your listeners and convince them that you have something important to say. Many possibilities were discussed in Chapter 7. For example, addressing the United Nations regarding prospects for peace in the Middle East, Israeli Prime Minister Benjamin Netanyahu (2009) began his speech by saying:

> ...Netanyahu (2009) began his speech by saying that he was speaking on behalf of the Jewish state. He lashed out against the President of Iran, whom he said was insisting that the Holocaust was a lie.

Israeli Prime Minister Benjamin Netanyahu often must motivate the people of his country in times of crisis.

The prime minister's keen use of irony and strong language surely engaged all who were listening. His opening also establishes his credibility and introduces his topic. In your attention step, you must catch your audience's attention, introduce and make your topic relevant, and establish your credibility.

STEP 2: NEED. In the need step, you describe the problem you will address in your speech. You hint at or suggest a need in your introduction, then state it in a way that accurately reflects your specific purpose. You motivate listeners to care about the problem by making clear a problem exists, it is significant, and it affects them. You illustrate need by using examples, intensifying it through the use of carefully selected additional supporting material, and *linking* it directly to the audience. Too often the inexperienced speaker who uses the motivated sequence will pass through the need step in haste to get to the third step, the satisfaction step.

The need step has four parts. It (1) establishes there is a problem, (2) explains the problem, (3) proves that the problem is serious, and (4) connects the problem to specific needs the audience holds dear.

STEP 3: SATISFACTION. The satisfaction step presents a solution to the problem you have just described. You offer a proposition you want your audience to adopt and act on. A clear explanation as well as statistics, testimony, examples, and other types of support ensure that your audience understands what you propose. Show your audience how your proposal meets the needs you presented earlier in your speech. You may use several forms of support accompanied by visuals or audiovisual aids.

An audience is usually impressed if you can show where and how a similar proposal has worked elsewhere. Before you move to the fourth step, meet objections that you predict some listeners may hold. We are all familiar with the persuader who attempts to sell us a product or service and wants us to believe it is well worth the price and within our budget. In fact, a considerable amount of sales appeal today aims at selling us a payment we can afford as a means to purchasing the product, whether it is an automobile, a vacation, or some other attractive item. If we can afford the monthly payment, a major objection has been met.

Here is how a citizen and mother suggested solving the problem of head injuries in Little League baseball:

> Well, "some sort" of protection has been developed. *American Health* reports that Home Safe, Inc. has found an all-star solution. Teams like the Atlee Little Leaguers in Mechanicsville, Virginia, have solved many of their safety problems by wearing face shields like this one [shown].
>
> This molded plastic shield snaps onto the earflaps of the standard batter's helmet. Most youth teams require the use of a batter's helmet, but with this shield they could add complete facial protection, including the eyes, for a cost of under $15 per shield. Some might say that is expensive, but former Little Leaguer Daniel Schwartz's head injuries have cost his family $23,000 so far.

In sum, a strong satisfaction step involves clearly stating an acceptable solution, offering strong evidence supporting the solution, demonstrating how the solution solves the problem, proving that it is a workable solution, and clarifying how the solution will satisfy the audience's unresolved needs.

STEP 4: VISUALIZATION. The visualization step compels listeners to picture themselves either benefiting or suffering from adopting or rejecting your proposal. It focuses on powerful imagery to create a vision of the future if your proposal is adopted or, just as important, if it is rejected. It may also contrast these two visions, strengthening the attractiveness of your proposal by showing what will happen if no action is taken.

Positive visualization is specific and concrete. Your goal is to help listeners see themselves under the conditions you describe. You want them to experience enjoyment and satisfaction. In contrast, negative visualization focuses on what will happen without your plan. Here you describe the discomfort with conditions that would exist. Whichever method you choose, make your listeners feel part of the future. For example, here would be an appropriate visualization step:

> Imagine yourself on a quiet and lazy summer afternoon watching your own child, a niece, a nephew, a cousin, or a neighborhood friend up at bat in an exciting youth league baseball game. Think about the comfort you will experience when you see that she or he has the proper safety equipment on so that there is no possibility that a speeding baseball will take his or her life, or result in any permanent disability. See for a moment the face and the form of a child enthusiastically awaiting the pitch and see as well this child effectively shielded from impact that could come from a missed pitch.

The visualization step can be enhanced with powerful visuals. Movie clips, sound tracks, interviews, and memorable photos have all been used successfully to help listeners fully engage their imagination in the future scenario.

STEP 5: ACTION. The action step acts as the conclusion of your speech. Here you tell your listeners what you want them to do or, if action is unnecessary, the point of view you want them to share. You may have to explain the specific actions you want and the timing for these actions. This step is most effective when immediate action is sought.

Many students find the call to action a difficult part of the persuasive speech. They are reluctant to make an explicit request for action. Can you imagine a politician failing to ask people for their vote? Such a candidate would surely lose an election. When sales representatives have difficulty in closing a deal because they are unable to ask consumers to buy their products, they do not last long in sales. Persuasion is more likely to result when direction is clear and action is the goal. Here is how we might conclude our Little League example:

> We must realize, however, that it may be awhile before this equipment scores a home run, so now it is your turn

up at bat. If you are personally interested in protecting these young ball players, spread the word about these injuries, especially to businesses that sponsor youth teams. Encourage them to purchase safety equipment for the teams and then to sponsor them only on the condition that the equipment be used. Additionally, I ask for your signature on the petition I am circulating. This will send a loud message to our representatives in Congress.

To create closure and reinforce the need to act, our final comment might be:

Now that we have discovered how children are being seriously injured and even killed while playing baseball, I know you agree that, given the children's lack of skill, we need to mandate the use of face shields. So take them out to the ball game, but make it one that children can play safely, because children may be dying to play baseball, but they should never die because of it.

From *Winning Orations of the Interstate Oratorical Association* by C. Spurling. Copyright © 1992 by Interstate Oratorical Association. Reprinted by permission.

In review, remember the five-step sequence if you want to lead your audience from attention to action. The motivated sequence is effective but, like all tools of persuasion, can be misused. The line between use and abuse of persuasive tools warrants further examination.

Ethics and Persuasive Speaking

The importance of ethics is stressed both implicitly and explicitly throughout this textbook. Ethics provide standards of conduct that guide us. The ethics of persuasion call for honesty, care, thoroughness, openness, and a concern for the audience without manipulative intent. The end does *not* justify the means at all costs. In a world as complex as ours, one marked in part by unethical as well as ethical persuaders, the moral imperative is to speak ethically.

The choice between right and wrong is not simple. Informing people about a particular topic assumes providing knowledge to an audience that, in turn, learns more about the topic. In a persuasive speech, however, you are asking listeners to think or act in ways called for to achieve your specific purpose.

As members of an audience, many of the choices we make are inconsequential, such as which soft drink to buy at a convenience store or which magazine to read in a doctor's waiting room. Far more important, however, is the decision to reject our religious, social, or political beliefs in order to embrace new ones. Even the purchase of an expensive automobile is a considerable decision for us when weighed against the selection of a soft drink.

ETHICS MATTER

Shirley is the Human Resources Director for her company. A major part of her job involves presenting news about policy changes (good or bad) to her employees. Recently, Shirley's company implemented a policy that requires salaried employees to work multiple weekends a month without an increase in pay or vacation time. As Shirley contemplated the best way to present this news to her employees, she came across an internal company memo that covered a new state law going into effect. The new law requires companies (like Shirley's) to increase certain medical benefits to full-time employees. Although the company is already mandated by the state to comply, Shirley presents the news about increased medical coverage as a reward for the extra hours being worked to her employees. Because the new rules didn't gain significant media attention, Shirley's employees remained unaware of the state requirement and saw the new weekend policy as an even trade.

QUESTIONS TO CONSIDER:

1. What ethical concern did Shirley breach in persuading her employees to accept the new weekend work policy?
2. What possible backlash could Shirley face if word got out that the new medical coverage was a state requirement and not a reward for working more hours?
3. What are some other ways Shirley have presented the new policy in a more ethical manner?

As a speaker, you must decide not only what to tell your audience but what you should avoid saying. Be mindful of your audience's needs and values, and weigh benefits of successful persuasion against possible risks or harms. If a doctor, for example, prescribes a medication for a patient that results in the patient having to fight addiction to the medication, was that an appropriate act on the part of the doctor? Depending upon the circumstances, it may be unethical.

As you prepare for any persuasive speech, respect your audience. Be informed, truthful, and clear about your motives, use various appeals ethically, avoid misleading your audience through faulty argument, and work to create your most effective, honest persuasive message.

ESSENTIALS FOR EXCELLENCE

In this chapter, we have examined the elements of persuasive speech as well as the foundations of creating effective persuasive messages. We have learned about the hierarchy of needs that people want fulfilled, as well as sequences needed to motivate an audience toward your persuasive message. To conclude this chapter, it is necessary to offer practical advice that can enhance your persuasive presentations. Adam Frankel, Senior Speechwriter to President Barack Obama, offers several tips to writing a persuasive speech on any topic.

Write like you talk.
A speech is meant to be spoken, not read (Frankel, 2015). Use short words and write short sentences. Try to avoid awkward speech constructions that might cause you to stumble over your words.

Structure matters.
The order of the points you wish to make are as important as the words themselves. Order of points matters because arguments that are clear and logical are more likely to be persuasive. Lists (like this one) are one way to create the structure of a speech.

Be authentic.
Think about the moment you are in, and speak something that feels true. Don't rely on soundbites and generic language; simply say something you believe in as simply as you can. Sharing personal stories can help you find your voice and create a connection with the audience (Frankel, 2015).

![] WHAT YOU'VE LEARNED:

Now that you have studied the chapter, you should be able to:

1. Identify the three different levels on which persuasive communication takes place.
   - Persuasion takes place on an *interpersonal level*. This can include convincing a friend to go to dinner or persuading someone to help you move.
   - Persuasion takes place on a *professional level*. This could involve persuading your supervisor that you deserve a promotion, or convincing your company to fund a business trip.
   - Persuasion takes place on a *societal level*. Sending a letter to your legislator to vote in favor of a health bill, or persuading your local city council to enact curbside recycling are examples of societal persuasion.
2. Define the five levels of Maslow's Hierarchy of Needs.
   - Physiological needs. The foundation of the hierarchy includes our biological needs for food, water, oxygen, procreation, and rest.
   - Safety needs. These include the need for security, freedom from fear and attack, a home that offers tranquillity and comfort, and a means for earning a living.
   - Belongingness and love needs. These needs refer to our drive for affiliation, friendship, and love.
   - Esteem needs. Esteem needs include the need to be seen as worthy and competent and to have the respect of others.
   - Self-actualization needs. People who reach the top of the hierarchy seek to fulfill their highest potential through personal growth, creativity, self-awareness and knowledge, social responsibility, and responsiveness to challenge.
3. Recognize the different types of argument fallacies.
   - Attacking a person (also known as *ad hominem*) occurs when a speaker attacks the person rather than the substance of the person's argument. A personal attack is often a cover-up for lack of evidence or solid reasoning.
   - A hasty generalization is a fallacy based on quantity of data. A faulty argument occurs because the sample chosen is too small or is in some way not representative. Therefore, any conclusion based on this information is flawed.
   - False cause fallacies occur when a speaker points out that because one event happened before another event, the first event caused the second event.
   - A false analogy compares two things that are not really comparable.
   - A slippery slope fallacy warns that a course of action will set off a chain reaction that will end in some dire consequence.
4. How to organize a persuasive speech using Monroe's Motivated Sequence.
   - Step 1: Attention. Persuasion is impossible without attention. Your first step is to capture the minds of your listeners and convince them that you have something important to say.
   - Step 2: Need. In the need step, you describe the problem you will address in your speech. You hint at or suggest a need in your introduction, then state it in a way that accurately reflects your specific purpose.
   - Step 3: Satisfaction. The satisfaction step presents a solution to the problem you have just described. You offer a proposition you want your audience to adopt and act on.
   - Step 4: Visualization. The visualization step compels listeners to picture themselves either benefiting or suffering from adopting or rejecting your proposal. It focuses on powerful imagery to create a vision of the future if your proposal is adopted or, just as important, if it is rejected.
   - Step 5: Action. The action step acts as the conclusion of your speech. Here you tell your listeners what you want them to do or, if action is unnecessary, the point of view you want them to share.

Key Terms

adoption, 417
attacking, 413
cause-and-effect pattern, 422
claim, 407
comparative-advantages
 organizational pattern, 422
continuance, 417
criteria-satisfaction pattern, 423
data, 407
deductive reasoning, 407

deterrence, 418
discontinuance, 417
ethos, 401
false analogy, 414
false cause, 414
hasty generalization, 413
inductive reasoning, 407
logos, 406
mythos, 411
opposed audience, 398

pathos, 404
problem–solution pattern, 422
proposition of fact, 419
proposition of policy, 420
proposition of value, 419
red herring, 413
slippery slope, 414
supportive audience, 397
uncommitted audience, 398
warrant, 407

Reflect

1   What are the dimensions of credibility, and how important is credibility to the overall effectiveness of a persuasive speech? What strategies can improve low credibility?

2   How would you define persuasion, persuasive goals, and persuasive aims? Illustrate your definitions with specific examples.

3   Why is the motivated sequence audience-centered? How does the motivated sequence relate to Maslow's Hierarchy of Needs?

4   When would comparative-advantages or criteria-satisfaction be more appropriate organizational patterns than Monroe's Motivated Sequence?

5   What are ethical, logical, emotional, and mythic appeals? How are these appeals distinct, yet interrelated?

6   How important is evidence in a persuasive speech? How important are ethics in persuasive speaking? Does the importance depend on the audience and its shared needs and expectations?

Review Questions

1   A(n) _____ audience is one that agrees with you.

2   A(n) _____ audience is one that does not agree with you, is not friendly or sympathetic, and will search for flaws in your argument.

3   A(n) _____ audience is one that is neither friendly nor hostile, but most likely not sympathetic.

4   _____ refers to speaker credibility.

5   Persuading through emotional appeals involves the use of _____.

6   _____ uses an appeal that is rational and reasonable based on the evidence provided.

7   When you generalize from specific examples and draw conclusions from what you observe, you are using _____.

8   When you draw conclusions based on the connections between statements that serve as premises, you are using _____.

9   _____ is a term given when content supports a claim by reminding an audience how the claim is consistent with cultural identity.

10 _____ occurs when a speaker attacks the person rather than the substance of the person's argument.

11 A(n)_____ occurs when a speaker attempts to divert the attention of the audience from the matter at hand.

12 A fallacy based on quantity of data is known as a(n) _____.

13 When a speaker uses a fallacy to point out that because one event happened before another event, the first event caused the second event, this is known as _____.

14 A(n) _____ compares two things that are not really comparable.

15 A(n) _____ fallacy claims there will be a chain reaction that will end in some dire consequence.

16 When you want your audience to start doing something, you are persuading _____.

17 _____ is when your listeners are already doing the thing you want them to do.

18 An attempt to persuade your listeners to stop doing something is known as _____.

19 _____ tasks you to convince your listeners to not start something.

20 When you persuade your listeners that your interpretation of a situation, event, or concept is accurate, you are offering a(n) _____.

21 A _____ involves persuading your listeners based on deep-seated beliefs.

22 _____ requires a speaker to present an audience with a problem and then examine one or more likely solutions.

23 Arranging main points into causes and effects creates a(n) _____.

24 A(n) _____ organizational pattern places alternative solutions to a problem side-by-side and discusses the advantages and disadvantages of each.

25 Demonstrating how your idea has the features your audience needs forms a(n) _____ pattern.

434

Stephen Colbert has given several notable commencement speeches throughout his career.

CHAPTER THIRTEEN
SPECIAL-OCCASION SPEAKING

OUTLINE

▰ WHAT YOU'LL LEARN

After studying this chapter, you should be able to:

1. Identify the guidelines for speeches of introduction.
2. Understand the importance of commemorative speeches.
3. Define and describe an after-dinner speech.
4. Know the strategies to give an effective acceptance speech.

SPEAKING IN CONTEXT

Wake Forest University's Class of 2015 was treated to one of the most memorable commencement speeches in recent history, courtesy of Stephen Colbert. Colbert, host of *The Late Show*, masterfully blended sage advice with humorous sound bites in his presentation to the recent college graduates.

"It's time to say goodbye to the person we've become, who we've worked so hard to perfect, and to make some crucial decisions in becoming who we're going to be," said Colbert. "For me, I'll have to figure out how to do an hour-long show every night. And you at some point will have to sleep. I am told the Adderall wears off eventually." (Bradley, 2015).

Colbert encouraged students to set their own standards and to be fair when evaluating themselves. He called for students to never relent, even when detractors tell them that improvement is impossible. Colbert kept his audience engaged with moving earnestness peppered with bits of hilarity.

As you learn about different types of special occasion speeches, remember the importance of blending speaking styles. Stephen Colbert's speech resonates years later because it combines many of the strategies you have learned during your communication studies. No matter what the occasion, be sure you make the moment special.

Special-Occasion Speeches

As with other forms of public speaking, a speech delivered on a special occasion can rise to the level of the extraordinary. Certainly as a college student, few ceremonies are likely to be more important than your commencement ceremony. In the following excerpt from his 2010 commencement address at Syracuse University, CEO of JPMorgan Chase Jamie Dimon acknowledged the mixed feelings individuals have about Wall Street executives by setting up the speech in the following manner:

> Graduating today means you are through with final exams, through with submitting term papers, all that nervousness, the cold sweat of sleepless nights preparing to answer seemingly impossible questions. Well, that's a feeling we banking executives know pretty well these days—we call it "testifying before Congress."

> I am honored to be here today, but I also know that some of your fellow students have raised questions about me being your commencement speaker... Today I will talk about what it takes to be accountable, in the hope that it might be valuable to you in years to come.

Like all good ceremonial speeches, Dimon expressed sincere feelings about the event and his audience. As his method for setting the tone, he chose humor—but only briefly. He quickly moved on to address the banking controversy head-on, and his interest in accountability is relevant to an audience of college graduates.

To parents and students alike, commencement is, indeed, a special occasion. Other special occasions, to name a few, include marriages, anniversaries, deaths, retirements, award ceremonies, special events, and important dates in history. Some speeches may include a little humor or even a great deal of humor; others do not. An overriding principle to remember is that, no matter how short or long, a special-occasion speech has a specific purpose; it should be designed to achieve some objective.

Seven General Guidelines for Special-Occasion Speeches

Most likely, you will be called on to give a special-occasion speech at least once in your lifetime. Special-occasion speeches, while aptly named, are given every day. To prepare you to provide an impromptu toast or say a few words of praise or thanks, this chapter provides some general suggestions for the special-occasion presentation, and then offers guidelines for several of the most common speaking situations.

Whether you are introducing a guest speaker at your church, presenting an award honoring the volunteer of the year, or toasting the marriage of your sister, the following seven guidelines will help you decide what to say and how best to say it. Although differences exist among the types of special-occasion speeches, as addressed later in this chapter, these guidelines apply in most cases.

1. Make Sure Your Speech Meets Expectations

Ceremonies and the speeches that mark them are surrounded by sets of expectations. Mourners listening to a eulogy, graduates listening to a commencement address, and members of a wedding party toasting the new couple expect certain words, gestures, and acts. Do not disappoint them. The words you choose to mark the occasion should remind people of the event they are commemorating. Even if you are sure everyone realizes the reason for your speech, explain it anyway. Following are a few brief examples of special-occasion speeches and some corresponding expectations:

- PRESENTING AN AWARD. Audiences expect the speaker to mention the background and purpose of the award and reasons the recipient was chosen.
- A SPEECH OF ACCEPTANCE. Audiences expect the speaker to acknowledge the people who deliberated on the award, and to say thank you to individuals who bestowed the award and people who helped the recipient reach this level.
- A EULOGY. Audiences expect to hear some background information on the deceased, a few stories about the person's life, and acknowledgment of the mourners' grief.
- TOAST. Audiences expect the speech to be brief, to identify the purpose of the toast, and to provide some memorable comment that reflects well on the occasion or individuals involved.

2. Tailor Your Remarks to the Audience/Occasion

Saying what people expect is not the same as delivering a generic speech that could be given before any audience on a similar occasion. It is not enough to change a few facts here and there and give the same speech of introduction no matter who the audience is. For example, introducing a candidate at a fundraiser attended by close friends and colleagues is different than introducing that same candidate before a group of citizens gathered for a candidates' forum. In the first situation, the audience knows the candidate and supports his or her positions on issues. In the second situation, the audience may not know the candidate, and may be unclear as to his or her stance on various positions.

3. Use Personal Anecdotes and Appropriate Humor

The more you say about the people gathered and the occasion, the more intimate and fitting your speech becomes. Personal anecdotes—especially sentimental or humorous ones—create the feeling that the speech was written for that event and no other.

Actress Lisa Kudrow gave the 2010 commencement address at Vassar College, her alma mater. She begins the speech by saying:

© Joe Seer/Shutterstock.com

> Thank you, President Hill, for inviting me to speak, and thank you to the Class of 2010 for not protesting ... seriously. I was wondering what I should say to you—there are so many possibilities, you know? So I asked some of you—and by "some" I mean two— who I happened to see in passing (It was convenient for me). Well I couldn't ask every one of you. It's not like there's some kind of social network wherein I could communicate with such a large number of people at once ...

After including some humor in her introductory remarks, Kudrow connected with the audience further by describing her graduation from Vassar in 1985. She provided a personal anecdote, with humor, that described the quick transformation from biology major to actress.

Actors like Lisa Kudrow know the importance of humor in special occasion speeches.

Not every occasion is one in which humor is anticipated or expected, but as Lisa Kudrow illustrates, it can draw the audience in, and personal anecdotes keep listeners interested.

Speaking Well with Technology Is an Essential for Excellence

When running a creative digital agency, it's often necessary to stay at the running edge of technology. New Zealand-based digital agency Resn prides itself in staying current, but also enjoys poking fun at its contemporaries in the industry.

In the last year, Resn has received numerous advertising awards across the international community. Most recently, the organization has cleaned house at the Cannes Lions, a global awards ceremony for individuals and organizations working in the creative communications, advertising, and other related fields. Representatives of Resn were also delighted to find out they won several Webby Awards, an award for excellence on the Internet presented annually by The International Academy of Digital Arts and Sciences. Resn played a key role in New Zealand's McWhopper campaign, a popular viral campaign where Burger King offered to "set aside" its differences with competitor McDonalds by creating a hybrid "McWhopper" sandwich, ostensibly for world peace. What was particularly interesting is that Resn representatives did not attend or accept any of their awards in person. Instead, the organization delivered a satirical videotaped speech on a VHS cassette.

"Since technological change has been so rapid in recent years and we're not sure if the rest of the world has kept pace with New Zealand, we used VHS to ensure that technology wasn't a barrier to accessing the speech," said Resn Managing Director Rik Campbell. "Ironically, they didn't have the equipment to play it. Last year we tried laser disc and the same thing happened. I mean, how far back do we have to go? Stone tablets?" (Campbell, 2016).

Although we tend to view special occasion speeches as more informal when they are detached from the office, many professional agencies benefit by practicing these strategies effectively. In this case, Resn was presented a prestigious award in their field, and accepted their award with playful tact. For many companies, the way they accept public awards can also be a golden opportunity to increase positive public opinion.

4. Avoid Clichés

Although speeches for special occasions should follow a predictable form, they should not be trite. To avoid delivering yet another tired introductory, presentation, acceptance, or commemorative speech, dodge the clichés that seem to be part of every speaker's vocabulary. The fact that clichés are overused makes them fairly meaningless, and certainly shows a lack of creativity. These include:

"And now ladies and gentlemen …"

Use this line only if you are introducing Conan O'Brien or David Letterman. Simply avoid saying "ladies and gentlemen." Try saying something like, "And now I am honored to introduce …," or make reference to the occasion. Other meaningless, annoying, and overworked phrases to avoid include:

"Without further ado …"

How many times have you heard this expression in ordinary conversation? We do not use the word "ado," so try "Finally" or "And now."

"I don't know what to say."

An alternative might be to express a statement of feeling, such as "I'm stunned!" or "How *wonderful* this is."

"My friends, we are truly honored tonight."

Is the audience filled with personal friends? Instead, it makes more sense to say, "I'm very honored tonight …"

"Ladies and gentlemen, here is a speaker who needs no introduction."

5. Be Aware That You Are Speaking for Others as Well

Whether you are presenting a gold watch to commemorate a vice-president's 25th year of employment or toasting the conference championship of your college football team, you are speaking as a representative of the group. Although your words are your own, your purpose is to echo the sentiments of those who have asked you to speak. In this capacity, you are the group spokesperson. It is acceptable to make "we" statements when you are referencing events and experiences shared by the audience and honoree. Remember, for the most part, it is not about you.

6. Be Sincere but Humble

You cannot fake sincerity. If you have been asked to give an award or to introduce a person you have never met, do not pretend an intimate relationship. You can make reference to the person's accomplishments that are well known, or you can ask others about the person you will introduce and use that information. Instead of saying "I've seen what Jim can do when he puts his mind to it," tell your listeners "I've spoken to the people who know Jim best—his supervisors and coworkers. They told me how, single-handedly, he helped two dozen of his coworkers escape a fire-filled office and how he refused medical attention until he was certain everyone was safe. I'm proud to honor Jim as our Employee of the Year." Generally speaking, using real information from people the speaker knows creates greater impact.

Being humble is also important. Even when you are accepting an award or being honored as Person of the Year, resist the temptation to tell everyone how great you are. It is in poor taste. Be appropriately humble, remembering that your audience is aware of your accomplishments. When Philip Seymour Hoffman won Best Actor in a Leading Role for his portrayal of Truman Capote in *Capote* at the March 2005 Academy Awards, he started his acceptance speech with these words:

> Wow, I'm in a category with some great, great, great actors. Fantastic actors, and I'm overwhelmed. I'm really overwhelmed. I'd like to thank Bill Vince and Caroline Baron. And Danny Rosett. The film wouldn't have happened without them. I'd like to thank Sarah Fargo, I'd like to thank Sara Murphy. I'd like to thank Emily Ziff, my friends, my friends, my friends. I'd like to thank Bennett Miller and Danny Futterman, who I love, I love, I love, I love. You know, the Van Morrison song, I love, I love, I love, and he keeps repeating it like that. And I'd like to thank Tom Bernard and Michael Barker. Thank you so much. And my mom's name is Marilyn O'Connor, and she's here tonight. And I'd like if you see her tonight to

The late Philip Seymour Hoffman practiced sincerity when accepting his award for Best Actor.

> congratulate her, because she brought up four kids alone, and she deserves a congratulations for that.

It was not necessary to attend the ceremony to experience Seymour Hoffman's enthusiasm and gratitude. It may not be the most eloquent acceptance speech, but he avoids bragging, and even requests that his mother be congratulated.

7. Be Accurate

Avoid embarrassing yourself with factual mistakes. If you are introducing a guest speaker, find out everything you need to know before the presentation by talking with the person or reading his or her résumé. If you are giving a commencement address, learn the names of the people who must be acknowledged at the start of your talk as well as the correct pronunciation of the names. If you are toasting an employee for years of dedicated service, make sure you get the number of years right! You do not want to give people higher or lower rank (captain/lieutenant, CEO/CFO), or state incorrect marital status (Ms./Mrs./Miss), or give incorrect information about children, current and past employment, or education.

The guidelines we provided above fit almost any special-occasion speech. As we have mentioned throughout the book, the speech should be audience-centered. While all special-occasion speeches should follow general guidelines, we now turn to some of the specific types of special-occasion speeches to see how these general guidelines apply and how other, more specific rules define these speech forms. Several types of special-occasion speeches are not covered here. At the end of the chapter we identify other special-occasion speeches and provide brief outlines to help you plan for most of the occasions you may encounter.

Speeches of Introduction

The purpose of a speech of introduction is to introduce the person who will give an important address. Keynote speakers are introduced, as are commencement speakers and speakers delivering inaugural remarks. When you deliver this type of speech, think of yourself as the conduit through which the audience learns something about the speaker. This speech is important because it has the potential to enhance the introduced speaker's credibility.

A **speech of introduction** can be viewed as a creative minispeech. Even the speech of introduction has an introduction, body, and conclusion. It is your job to heighten anticipation and prepare your audience for a positive experience. You can accomplish these goals by describing the speaker's accomplishments appropriately. Tell your listeners about the speaker's background and why he or she was invited to address the gathering.

Speech of introduction

Introduces the person who will give an important address.

Specific Guidelines for Speeches of Introduction

The following four guidelines will help you prepare appropriate introductory remarks:

Set the Tone and Be Brief but Personal

The tone for the speech of introduction should match the tone of the speech to follow. If a comedian is going to do his/her act following the speech of introduction, then a humorous tone is warranted. If the main speaker will discuss something serious, then the speech of introduction should set that tone.

If you are going to err in an introductory speech, err on the side of brevity and personalization. In other words, an introductory speech should be relatively short, set the appropriate tone, and be specifically designed for the individual being introduced.

Recently, we heard a speech introducing a member of Congress at a U.S. Naval retirement ceremony. The speaker went into great detail introducing the man, detailing his education, military service, activities in community service organizations, campaigns for Congress, and so on. This introductory speech was too long, it was not personal, and the speaker failed to set the appropriate tone for the featured speaker. As a result of this information overload, members of the audience shifted restlessly, coughed, yawned, and may have even dozed off. The main speaker began his speech at a big disadvantage.

As part of your preparation, it is helpful to talk with the featured speaker. Doing so may give you important information for the speech as well as some indication of the person's expectations for the introduction. Oftentimes, professional or experienced speakers will have prepared a short introduction for you to weave into your remarks.

Create Realistic Expectations

By telling the audience, "This is the funniest speech you'll ever hear" or "This woman is known as a brilliant communicator," you are making it difficult for the speaker to succeed. Few speakers can match these expectations. Instead, the audience may "appreciate the wisdom" of someone's remarks, or "be inspired" or "be entertained fully" by the speaker. Identify what you hope the audience will experience without creating a bar too high for anyone to clear.

When you read the "A" and then the "B" statements that follow; reflect on how the audience might feel if the speaker did not achieve what is indicated in the "A" statement.

At a gathering of salespeople who are about to listen to a motivational speaker:

A: "Starting tonight, he will change how you think forever."

B: "He will challenge you to think in ways you haven't considered before."

In an auditorium where individuals are gathered who are experiencing significant credit card and loan debt:

A: "Her understanding of personal finance is truly amazing. She will solve all your financial problems."

B: "Her background and experience give her insight into many aspects of personal finance. She will give you the tools to begin your climb to financial success."

Avoid Summarizing the Speaker's Intended Remarks

Your job is to provide an enticement to listen, not a summary of the remarks to follow. You might tell an audience of college students that you brought a well-known financial advisor to your college to help them make wise financial decisions. Avoid saying, "This speaker will tell you to reduce your spending, save a little money each month, distinguish between wants and needs, and pay your credit card balance on time." This is clearly interfering with the speaker's plan. Teasing a message means providing your audience with a hint of what is to come by mentioning something specific they will want to learn from the speaker. If you have any questions about how much to include in the introduction, share your proposed comments with the main speaker before your presentation.

Recognize the Potential for Spontaneity

Spontaneous introductions are sometimes appropriate. An unexpected guest whom you want to acknowledge may be in the audience. Something may have happened to the speaker, to the audience, or in the world just before the introductory speech, making the planned introduction less effective. For example, when actor Dustin Hoffman was taking his curtain calls after completing a performance of a Shakespeare play on Broadway, he noticed that Arthur Miller, well-known playwright, was seated in the audience. Hoffman raised his hands, asked for quiet, and said:

> When we were doing the play in London, we had the pleasure of playing one night to an audience that included Dame Peggy Ashcroft, who was introduced from the stage. We do not have knights in America, but there is someone special in the audience tonight. He is one of the greatest voices and influences in the American theater— Mr. Arthur Miller (Heller Anderson, 1990).

Hoffman's impromptu introduction demonstrated that brevity and grace are the hallmarks of an effective introduction.

The Academy Awards ceremony is perhaps the biggest stage for speeches of presentation and acceptance.

© Tinseltown/Shutterstock.com

Speeches of Presentation

The presentation speech is delivered as part of a ceremony to recognize an individual or group chosen for special honors. Our personal and professional lives are marked, in part, by attendance and participation in award ceremonies to recognize personal achievement. Some occasions for presentation speeches include commencements (high school, college, and graduate school), where special presentations are made to students with exceptional academic and community service records, and corporate awards ceremonies, where employees are honored for their years of service or exemplary performance. Televised ceremonies involve award presentations such as the Academy Awards, the Emmy Awards, and Country Music Awards. Other ceremonies recognize achievement in a sport, such as the Heisman Memorial Trophy, presented each year to the nation's most outstanding college football player. Each of these ceremonies includes one or more presentation speeches.

Specific Guidelines for Speeches of Presentation

Every **speech of presentation** should accomplish several goals. Using an example of a speech marking the presentation of the "Reporter of the Year" award for a student newspaper we will illustrate our four guidelines for speeches of presentation.

Speech of presentation
Delivered as part of a ceremony to recognize an individual or group chosen for special honors.

State the Importance of the Award

Many departmental scholarships and awards are available in college to qualified students. A scholarship may be significant because the selection criteria include finding the individual with the most outstanding academic achievement. Other scholarships may have been established to help single mothers, residents of the town, or students who engage in significant community service. Some awards are established in the names of people living and deceased or companies and organizations.

The award may be worth $100 or it may be $5,000. Regardless of the monetary value, the audience wishes to understand why the award is important. You may need to describe the achievements of the individual or individuals for whom the award has been established.

Here is the beginning of a speech of presentation, as Tom speaks about his fellow reporter, Kathryn Remm.

> I am pleased to have been asked by our editorial staff to present the Reporter of the Year award—the college's highest journalistic honor. This award was established six years ago by a group of alumni who place great value on maintaining our newspaper's high standard of journalism.

In this example, Tom clearly states the importance of the award when he mentions that it is the college's highest journalistic honor. Further, he clarifies how the award came to be by mentioning who began the award and why.

Explain the Selection Process

The audience needs to know that the award was not given arbitrarily or based on random criteria. Explaining the criteria and selection process helps establish the significance of the award. If the award is competitive, you might mention the nature of the competition, but do not overemphasize the struggle for victory at the expense of the other candidates.

SPEAKING EXCELLENCE IN YOUR CAREER

As advertising has become more intertwined with entertainment and new (viral) media, so has its importance in the field of communication studies. In the same vein as the Academy Awards, Grammys, and other accolade ceremonies, advertising awards have become a major point of interest in mainstream media. Besides acknowledging successful achievements in advertising, awards ceremonies are also breeding grounds for innovation in new communication strategies. When a company makes a landmark achievement in advertising success (The GEICO gecko comes to mind), it sets a benchmark for other advertising companies. Researchers María Galmés, Inmaculada Berlanga, and Juan Victoria analyze the new era of advertising communication.

For many of the advertising awards ceremonies examined, the researchers noticed a forum-like field that developed among attendees. Unlike traditional awards shows for movies, television, or music, the main purpose of these awards ceremonies appeared to be the exchange of ideas and strategies for reaching new markets. In the course of researching this paper, the researchers identified five major trends addressed at these awards ceremonies: digitization, new alternatives, innovation, integration, and results (Galmés, Berlanga, & Victoria, 2016). Research indicated that digitization of communications has integrated with mainstream media so thoroughly that it has become the norm; for advertisers, innovation (something consumers have never seen before) has become the greatest value in advertising research. The researchers indicate that future directions of advertising communications will trend towards integration of all aspects of traditional and new (social media).

The following passage illustrates how this guideline can be followed effectively. Tom continues:

> The award selection process is long and arduous. It starts when the paper's editorial staff calls for nominations and then reviews and evaluates dozens of writing samples. The staff sends its recommendations to a selection committee made up of two alumni sponsors and two local journalists. It is this group of four who determines the winner.

Note the Honoree's Qualifications

Many organizations honor their members and employees for specific accomplishments. For example, the Midas Auto Service "South Central Regional Dealer of the Year" award honors an employee for excellence in regional retail sales, overall retail image, and customer satisfaction. The Edward Jones Investing firm chooses employees for the "Partner's Award" based on sales and service efforts over the past year. The nature of the award suggests what to say about the honoree. The following example shows why the reporter is being recognized.

> This year's honoree is Kathryn Remm, the community affairs reporter for the paper. Almost single-handedly, Kathryn reached out to noncollege community residents and established channels of communication that have never before been open. In a series of articles, she told students about the need for literacy volunteers at the community library and for Big Brothers/Big Sisters at our local youth club.

Be Brief

Like speeches of introduction, the key to a successful presentation speech is brevity. Choose your words with care so that the power of your message is not diminished by unnecessary detail. Within this limited context, try to humanize the award recipient through a personal—perhaps humorous—anecdote.

As a final note about speeches of presentation, occasionally it is appropriate to ask past recipients of the award to stand up and receive applause. This decision should be based, in part, on your conviction that this acknowledgment will magnify the value of the award to the current recipient as well as to the audience.

Here is how Tom finishes his speech:

> Kathryn was a bit surprised when she learned that student volunteerism for Big Brothers/Big Sisters rose 150 percent after her outreach and articles. This makes her the biggest sister in our community. Please help me acknowledge Kathryn Remm as our reporter of the year.

Speeches of Acceptance

The main purpose of an acceptance speech is to express gratitude for an award. It is personal, gracious, and sincere. Most speakers begin with something like "I am genuinely grateful for this award, and I want to express my sincere thanks to everyone here."

Most acceptance speeches are brief. In many instances, such as an awards night in high school and departmental recognition in college, several individuals are honored for their achievements. If acceptance speeches are long, the event will seem interminable. However, in some cases, such as the Nobel Peace Prize ceremony, recipients are asked to do more than express gratitude. These speeches fit within the category of "keynote speeches," which are discussed later in this chapter. Following are four guidelines for the successful speech of acceptance.

Acceptance speech

A speech given to express gratitude for an award.

Specific Guidelines for Speeches of Acceptance

Restate Importance of the Award

Restating the importance of the award shows the audience as well as those involved in the award that the recipient values and acknowledges the importance of the award. For example, scholarships are generally established by an individual, an organization, or a group of individuals who have contributed financially. Representatives of the scholarship, along with the scholarship committee, appreciate hearing that the scholarship is viewed as important. Along with this, communicate to your audience what receiving the award means to you.

Be Sincere

An acceptance speech is built around the theme of "thank you." You thank the person, group, or organization bestowing the award. You recognize the people who helped you gain it. Your acceptance should be sincere and heartfelt. The audience wants to feel that the individuals bestowing the award have made the right choice.

ENGAGING IN COMMUNITY

Actress Yara Shahidi's community engagement was recognized at the Points of Light Conference.

Although only 16, actress Yara Shahidi has already made an enormous impact engaging in her community. Shahidi, costar of the sitcom *Black-ish*, recently accepted the Daily Point of Light Award at the annual Points of Light Conference. The award was created by President George H.W. Bush to recognize individuals who dedicate their lives to public service and volunteering (Smith, 2016). The actress gave a heartfelt acceptance speech in front of 1,000 people. After accepting the award, Shahidi reminded her audience about the importance of bettering communities.

© Helga Esteb/Shutterstock.com

"I express my activism through my art," said Shahidi. "I see myself as a child of the world. Giving back isn't something you do when you're old, it's something you do when you're young as well, and that means right now" (Smith, 2016).

Shahidi spent time after the ceremony answering questions about her community service and the types of stereotypes and social labels her character deals with on *Black-ish*. Shahidi credited her experience and exposure as an actress as resources she has successfully used to spread her community efforts. "Acting is cool, but it's not who I am. It's not at all my end all and be all. For me, wanting to be a humanitarian pushed me to be an actress and a volunteer and everything else."

As you continue your studies, remember the importance of aiding your local communities. If you ever find yourself lucky enough to be recognized for your service, be sure to use the strategies presented in this chapter to deliver a graceful acceptance speech. Above all, remember to place your pride in community service above the pride in yourself.

So if you know you will be asked to give a brief acceptance speech, think about who deserves recognition. It is not necessary to give a long list of all the individuals who have influenced you in your lifetime, but you want to acknowledge those who have had an impact on you in some way that relates to your accomplishing this goal. A well-developed and appropriately delivered acceptance speech allows the listeners to be part of the moment and share the recipient's joy or amazement.

Describe How You Reached This Point of Achievement

As you thank people, you can mention in a humble tone how you reached this point of recognition. If you are a gymnast, you can talk about your training and gymnastic meets. If you are a pianist, you can talk about practice and recitals. The audience wants to know that you worked for this award, that you deserve it, but that you are gracious and humble, too.

Use Anecdotes

As you express gratitude and explain how you have reached this point of achievement, select with care the events you want to mention in order to avoid an endless chronology of your life. Stories about your life, or personal anecdotes, give people a lasting impression of your achievements

Anecdotes engage the audience and help them understand more clearly why this person was a good choice for the award. Be careful not to be arrogant with the anecdotes you select, or you may leave the audience with regrets.

Anecdote
A short account of an interesting or humorous incident.

Commemorative Speeches

When we commemorate an event, we mark it through observation and ceremony. Public or private, these ceremonies are often punctuated by speeches appropriate for the occasion. Commencement speeches at college graduation, eulogies at the funeral of a loved one, speeches to celebrate the spirit of a special event or a national holiday like the Fourth of July, toasts at a wedding or the birth of a baby or a business deal, inaugural speeches, and farewell addresses all fit into this category.

Although commemorative speeches may inform, their specific purpose is not informational. Although they may persuade, their primary purpose is not persuasive. They are inspirational messages designed to stir emotions. These speeches make listeners reflect on the message through the use of rich language that lifts them to a higher emotional plain. More than in any other special-occasion speech, your choice of words in the commemorative address will determine your success.

The next section covers three common forms of commemorative speeches: toasts, commencement speeches, and eulogies.

Commemorative speech
An inspirational message designed to stir emotions.

Toasts

Toast

Brief message of good will and congratulations.

Some credit the custom of toasting to the Norsemen, Vikings, and Greeks who lifted their glasses in honor of the gods. But the newer "toast" derives from the 17th-century British custom of placing toasted bits of bread in glasses to improve the taste of the drink. As the concept of the toast evolved, so did the customs surrounding it. In England, those proposing the toast knelt on "bended" knee. In France, elaborate bows were required. In Scotland, the toast maker stood with one foot on a chair, the other on a table. Today, Western tradition dictates the clinking of glasses while making strong eye contact (Bayless, 1988).

You are more likely to be asked to deliver a toast than any other form of commemorative speech. Toasts are given at engagements, weddings, graduations, quinceañeras, confirmations, births, the sealing of business deals, at dinner parties, and so on. They are brief messages of good will and congratulations.

Humor is a part of many occasions where toasts occur. However, it is imperative that boundaries on humor be observed. Tasteful humor is preferable to humor that can end up embarrassing or hurting individuals involved in the toast.

Following are three guidelines to help you deliver a memorable toast:

1   PREPARE A SHORT, INSPIRATIONAL MESSAGE AND MEMORIZE IT. If you are the best man at your brother's wedding, the mother of the new college graduate at his graduation dinner, a close associate of an executive just promoted to company president, you may be asked in advance to prepare a toast to celebrate the occasion. Even though most toasts are generally no more than a few sentences long, do not assume that you will be able to think of something appropriate to say when the glasses are raised. To avoid drawing a blank, write—and memorize—the toast in advance.

2   CHOOSE WORDS WITH CARE THAT ADDRESS THE AUDIENCE AND OCCASION. There is a time to be frivolous and a time to be serious. The audience and the occasion indicate whether it is appropriate to be humorous or serious, inspirational or practical. Here is an example of an appropriate toast to a new law partner:

> Ken has been a portrait of strength for all of us. When four partners were sick with the flu at the same time last year, Ken worked tirelessly, seven days a week, to meet

our deadlines. Here's to Ken—the best lawyer in town and the newest partner of our law firm.

3   BE POSITIVE AND AVOID CLICHÉS. A toast is upbeat. Look to the future with hope. It is inappropriate to toast a college graduate saying, "If John does as poorly at work as he did at college, we may all be asked to help pay his rent," or at a wedding to say, "After all those other women you brought home, your bride looks pretty good." Such comments will bring a big laugh, but will also wound, and therefore should not be used.

Remember that public speaking is a creative activity. Clichés such as "Down the hatch," "Here's mud in your eye," and "Cheers" waste an ideal creative moment. Instead, you can say something simple like, as is noted in the previous example, "Here's to Ken—the best lawyer in town and the newest partner of our law firm." If the tone is lighter, you might opt for something more creative.

Author John Grisham's commencement speech at the University of North Carolina resonates years after its original presentation.

Commencement Speeches

Most of us believe we will not be asked to give a commencement speech. However, colleges and universities have students and guests give commencement speeches every year. Either they are voted on by the student body or they are asked to speak because they were elected to a position, such as student senate president. A speaker may be a distinguished alumnus or may have achieved celebrity status.

No other speech offers greater potential to achieve the aims of a ceremonial speech than the commencement address delivered by an honored guest. Following are several guidelines for developing a commencement speech.

Author John Grisham began his May 9, 2010 commencement speech at the University of North Carolina, Chapel Hill with a brief *expression of honor*, giving thanks for the invitation to speak. Later in his speech, he makes tribute to the college as a place of excellence, saying how proud he is to be a Tar Heel.

Later in his speech, he makes *tribute to the college as a place of excellence.*

Traditional commencement speeches *offer counsel to the graduating members of the audience.*

All commencement speakers *should impart some memorable message.* Grisham moves on to the main point of his speech, which is the importance of finding and using one's "voice."

He concludes on a *congratulatory* note by telling the audience that their future has arrived and they should remember what they want to be right now, wishing them good luck.

Although Grisham's speech lasted only 17 minutes, the strength of its message endures, and it is a model commencement speech.

Eulogies

Eulogy

A commemorative speech that involves paying tribute to a family member, friend, colleague, or community member who died.

Eulogies are perhaps the most difficult commemorative speeches to make, since they involve paying tribute to a family member, friend, colleague, or community member who died. It is a difficult time for the speaker as well as the audience. A eulogy focuses on *universal themes* such as the preciousness and fragility of life, the importance of family and friends at times of great loss, and the continuity of life, while avoiding impersonal clichés. Here are five guidelines to help you develop and present a eulogy:

ACKNOWLEDGE THE LOSS AND REFER TO THE OCCASION. Your first words should focus on the family and/or significant others of the deceased. Talk directly to them, taking care to acknowledge by name the spouse, children, parents, and special friends of the deceased. It is safe to assume that all members of the audience feel loss. People come together to mourn because they want to be part of a community; they want to share their grief with others. By using "we" statements of some kind, you acknowledge the community of mourners. For example, you might say, "We all know how much Andrew loved his family" or "I am sure we all agree that Andrew's determination and spirit left their mark."

Kevin volunteers at a local soup kitchen in his community. Recently, a long-time volunteer for the shelter passed away, and Kevin was asked to deliver a eulogy at the funeral service. Although Kevin knew very little about the man, he agreed. Kevin began by asking other volunteers at the shelter if they had any heartwarming or good-natured stories to share about the deceased, but they had none to offer. After searching online and at the local library, Kevin was unable to find any relatives he could talk to either. Kevin exhausted the few resources he had left, discovering that he had virtually no information to offer about his deceased co-volunteer. Although Kevin didn't want to be dishonest, he knew the ceremony would be awkward if his eulogy was overly brief. After much deliberation, Kevin decided to add a few innocent, good-natured (untrue) stories about his experiences with the old volunteer. The ceremony proceeded without any issues, but Kevin was troubled with the lack of sincerity in his speech.

QUESTIONS TO CONSIDER:
1. Are the ethical issues of lying removed in this particular instance?
2. Do you believe it would have damaged the ceremony if Kevin had only offered a few, brief words about the volunteer's service at the shelter?
3. How would you have crafted the eulogy had you been in Kevin's place?

CELEBRATE LIFE RATHER THAN FOCUSING ON LOSS. Some deaths are anticipated, such as dying from ailments related to old age or after a lengthy illness. Others are shocking and tragic, and those left behind may have unresolved issues. Although it is appropriate to acknowledge shared feelings of sadness and even anger, the eulogy should focus on the unique gifts and lasting legacy the person brought to their world.

USE QUOTES, ANECDOTES, AND EVEN HUMOR. Nothing is better than a good story to celebrate the spirit of the deceased. A well-chosen anecdote can comfort as it helps people focus on the memory of the person's life. Fitting anecdotes need not be humorless. Rather than using ambiguous phrases such as he was "a loving husband," "a loving father," or "a wonderful person," it would mean more to provide a brief story or a humorous account of some incident in the person's life. Saying something like "Getting an ice cream cone was a reward from Dad, even in my 30s" or "He was a great teacher who liked to experiment with new ideas, such as teaching class outdoors, until the day a bird pooped on his head." Stories and humor help mourners get through the experience of attending the memorial as they recall pleasant memories and laugh along with the speakers.

Quote others. You may choose to turn to the remarks of noted public figures such as Winston Churchill, John F. Kennedy, and Mark Twain, whose words are fitting for your speech. Know that you do not need to rely on quotations from famous writers, poets, actors, or politicians. You may choose to include the words of friends and family members of the deceased.

CONTROL YOUR EMOTIONS. Composure is crucial. If you have any questions about your ability to control your grief, suggest that someone else be chosen. As you offer comfort to others, try not to call undue attention to your own grief. While an expression of loss and its attending emotions is appropriate, uncontrolled crying will prevent you from providing the needed healing your eulogy offers. If you do not think you can make it through without falling apart, have someone else do it or bring someone up to the podium with you who can take over, if necessary.

BE SINCERE AND BE BRIEF. Speak from the heart. Avoid "Words cannot express our sorrow," "The family's loss is too much to bear," and "She's in a far better place now." Rely instead on personal memories, anecdotes, and feelings. Eulogies need not be lengthy to be effective.

Depending on the wishes of the family, several individuals may be called on to eulogize the deceased. A brief, sincere speech will be greatly appreciated by those attending the memorial service.

Keynote Speeches

Keynote speaker

Featured speaker at an event.

A **keynote speaker** is the featured speaker at an event. There may be several people who speak briefly, but the keynote speaker has the top billing of the event. Whatever the setting, whether it is a gathering of members of the American Society of Journalists and Authors or the annual convention of the American Bar Association, the keynote address is usually anticipated as a highlight that has the potential to compel the audience to thought and action. Unlike many special-occasion speeches, the keynote speech is not brief. You may be called on to give a keynote speech at some point. We offer the following guidelines.

Remember That Your Speech Sets the Tone for the Event

Think of keynote speakers as cheerleaders and their speeches as the cheers that set the tone for an event. The purpose of the gathering may be to celebrate the group's achievements, to share information with each other, or to give individuals the opportunity to interact with people who are in similar positions or situations. The keynote speaker is there to excite people, and to stimulate thought and action.

Keynote addresses at political conventions are known for their hard-hitting approach and language. When he was a candidate for the U.S. Senate in Illinois, Barack Obama delivered the keynote address at the Democratic National Convention in Boston in July 2004. Following is an excerpt from that speech:

> Tonight, we gather to affirm the greatness of our nation not because of the height of our skyscrapers, or the power of our military, or the size of our economy; our pride is based on a very simple premise, summed up in a declaration made over two hundred years ago: "We hold these truths to be self-evident, that all men are created equal ... that they are endowed by their Creator with certain inalienable rights, that among these are life, liberty, and the pursuit of happiness."

Obama's speech makes patriotic references that stirred many Americans' sense of pride in their country. But he also suggested that things could be better. His words clearly set the tone for Democrats at that convention.

President Barack Obama (and all other U.S. Presidents) are obligated to give countless keynote speeches throughout their career.

Select Your Topic and Language *After* Analyzing the Audience and Occasion

There is a reason you were asked to be the keynote speaker. It may be fame, fortune, or simply achievement based on hard work. You may be provided with some basic guidelines for your speech, such as "motivate them," or "talk about success." Decisions about how you develop the content of your speech and the words you choose to express yourself should be made after reflecting on the audience and occasion. As one of the keynote speakers at the Microsoft India, NGO (nongovernmental organization) Connection workshop in April 2010 in Jaipur, India, Rajendra Joshi, one of the organization's trustees, started her speech by making a specific connection between technology and governance.

> The most powerful weapon on the earth is public opinion [Paul Crouser]. *Governance* encompasses not just government, but also the civil society and the corporate sector.

Joshi asserts the importance of public opinion at the very beginning. Since her speech was presented to individuals connected with Microsoft and nongovernmental organizations, she tied technology together with governance to highlight an important aspect of nongovernmental organizations trying to improve the world.

Time Is Still a Factor

Yes, people are gathered to hear you. You are the focus of attention. Say what you need to say, but do not waste their time. Think about what has happened in the time before your speech, and what will happen after your speech. Even if you have what seems to be an unlimited amount of time, realize that your audience may have other things to do.

Consider the audience's attention span. Have they been in the same room for the last four hours? An audience can be enthralled for some period of time, but there is a limit as to how long they can pay attention. One of your authors attended a ceremony celebrating the university's 100-year anniversary, and slipped out of the room after 45 minutes of listening to the keynote speaker. (The speech lasted another 20 minutes!) Time is a factor. You do not want to have your audience dreaming of an escape plan.

After-Dinner Speeches

If the keynote address is the meat-and-potatoes speech of a conference, the after-dinner speech is the dessert. It is a speech delivered, literally, after the meal is over and after all other substantive business is complete. Its purpose is to entertain, often with humor, although it may also convey a thoughtful message. Keep in mind, a more accurate description of this speech would be "after-meal" as an after-dinner speech can occur after any meal. Two suggestions for after-dinner speaking are to focus on the specific purpose, which is to entertain, and use the opportunity to inspire action or renewed commitment.

After-dinner speech
Purpose is to entertain, often with humor, although it usually conveys a thoughtful message.

Outlines for Other Special-Occasion Speeches

Following are 14 outlines for you to consider. Each commemorates an event you will probably encounter in the future. These outlines spell out both what is expected and the traditional order in which we expect to hear them.

Speech of Introduction
1. Greeting and reference to the occasion
2. Statement of the name of the person to be introduced
3. Brief description of the person's speech topic/company position/role in the organization, etc.
4. Details about the person's qualifications
5. Enthusiastic closing statement
6. Inviting a warm reception for the next speaker

Speech of Welcome
1. Expression of honor this person's visit brings to the group
2. Description of the person's background and special achievements
3. Statement of the reason for the visit
4. Greeting and welcome to the person

Speech of Dedication
1. Statement of reason for assembling
2. Brief history of efforts that have led to this event
3. Prediction for the future success of the company, organization, group, or person

Anniversary Speech

1. Statement of reason for assembling
2. Sentimental significance of the event
3. Explanation of how this sentiment can be maintained
4. Appeal for encouraging the sentiment to continue in future years

Speech of Presentation

1. Greeting and reference to the occasion
2. History and importance of the award
3. Brief description of the qualifications for the award
4. Reasons for this person receiving the award
5. Announcement of the recipient's name
6. Presentation of the award

Speech of Acceptance

1. Expression of gratitude for the award
2. Brief praise of the appropriate people
3. Statement of appreciation to those giving the award
4. Closing of pleasure and thanks

Speech of Farewell

1. Expression of sorrow about the person's departure
2. Statement of enjoyment for the association with this person
3. Brief description of how the person will be missed
4. Announcement of friendship and best wishes for the future
5. Invitation to return again soon

Speech of Tribute (if honoree is alive) or the Eulogy (if deceased)

1. Expression of respect and love for the honoree
2. Reasons for paying tribute to this person
3. Review of the person's accomplishments and contributions
4. Clarification of how this person has touched the lives of others
5. Closing appeal to emulate the good qualities of this person

Speech of Installation

1. Orientation of the audience to the occasion and the theme of this installation
2. Introduction of the current officers
3. Praise of the current officers for the work they have accomplished

4. Announcement for the new officers to come forward
5. Explanation of the responsibilities for each office
6. Recitation of the organization's installation of officers pledge
7. Declaration of the installation of the new officers

SPEECH OF INAUGURATION
1. Expression of appreciation for being elected or placed in office
2. Declaration of the theme or problem focus while in office
3. Explanation of policy intentions
4. Announcement of goals to achieve while in office
5. Closing appeal for confidence in a successful future

KEYNOTE ADDRESS
1. Orientation of the audience to the mood and theme of the convention
2. Reference to the goals of the organization and their importance
3. Brief description of the convention's major events
4. Closing invitation for active participation in the convention

COMMENCEMENT ADDRESS
1. Greeting to the graduates and the audience
2. Review of the graduates' successful accomplishments
3. Praise to the graduates for reflecting respected values
4. Prediction and discussion of future challenges
5. Closing inspiration for the graduates to meet these new challenges successfully

AFTER-DINNER SPEECH
1. Statement of reference to the audience and the occasion
2. Humorous transition into the central idea or thesis
3. Presentation of major points developed with humorous supporting materials
4. Closing that is witty and memorable

HUMOROUS SPEECH
1. Humorous attention-getter
2. Preview of the comic theme and intent of the speech
3. Presentation of humorous points and supporting materials that are typical of the audience in terms of events, feelings, experiences, or thoughts
4. Closing that presents a strong punch line (Harrell 1997)

ESSENTIALS FOR EXCELLENCE

In this chapter, you have learned about the research, strategies, and skills needed to deliver memorable special occasion speeches. We hope that you have noticed one of the most crucial factors in creating an effective presentation: the ability to relate to the audience. This skill is especially important in wedding toasts, which is one of the most expressive social occasions across many cultures. Writer Lisa Bonos offers several tips to nailing the best wedding toast.

If you don't have anything good to say, don't give a toast.
Many times, nervous best men (and women) will try to relieve their anxiety by poking fun at the bride and/or groom. While humor can have its place in a toast, remember that this is their special occasion; your goal should never be to embarrass the guests of honor.

The toast shouldn't be all about you and your relationship with the bride or groom.
In this situation, you are not the centerpiece of conversation. While you want to use personal anecdotes to relate with the bride and groom, make sure they stay the focal point of your speech. Any personal story you share should also paint the marriage couple as the main protagonist.

Keep it short.
Jen Glantz, a professional bridesmaid and notable ghostwriter of many wedding toasts, recommends a three-minute maximum when giving your toast (Bonos, 2015). Remember, your toast should never take longer than the actual wedding vows!

▨ WHAT YOU'VE LEARNED:

Now that you have studied the chapter, you should be able to:

1. Identify the guidelines for speeches of introduction.
    *   Set the tone but be brief and personal. The tone for the speech of introduction should match the tone of the speech to follow. Also, if you are going to err in an introductory speech, err on the side of brevity and personalization.
    *   Create realistic expectations. Identify what you hope the audience will experience without creating a bar too high for anyone to clear.
    *   Avoid summarizing the speaker's intended remarks. Your job is to provide an enticement to listen, not a summary of the remarks to follow. Teasing a message means providing your audience with a hint of what is to come by mentioning something specific they will want to learn from the speaker.
    *   Recognize the potential for spontaneity. Spontaneous introductions are sometimes appropriate. Something may have happened to the speaker, to the audience, or in the world just before the introductory speech, making the planned introduction less effective.

2. Understand the importance of commemorative speeches.
    *   Commemorative speeches are inspirational messages designed to stir emotions. These speeches make listeners reflect on the message through the use of rich language that lifts them to a higher emotional plain. More than in any other special-occasion speech, your choice of words in the commemorative address will determine your success.

3. Define and describe an after-dinner speech.
    *   After-dinner speeches are designed to entertain (often with humor), although they usually convey a thoughtful message. It is a speech delivered, literally, after the meal is over and after all other substantive business is complete.

4. Know the strategies to give an effective acceptance speech.
    *   Restate the importance of the award. This shows the audience as well as those involved in the award that the recipient values and acknowledges the importance of the award.
    *   Be sincere. The audience wants to feel that the individuals bestowing the award have made the right choice.
    *   Describe how you reached this point of achievement. As you thank people, you can mention in a humble tone how you reached this point of recognition. The audience wants to know that you worked for this award, that you deserve it, but that you are gracious and humble, too.
    *   Use anecdotes. As you express gratitude and explain how you have reached this point of achievement, select with care the events you want to mention in order to avoid an endless chronology of your life. Stories about your life, or personal anecdotes, give people a lasting impression of your achievements.

Key Terms

acceptance speech, 451   **commemorative speech, 453**   **speech of introduction, 444**
after-dinner speech, 461   **eulogy, 456**   **speech of presentation, 447**
anecdote, 453   **keynote speaker, 458**   **toast, 454**

Reflect

1   What is memorable from the speeches you heard when you graduated from high school? If you were giving one of those speeches, what could you have included to personalize it and make it more memorable?

2   When is it appropriate to use humor? Should speakers tell jokes? When/Why/Why not? Can there be too much of a good thing with humor for a speaker? Can humor hurt credibility?

3   Do you know any good toasts? What are the elements of an effective toast? How can you tell the difference between a good one and a bad one?

4   Have you seen someone introduce someone else in a formal speech setting? How did they do? What are the elements of an effective speech of introduction? Did the speech you are recalling satisfy these elements? What should speakers avoid?

5   Why are brevity and gratitude key elements of an effective acceptance speech? Is it appropriate for recipients to use the platform of their acceptance speech to further a cause they care about? What causes or issues are out of bounds? If there are some, why are they not appropriate?

Review Questions

1   The speech of _____ introduces the person who will give an important address.

2   The speech of _____ is delivered as part of a ceremony to recognize an individual or group chosen for special honors.

3   A speech given to express gratitude for an award in a(n) _____ speech.

4   A(n) _____ is a short account of an interesting or humorous incident.

5   The _____ speech is an inspirational message designed to stir emotions.

6   A(n) _____ is a brief message of good will and congratulations.

7   A commemorative speech that involves paying tribute to a family member, friend, colleague, or community member who died is known as a(n) _____.

8   A(n) _____ speaker is the featured speaker at an event.

9   A(n) _____ speech's purpose is to entertain, often with humor, although it usually conveys a thoughtful message.

Recall Snyder !
Sign the petition here!
Repeal the "emergency manager" law.

468

Governor Rick Snyder faced severe public backlash over his handling of the Flint water crisis.

CHAPTER FOURTEEN
PRESENTING TO AND WORKING WITH SMALL GROUPS

OUTLINE

◼ WHAT YOU'LL LEARN

After studying this chapter, you should be able to:

1. Define the purposes of a primary group and secondary group.
2. Identify the three types of small-group formats.
3. List the seven-step reflective thinking process.
4. Describe the strategies for presenting in a small group.

SPEAKING IN CONTEXT

In July of 2016, Heidi Grether was appointed as the Department of Environmental Quality director by Michigan Governor Rick Snyder. The appointment comes as the Michigan government struggles with the fallout of the Flint water crisis, when the city of Flint found its water supply was contaminated with lead, creating a serious public health danger. The Department of Environmental Equality (DEQ) has been deemed responsible for the lead-tainted tap water emergency, when the agency switched Flint's water source from Lake Huron/Detroit River to the Flint River (Eggert, 2016). Officials for the DEQ failed to apply corrosion inhibitors to treatment facilities along the Flint River, leading to many residents losing access to safe running water.

Before her appointment, Heidi Grether worked for British Petroleum (BP), notably managing external affairs in the Gulf of Mexico after the disastrous 2010 oil spill. Governor Snyder noted that Grether was chosen largely because of her experience with crisis management and environmental quality issues. Grether, along with a small group of crisis management experts, made significant gains in reducing the public relations fallout BP faced after its role in the Gulf of Mexico oil spill. With many citizens of Michigan without safe water and public opinion of his office failing, Snyder is banking on this new DEQ chief to fix the health crisis and his public image.

This chapter will discuss the responsibilities, guidelines, and strategies for small-group communication. However, the most critical aspect of this chapter will discuss the significance of small-group communication. When working together efficiently and effectively, small groups are capable of reaching communication goals that individual members cannot obtain on their own. As terrible as the 2010 oil spill was (as well as the public image of British Petroleum), crisis management leaders like Heidi Grether were able to deflect the worst of public backlash, and respond as best they could to the environmental fallout. As you learn to work in small groups, remember that you can make a presentation greater than the sum of its parts.

The Significance of Small-Group Communication

Small groups are a part of life. The small group has been a common phenomenon in every society from the beginning of civilization. Generally speaking, the family is the first group to which we belong. We are born into this group or brought into the family, but it is not something we choose. The same is true of some of our early groups that develop once our formal education begins. We may be placed in work or task groups in class as well as reading groups or sports groups. Sometimes, we take part in some activity, not because of a conscious effort to belong to a group, but because of our interests. If you are on the editorial board of your school newspaper or are an organizer of the community blood drive, you are a member of a small group. If you are a member of a church, a musical, athletic, or academic group, you are a member of a small group.

Given our interest in helping you become the most effective speaker possible regardless of context, this chapter discusses the small-group experience and identifies small-group characteristics. Then, we discuss (1) different ways to present to and participate in small groups, (2) small-group members' roles and responsibilities, and (3) guidelines for group problem solving and presenting.

Small-Group Purposes

Any time you work with a group, that group belongs in one of two categories—primary or secondary. According to Beebe and Masterson (2014), the purpose of a primary group is to "fill the basic need to associate with others" (p. XX). Included in this first category are your family and best friends. Beebe notes that the main task of the primary group is to "perpetuate the group so that members can continue to enjoy one another's companionship" (p. 16). Tubbs (2011), another small-group researcher, states that our primary groups "influence self-concept as well as personality from childhood to adulthood" (p. XXX).

Primary group
A group that fills the basic need to associate with others, such as family and best friends.

The purpose of a secondary group is to accomplish a task or achieve a goal. Groups you belong to in college and in your professional life are secondary groups, such as study groups, social groups, therapy groups, and problem-solving groups. In college, you may want to join a *study* group to do better on a test. You may join a fraternity or sorority to engage in *social* activities. There may be a *therapy group* you belong to designed to help you with personal or social issues. And you may be asked to join a committee or Habitat for Humanity, and engage in *problem-solving* or

Secondary group
A group that accomplishes a task or achieves a goal.

decision-making activities. A group may have multiple purposes. For example, a sorority may be a social group, but to do fundraising, members need to engage in decision-making activities. Also, you may form a subgroup within the sorority that gets together to study for a class.

Habitat for Humanity is a type of secondary group that combats the problem of homelessness in the United States.

ENGAGING IN COMMUNITY

As part of their bus tour across the country, members of the Nuns on the Bus organization have traveled to many cities and small towns to foster small-group discussion about public policy. The nuns affiliated with the network organization began their "Mend the Gaps: Reweaving the Fabric of Society" bus tour in Janesville, Wisconsin. The 20-city tour includes stops at both the Democratic and Republican National Conventions, as well as many community-oriented non-profit organizations. As part of their community work, the nuns invite citizens to break into small groups to discuss seven areas they consider "gaps" in federal government social policy: income taxes, livable wages, family-friendly workplaces, voting rights and proper representation, health care, paths to citizenship, and adequate housing (Kilbane, 2016).

As the Nuns on the Bus travel to new locations, they take the time to listen to the stories and struggles of local communities in order to better represent their interests. While visiting Fort Wayne, Indiana, the sisters heard inspiring stories from four of its citizens; women who were living in the Vincent Village homeless shelter and trying to get back on their feet. Facing issues such as racism, lack of transportation, and injured spouses, these women brought their needs and concerns to the Nuns on the Bus.

"You four are such fabulous representatives of good strong women who take care of your families," Sister Simone Campbell, the executive director of the organization, told the women afterward (Kilbane, 2016).

Cambell urges people to work together to create change in U.S. government social policies that create gaps between the wealthy and those of lower incomes. Using the power of small-group communication, Campbell and her organization hope to foster constructive discussion that will help the communities they visit. As you collaborate in small groups in both school and the professional workplace, remember the previous story as a reminder of how effective small-group communication can be.

In the public speaking classroom, group speeches may have different tasks, including, among other possibilities, presenting:

- A chapter of a book or a text
- Results of research on some topic
- A cohesive, informative speech
- Results of a problem-solving activity
- Results of some group activity
- Two sides of an issue (pro/con)
- A minilecture on some topic

In a college classroom, you may not have chosen your "group mates," but these are the individuals with whom you must interact and cooperate. Research suggests that students believe they accomplish more by working in groups than by working alone (Winter & Neal, 1995). Each person brings to the group his or her own predispositions, attitudes, work ethic, personality, knowledge, and ability. You may find your group mates friendly, fascinating, frustrating, or infuriating. Likewise, they will have their own perceptions of you and of each other. Regardless, in all but the most dire circumstances, you will traverse the hills and valleys of group work with these people.

Small-Group Characteristics

We acknowledge that many academic institutions have semester-long courses devoted to the topic of small-group communication, and research is voluminous. However, Forsyth's (1999) following five characteristics that define a small group seem to be most relevant to the public speaking classroom.

1 INTERACTION. Seven people waiting in line for tickets to see the Los Angeles Lakers are not considered members of a small group. Neither are five people sharing a taxi from the Dallas-Fort Worth airport or eight people sitting in a dentist's waiting room. People walking down the sidewalk on a city street may have a goal (get to work), but that goal may be different than those around them (go to lunch, run errands, go home). Perhaps the most basic function of a group is to *communicate with each other*. The amount of communication, formality, type of communication all influence interactions, but speaking (or using a keyboard, if not face-to-face) is fundamental to group communication.

2 STRUCTURE. Whether a group is loosely or tightly structured, every group member contributes to the structure in some way, whether as a leader or a follower. *Structure relates to how members are organized into certain roles.* The basic family structure includes parents and children. The parents, in general, are the "leaders" of this primary group, and children are the "followers." However, even within any family structure, we have different roles: mother, daughter, sister, wife, primary wage earner, caretaker, disciplinarian, financial advisor, and so on.

Within most groups, we also enact different roles. Decades ago, Benne and Sheats (1948) proposed a classification of roles into three broad categories: *task, maintenance, and individual roles.* In an ideal world, individual roles would not exist, since they are self-centered roles that can lead to conflict and greatly harm the group's process.

Task roles are directed toward completing the group's goal. Asking for information, giving information, asking for opinions, giving opinions, and initiating ideas are all examples of task roles. Encouraging, observing, following, and harmonizing are examples of maintenance roles. These keep the group functioning interpersonally. Individual roles include blocking, aggressing, dominating, and seeking recognition. These take energy away from the task at hand.

A leader can engage in task and maintenance functions during the group's process, and individual members can enact different roles. One person might ask for information, give information, and harmonize during one group meeting.

3 GROUP COHESION. The concept of group cohesion relates to how strongly *members feel a sense of unity*. A cohesive group works together, handles conflict effectively, and enacts both task and maintenance roles. A highly cohesive group, according to Janis (1982), can produce negative consequences. Groupthink, Janis said, is the deterioration of the mental processes of a group. In other words, if we agree with each other too much, trust each other implicitly and explicitly, we may forget to engage in the critical thinking process.

Groupthink

Conformity in thought and behavior among the members of a group.

4 SOCIAL IDENTITY. Perhaps the most abstract characteristic of a group relates to the concept of social identity, which occurs when *group members share a perception of being members of the group*. It does not take much to see overt signs of social identity. Think of the T-shirts you own. Do you have a sports team's name on one? Name of

a college? Department? Club? Community event? High school event? If you were to describe yourself in a two-minute speech, it is possible you would name several groups with which you identify. Having social identity with a group means there is some sense of responsibility to the group members and to its final product or outcome.

5   GOALS. Members of small groups usually have both group-oriented and self-oriented goals. **Group-oriented goals** center around specific tasks to be performed to accomplish the group's purpose, whereas **self-oriented goals** relate to the individual's personal needs and ambitions. For example, as a member of a small group charged with the responsibility of determining policies of a new campus radio station, some of the tasks you face are developing station operating policies, purchasing equipment, and attracting advertisers. As an individual, however, a self-oriented goal may be to emerge as leader of the group in order to demonstrate leadership potential. Self-oriented goals may complement group-oriented goals or they may provide distracting roadblocks.

Group-oriented goals
Center around specific tasks to be performed.

Self-oriented goals
Relate to the individual's personal needs and ambitions.

In summary, groups are distinguished from a collection of individuals by their behavior and goals. They communicate with each other, develop roles, bond in some way, and see themselves as a group. They have at least one shared goal.

Presenting to and Participating in Small Groups

Just as different groups have different purposes, there are three ways to be involved in the small-group setting. First, you may be part of a group that meets regularly to discuss issues on campus. In this case, you are participating in a small group. Second, as a concerned citizen you speak before the zoning board to ask them to reject a request for a zoning variation so large apartment buildings cannot be built in your neighborhood. Here, you are speaking before a group. Third, you may find yourself in a group presenting before another group for some reason. Each of these ways is clarified briefly below.

Participating in the Small Group

The most common way to be involved in groups is to participate in a small group. Groups meet for a variety of purposes. Sometimes the purpose of a small-group meeting is to discuss a current problem. For example, if your

Speaking Well with Technology Is an Essential for Excellence

July of 2016 saw the release of the Pokémon Go, a GPS-based augmented reality game that combined the features of geocaching and video game play. The new take on the classic Nintendo game received massive positive reception; within the first two weeks of its release, the app had more than 9.5 million daily active users (Wagner, 2016). Using the app on their phones, players walk around the real world in search of Pokémon and visit actual landmarks that have been designated spots known as "Pokéstops" and "Gyms." When a Pokémon is in their vicinity, the app turns on the camera on the player's phone, allowing them to see an animated creature as if it's right in front of the player (Stevenson, 2016).

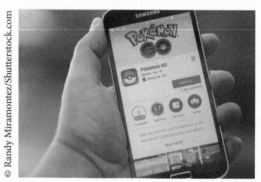

© Randy Miramontez/Shutterstock.com

Pokémon Go rapidly became one of the most popular mobile apps in the country.

The game is significant in that it has reached across a wide range of demographics. Although the game was initially geared toward a younger audience, many adults are playing the game as well. Many players are creating small, local groups to play together, and the "gyms" are attracting many players to come together and discuss strategies for capturing and battling different Pokémon. Although the professional applications of Pokémon Go remain to be seen, its social impact cannot be ignored. The app has created a new dimension for small-group interaction in the new media environment.

As you learn the significance of small-group communication as it applies to public speaking, remember to pay attention to social developments in the communication field. Many trends that begin at the social level make their way to the professional environment; take a look at the net value of Facebook and Twitter. Speaking excellence also requires you to develop good assessment skills about the value of new communication technologies.

organization is low on funds, you must find a way to raise money. A group of individuals wanting to become a recognized group on campus needs to think of a strategy for presenting its case to the appropriate governing body. Everyone contributes to the discussion, and usually a designated leader facilitates the discussion. In college, you may connect with others through membership in one or more of the following groups:

- Study groups
- Sororities and fraternities
- Residence halls
- Honorary societies
- Academic groups
- Athletic groups
- Church groups

For those who spend little time on campus or are part-time students and full-time employees, you may find yourself participating in a variety of other groups.

Speaking as an *Individual* to a Group

A second way to be involved with a small group is by speaking before one. This is considered public speaking and is the focus of this textbook. Unlike regular public speaking, however, you may have two audiences, not one. The *primary audience* is the small group, such as a seven-member school board, a five-member city council, or a ten-member apportionment board. Your purpose is to provide information, to express a concern, or attempt to persuade. Also in attendance, however, may be a *secondary audience*. This is a collection of individuals who attend the open meeting for any number of reasons, including observing its proceedings. It is possible these individuals have no knowledge or interest in your specific topic, and did not know you planned to speak.

In a situation involving both primary and secondary audiences, do you construct a message for the primary audience, accepting the fact that the secondary audience may not understand the context, concern, or content? Or do you construct a message that takes into account both audiences, knowing that for members of the primary audience, some of the information will be unnecessary or redundant? Complexity of the issue, size of the secondary audience, and time constraints are a few of the factors to consider before developing your message.

Speaking as a *Member of a Group* to a Group

Alternatively, you may find yourself in a third speaking situation where you are a member of a small group presenting before another group. This may occur in your business class when you are part of a group presenting a case study, in a psychology class when your group presents results of its research project, or in a public relations class when you are asked, as a group, to present your public relations campaign. There are many instances in college when you work as a group to accomplish a task and report the results to your classmates. In your community, as a health care professional, you may be asked to join a panel with several other health care professionals to discuss the health care crisis before a group of senior citizens. The focus is not only on you, but on your group.

Small-Group Formats

If you have the opportunity to meet as a group at the beginning of the group process, you will spend time defining your purpose, setting goals, distributing the workload, researching your topic/issues, and organizing your research into something meaningful. In business or civic life, you may be known as an expert on the topic. In this case you may focus primarily on what information and resources you need to bring to a particular presentation. Sometimes, you may not meet the other group members until moments before the presentation.

In a public speaking class, your instructor may suggest a particular small-group format. In business or civic life, a moderator or facilitator decides how the group should present. It is also possible that you determine your format. Regardless, there are three main small-group formats: panel discussion, symposium, and forum.

Panel Discussion

Panels are public discussions and, as such, are presented for the benefit of the audience. It involves an informal interchange on some issue(s). The positive and negative features of issues are debated in front of an audience. When you are part of a panel discussion, it is important to remember that you are talking for the benefit of the audience rather than for other group members. Although your responses are spontaneous, ideas should be thought out in advance, just as in any other public speaking presentation.

SPEAKING EXCELLENCE IN YOUR CAREER

In recent times, many communication studies departments are building service learning projects into their curricula. Service learning is defined as "linking academic study and civic work through structured reflection" (Ehrlich, 2011). While the idea of service learning has gained acceptance, some scholars question the methods by which its effectiveness is measured. Namely, critics argue that service learning is driven by academic concerns; a program's effectiveness is based chiefly on student and faculty perceptions of learning rather than the perceptions of community participants of service learning. Researcher Sarah Steimel assesses community partners' perception of service learning as it impacts their community.

Through semi-structured interviews with community service partners, Steimel asked participants (directors, volunteer coordinators, community coordinators, etc.) to assess the value and effectiveness that service learning programs had in their community. Results indicated that community partners believed that students were providing a needed and valuable service, and that students were learning about their local communities (Steimel, 2013). However, in these same interviews, community partners also felt that the students were unaware of or did not care about what they should be learning; students were more concerned with completing the service requirement than applying their experiences to their field of study. Also, community partners expressed their frustration with their lack of contact with faculty members. Almost all participants reported little to no contact with faculty before, during, or after the service learning project. Overall, the research pointed to both promising and limiting trends in the implementation of service learning. Steimel proposes that more emphasis should be placed on developing relationships between community partners and faculty, as well as clearly defining what the learning outcomes should be for students participating in service learning.

Panel discussions are directed by a moderator who attempts to elicit a balanced view of the issues and to involve all group members. The role of the moderator is to encourage the discussion—this person does not take part in the debate. Moderators coordinate and organize the discussion, ask pertinent questions, summarize conclusions, and keep the discussion

Panel discussion

Group members have an informal interchange on the issues in front of an audience.

moving. Once the discussion is over, the moderator often opens the discussion to audience questions.

As you can tell from the previous description, the critical elements of a panel discussion are: (1) it is an informal discussion moderated or facilitated by someone who is not an active participant, (2) interaction should be distributed equitably among group members with no predetermined time limit for each group member, and (3) generally, there are no prepared remarks.

Audience analysis is important to the panel discussion because you need to be aware of the demographics of your audience. If the panel is discussing health care, it makes a difference whether the audience is composed of mostly college students or senior citizens. Both audiences are certainly interested in health care access and cost, but since college-aged individuals are a generally healthy population, the senior citizen audience is more likely to want to hear about long-term care, chronic diseases, and relevant health care screenings. Also, an audience of health care professionals will have a different level of knowledge than an audience of concerned citizens.

Symposium

Prepared speeches on a specified subject given by group members who have expertise on the subject.

Symposium

A **symposium** is more formal and predictable than a panel discussion. Instead of focusing on the interaction among group members, it centers on prepared speeches on a specified subject given by group members who

Symposiums are effective small-group formats, especially in business settings.

© Matej Kastelic/Shutterstock.com

have expertise on the subject. The topic and speakers are introduced by a moderator. A symposium is structured, and speakers are generally given a time frame for their comments. After the formal presentation, a panel discussion or forum may follow. This allows for interaction among group members, and for the audience to ask questions of individual speakers.

Forum

In a forum, group members respond to audience questions. Someone may provide a prepared statement, but it is also possible to introduce group members and their credentials, and then go straight to audience questions. Unlike a panel discussion or the second half of a symposium, a forum does not include interactions among group members. The forum is audience-centered.

Forum
Group members respond to audience questions.

Small-Group Role Responsibilities

When you become a group member, how you communicate is shaped, in large part, by your role in the group. If you have been appointed leader or have expertise that sets you apart from the other members, you may be given more responsibility than the other members.

According to Kreps (1990), norms are often invisible social structures that group members develop that govern behavior. Norms define the general roles that group members are expected to perform. Roles quickly emerge in small groups. While one group member emerges as the leader, taking the initiative in setting the group's agenda, another is uncommunicative and plays a minor role in group discussions. Still other members may try to dominate the discussion, oppose almost every point raised, and close their minds before the discussion begins.

The role you assume influences how you communicate in the group and how effective the group is. Although there are many types of roles, we focus on two broad categories: your role as a group leader and your role as a group member.

Norms
Often invisible social structures that group members develop that govern behavior.

Leader Responsibilities

Whether you are elected, appointed, or emerge as leader over time, you need to be aware of the group's *process and the relationships* among group members. Behaviors that relate to *process* are designed to help the group complete the task. These include *providing direction and purpose, keeping the group on track, and providing clarifying summaries.*

Leader Process Roles

PROVIDE DIRECTION AND PURPOSE. As part of your responsibility to provide direction and purpose, you may choose to open the meeting with action-directed comments (We are here to establish whether it is feasible to add another organization to our college.) or by examining items on an agenda. Once the discussion begins, others will contribute, but it is the leader's role to focus the meeting at the start.

STAY ON TRACK. Staying on track means making sure the group does not drift too far from the task at hand. If you are talking about offering healthy alternatives in the cafeteria, it is easy to start talking about favorite foods or incidents that occurred in the cafeteria or people who work or eat in the cafeteria. While *some* extraneous conversation helps build relationships among group members, the leader is responsible for making sure time is not wasted and the group does not get side-tracked on irrelevant issues.

PROVIDE A CLARIFYING SUMMARY. Groups, like the individuals who comprise them, can be confused by the information they hear. Warning signs include questions for clarification, puzzled looks, and drifting attention. When the leader senses confusion, one of the best ways to move forward is to provide a clarifying summary that recaps what has just occurred.

Leader Relationship Roles

In addition to facilitating the group's *process*, an effective group leader is concerned with *relationship* aspects, which facilitate communication. An effective leader draws information from participants, keeps group communication from being one-sided, and tries to maintain cohesiveness within the group. Ultimately, the relationship aspects allow the group to accomplish its task.

DRAW INFORMATION FROM PARTICIPANTS. Each person has something to contribute to the group, whether it is in the form of offering specific information, analyzing the issue, or being creative. However, some people are hesitant to speak even when they have something valuable to contribute. Their reasons may range from communication anxiety to uncertainty about their role in the group to cultural differences.

Keep group communication from being one-sided. A leader should keep group communication from being one-sided. We often have preconceived ideas of how something should be done. These ideas may become obstacles to group communication if the leader allows the discussion to become one-sided. The leader needs to recognize when one point of view is dominating the discussion. Inviting others into the discussion or offering a varying opinion may open up the discussion for multiple perspectives.

Maintain cohesion. As a leader, you should maintain the cohesiveness of the group. You want the group to see themselves as a group and function as a group, not as a collection of individuals. Everyone needs to work toward the group goal, while not ignoring his or her personal goals. Nothing is inherently wrong with a heated discussion, especially when the issue is controversial. But when the discussion turns into a shouting match, it is no longer productive. In a conflict situation, the leader should acknowledge the person's point of view but suggest that the problem be analyzed from other perspectives as well. Conflict is healthy, but unproductive conflict is a major obstacle to task completion. Keeping communication flowing effectively and making sure members feel their contributions are valued are important to the overall cohesiveness of the group.

Member Responsibilities

Being an active participant is the most important responsibility of each group member. An active participant contributes to the discussion, shares responsibility for task completion, and works effectively with other group members. Some group members, however, believe that their participation is unnecessary because others will pick up their slack. Others view the experience as less important than other college work or activities. Complaining about group members is nothing new. The following is a partial list of common complaints about other group members.

- Doesn't work or prepare enough
- Socializes too much
- Information in presentation overlaps too much
- Information is excessive or too brief

- Difficult to contact
- Has reasons/excuses why it is not possible to meet *at any time*
- Consistently arrives late and/or leaves early
- Doesn't come to class on group work days
- Doesn't proofread PowerPoint

In research on *slackers* in classroom activities, Myers and colleagues (2009) found that not only are group members frustrated by their lack of participation, but that slackers receive credit for work they do not complete and they make excuses for their behavior. Further, group members believe that slackers are aware of their dysfunctional behavior, and that they do not care about the group tasks or group members. Their lack of motivation affects the group in negative ways and can lead to "group hate." This refers to "feelings of dread that arise when faced with the possibility of having to work in a group" (p. 598).

We understand that students take several academic courses. They have social and work lives, and priorities differ among students. But, as you can see by the list of complaints and the research on slackers, once you are part of a group, your actions impact the other people in that group. In a classroom setting, you may not be thrilled with the topic, the assignment, or the other group members. But you do need to work with your group to complete the required assignment. Actively working to complete your individual tasks and being available and cooperative will make the situation better for all involved.

Suggestions for Group Members

The following eight suggestions are designed to create the most effective small-group experience within the context of your classroom. Many of these translate easily to experiences outside the college classroom. The suggestions are derived partially from *Speak from Success* by Eugene Ehrlich and Gene Hawes (1984, p. 133).

1   KNOW THE CONSTRAINTS OF THE ASSIGNMENT. Read the syllabus or other material given to you related to the assignment. Make sure everyone agrees as to the constraints of the assignment. Following are some questions that may guide your group:
    - When does the group present?
    - How much time does the group have to present?
    - Does each speaker have the same amount of time?

- What information needs to be included in the presentation?
- Are presentational aids required?
- Does each speaker use a set of note cards? Is there a restriction?
- Is there audience involvement at some point during the group presentation?
- Can group members interrupt each other to comment or add insight?
- Is there a paper required? Or an outline?
- How many and what type of sources are required, and should they be cited during the presentation?
- Does the group choose its format, or is there a particular format required?
- Are students being graded individually, as a group, or both?
- Will there be any peer evaluations?

2   DEVELOP A COMMUNICATION PLAN. Not all communication occurs during class. Therefore, you need to figure out how the group can communicate most effectively. Some people don't check email or Facebook regularly. Others are not at their place of residence often enough to use their telephone. Some prefer to text; others prefer to talk on the cell phone. Groups who want to be successful begin with an effective communication plan.

Products and services like Mary Kay, Inc. rely on sound communication plans to create a successful product.

© dcwcreations/Shutterstock.com

One speech instructor described a group that chose to put together an informative presentation on Mary Kay cosmetics. One group member was assigned the task of setting communication standards and considered the following:

- How will we contact each other?
- Which technological medium will be used to create our outline and all the material for our speech?
- Will the group use only one form of technology for communication?
- What is the acceptable response time for returning communication?
- The day of the speech, how will the group communicate that everyone will be on time and ready for the presentation?

3   WORK TO ACHIEVE GROUP GOALS. Instructors understand that each individual is concerned about his or her own grade. However, the purpose of a group assignment is to work collectively and collaboratively. Make group goals your top priority. When you

feel strongly about your position, it is legitimate to try to convince the group you are correct. But if others disagree, it is important that you listen to their objections and seek merit in them. You need an objective detachment from your own proposals to enable you to place the group's goals above your own. A group needs a shared image of the group, in which individual aspirations are subsumed under the group umbrella that strives for the common good.

4   BE RESPONSIBLE FOR COMPLETING YOUR PART OF THE ASSIGNMENT. Group membership brings with it a set of roles and responsibilities. If a group member volunteers to create the PowerPoint presentation so it is consistent from speaker to speaker, you need to make sure that person has your slides when they are requested. If you are supposed to make contact with city officials or individuals who may help with a fundraising idea, you need to come to the group with that information. Do not be responsible for the group's progress being delayed or the task not finished. If you cannot attend a meeting, make sure someone knows. Send your work to or with someone else. If you do get behind, make sure group members know so they have an opportunity to respond in some way.

5   RESEARCH SUFFICIENTLY. Most group work involves research of some type. When you are finished researching, you should feel confident that you have ample support or that the topic or issue has been covered in enough depth. If your group seeks to determine what Americans consider the most important political issues for the 2016 presidential campaign, locating *one* website or *one* magazine article is not sufficient. If your group wants to determine which pizza place in town serves the best pizza, selecting the top two from a Google search is not sufficient, particularly in a city that has 10 or more places that sell pizza. If you have been assigned to interview city council members, talking to one person for five minutes is not sufficient.

6   COMMUNICATE EFFECTIVELY AND EFFICIENTLY. Different people bring to a group a wide range of knowledge and views that help complete the task. Group discussion often produces creative approaches that no one would have thought of alone. Group involvement through communication increases the likelihood that the group's decision will be accepted and supported by all group members and by the broader community. Do not waste time and do not monopolize the group discussions or the presentation.

7   AVOID PERSONAL ATTACKS. Comments like "You're not bright, are you?" or "My six-year-old cousin has better ideas than this" accomplish

nothing. On the contrary, these comments are so antagonistic that they make it virtually impossible for people to work together. If you do not like an idea, say so directly by focusing on the idea, not the person, such as "It may be difficult to get funds for that project" or "I don't think parents will want to volunteer their time for that." Try not to make your disagreement too negative. Find areas of agreement, where possible.

ETHICS MATTER

Chris is a senior undergraduate at his local university. For his final public speaking assignment, Chris is tasked with creating a small-group presentation with three of his classmates. Although this project is assigned to the entire group, Chris' professor stated that the majority of the project grade would be dependent on individual performance.

Chris knows that he needs a very good grade to finish the class with an A average. In an attempt to make his performance look better by comparison, Chris decided to attack and belittle the ideas forwarded by his other group members. He would often dismiss ideas by saying they had no merit or would never work in a presentation. While dismissing his teammates' ideas, however, Chris was also incorporating their designs into his part of the presentation. On the day of his group's presentation, Chris presented on many of the points his group had brainstormed, without giving them proper credit. Although Chris initially received a good grade, his teammates went to the professor with accusations of plagiarism. Chris is currently waiting for the results of an academic investigation.

QUESTIONS TO CONSIDER:
1. What ethical issues did Chris breach while working with members of his group?
2. How significantly did Chris damage group dynamics and cohesion with his actions?
3. What steps could other members of Chris' group take to remove his negative influence on group discussion?

8   LEAVE PERSONAL PROBLEMS AT HOME. Group conflicts are often the result of personal problems brought to the group meeting. A fight with a family member, a poor test grade, an alarm clock that failed to go off, a near-accident on the highway, school pressure, or work pressure can put you in a bad mood for the meeting and lessen your tolerance for other group members. Although an outburst of anger may make you feel better for the moment, it can destroy the relationships you have with other members of the group.

Guidelines for Group Problem-Solving and Presenting

Individuals end up in problem-solving or decision-making groups for a variety of reasons. A few examples of task-oriented groups in college are:

- APPORTIONMENT BOARD: Distributes money to student organizations
- ACADEMIC OR SOCIAL GROUP: Raises funds so the group can participate in activities
- COMMUNITY SERVICE GROUP: Raises money for specific causes, such as Habitat for Humanity or Relay for Life
- STUDENT SENATE: Creates initiatives and solves problems related to the student body
- ADVISORY GROUP: Provides input to a particular department or organization on campus, such as serving on a student advisory committee within an academic department or being on a city advisory group searching for ways to get students to attend local events

The groups listed above are different from each other, but they all involve effort and collaboration in the problem-solving process. Nontraditional students are most likely involved with problem-solving or decision-making groups within their community. Following are a few such groups.

- CHAMBER OF COMMERCE: Seeks ways to entice new businesses to the community and increase membership
- CITY COUNCIL: Explores ways to maintain and improve the community
- CHURCH TRUSTEE: Works to keep the church solvent and moving in the agreed-on direction through property maintenance, providing financial advice, and giving pastoral direction
- LEAGUE OF WOMEN VOTERS: Dedicated to maintaining an informed citizenry through research of political issues, moderating political debates, and taking political action
- BOARD OF A CHARITY: Finds ways to raise money to provide resources for people in need, such as a soup kitchen, rehabbing houses, or helping victims of disaster

Groups are faced with small and large problems on a regular basis. Group members may walk into the discussion with a solution in mind. Group members may throw out ideas, vote quickly, and report on the winning solution. Sometimes, the leader has a solution, and spends most of the discussion trying to persuade other group members to accept said solution. These situations occur regularly, but they are not the most effective way to problem-solve.

The Seven-Step Reflective Thinking Process

Over one hundred years ago, John Dewey (1910) developed a theory of reflective thinking that is now applied to group communication. The basic notion of *reflective thinking* is that individuals conduct a careful analysis of the problem and the facts at hand. Groups determine what they know, what they need to know, and work persistently to solve the existing problem. For the seven-step Reflective Thinking Process to work best, it should be accomplished in order. Following these steps helps group members complete a deliberate process that may lead to an effective solution accepted by all stakeholders. Each step should be completed satisfactorily before moving to the next step.

1. Identify and Define the Problem

The first step of this process is to make sure group members understand and agree on what the problem is. Otherwise, the discussion may scatter into many directions and time will be misused. Suppose a newly elected Student Senate member wants to work with a group to handle student complaints about residence hall assignments. One problem students identify is that they are not given enough options about where they may live or with whom. A second problem is that the administration does not process complaints effectively. Third, students are unhappy about meal plan options, and, fourth, they are frustrated by all the residence hall rules and contracts. Does the group want to work on all these problems, or focus on the complaint process? The first thing the group needs to do is identify the problem.

U.S. philosopher, psychologist, and education reformer John Dewey is responsible for the notion of reflective thinking.

© Bettman/Contributor/Getty Images

2. Analyze the Problem

In the process of analyzing the problem, group members need to identify what they know about the problem, what they do not know, and what resources are available to help them acquire more information. In this step, group members should find out what caused the problem, how long the problem has been an issue, and the extent of the problem. If only one student has complained about her residence hall assignment, there is not much of a problem. But if lots of staff time is devoted to addressing students' complaints, then the problem is significant. Perhaps the problem started when a new administrator took office. Perhaps the problem is ongoing. This is the information-gathering, sorting, and evaluation stage of the reflective thinking process.

3. Determine Criteria for an Acceptable Solution

Many groups skip this step, whether they are newly formed groups in a college classroom or well-established policy groups in a community. However, it is a mistake to come into the problem-solving process with a firm idea of what you think is the best solution. Whatever solution your group suggests must meet agreed-on criteria or standards. Criteria will differ from situation to situation. For example, if four students turned in a group paper that was clearly plagiarized, before determining the punishment, an instructor might consider the following criteria:

- Is it (the punishment) fair (to the four students and the rest of the class)?
- Is it appropriate (given the nature of the misconduct)?
- Will it deter future misconduct (on the part of the students who cheated as well as other students who might be contemplating misconduct)?

Criteria related to the residence hall complaints issue might include the following:

- Does the solution consider the needs of both students and college administrators?
- Does the solution apply to all students living in residence halls, not just incoming freshmen?
- Does the solution allow students to change residence halls?
- Does the solution recognize that freshmen do not have cars?

Establishing criteria keeps group members from simply proposing their solution. Any solution presented needs to meet the criteria established by group members.

4. Generate Possible Solutions

According to Dewey, suspended judgment is critical at this point in the decision-making process (Ross & Ross, 1989, p. 77). Group members need to identify available options without stifling the process by providing immediate evaluation. Brainstorming, which was mentioned earlier in the text, involves generating as many solutions as possible without critical evaluation. This may be useful when trying to generate possible solutions. Be creative. Encourage group members to think "outside the box." Avoid the temptation to say, "That won't work," "That's not possible," or worse, "That's a dumb idea," and "Your ideas are worse than your breath." Instead, generate ideas until you agree you have exhausted the possibilities. If possible, give yourselves time to think about these solutions before evaluating or moving on to the next step. For the teacher who caught the group of students plagiarizing, some of the punishment options include ignoring it, talking to the students, requiring them to give a group presentation on the evils of plagiarism, requiring them to write another paper, lowering their grade on the paper, failing them for the assignment, failing them for the semester, and reporting the students to the Office of Judicial Affairs.

Regarding the problem of residence hall complaints, the group may develop several options, including changing the forms students fill out, suggesting a policy change, providing clearer, more specific information to students, and establishing a committee to hear complaints not resolved between students and administration. The important thing is to *have* alternatives, and not be single-minded in your approach.

5. Choose the Solution That Best Fits the Criteria

Each solution identified in Step 4 needs to be evaluated based on the criteria established in Step 3. Ideally, the best solution is one that meets all the established criteria. If that does not happen, the group may need to revisit the possible solutions, and determine if amending one of the solutions might result in it meeting all the established criteria. The instructor who caught students plagiarizing needs to evaluate her possible options by the criteria she has set. For example, if she ignores the misconduct, is that fair to those in the class who did not plagiarize? Is failing students for the course an appropriate punishment for the students' misconduct?

In terms of the residence hall complaints, does changing the form students fill out meet the needs of both students and administrators? Will the form address the issue of changing residence hall assignments? Will a committee be formed to hear complaints from all students in residence halls? An option might not meet each of the criteria perfectly, but the point of this step is to choose the solution that best meets the criteria. If multiple options are acceptable, the group needs to determine how it will decide on which solution to implement.

6. Implement the Solution

Implementing the solution means putting it into effect. It is one thing for a group needing a fundraiser to decide that a car wash will raise the most money. It is another thing to advertise, staff, supply, and conduct the fundraiser. The work involved in implementing the solution varies according to the problem. For example, an instructor dealing with plagiarism can determine the best solution, and then communicate that decision to the students and/or administration. If the group dealing with residence hall complaints decides to form a committee to hear complaints, then implementing the solution entails setting up a committee structure, writing policies and procedures, soliciting membership, and informing students about the committee.

In a public speaking class, your group may be involved in determining a solution and suggesting how it could be implemented, but it is possible the group will not be involved with the actual implementation. For example, your group may be given the task of determining how to get students more involved in their department's activities. Your group could work through Step 5 and decide that the best solution is to advertise activities earlier so that students can work them into their schedules. As a group, you may present Steps 1 through 5 to a faculty committee, but ultimately, Step 6 might be the committee's responsibility.

7. Reassess

Reassessing at some point prevents the group from saying, "We're done" after implementing the solution. It is an important part of the process that you evaluate your group's success or lack thereof. Fundraisers are carefully planned and executed, but still may fail. New policies are developed with the best intentions, but may still be ineffective. Do you try the same fundraiser again? Do you keep the new policy? Before you answer "yes" or "no" to these questions, the group needs to answer other questions. Did the fundraiser fail because it was held at a bad time? Was it advertised sufficiently? Did it ask too much of the people working it or attending the fundraiser? In other words, the group needs to decide what contributed to the lack of success. Similarly, in the case of the ineffective policy, did the administration evaluate its effectiveness too soon? Were students inadequately informed? Was administration insufficiently trained? Those engaged in reassessment need to discuss what factors influenced the lack of success. In a sense, this final step can be the beginning step of a new process, if the solution has not been effective.

The seven-step reflective thinking process is one way to help groups move through the problem-solving process. It is certainly not the only way. However, regardless of the approach groups take, it is important that a clear process be established that allows for rational, deliberative discussion of all relevant aspects of the problem. A leader should help the group through this process, and group members should contribute productively throughout the process.

Presenting in Small Groups

Just because you are part of a small-group discussion does not mean that you will report your results through some type of oral presentation. Some groups prepare written reports that some administrator, council, or committee will evaluate. Sometimes the results of your deliberation are presented before a group, and in many instances a group presents before another group for other reasons. For example, a group of teachers who attended a workshop on gifted students may present their observations of the workshop to the group of teachers who were unable to attend. Members of the League of Women Voters who attended the national convention may present a summary of their experiences to the rest of the membership. Also, many professions have national conferences where people with similar interests have the opportunity to attend or present seminars and panel presentations.

Whether presenting as a group or as an individual to a group, successful public speaking strategies are necessary. Audience analysis is essential. Each presentation you prepare should have a clear introduction, body, and conclusion. Your presentation needs to be well researched, sufficiently supported, and organized effectively. Delivery must be engaging and extemporaneous. Avoid overdependence on notes.

Speaking as a member of a group, however, involves additional review. First, it is important to find a small-group format that best suits your purpose. This was discussed earlier in the chapter. Second, it is important that the speeches all group members give flow as though they were one coherent speech. This next section of the chapter describes a variety of small-group formats, concerns that need to be addressed before the group speaks, and suggestions for the presentation.

Preparing to Present as a Group

When you prepare a speech for class, you are responsible for all aspects of the speech. As an individual, you prepare, practice, and present. Once you join a group, however, you must be prepared, but you also need to know how your speech fits in with the other speeches, and the whole group needs to view the presentation from a similar perspective. With this interest in mind, we present issues for the group to consider *before* the group speaks. All group members should know and be in agreement regarding the following:

1 Speaker order
2 Formality of the presentation:
   Can group members interrupt each other?
   Can group members wander from their prepared remarks?
3 Determine where the group will sit/stand:
   If they are all in front of the class, whether standing or speaking, audience members will be aware of them, even when they are not speaking. Avoid standing too close to the person speaking.
   Will all sit and then stand up to speak or will all stand throughout the entire presentation?
   Should the group sit to the side and have the speaker stand in the middle of the front of the class?
4 Delivery:
   Use note cards? Legal pad? PowerPoint slides?
   Prepare individually—think about eye contact (speak to the group, not the instructor), gestures, and vocal aspects
5 Time constraints for each speech
6 Determine how to signal if someone is speaking too long or if the

group is going too long

7 Introduction, body, conclusion:

Who will deliver the group's introduction and conclusion?

How will each person's introduction and conclusion relate to the group? The goal is to have a group presentation that appears to be one cogent speech. In some cases, it may make sense to introduce the next speaker and provide a preview statement (And now Melissa will identify the pros and cons of the three solutions we developed).

How do you make transitions between speeches so all presentations are connected? Speakers often create their own "part" of their speech, and then deliver it in a predetermined order. Each speaker should link the previous speech to his/her own, and his/her speech should also be linked to the next speech.

8 Presentational aids:

What is available in the classroom?

Will they complement the presentation?

Who is responsible for making them and setting them up?

9 Setting:

Have you taken into consideration that you may have audience members with disabilities who may not be able to climb stairs, sit in a regular chair, hear the presentation, or see the presentational aids?

If group members wait until they approach the front of the room to address these concerns, they will appear unprepared. Deciding where to stand, how to signal each other, and the speaking order reduces awkwardness and uncertainty, and gives a more professional, polished look to the presentation. Before the day of the group presentation, consider what group members will wear. If one group member wears a suit, and another has jeans with holes in them, you will not look as cohesive and credible as if you all agreed on business casual or a particular color palette. Dress as a team.

Strategies for Presenting in a Small Group

The following guidelines will help you succeed as a participant in a panel discussion, symposium, or forum. Many of the guidelines apply to all three group formats, but others apply just to one.

LIMIT THE NUMBER OF POINTS YOU MAKE. Since you will be given some time constraints, limit the number of points you make. Remember that each person has information to present. Your audience cannot process an overload of material. Be brief. Make your point as clearly as possible and do not confuse your listeners with too many details.

AVOID REPETITION. Avoid repeating another group member's content by learning in advance what the other panelists will cover in their speeches. The job of assigning topics should be the responsibility of the presentation organizer. If the organizer is negligent, you may want to get in touch with the other panelists yourself. Keep communication channels open with your group members so you do not find yourself giving the same presentation as the person who spoke before you.

MEET IN ADVANCE. Meet your fellow panelists in advance, if possible. When group members meet for the first time on stage, their interchange may sound awkward because they don't know each other. This discomfort may be communicated to the audience.

RESTRICT YOUR SPEECH TO THE ALLOTTED TIME. If speakers exceed the time limit, the audience will find it difficult to sit through the entire program, and little opportunity will remain for panel interaction or a question-and-answer period. In addition, by violating the time constraints, you may cause another speaker to modify his or her speech significantly. Staying within the allotted time frame is a necessary courtesy to the other group members.

PREPARE FOR AUDIENCE QUESTIONS. Because the question-and-answer period may be the most important part of the program, spend as much time preparing for questions as you did for your formal remarks. Anticipate the questions you are likely to be asked and frame your answers. During the question-and-answer period, be willing to speak up and add to someone else's response if none of the questions are being directed to you. When a fellow panel member finishes a response, simply say, "I'd like to make one more point that . . ." If, on the other hand, a question is directed to you that you think would be better handled by another panel member, say, "I think that considering her background, Therese is better able to answer that question."

CONSIDER ENHANCING YOUR PRESENTATION WITH PRESENTATIONAL AIDS. Simple visual aids are as appropriate in group presentations as they are in single-person public speaking. Coordinate the use of visual aids so information is not repeated by multiple speakers. Be consistent and professional. It is inconsistent to have one group member use the blackboard when the rest of the group has PowerPoint slides.

ESSENTIALS FOR EXCELLENCE

In this chapter, you have learned the strategies needed to be an effective member of a small group, as well as the skills needed to be a leader of a small group. We have also covered the significance of small-group learning, as well as guidelines needed to solve problems and present effectively. However, it is important to remember one of the core aspects of group communication: learning. Besides creating effective presentations, small-group interactions should also help you as a scholar and professional. International marketing director Carolyn Hollowell offers several tips to facilitate small-group learning.

Define a goal.
Always have a clear end goal in mind. Don't create vague benchmarks for your group; the goals should be specific and achievable. Once you have a clear direction in mind, you can better figure out how to get there.

Identify the right activity.
You need to choose the right kind of activity and group structure to reach your goal (Hollowell, n.d.). Study different types of group organizations commonly used in the professional environment and practice different strategies until you find an optimal one.

Revise, reassess, restructure.
Once your group is comfortable in the small-group setting, try new dynamics. Pair group members with different partners to familiarize them with one another. Try to revise group structures to identify the optimal role for members of your group.

WHAT YOU'VE LEARNED:

Now that you have studied the chapter, you should be able to:

1. Define the purpose of a primary group and secondary group.
   - The purpose of a primary group is to fill the basic need to associate with others. The main task is to perpetuate the group so that members can continue to enjoy one another's companionship.
   - The purpose of the secondary group is to accomplish a task or achieve a goal. Groups you belong to in college and in your professional life are secondary groups, such as study groups, social groups, therapy groups, and problem-solving groups.

2. Identify the three types of small-group formats.
   - Panel discussions are directed by a moderator who attempts to elicit a balanced view of the issues and to involve all group members. The role of the moderator is to encourage the discussion—this person does not take part in the debate.
   - A symposium is more formal and predictable than a panel discussion. Instead of focusing on the interaction among group members, it centers on prepared speeches on a specified subject given by group members who have expertise on the subject.
   - In a forum, group members respond to audience questions. Someone may provide a prepared statement, but it is also possible to introduce group members and their credentials, and then go straight to audience questions. Unlike a panel discussion or the second half of a symposium, a forum does not include interactions among group members.

3. List the seven-step reflective thinking process.
   - Identify and define the problem. The first step of this process is to make sure group members understand and agree on what the problem is. Otherwise, the discussion may scatter into many directions and time will be misused.
   - Analyze the problem. In the process of analyzing the problem, group members need to identify what they know about the problem, what they do not know, and what resources are available to help them acquire more information.
   - Determine criteria for an acceptable solution. Whatever solution your group suggests must meet agreed-on criteria or standards. Criteria will differ from situation to situation.
   - Generate possible solutions. Group members need to identify available options without stifling the process by providing immediate evaluation. Brainstorming, which was mentioned earlier in the text, involves generating as many solutions as possible without critical evaluation.
   - Choose the solution that best fits the criteria. Ideally, the best solution is one that meets all the established criteria. If that does not happen, the group may need to revisit the possible solutions, and determine if amending one of the solutions might result in it meeting all the established criteria.
   - Implement the solution. Implementing the solution means putting it into effect. The work involved in implementing the solution varies according to the problem.
   - Reassess. This is the part of the process when you evaluate your group's success or lack thereof. Those engaged in reassessment need to discuss what factors influenced the lack of success. In a sense, this final step can be the beginning step of a new process, if the solution has not been effective.

4. Describe the strategies for presenting in a small group.
   - Limit the number of points you make. Remember that each person has information to present. Your audience cannot process an overload of material. Be brief.

- Avoid repetition. Avoid repeating another group member's content by learning in advance what the other panelists will cover in their speeches. The job of assigning topics should be the responsibility of the presentation organizer.
- Meet in advance. Meet your fellow panelists in advance, if possible. When group members meet for the first time on stage, their interchange may sound awkward because they don't know each other.

Key Terms

forum, 481

group-oriented goals, 475

groupthink, 474

norms, 481

panel discussion, 479

primary group, 471

self-oriented goals, 475

secondary group, 471

symposium, 480

Reflect

1 What is the difference between being a member of a small group that works together and then presents before another group, and being a member of a panel that never meets before it presents?

2 How would your presentation differ if you had a primary audience only or you had both a primary and a secondary audience?

3 When you work with others to accomplish tasks in college, can you usually identify who the leader is? How? What seems to be the most difficult aspect of being a leader in a college classroom project?

4 Can you think of a situation when your fellow group members did not fulfill their group responsibilities? If so, how did you react? How did other group members react?

5 Under what circumstances would it make sense to present as a member of a panel? Of a symposium? When is a forum appropriate?

6 If you were giving advice to a friend who had not participated in a small-group presentation, what would you tell your friend about speaking as a member of a group before another group?

7 Have you traveled abroad and noticed differences in how other cultures communicate? What are some differences you noted? How might these differences impact the group's task at hand?

Review Questions

1 A(n) _____ group fills the basic need to associate with others, such as family and best friends.

2 A(n) _____ group is one that accomplishes a task or achieves a goal.

3 Goals that center around specific tasks to be performed are _____.

4 Goals that relate to an individual's personal needs and ambitions are _____.

5 _____ task group members to have an informal interchange on an issue in front of an audience.

6 In a(n) _____, group members who have expertise on a subject give prepared speeches on a specified subject.

7 In a(n) _____, group members respond to audience questions.

GLOSSARY

Abstract topics Ideas, theories, principles, and beliefs.

Acceptance speech A speech given to express gratitude for an award.

Accurate Reliable, current, and error-free.

Adapting Making your speech fit the audience's needs.

Adoption When you want your audience to start doing something.

After-dinner speech Purpose is to entertain, often with humor, although it usually conveys a thoughtful message.

Alliteration The repetition of the initial consonant or initial sounds in a series of words.

Analogy Establishes common links between similar and not-so-similar concepts.

Anaphora The repetition of the same word or phrase at the beginning of successive clauses or sentences.

Anecdote A short account of an interesting or humorous incident.

Antithesis The use of contrast, within a parallel grammatical structure, to make a rhetorical point.

Articulation The verbalization of distinct sounds and how precisely words are formed.

Asyndeton The deliberate omission of conjunctions between a series of related clauses.

Attacking Occurs when a speaker attacks the person rather than the substance of the person's argument.

Attitudes Predispositions to act in a particular way that influences our response to objects, events, and situations.

Audience-centered Showing your audience you understand their needs and want to help them achieve their goals.

Authority An individual cited or considered to be an expert; power to influence or command thought; credible.

Bandwagoning Unethical speakers may convince listeners to support their point of view by telling them that "everyone else" is already involved.

Beliefs Represent a mental and emotional acceptance of information. They are judgments about the truth or the probability that a statement is correct.

Body Includes your main points and supporting material that reinforces your specific purpose and thesis statement.

Brainstorming Generating a list of ideas consistent with the goals of your speech.

Calculated ambiguity A speaker's planned effort to be vague, sketchy, and considerably abstract.

Captive audience Those who are required to attend.

Cause-and-effect pattern Arranging main points into causes and effects.

Claim A statement or contention the audience is urged to accept.

Cliché A trite phrase.

Cognitive dissonance The tendency to agree with ideas that fit our value system and disagree with those ideas that conflict with our value system.

Commemorative speech An inspirational message designed to stir emotions.

Communication The creation of shared meaning through symbolic processes.

Communication apprehension An individual's level of fear or anxiety associated with either real or anticipated communication with another person or persons.

Comparative-advantages organizational pattern Place alternative solutions to a problem side-by-side and discuss the advantages and disadvantages of each.

Computer-based system Includes a webcam and free software.

Conclusion Supports the body of your speech, reinforces your message, and brings your speech to a close.

Connotation The meaning we ascribe to words as framed by our personal experience.

Continuance When your listeners are already doing the thing you want them to do.

Coverage The depth and breadth of the material.

Credibility The extent to which a speaker is perceived as a competent spokesperson.

Criteria-satisfaction pattern Demonstrating how your idea has the features your audience needs.

Critical thinking The application of the principles of reasoning to your ideas and the ideas of others.

Culture The rules people follow in their relationships with one another; values; the feelings people share about what is right or wrong, good or bad, desirable or undesirable; customs accepted by the community of institutional practices and expressions; institutions; and language.

Currency The timeliness of the material.

Data Evidence in support of an idea you advocate.

Deductive reasoning Drawing conclusions based on the connections between statements that serve as premises.

Delayed feedback Audience response after the speech is performed.

Demographics Age, gender, race and ethnicity, education/knowledge, group affiliation, occupational group, socioeconomic status, religious background, political affiliation, and geographic identifiers of listeners.

Denotative Literal, objective definition provided by a dictionary.

Desktop system Dedicated software improves the audio and video quality.

Deterrence Your goal is to convince your listeners not to start something.

Dialogic communication Demonstrates an honest concern for the welfare of the listeners.

Discontinuance An attempt to persuade your listeners to stop doing something.

Dynamic variables Those things that are subject to change.

Emphasis Stressing certain words or phrases to draw attention.

Epistrophe The repetition of a word or expression at the end of phrases, clauses.

Equality pattern Giving equal time to each point.

Ethics The rules we use to determine good and evil, right and wrong. These rules may be grounded in religious principles, democratic values, codes of conduct, and bases of values derived from a variety of sources.

Ethnocentrism The belief that one's own culture is superior to other cultures.

Ethos Speaker credibility.

Eulogy A commemorative speech that involves paying tribute to a family member, friend, colleague, or community member who died.

Euphemism A word or phrase substituted for more direct language.

Evaluation Assessing the worth of the speaker's ideas and determining their importance to you.

Examples Support that illustrates a point or claim.

Extemporaneous speaking A method of delivery that involves using carefully prepared notes to guide the presentation.

Extrinsic ethos A speaker's image in the mind of the audience.

Eye contact The connection you form with listeners through your gaze.

Facts Verifiable and irrefutable pieces of information.

Fallacies Appealing to audience emotions to disguise the deficit of the speaker's logic not holding up under scrutiny.

False analogy Compares two things that are not really comparable.

False cause When a speaker uses a fallacy to point out that because one event happened before another event, the first event caused the second event.

Figurative analogy Drawing comparisons between things that are distinctly different in an attempt to clarify a concept or persuade.

Fixed-alternative questions Limit responses to several choices, yielding valuable information about such demographic factors as age, education, and income.

Flow chart Used to display the steps, or stages, in a process.

Forum Group members respond to audience questions.

General encyclopedias Cover a wide range of topics in a broad manner.

General purpose There are three general purposes for speeches: to inform, to persuade, and to entertain or inspire.

Gestures Using your arms and hands to illustrate, emphasize, or provide a visual experience that accompanies your thoughts.

Glittering generalities Rely on the audience's emotional responses to values such as home, country, and freedom.

Group-oriented goals Center around specific tasks to be performed.

Groupthink Conformity in thought and behavior among the members of a group.

Hasty generalization A fallacy based on quantity of data.

Hearing The physical ability to receive sounds.

Hidden agenda Private motivation for acting in a certain way. This is unethical behavior.

Hypothetical example A fictional example; the circumstances a hypothetical example describes are often realistic and thus effective.

Imagery Creating a vivid description through the use of one or more of our five senses.

Immediate feedback Audience response as the speech is performed.

Impromptu speaking Speaking with little or no preparation time; using no notes or just a few.

Inductive reasoning Generalizing from specific examples and drawing conclusions from what we observe.

Informative speech Communicates information and ideas in a way that your audience will understand and remember.

Innuendos Veiled lies, hints, or remarks that something is what it is not.

Internal previews Extended transitions that tell the audience, in general terms, what you will say next.

Internal summaries Follow a main point and act as reminders; useful to clarify or emphasize what you have just said.

Interpreting Attaching meaning to a speaker's words.

Intrinsic ethos Ethical appeal found in the actual speech, including such aspects as supporting material, argument flow, and source citation.

Introduction Supports the body of your speech and should capture your audience's attention and indicate your intent.

Jargon Technical terminology unique to a special activity or group.

Keynote speaker Featured speaker at an event.

Line graph Used to show a trend over time.

Listener Perceives through sensory levels and interprets, evaluates, and responds to what he or she hears.

Listening The attending, receiving, interpreting, and responding to messages presented aurally.

Literal analogy Compares like things from similar classes, such as a game of professional football with a game of college football; drawing comparisons between things that are similar in an attempt to clarify a concept or persuade.

Logos An appeal that is rational and reasonable based on evidence provided.

Metaphor A symbol that tells your listeners that you are saying more; state that something is something else.

Monologic communication From this perspective, the audience is viewed as an object to be manipulated and, in the process, the speaker displays such qualities as deception, superiority, exploitation, dogmatism, domination, insincerity, pretense, coercion, distrust, and defensiveness.

Mood The overall feeling you hope to engender in your audience.

Mythos A term given when content supports a claim by reminding an audience how the claim is consistent with cultural identity.

Name calling Linking a person or group with a negative symbol.

Nonfluencies Meaningless words that interrupt the flow of our speech; also known as vocalized pauses or vocal fillers.

Norms Often invisible social structures that group members develop that govern behavior.

Objectivity Information that is fair and unbiased.

Open-ended question Audience members can respond however they wish

Opinions Points of view that may or may not be supported in fact.

Opposed audience This audience does not agree with you, is not friendly or sympathetic, and will search for flaws in your argument.

Organization of ideas The placement of lines of reasoning and supporting materials in a pattern that helps to achieve your specific purpose.

Organizational chart Organized according to official hierarchies that determine the relationships of people as they work.

Panel discussion Group members have an informal interchange on the issues in front of an audience.

PARTS A mnemonic for building your information literacy through consideration of the point of view, accuracy, reliability, timeliness, and scope of your sources.

Pathos Persuading through emotional appeals.

Personification Investing human qualities in abstractions or inanimate objects either through metaphor, simile, or analogy.

Physical noise Anything in the environment that distracts the speaker or listeners.

Physiological noise A result of our senses failing us in some way.

Pictograph Most commonly used as a variation of the bar graph. Instead of showing bars of various lengths, comparing items on the graph, the bars are replaced by pictorial representations of the graph's subject.

Pie graph Also known as a circle graph, shows how the parts of an item relate to the whole.

Pitch Vocal range or key, the highness or lowness of your voice produced by the tightening and loosening of your vocal folds.

Plagiarism Using another's work, words, or ideas without adequate acknowledgment.

Plain folks An effort to create false identification with the audience.

Positive visualization Creating powerful mental images of skillful performances and winning competitions.

Primacy effect The belief that it is the first point in your speech that listeners will most likely remember.

Primary group A group that fills the basic need to associate with others, such as family and best friends.

Primary sources Firsthand accounts such as diaries, journals, and letters, as well as statistics, speeches, and interviews. They are records of events as they are first described.

Problem–solution pattern Presenting an audience with a problem and then examining one or more likely solutions.

Progressive pattern Progression from least important argument to most important argument.

Pronunciation Knowing how to say a word and saying it correctly.

Proposition of fact Persuading your listeners that your interpretation of a situation, event, or concept is accurate.

Proposition of policy Easily recognizable by their use of the word "should."

Proposition of value Assertions rooted in judgments based on ideals.

Psychographics Refer to the behaviors, attitudes, beliefs, and values of your listeners.

Psychological noise A distraction that exists in an individual's mind.

Rate The pace at which you speak.

Reacting/responding Providing feedback to the speaker's message.

Recency effect The belief that it is the last point in your speech that listeners will remember.

Red herring Occurs when a speaker attempts to divert the attention of the audience from the matter at hand.

Research The raw material that forms the foundation of your speech.

Scale questions A type of fixed-alternative question that asks people to respond to questions set up along a continuum.

Secondary group A group that accomplishes a task or achieves a goal.

Secondary sources Generally provide an analysis, an explanation, or a restatement of a primary source.

Self-oriented goals Relate to the individual's personal needs and ambitions.

Semantic noise The disconnect between the speaker's words and the listener's interpretation.

Sensing To become aware of or to perceive.

Similes Create images as they compare the characteristics of two different things using words "like" and "as."

Slang Use of informal words and expressions that are not considered standard in the speaker's language.

Slippery slope This fallacy claims there will be a chain reaction that will end in some dire consequence.

Specialized encyclopedias Focus on particular areas of knowledge in more detail.

Specific purpose The precise response you want from your audience.

Speech of demonstration When the focus is on how something is done.

Speech of description Helps an audience understand what something is.

Speech of explanation Helps an audience understand why something is so.

Speech of introduction Introduces the person who will give an important address.

Speech of presentation Delivered as part of a ceremony to recognize an individual or group chosen for special honors.

Static variables Those things that remain stable from speaking situation to speaking situation.

Statistics The collection, analysis, interpretation, and presentation of information in numerical form.

Stereotypes Avoid generalizations related to race, ethnicity, or nationality, even if these groups are not present in your audience.

Strongest point pattern You spend the most time in your speech on the first point, less time on the second point, and even less time on the last point of your speech.

Studio-based system Offers the best quality, but also is most expensive.

Supporting material The information used in a particular way to make your case.

Supportive audience An audience that agrees with you.

Symposium Prepared speeches on a specified subject given by group members who have expertise on the subject.

Systematic desensitization A premise that people have learned to associate anxious states with public speaking.

Testimonials Statements testifying to benefits received; can be both helpful and destructive.

Thesis statement The core idea; identifies the main ideas of your speech.

Toast Brief message of good will and congratulations.

Tone The emotional disposition of the speaker as the speech is being delivered.

Transitions Verbal bridges between ideas, words, phrases, or sentences that tell your audience how ideas relate.

Uncommitted audience An audience that is neither friendly nor hostile, but most likely not sympathetic.

Values Socially shared ideas about what is good, right, and desirable; deep-seated abstract judgments about what is important to us.

Volume The loudness of your voice, controlled by how forcefully air is expelled through the trachea onto the vocal folds.

Voluntary audience Those who choose to attend.

Warrant An inference that links the evidence with the claim.

REFERENCES

Chapter 1

Anderson, C. (2016). *TED talks: the official TED guide to public speaking.* Boston, MA: Houghton Mifflin Harcourt.

Bradley, B. (1988). *Fundamentals of speech communication*, 5th Ed. Dubuque, IA: Wm. C. Brown.

Duncan, J. (1973, May 12). 'The mouth': Muhammad Ali talks candidly about boxing, beliefs with sports editor. *The Auburn Plainsman*. Retrieved from http://www.theplainsman.com/article/2016/06/from-the-archives-muhammad-ali-at-auburn

Hoff, R. (1998). *I can see you naked: A guide to making fearless presentations.* Kansas City: Andrews McMeel Publishing.

Hunter, K. M., Westwick, J. N., & Haleta, L. L. (2014). Assessing success: the impacts of a fundamentals of speech course on decreasing public speaking anxiety. *Communication Education, 63*(2), 124-135. doi:10.1080/03634523.2013.875213

Jandt, F. E. (2009). *An introduction to intercultural communication: Identities in a global community*, 6th Ed. Thousand Oaks, CA: Sage Publications, Inc.

McCroskey, J. C. (1970). Measures of communication-bound anxiety. *Speech Monographs, 37*, 269–277. doi: 10.1080/03637757009375677

Michaels, J. (2016, June 7). Three tips for amplifying your event to a social-first audience. *The Globe and Mail*. Retrieved from http://www.theglobeandmail.com/report-on-business/careers/leadership-lab/three-tips-for-amplifying-your-event-to-a-social-first-audience/article30248418/dxs

Morrison, T., Conaway, W. A., & Douress, J. J. (2001). *Dun & Bradstreet's guide to doing business around the world.* Paramus, NJ: Prentice Hall Press.

Phillips, P. & Demuro, R. (2016, May 25). Head "TED TALKS" curator offers tips to become a better public speaker. KTLA 5. Retrieved from http://ktla.com/2016/05/25/ted-talks-guide-to-public-speaking/

Rae, C. (2011). *The septic's companion: A British slang dictionary*. Retrieved July 8, 2011 from www.septicscompanion.com/index.htp.

Samovar, L. A., Porter, R. E., & McDaniel, E. R. (2007). *Communication between cultures*, 6th Ed. Belmont, CA: Thomson Wadsworth.

Sweeney, C. (2016, June 7). From gangs to motivation: Napa teen inspires community with TEDxNapaValley talk. *North Bay Business Journal*. Retrieved from http://www.northbaybusinessjournal.com/northbay/napacounty/5636240-181/napa-teen-inspiration-tedx#page=0

Toogood, G. N. (1996). *The articulate executive*. New York: McGraw-Hill, Inc.

Welch, J., & Byrne, J. A. (2001) *Jack; straight from the gut*. New York: Grand Central Publishing.

What Americans do online: Social media and games dominate activity. (2010, August 2). Retrieved July 11, 2011 from blog.nielsen.com/nielsenwire/online_mobile/what-americans-do-online-social-media-and-games-dominate-activity.

Williams, C. (2016, June 4). From the archives: Muhammad Ali at Auburn. *The Auburn Plainsman*. Retrieved from http://www.theplainsman.com/article/2016/06/from-the-archives-muhammad-ali-at-auburn

Wolfe, A. (2005). *The transformation of American religion: How we actually live our faith*. Chicago: The University of Chicago Press.

Chapter 2

Brady, J. (2015). Judge nullifies Tom Brady's Deflategate suspension. *SB Nation*. Retrieved from http://www.sbnation.com/nfl/2015/9/3/8804543/tom-brady-suspension-appeal-nfl-roger-goodell-deflategate

Bruner, B., & Haney, E. (n.d.). *Civil Rights timeline: Milestones in the Civil Rights Movement*. Info Please. Retrieved August 4, 2011 from www.infoplease.com/spot/civilrightstimeline1.html

Cebeci, U. (2013). Presenting via video: Five questions for public-speaking expert Matt Abrahams. *Workspace Blog*. Retrieved from http://blogs.skype.com/2013/04/03/presenting-via-video-five-questions-for-public-speaking-expert-matt-abrahams/

Cooper, L. (1960). *The rhetoric of Aristotle*. Upper Saddle River, NJ: Prentice Hall.

Corn-Revere, R. (2006). *Internet and the First Amendment*. Retrieved from www.firstamendementcenter.org.

Hart, R. (1985). The politics of communication studies: An address to undergraduates. *Communication Education, 34,* 162.

Johannesen, Richard L. (1971). The emerging concept of communication as dialogue. *Quarterly Journal of Speech, 57,* 373–382.

Johannesen, R. L. (1990). *Ethics in communication*. Prospect Heights, IL: Waveland Press.

Kudooski, J. (2014). The ethics in public speaking: Why so important? *Hubpages*. Retrieved from http://hubpages.com/business/the-ethics-in-public-speaking

Martin, D. E., Rao, A., & Sloan, L. R. (2009). Plagiarism, integrity, and workplace deviance: A criterion study. *Ethics & Behavior, 19*(1), 36-50. doi:10.1080/10508420802623666

McCroskey, J. C., & Young, T. J. (1981). Ethos and credibility: The construct and its measurement after three decades. *The Central States Speech Journal, 22,* 24–34.

Pilkington, E. (2009, January 29). Barack Obama inauguration speech. *The Guardian.* Retrieved August 4, 2011 from www.guardian.co.uk/world/2009/jan/20/barack-obama-inauguration-us-speech.

Quintanilla, K.M., & Wahl, S.T. (2016). *Business and professional communication: Keys for workplace excellence* (3rd. ed). Thousand Oaks, CA: Sage.

The Y, Share the News. (2010, July 12). A Brand New Day: The YMCA Unveils New Brand Strategy to Further Community Impact. Washington, DC. Retrieved August 4, 2011 from www.ymca.net/ news-releases/20100712-brand-new-day.html.

Sifri, D. (2006). *Chinese bloggers top 17 million.* Retrieved May 26, 2006 from www.vnunet.com.

Wahl, S.T., & Maresh-Fuehrer (2016). *Public relations principles: Strategies for professional success.* Dubuque, IA: Kendall Hunt.

Walding, S. (2015). CASA needs volunteers. *San Angelo Standard-Times.* Retrieved from http://www.gosanangelo.com/news/local/casa-needs-volunteers-267c9769-f093-39a6-e053-0100007f938b-363039341.html

Wallace, K. 1987. An ethical basis of communication. *The Speech Teacher, 4,* 1–9.

Chapter 3

Brunner, B., & Haney, E. (2007). *Civil rights timeline: Milestones in the civil rights movement.* Information Please. Retrieved August 4, 2011 from www.infoplease.com/spot/civilrightstimeline1.html.

Churchill, G. A., Jr. (1983). *Marketing research: Methodological foundations,* 3rd Ed. Chicago: The Dryden Press.

Clanton, J. (1988). Title unknown. *Winning orations of the Interstate Oratorical Association.* Mankato, MN: Interstate Oratorical Association.

Griffin, J. D. (1989, July 16). To snare the feet of greatness: The American dream is alive (Speech). Reprinted in *Vital Speeches of the Day, September 15, 1989,* 735–736.

Guerra, J. (2014, July 16). Teaching students how to switch between black English and standard English can help them get ahead. *State of Opportunity.* Retrieved from http://stateofopportunity.michiganradio.org/post/teaching-students-how-switch-between-black-english-and-standard-english-can-help-them-get-ahead

Holland, J. (1988). Whose children are these? The family connection (Speech). Reprinted in *Vital Speeches of the Day, July 1, 1988,* 559.

Kiechel, W., III. (1987, June 8). How to give a speech. *Fortune,* 179.

Kushner, Harold S. (2002). *When all you've ever wanted isn't enough: the search for a life that matters.* New York: Random House.

Mazur, M. (2015, January 29). 5 ways to make the audience the star of your presentation. *Fast Company*. Retrieved from http://www.fastcompany. com/3041558/5-ways-to-make-the-audience-the-star-of-your-presentation

Melendez, S. (2016, April 27). What it's like to use a chatbot to apply for jobs. *Fast Company*. Retrieved from http://www.fastcompany.com/3059265/the-future-of-work/what-its-like-to-use-a-chatbot-to-apply-for-jobs

Noonan, P. (1989, October 15). Confessions of a White House speechwriter, *New York Times*, 72.

Pilkington, E. (2009, January 29). Barack Obama inauguration speech. *The Guardian*. Accessed August 4, 2011 from www.guardian.co.uk/world/2009/jan/20/barack-obama-inauguration-us-speech.

Rackleff, R. B. (1987, September 26). The art of speechwriting: A dramatic event (speech). Reprinted in *Vital Speeches of the Day, March 1, 1988.*

Rokeach, M. (1968). The role of values in public opinion research. *Public Opinion Quarterly, 32*(4), 547–559.

Sharples, A. J. (2014). "Do you know why that's funny?" Connecting the scholarship of humor to the practice of after-dinner speaking. *National Forensic Journal, 32*(1), 4-20.

The Y, Share the Day. (2010, July 12). A Brand New Day: The YMCA Unveils New Brand Strategy to Further Community Impact. Retrieved August 4, 2011 from www.ymca.net/news-releases/20100712-brand- new-day.html.

Wahl, S.T., & Scholl, J. (2014). *Communication and culture in your life.* Dubuque, IA: Kendall Hunt

Wrege, L. (2016, April 25). Overcoming cerebral palsy. *The Herald Palladium*. Retrieved from http://www.heraldpalladium.com/news/local/overcoming-cerebral-palsy/article_47073098-4f76-5713-87a7-16464f4f1b8e.html

Chapter 4

AICPA. (2005). *Highlighted Responses from the Association for Accounting Marketing Survey. Creating the Future Agenda for the Profession—Managing Partner Perspective.* Retrieved April 8, 2005 from www. aicpa.org/pubs/tpcpa/feb2001/hilight.htm.

Adams, W. C., & Cox, E. Sam. (2010). The teaching of listening as an integral part of an oral activity: An examination of public-speaking texts. *The International Journal of Listening, 24,* 89–105.

Adler, M. J. (1983). *How to speak, how to listen.* New York: Macmillan.

Aldrich, R. (2016, May 9). Generation NEXT: Multimedia artist, advocate has a heart for community. *The New Pittsburgh Courier*. Retrieved from http://newpittsburghcourieronline.com/2016/05/09/generation-next-multimedia-artist-advocate-has-a-heart-for-community/

Argenti, P. A. (2013). *Corporate communication* (6th ed.). New York, NY: McGraw-Hill/Irwin.

Bommelje, R., Houston, J. M., & Smither, R. (2003). Personality characteristics of effective listeners: A five-factor perspective. *International Journal of Listening, 17,* 32–46.

Botella, C., Gallego, M. J., Garcia-Palacios, A., Guillen, V., Baños, R. M., Quero, S. et al. (2010). An Internet-based self-help treatment for fear of public speaking: a controlled trial. *Cyberpsychology, Behavior, and Social Networking, 13*(4), 407–421. doi:10.1089/cyber.2009.0224.

Clark, A. J. (1989). Communication confidence and listening competence: An investigation of the relationships of willingness to communicate, communication apprehension, and receiver apprehension to comprehension of content and emotional meaning in spoken messages. *Communication Education, 38*(3), 237–249.

Cohe, S. (2016, May 9). Q&A: Gloria Steinem talks about her new TV series, 'Woman.' *The Miami Herald*. Retrieved from http://www.miamiherald.com/entertainment/celebrities/article76497997.html

Cruz, C. (2016, May 10). Taco Bell's snapchat game is strong among teens, but does it sell tacos?. *National Public Radio*. Retrieved from http://www.npr.org/sections/thesalt/2016/05/10/477336641/taco-bell-s-snapchat-game-is-strong-among-teens-but-does-it-sell-tacos

Festinger, L. (1957). *A theory of cognitive dissonance.* Palo Alto, CA: Stanford University Press.

Friedman, P. G. (1986). *Listening processes: Attention, understanding, evaluation* 2nd Ed., (pp. 6–15). Washington, DC: National Education Association.

Grohol, J. (2015, October 30). Become a better listener: Active listening. *Psych Central*. Retrieved from http://psychcentral.com/lib/become-a-better-listener-active-listening/

Haas, J. W., & Arnold, C. L. (1995). An examination of the role of listening in judgments of communication competence in co-workers. *Journal of Business Communication, 32*(2), 123–139.

Janusik, L. A., & Wolvin, A. D. (2006). 24 Hours in a Day. A Listening Update to the Time Studies. Paper presented at the meeting of the *International Listening Association*, Salem, OR.

Job Outlook Survey. (2011). National Association of Colleges and Employers (NACE). Retrieved from naceweb.org/press/frequently_asked_ questions.aspx.

Johnson, S. D., & Bechler, C. (1998). Examining the relationship between listening effectiveness and leadership emergence: Perceptions, behaviors, and recall. *Small Group Research, 29*(4), 452–471.

Klerk, W. G., & Maritz, A. C. (1997). A test of Graham's stock selection criteria. *Investment Analysis Journal, 45,* 26–33. Retrieved July 27, 2011 from www.iassa.co.za/articles/045_1997_03.pdf.

Leavitt, D. (1989, July 9). The way I live now. *The New York Times Magazine*, p. 30.

Leberecht, T. (2012). 3 ways to (usefully) lose control of your brand. [video file]. Retrieved from: http://www.youtube.com/watch?v=_xM- WqUe8FdU

Lewis, T. R., & Nichols, R. (1965). *Speaking and listening: A guide to effective oral-aural communication.* Dubuque, IA: W. C. Brown.

Naistadt, I. (2004). *Speak without fear.* New York: HarperCollins.

Nichols, R. G. (1961). Do we know how to listen? Practical helps in a modern age. *Speech Teacher, March,* 118–124.

REFERENCES

Priorities of Listening Research: Four Interrelated Initiatives. (2008). A White Paper sponsored by the Research Committee of the International Listening Association, 1–27. Accessed August 2, 2011 from www.listen.org/Resources/Documents/White_Paper_PrioritiesResearch.pdf.

Rosendale, J. A. (2015). New communication technologies in organization communications and branding: The integral role social media now play. *Florida Communication Journal, 43*(2), 49-59.

Timm, S., & Schroeder, B. L. (2000). Listening/nonverbal communication training. *International Journal of Listening, 14,* 109–128.

Tubbs, S. (2008). A *systems approach to small group communication.* New York: McGraw-Hill.

Wolf, F. L., Marsnik, N. C., Taceuy, W. S., & Nichols, R. G. (1983). *Perceptive listening.* New York: Holt, Rinehart and Winston.

Chapter 5

About LexisNexis. Retrieved August 31, 2011 from www.lexisnexis.com/about-us/.

Brook, S. (2010, February 15). *New York Times investigates plagiarism incident.* Retrieved June 20, 2011 from www.guardian.co.uk.

Agnew, T. (2016, June 7). *Schools recognize volunteers.* Suffolk News-Herald. Retrieved from http://www.suffolknewsherald.com/2016/06/07/schools-recognize-volunteers/

Behrman, E. & Lindstrom, N. (2016, June 8). New Pittsburgh schools leader caught plagiarizing. TribLive. Retrieved from http://triblive.com/news/education/10601208-74/hamlet-resume-board

Cookie fun fact. Retrieved August 31, 2011 from www.littlebrowniebakers.com/cookies/cookie-fun-facts/.

Ehrlich, P. (1970, June 9). *Speech delivered to First National Congress on Optimum Population and Environment.*

The face of Egypt's networking revolution. Retrieved August 31, 2011 from CBSnews.com/stories/2011/02/12/eveningnews/20031662.shtml.

Google exec tells of a 12-day Egypt ordeal. Retrieved August 1, 2011 from www.adelaidenow.com/au/news/breaking-news/google-exec-tells-of-a-12-day-Egypt-ordeal/story/.

Harris, R. (2002). *Using sources effectively: Strengthening your writing and avoiding plagiarism.* Glendale, CA: Pyrczak Publishing.

Henson, P. (2016, May 30). *Learn how to practice basic online research techniques.* The Telegraph. Retrieved from http://www.macon.com/news/business/article80764627.html

Heumann, J. (1988). *Education: Engine of empowerment* (Speech). Retrieved August 31, 2011 from www.dinf.ne.jp/doc/english/conf/z20/z20001/z200100.html.

Jimmy Carter slams Iraq War. Retrieved February 11, 2009 from www.cbsnews.com/stories/2005/07/30/politics/main712910.shtml.

Levine, T. R. (2012). The problems with some means: cautionary advice regarding reporting and interpreting averages in communication research.

Communication Research Reports, 29(1), 80-85. doi:10.1080/08824096.2012
.640914

Luthra, S. (2016, June 13). Doctors are overloaded with electronic alerts, and
that's bad for patients. The Washington Post. Retrieved from https://www.
washingtonpost.com/national/health-science/doctors-are-overloaded-
with-electronic-alerts-and-thats-bad-for-patients/2016/06/10/0cae6b4a-
20fa-11e6-   9e7f-57890b612299_story.html

Major League Baseball salaries: 2011 MLB salaries by team. Retrieved August 1,
2011 from content.USAtoday.com/sportsdata/baseball/mlb/salaries/team.

Obama, Barack. (2009, October). Presidential Proclamation for Information
Literacy Awareness Month. Accessed October 1, 2009 from www.
whitehouse.gov.

Owl.english.purdue.edu. Retrieved June 22, 2011.

Pierse, C., & Simons, P. (2011, June 17). University's dean of medicine resigns after
plagiarism accusations. Retrieved June 20, 2011 from montrealgazette.com.

Plagiarism incidents featured in world press reports. (2008, November 17).
Retrieved June 20, 2011 from www.globalethics.org.

Radford, M. L., Barnes, S. B., & Barr, L. (2006). Web research: Selecting,
evaluating, and citing. Boston: Allyn & Bacon.

Raimes, A. (2008). Keys for writers, 5th Ed. Boston: Houghton Mifflin Harcourt
Publishing Company.

Samovar, L. A., Porter, R. E., & McDaniel, E. R. (2007). Communication between
cultures, 6th Ed. Belmont, CA: Thompson Wadsworth.

The seven steps of the research process. Retrieved June 20, 2011 from www.
olinuris.library.cornell.edu.

Steves, Rick. (n.d.). Tourist scams in Europe. Retrieved August 31, 2011 from
www.ricksteves.com/plan/tips/298scam.htm.

U.S. & world population clocks. Retrieved August 31, 2011 from www.census.
gov/main/www/popclock.html.

What is citation? Retrieved June 20, 2011 from www.plagiarism.org.

What is Google Scholar? Retrieved August 31, 2011 from scholar.google.com/
intl/en/scholar/about/html.

Chapter 6

Barber, C. (2016, June 7). Stop faking it: four tips for giving a memorable public
speech. City   A.M. Retrieved from http://www.cityam.com/242730/stop-
faking-it-four-tips-for-

Clarke, M. L. (1963). Rhetoric at Rome: Historical survey. New York: Barnes &
Noble.

Creating and using presentation note cards. Retrieved September 2, 2011 from
www.wisc-online.com/objects/ViewObject.aspx?ID=SPH3102.

Daniels, T. D., & Witman, R. F. (1981). The effects of message structure in verbal
organizing ability upon learning information. Human Communication
Research, Winter, 147–160.

Díaz-Galaz, S., Padilla, P., & Bajo, M. T. (2015). The role of advance preparation in simultaneous interpreting. *Interpreting. International Journal Of Research & Practice In Interpreting*, 17(1), 1-25. doi:10.1075/intp.17.1.01dia

Express News Service (2016, June 16). *Interactive seminar on speech disorder.* The New Indian Express. Retrieved from http://www.newindianexpress.com/cities/thiruvananthapuram/Interactive-seminar-on-speech-disorder/2016/06/16/article3484225.ece

Harkins, E. (2016, June 15). *Tribune profile: Mary Stanton: she made a career of helping others.* The Waunakee Tribune. Retrieved from http://www.hngnews.com/waunakee_tribune/community/arts_and_entertainment/article_c3e83e78-326e-11e6-832a-37ae08058822.html

Horner, W. B. (1988). *Rhetoric in the classical tradition.* New York: St. Martin's Press.

Lemonick, M. D. (2007, July 5). How we get addicted. *Time.* Retrieved February 15, 2011 from time.com.

Makay, J., & Fetzger, R. C. (1984). *Business communication skills: Principles and practice,* 2nd Ed. Englewood Cliffs, NJ: Prentice-Hall.

Mathew, S. (2016, August 1). Interactive Disability Awareness Seminars. *National Institute of Speech and Hearing.* Retrieved from http://www.schoolius.com/school/167315796634809/National+Institute+of+Speech+and+Hearing+(NISH),+Trivandrum,+India

National Institute of Speech and Hearing (NISH), Trivandrum, India, NISH Road, Ulloor-Akkulam Road, Sreekariyam P.O., Trivandrum www.schoolius.com

Respers, L. (2016, May 11). *Gene Simmons apologizes for calling Prince's death 'pathetic'.* CNN. Retrieved from http://www.cnn.com/2016/05/11/entertainment/gene-simmons-prince-death/index.html

Sprague, J., & Stuart, D. (1992). *The speaker's handbook,* 3rd Ed. San Diego: Harcourt Brace Jovanovich.

Supporting a speech. Retrieved September 2, 2011 from www.hawaii.edu/mauispeech/html/supporting_materials.html.

Tardiff, E., & Brizee, A. (2011). Four main components of an effective outline. Retrieved September 8, 2011 from www.owl.english.purdue.edu/owl/resource/544/01.

Turner, F. H., Jr. (1970). The effects of speech summaries on audience comprehension. *Central States Speech Journal, Spring,* 24–39.

Willerton, D. R. (1999, December). *Toward a rhetoric of marketing for high-tech service.* Published Master's Thesis, University of North Texas. Retrieved August 31, 2011 from digital.library.unt.edu/ark:/67531/metadc2432/m1/1/high_res_d/thesis.pdf.

Chapter 7

Baird, John E., Jr. (1974). The effects of speech summaries upon audience comprehension of expository speeches of varying quality and complexity. *Central States Speech Journal, Summer,* 119–127.

Barber, C. (2012, April 11). How to END a speech with power and impact. *Vivid Method*. Retrieved from http://vividmethod.com/how-to-end-a-speech-with-power-and-impact/

Beyer, A. & Figenschou, T. U. (2014). Human-interest fatigue: audience evaluations of a massive emotional story. *International Journal of Communication (19328036)*, 81944-1963.

Bush, George W. (2001). *Speech to the nation on 9/11*. Retrieved September 8, 2011 from www.americanrhetoric.com/speeches/gwbush911addresstothenationon.htm.

Childhood Overweight and Obesity Prevention Program: Fact Sheet. (2011). Retrieved September 7, 2011 from www.surgeongeneral.gov/obesityprevention/factsheet/index.html

Corbett, E., & Connor, R. (1999). *Classical rhetoric for the modern student*, 4th Ed. London: Oxford University Press.

Donovan, Shaun. (2010, November 18). *Speech given at the Virginia Housing Conference*. Retrieved September 8, 2011 from portal.hud.gov/hudportal/HUD/press/speeches_remarks.2010.htm.

Emanuel, Rahm. (2009). *Commencement speech at George Washington University*. Retrieved September 8, 2011 from www.blogs.gwhatchet.com/newsroom/2009/05/17/transcript-of-rahm-emanuels-commencement-address/.

Flaherty, B. (2016, July 14). Craig Sager delivers emotional speech while accepting Jimmy V Award at ESPY's. *The Washington Post*. Retrieved from https://www.washingtonpost.com/news/early-lead/wp/2016/07/14/craig-sager-delivers-emotional-speech-while-accepting-jimmy-v-award-at-espys/

Firth, Colin. (2011). *Oscar acceptance speech 2011*. Retrieved September 8, 2011 from www.nowpublic.com/colin-firth-oscar-acceptance-speech-2011-video-transcript.2761763.html.

Gaskell, A. (2016, July 14). How to make your presentations funnier. *Forbes*. Retrieved from http://www.forbes.com/sites/adigaskell/2016/07/14/how-to-make-your-presentations-funnier/#294d7dc03cdb

Hrynkiw, I. (2016, July 18). Alabama animal shelter giving dogs another chance at life. *Alabama Media Group*. Retrieved from http://www.al.com/news/birmingham/index.ssf/2016/07/second_chance_shelter.html

Jagland, Thorbjorn. (2010). *Nobel Peace Prize speech*. Retrieved September 8, 2011 from www.nobelprize.org/prizes_peace/presentation-speech.html.

Kamkwamba, William. (2009). How I harnessed the wind. *TED: Ideas Worth Spreading*. Retrieved July 28, 2011 from www.ted.com/talks/william_kamkwamba_how_i_harnessed_the_wind.html.

Lady Gaga. (2010, September). *The prime rib of America* (Speech). Retrieved September 8, 2011 from www.mtv.com/news/articles/1648304/lady-gagas-don't-ask-don't-tell-speech-full-transcript.jhtml.

Merkel, Angela. (2009, November 3). *We have no time to lose* (Speech). Retrieved March 2, 2011 from www.spiegel.de/international/europe.

Notable quotes from HealthCare Summit. (2010, February 25). Retrieved September 7, 2011 from www.msnbc.msn.com/id/35585513/ns/politics/t/notable-quotes-health-care-summit/.

REFERENCES

Reagan, Ronald. (1986). *Challenger* (Speech). Retrieved September 8, 2011 from www.americanrhetoric.com/speeches/ronaldreaganchallenger.htm.

Shapiro, L. (1990, February 26). The zap generation. *Newsweek, 56.*

Sigurdardottir, J. Address of the Prime Minister of Iceland at official ceremonies on the parliament square Austurvollur, 17 June 2011. Retrieved on Februrary 2, 2012 on http://www.forsaetisraduneyti.is/.

Tse-tung. Mao. (1942, February 1). *Rectify the party's style of work* (Speech). Retrieved March 2, 2011 from www.marxists.com.

Tsuji, A. (2016, July 13). Craig Sager gives emotional, inspiring speech after receiving the Jimmy V Award for Perseverance. *USA Today Sports.* Retrieved from http://ftw.usatoday.com/2016/07/craig-sager-espys-jimmy-v-award-speech

Weiner, Edith. (1989, October 10). Personal interview.

Winfrey, Oprah. (2002, September 22). *Speech.* Retrieved September 8, 2011 from www.famousquotes.me.uk/speeches/Oprah-Winfrey/.

Zucker, Jerry. (2003). *Commencement* (Speech). Retrieved September 8, 2011 from www.news.wisc.edu.8682.

Chapter 8

Agarwal, A., Mulgund, A., Hamada, A., & Chyatte, M. R. (2015). A unique view on male infertility around the globe. *Reproductive Biology & Endocrinology,* 13(1), 1-9. doi:10.1186/s12958-015-0032-1

Berg, K., & Gilman, A. (1989). *Get to the point: How to say what you mean and get what you want.* New York: Random House.

Buscaglia, Leo. (2007). *I helped him cry.* Children's Thoughts on Love. Utah Government Document. Retrieved July 28, 2011 from www.schools.utah.gov/cte/documents/.../6_8ChildrensThoughtsOnLove.

Burton, G. O. (n.d.). Silva Rhetoricae: *The trees of rhetoric* (Online resource). Brigham Young University. Retrieved September 1, 2011 from rhetoric.byu.edu/.

Chang, M., & Gruner, C. R. (1981). Audience reaction to self-disparaging humor. *Southern Speech Communication Journal, 46,* 419–426.

Colin Firth oscar acceptance speech 2011: Video, Transcript. Retrieved September 3, 2011 from www.nowpublic.com/culture/colin-firth-oscar-acceptance-speech-2011-video-transcript-2761763.html.

Derose, S. (2011). *Business meeting bingo.* Retrieved August 1, 2011 from www.derose.net/steve/resources/papers/Bingo.html.

Detz, J. (1984). *How to write and give a speech.* New York: St. Martin's Press.

Dosomething.org. (2011). *Tips and tools, 11 facts about the BP oil spill.* Retrieved August 1, 2011 from www.dosomething.org/tipsandtools/11-facts-about-bp-oil-spill.

Duarte, N. (2011). *Congress, preparers urge IRS to clarify publications by using plain language.* Retrieved July 28, 2011 from www.tax.com/taxcom/features.nsf/Articles/054E880A97191EFF852576E3006878C5?OpenDocument.

Dutta, M. C. (2015). Exploring social construction of victims through gendering of language: an untold account. *Language In India, 15*(5), 35-50.

Ehrlich, E., & Hawes, G. R. (1984). *Speak for success.* New York: Bantam Books.

Farhi, P. (2010, November 15). PBS edits Tina Fey's remarks from Twain event. *The Washington Post Online.* Retrieved September 3, 2011 from www.voices. washingtonpost.com/arts-posts/2010/11/by_paul_farhi_tina_fey.html.

Gruner, C. R. (1985, April). Advice to the beginning speaker on using humor— what the research tells us. *Communication Education, 34*, 142.

Gustainis, J. J. (1987). Jesse Louis Jackson. In B. K. Duffy & H. R. Ryan (Eds.), *American orators of the twentieth century: critical studies and sources.* New York: Greenwood Press.

Harrell, A. (1997). *Speaking beyond the podium: a public speaking handbook*, 2nd Ed. Harcourt Brace College Publishing: Fort Worth.

Kadian-Baumeyer, K. (2016). Using vivid language in public speaking. *Study.* Retrieved from http://study.com/academy/lesson/using-language-vividly.html

Kaplan, R. M., & Pascoe, G. C. (1977). Humorous lectures and humorous examples: some effects upon comprehension and retention. *Journal of Educational Psychology, 69*, 61–65.

Kleinfeld, N. R. (1990). Teaching the 'Sir Winston' method. *New York Times, March 11*, 7.

Knowlton, B. (2008). Obama vows to cut budget waste. *New York Times. November 25.* Retrieved September 3, 2011 from www. newyorktime/2008/11/26/us/politics/25-cnd-transition/html.

Kurtzman, D. (n.d.). *Political humor, top 10 Bushisms*, About.com. Retrieved July 29, 2011 from politicalhumor.about.com/cs/georgewbush/a/top10bushisms. htm.

McKenzie, J. (2016, April 1). April Fools' Day pregnancy jokes aren't funny to women struggling with infertility. *ABC News.* Retrieved from http:// abcnews.go.com/Lifestyle/april-fools-day-pregnancy-jokes-funny-women-struggling/story?id=38085191

Mooney, A. (2011, June 22). Michelle Obama brings 'yes, we can' to Africa. *CNN Politics, The 1600 Report.* Retrieved July 29, 2011 from whitehouse.blogs.cnn. com/2011/06/22/michelle-obama-brings-yes-we-can-to-africa/.

Phillips, M. (2009, January 21). President Barack Obama's inaugural address. *The White House Blog.* Retrieved July 29, 2011 from www.whitehouse.gov/blog/ inaugural-address/.

Purdue OWL. (2011). *Active and passive voice.* Purdue Online Writing Lab, Purdue University. Retrieved July 29, 2011 from owl.english.purdue.edu/ owl/resource/539/4/.

Rackleff, R. B. (1987, September 26). The art of speech writing: a dramatic event (speech). Reprinted in *Vital Speeches of the Day*, March 1, 1988.

Sanchez, X. (2016, June 23). Marco: student puts community first. *The San Diego Union-Tribune.* Retrieved from http://www.sandiegouniontribune.com/ news/2016/jun/23/community-journalism-scholar-marco-barron/

Schmich, M. (1997). Advice, like youth, probably just wasted on the young. *Chicago Tribune, June 1.* Retrieved June 10, 2007 from www.chicagotribune. com.

REFERENCES

Smith, M. (2016, June 28). Wife cake and evil water: the perils of auto-translation. *BBC News*. Retrieved from http://www.bbc.com/news/business-36638929

Tarver, J. (1988, March 2). Words in time: some reflections on the language of speech. Reprinted in *Vital Speeches of the Day*, April 15, 410–412.

Valenti, J. (1982). *Speak up with confidence*. New York: William Morrow and Company, Inc.

Ziv, A. (1982). Cognitive results of using humor in teaching. Paper presented at the *Third International Conference on Humor*, Washington, DC. (Cited in Gruner, Advice to the Beginning Speaker, p. 144).

Chapter 9

Ayers, J. (1996). Speech preparation processes and speech apprehension. *Communication Education, 45*(4), 228–234.

Ayers, J., Ayers, F. E., Baker, A. L., Colby, N., DeBlast, C., Dimke, D. et al. (1993). Two empirical tests of a videotape designed to reduce public speaking anxiety. *Journal of Applied Communication Research, 21*(2), 132–147.

Ayers, J., & Hopf, T. (1992). Visualization: Reducing speech anxiety and enhancing performance. *Communication Reports, 5*(1), 1–10.

Ayers, J., Hopf, T., & Myers, D. M. (1997). Visualization and performance visualization: application, evidence, and speculation. In J. A. Daly, J. C. McCroskey, J. Ayers, T. Hopf, & D.M. Ayers (Eds.), *Avoiding communication* (pp. 305–330). Cresskill, NJ: Hampton Press.

Ayers, J., Hopf, T., & Will, A. (2000). Are reductions in CA an experimental artifact? A Solomon four-group answer. *Communication Quarterly, 48*(1), 19–26.

Babej, M. C. (2011). Botox may deaden ability to empathize, new study says. *Forbes*, April 23. Retrieved September 1, 2011, from www.forbes.com/sites/marcbabej/2011/04/23/botox-may-deaden-ability-to-empathize-new-study-says/.

BBC. (2011, January 28). *Mandela's life and times*. BBC/Mobile/Africa. Retrieved May 29, 2011 at www.bbc.co.uk/news/world-africa-12305154.

Behnke, R. R., & Sawyer, C. R. (2004). Public speaking anxiety as a function of sensitization and habituation processes. *Communication Education, 53*(2), 164–173.

Brainyquote.com. (n.d.). *George Jessel Quotes*. Brainy Quotes. Retrieved August 26, 2011 from www.brainyquote.com/quotes/quotes/g/georgejess392909.html.

Botella, C., Gallego, M. J., Garcia-Palacios, A., Guillen, V., Baños, R. M., Quero, S. et al. (2010). An Internet-based self-help treatment for fear of public speaking: A controlled trial. *Cyberpsychology, Behavior, and Social Networking, 13*(4), 407–421. doi:10.1089/cyber.2009.0224.

Burke, K. (1969). *A rhetoric of motives*. Berkeley, CA: University of California Press.

Clapp, C. (2016). The 5 secrets of speaking with confidence. *American Bar Association*. Retrieved from http://www.americanbar.org/publications/tyl/topics/communications/5-secrets-speaking-confidence.html

Duffy, B., & Ryan, H. (Eds.). (1987). *American orators of the twentieth century: critical studies and sources.* New York: Greenwood Press.

Duff, D. C., Levine, T. R., Beatty, M. J., Woolbright, J., & Park, H. S. (2007). Testing public anxiety treatments against a credible placebo control. *Communication Education, 56*(1), 72–88.

Dwyer, K. K. (2000). The multidimensional model: teaching students to self-manage high communication apprehension by self-selecting treatments. *Communication Education, 49,* 72–81.

Fletcher, L. (1990). Polishing Your Silent Languages. *The Toastmaster* (March), 14.

Hardesty, A. (2016). Meals on Wheels route is a family tradition. *Independent Mail.* Retrieved from http://www.independentmail.com/news/meals-on-wheels-route-is-a-family-tradition-2d1819fe-afa6-586e-e053-0100007ff8c1-370993461.html

Hopf, T., & Ayres, D. M. (Eds.). (1997). *Avoiding communication: shyness, reticence, and communication apprehension.* Cresskill, NJ: Hampton.

Ivy, D.K., & Wahl, S.T. (2014). *Nonverbal communication for a lifetime.* (2nd ed.). Dubuque, IA: Kendall Hunt.

Jung, H. Y., & McCroskey, J. C. (2004). Communication apprehension in a first language and self-perceived competence as predictors of communication apprehension in a second language: a study of speakers of English as a second language. *Communication Quarterly, 52*(2), 170–181.

Levin-Epstein, A. (2011). Ace your Skype interview: 14 smart tips. *CBS News.* Retrieved from http://www.cbsnews.com/news/ace-your-skype-job-interview-14-smart-tips/

Lustig, M. W., & Koester, J. (2010). *Intercultural competence*, 6th Ed. Boston: Allyn & Bacon.

Mandela, Nelson. (1993). *Acceptance speech of the president of the African National Congress.* Retrieved September 1, 2011 from .db. nelsonmandela.org/speeches/pub_view.asp?pg=item&ItemID=NMS161 &txtstr=Nobel%20Peace

McCroskey, J. C. (1984). The Communication Apprehension Perspective. In J. Daly & J. C McCroskey (Eds.), *Avoiding communication: shyness, reticence, and communication apprehension.* Beverly Hills, CA: Sage Publications.

McCroskey, J. C. (2009). Communication Apprehension: What Have We Learned in the Last Four Decades? *Human Communication, 12*(2), 157–171.

Motley, T. M. (1988). Taking the terror out of talk. *Psychology Today,* 46–49.

Morrison, T., Conaway, W, A., & Douress, J. J. (2001). *Doing business around the world.* Paramus, NJ: Prentice Hall.

Mulac, A., & Sherman, A. R. (1974). Behavioral assessment of speech anxiety. *Quarterly Journal of Speech, 60*(2), 134–143.

Naistadt, I. (2004). *Speak without fear.* New York: HarperCollins Publishers Inc.

Praino, R., Stockemer, D., & Ratis, J. (2014). Looking good or looking competent? physical   appearance and electoral success in the 2008 congressional elections. *American Politics Research, 42*(6), 1096-1117.

Pryor, B., Butler, J., & Boehringer, K. (2005). Communication apprehension and cultural context: a comparison of communication apprehension in Japanese and American students. *North American Journal of Psychology, 7*(2), 247–252.

REFERENCES

Quintanilla, K.M., & Wahl, S.T. (2016). *Business and professional communication: Keys for workplace excellence.* (3rd. ed). Thousand Oaks, CA: Sage.

Robinson, T. E. (1989). Communication apprehension and the basic public speaking course: a national survey of in class treatment techniques. *Communication Education, 46*(3), 1997.

Samovar, L. A., Porter, R. E., & McDaniel, E. R. (2007). *Communication between cultures,* 6th Ed. pp. 209–211. Belmont, CA: Thomson Wadsworth.

Sawyer, C. R., & Behnke, R. R. (1999). State anxiety patterns for public speaking and the behavior inhibition system. *Communication Reports, 12*(1), 33–41.

Shannon, M. L., & Stark, C. P. (2003). The influence of physical appearance on personnel selection. *Social Behavior and Personality, 31*(6), 613–624.

Wahl, S.T., & Scholl, J. (2014). *Communication and culture in your life.* Dubuque, IA: Kendall Hunt

Whitworth, R. H., & Cochran, C. (2009). Evaluation of integrated versus unitary treatments for reducing public speaking anxiety. *Communication Education, 45*(4).

Chapter 10

Alley, M., & Neeley, K. A. (2005). Rethinking the design of presentation slides: a case for sentence headlines and visual evidence. *Technical Communication, 52*(4), 417–426.

Carey, R. (1999). Spice it up. *Successful Meetings, October,* 47–50.

CTIA Semi-Annual Wireless Industry Survey. Retrieved May 17, 2011 from ctia. org/research.

Cyphert, D. (2007). Presentation technology in the age of electronic eloquence: from visual aid to visual rhetoric. *Communication Education, 56*(2), 168–192.

Deighton, K. (2016, June 23). YouTube morphs into 'a 3D content experience', as 360 content uploads double in three months. *The Drum.* Retrieved from http://www.thedrum.com/news/2016/06/23/youtube-morphs-3d-content-experience-360-content-uploads-double-three-months

Foresman, C. *Wireless survey: 91% of Americans use cell phones.* Retrieved May 17, 2011 from arstechnica.com.

German twenty-somethings prefer internet to partner. Retrieved March 2, 2009 from reuters.com.

Haworth, T. (2016, June 6). NSPCC makes learning fun as kids are given lessons in safety. *Swindon Advertiser.* Retrieved from http://www. swindonadvertiser.co.uk/news/14539377.NSPCC_makes_learning_fun_as_ kids_are_given_lessons_in_safety/

Hickey, A. R. (2010, August 2). *Social networking dominates U.S. web use; Facebook leads the way.* Retrieved from www.crn.com.

Howell, D. D. (2008). four keys to powerful presentations in PowerPoint: Take your presentation to the next level. *TechTrends, 52*(6).

Internet usage statistics for the Americas. Retrieved June 30, 2010 from internetworldstats.com.

Ivy, D.K., & Wahl, S.T. (2014). *Nonverbal communication for a lifetime.* (2nd ed.). Dubuque, IA: Kendall Hunt.

Kalyuga, P., Chandler, P., & Sweller, J. (1991). When redundant on-screen text in multimedia technical instruction can interfere with learning. *Human Factors, 46*(3), 567–581.

Kraus, R. (2008). Presentation software: strong medicine or tasty placebo? *Canadian Journal of Science, Mathematics and Technology Education, 8*(1), 70–81.

Lapchick, R. E., Harrison, K., & Hill, F. *Keeping score when it counts: Academic rates for teams in the 2009–2010 NCAA Division bowl games.* Retrieved from www.tidessports.com.

Lapchick, R. E., Harrison, K., & Hill, F. *Keeping score when it counts: Academic rates for teams in the 2011 NCAA Division I Men's basketball study.* Retrieved from www.tidessports.com.

Mayer, R. E. (2001). *Multimedia Learning.* New York: Cambridge University Press.

Mirsky, S. (2015, March 2). Climate skeptic senator burned after snowball stunt. *Scientific American.* Retrieved from http://www.scientificamerican.com/podcast/episode/climate-skeptic-senator-burned-after-snowball-stunt/

Morales, X. Y. Z. G. (2010). *Networks to the rescue: Tweeting relief and aid during Typhoon Ondoy.* Thesis abstract. Retrieved from www.firstsearch.oclc.org.

Nicholson, D. T. (2002, Summer). Lecture delivery using MSPowerPoint: Staff and student perspectives at MMU. *Learning and Teaching in Action.* Retrieved from www.celt.mmu.ac.uk.

Paradi, D. (2009). *Results from the 2009 annoying PowerPoint Survey.* Retrieved from thinkoutsidetheslide.com.

Polycom Fact Sheet. *The top five benefits of video conferencing.* Retrieved from polycom.com/telepresence.

Purcell, K., Rainie, L., Rosenstiel, T., & Mitchell, A. (2011, March 14). *How mobile devices are changing community information environments.* Retrieved from pewinternet.org.

Smith, A. (2011, March 17). *The Internet and Campaign 2010.* Retrieved from pewinternet.org.

Stim, R. (n.d.). Websites: five ways to stay out of trouble. *Stanford University Libraries.* Retrieved from http://fairuse.stanford.edu/overview/website-permissions/websites/

Travel Weekly. (2008, October 16). Business travel: the rise of video-conferencing. Retrieved from travelweekly.com.

Tufte, E. R. (1997). *Visual explanations: images and quantities, evidence and narrative.* Cheshire, CT: Graphics Press.

Tufte, E. R. (2006). *The cognitive style of PowerPoint: Pitching out corrupts within,* 2nd Ed. Graphics Press: Cheshire CT.

U.S. Department of Education, National Center for Education Statistics. (2008). *Distance education at degree-granting postsecondary institutions: 2006–07.* Retrieved May 16, 2011 from nces.ed.gov/fastfacts.

Wazlawick, P., Bevelas, J. B., & Jackson, D. D. (1967). *Pragmatics of human communication: A Study of interactional patterns, pathologies, and paradoxes.* New York: Norton.

REFERENCES

Wrather, K. (2016). Making 'Maximum Fun' for fans: Examining podcast listener participation online. *Radio Journal: International Studies In Broadcast & Audio Media*, 14(1), 43-63. doi:10.1386/rjao.14.1.43_1

Wright, J. (2009). The role of computer software in presenting information. *Nursing Management, 16*(4).

Zetter, K. (2011). TED 2011: Wael Ghonim—Voice of Egypt's revolution. *Wired*, March 5. Retrieved from www.wired.com.

Chapter 11

Cyphert, D. (2007). Presentation technology in the age of electronic eloquence: from visual aid to visual rhetoric. *Communication Education, 56*(2), 168–192.

Gregory, R. J. (2004). *Psychological testing: history, principles, and application.* Needham, MA: Allyn & Bacon.

Griffin, I. (2013, February 1). 4 speaking essentials to inform an audience: don't be a 'foreign policeman'. *Jim Harvey*. Retrieved from http://www.jim-harvey.com/4-speaking-essentials-to-inform-an-audience-foreign-policeman/

Howard, B.C. (2015, December 2). Bill Nye tells you what you need to know about climate change. *National Geographic*. Retrieved from http://news.nationalgeographic.com/2015/12/151202-bill-nye-climate-change-101-video-science/

Jones, A. (2016, July 5). Aramark, American Heart Association offer community health education series. *The Philadelphia Tribune*. Retrieved from http://www.phillytrib.com/news/aramark-american-heart-association-offer-community-health-education-series/article_3c87df70-1f6d-581f-bd7e-88a8b5680619.html

Mazer, J. P., Simonds, C. J., & Hunt, S. K. (2013). Assessing evaluation fidelity: an examination of student comments and scores on speech self-evaluation forms in a general education communication course. *Ohio Communication Journal, 511-27.*

National Spiritualist Association of Churches. (2011). *Spiritualism. Definitions.* Retrieved June 16, 2011 from www.nsac.org/Definitions.aspx?id=3.0.

Official slam poetry history and beliefs. Retrieved June 16, 2011 from slampapi.com.

Reaves, J. (2003). Interview: Sarah Weddington. *Time* (January 16). Retrieved September 1, 2011 from www.time.com/time/nation/article/0,8599,409103,00.html.

Rocket, P.R. (2016, June 30). Focusky: PowerPoint alternative brings new HTML5 presentation technology. *Press Release Rocket*. Retrieved from http://www.pressreleaserocket.net/focusky-powerpoint-alternative-brings-new-html5-presentation-technology/466072/

Rockoff, H. (1995). The 'Wizard of Oz' as a monetary allegory. In R. Whaples & D. C. Betts (Eds.), *Historical Perspective on the American Economy*. New York: Cambridge University Press.

Spiritualism. Retrieved June 16, 2011 from Kheper.net.

U.S. Department of Housing and Urban Development. *Buying a home.* Retrieved June 17, 2011 from

300. American Rhetoric movie speeches. Retrieved July 8, 2011 from www.americanrhetoric.com/MovieSpeeches/moviespeech300queengorgo.html.

Emperor Akihito. (2011, March 16). *Speech to the Nation on disaster relief and hope*. Retrieved July 8, 2011 from www.americanrhetoric.com/speeches/emperorakitodisasterspeech.htm.

Frankel, A. (2015, January 12). 6 tips for writing a persuasive speech (on any topic). *Time*. Retrieved from http://time.com/3664739/6-tips-for-writing-a-persuasive-speech-on-any-topic/

Freeley, A. J. (1993). *Argumentation and debate: critical thinking for reasonable decision-making*, 8th Ed. Belmont, CA: Wadsworth Publishing.

Hample, D., Sells, A., & Valazquez, A. L. I. (2009). The effects of topic type and personalization of conflict on assessments of fallacies. *Communication Reports*, *22*(2), 74–88.

Hirsen, J. (2011, April 13). Tina Fey voices Palin parody pangs; 'Idol' voting needs reboot. Retrieved July 8, 2011 from www.newsmax.com/Hirsen/Tina-Fay-Palin-Parody/2011/04/13/id/392760.

Kennedy, G. A. (2007). Aristotle's 'On Rhetoric': A theory of civic discourse, 2nd Ed. (G. A. Kennedy, Trans.). New York: Oxford University Press. (Original work published 350 BCE.)

Kupor, D., & Tormala, Z. (2015). Persuasion, interrupted: The effect of momentary interruptions on message processing and persuasion. *Journal of Consumer Research*, *42*(2), 300-315.

Leveille, D. (2016, March 28). Florence tackles the problem of graffiti with 'playful, persuasive' technology. *Public Radio International*. Retrieved from http://www.pri.org/stories/2016-03-28/florence-tackles-problem-grafitti-playful-persuasive-technology

Maslow, A. H. (1943). A theory of human motivation, *Psychological Review*, *50*(4), 370–396.

Monroe, A. H. (1965). *The psychology of speech* (Seminar). Purdue University.

Netanyahu, Benjamin. (2009, September 24). *Speech delivered before the United Nations*. Retrieved July 8, 2011 from www.washingtontimes.com/news/2009/sep/transcript-Israeli-Prime-Minister-Benjamin-Netanya.

Osborn, M. (1990). In defense of broad mythic criticism—A reply to Rowland. *Communication Studies*, *41*, 121–127.

Pearson, J. C., Child, J. T., Mattern, J. L., & Kahl, D. H., Jr. (2006). What are students being taught about ethics in public speaking textbooks? *Communication Quarterly*, *54*(4), 507–521.

Pornpitakpan, C. (2004). The persuasiveness of source credibility: A critical review of five decades' evidence. *Journal of Applied Social Psychology*, *34*(2), 243–281.

Regan, D. T., & Fazio, R. (1977). On the consistency between attitudes and behavior: look to the method of attitude formation. *Journal of Experimental Social Psychology*, *13*, 28–45 (Cited in Zimbardo, p. 618.)

REFERENCES

Shen, A. (2016, July 7). Community and contribution: National Service Ride promotes a life of service. *Huffington Post*. Retrieved from http://www.huffingtonpost.com/anna-shen/a-veteran-takes-his-messa_b_10743090.html

Simons, H. (2001). *Persuasion in society*. Thousand Oaks, CA: Sage Publications.

Sprague, J., & Stuart, D. (1988). *Speaker's handbook*, 2nd Ed. San Diego: Harcourt Brace Jovanovich.

Spurling, C. (1992). Batter up-batter down. *Winning Orations of the Interstate Oratorical Association*. Mankato State University: The Interstate Oratorical Association.

Toulmin, S. (1958). *The uses of argument*. Cambridge, UK: Cambridge University Press.

Vancil, D. L. (1993). *Rhetoric and argumentation*. Boston: Allyn and Bacon.

Wahl, S.T. (2013). *Persuasion in your life*. Boston, MA: Pearson.

Wahl, S.T., & Maresh-Fuehrer (2016). *Public relations principles: Strategies for professional success*. Dubuque, IA: Kendall Hunt.

Wheeler, B. & Hunt, A. (2016, June 24). The UK's EU referendum: all you need to know. *BBC News*. Retrieved from http://www.bbc.com/news/uk-politics-32810887

Wicker, A. W. (1969). Attitudes versus actions. The relationship of verbal and overt behavioral responses to attitude objects. *Journal of Social Sciences*, *25*(4), 41–78.

Walker, F. R. (2005). The rhetoric of mock trial debate: Using logos, pathos and ethos in undergraduate competition. *College Student Journal*, *39*(2), 277–286.

Zimbardo, P. G. (1988). *Psychology and life*, 12th Ed. Glenview, IL: Scott, Foresman and Company.

Chapter 13

Averbuch, Yael. *Speech*. Retrieved January 20, 2010 from potomacsoccerwire.com.

Bangs, M. (2010, December 13). *Avoid clichés like the plague*. Retrieved June 19, 2011 from www.huffingtonpost.com

Bayless, J. (1988). Are you a master of the toast? *The Toastmaster*, November, 11.

Bonos, L. (2015, October 28). 5 tips for giving a wedding toast. Skip the inside jokes—and no roasting. *The Washington Post*. Retrieved from https://www.washingtonpost.com/news/soloish/wp/2015/10/28/5-tips-for-giving-a-wedding-toast-skip-the-inside-jokes-and-no-roasting/

Bradley, L. (2015, May 19.) Watch Stephen Colbert's surprisingly earnest Wake Forest commencement speech. *Slate*. Retrieved from http://www.slate.com/blogs/browbeat/2015/05/19/stephen_colbert_commencement_speech_at_wake_forest_may_you_ride_eternal.html

Dimon, Jamie. (2010, May 16). *Commencement remarks*. Retrieved December 11, 2010 from syr.edu.

Firth, Colin. (2011). *Oscar acceptance speech*. Retrieved September 6, 2011 from www.nowpublic.com/culture/colin-firth-oscar-acceptance-speech-2011-video-transcript-2761763.html.

Galmés, M., Berlanga, I., & Victoria, J. S. (2016). Advertising from the perspective of festivals: the present and future of commercial communication in the categories of awards (2013-2014). *Communication & Society*, *29*(2), 81-100.

Grisham, John. (2010, May 9). *Commencement speech*. Retrieved from Forbes.com.

Harrell, A. (1997). *Speaking beyond the podium: a public speaking handbook*, 2nd Ed. Fort Worth: Harcourt Brace College Publishing.

Heller Anderson, S. (1990). Chronicle: Interview with Professor Melvin Helitzer. *New York Times*, (January 18), B6.

Henmueller, P. (1989, June 11). Diamonds of hope: the value of a person (speech). Reprinted in *Vital Speeches of the Day, September 1, 1989*, 680–681.

Irish weddings toasts, blessings, proverbs, traditions. Retrieved September 6, 2011 from www.lollysmith.com/irwedtoasble.html.

Joshi, R. (2010, April 15–16). *Keynote speech*. Retrieved from saath.wordpress.com.

Kudrow, Lisa. (2010, May 23). *Commencement address*. Retrieved from commencement.vassar.edu/2010.

Nair, T. (2011). *Introduction speech examples*. Retrieved September 6, 2011 from www.buzzle.com/articles/introduction-speech-examples.html.

Obama, Barack. (2004). *Keynote speech*. Retrieved September 6, 2011 from americanrhetoric.com/speeches/convention2004/barackobama2004dnc.htm.

Praetorius, D. (2011, May 23). *The most viewed commencement speeches in the history of YouTube* (VIDEOS). Retrieved June 19, 2011 from www.huffingtonpost.com.

Resn. (2016, June 25). Resn caps off awards wins with even more awards. *Scoop Business*. Retrieved from http://www.scoop.co.nz/stories/BU1606/S00765/resn-caps-off-awards-wins-with-even-more-awards.htm

Smith, A. (2016, July 1). Yara Shahidi of "Black-ish" talks career, life, service. *Detroit Free Press*. Retrieved from http://www.freep.com/story/news/local/michigan/detroit/2016/06/30/yara-shahidi-black-ish-talks-career-life-service/86531620/

Swanger, J. (2010, May 8). *The tyranny of certainty* (Baccalaureate Address).

Wells, J. (2009). *Word choice*. Retrieved June 19, 2011 from www.owl.english.purdue/engagement.

Chapter 14

Beebe, S. A., & Masterson, J. T. (2014). *Communicating in small groups: Principles and practices,* 11th Ed. New York: Longman.

Barker, L. L., Wahlers, K. J., & Watson, K. W. (1995). *Groups in process: An introduction to small group communication.* Boston: Allyn and Bacon.

Benne, K. D., & Sheats, P. (1948). Functional roles of group members. *Journal of Social Issues, 4*(2), 41–49.

Bucher, R. D. (2000). *Diversity consciousness: opening our minds to people, cultures, and opportunities.* Upper Saddle River, NJ: Prentice Hall.

Colbeck, C. L., Campbell, S. E., & Bjorklund, S. A. (2000). Grouping in the dark: what college students learn from group projects. *Journal of Higher Education, 71,* 60–83.

Dewey, John. (1910). *How we think.* Boston: D. C. Heath.

Duin, A. H. (1990). Terms and tools: a theory and research-based approach to collaborative writing. *The Bulletin for the Association for Business Communication, 53*(2), 45–50.

Eggert, D. (2016, July 14). Veteran BP lobbyist named the Michigan environmental chief. *ABC News.* Retrieved from http://abcnews.go.com/Politics/wireStory/veteran-bp-lobbyist-named-michigan-environmental-chief-40586825

Ehrlich, T. (2011). Forward. In C. M. Cress & D. M. Donahue (Eds.), *Democratic dilemmas of teaching service learning: Curricular strategies for success* (pp. xixvi). Sterling, VA: Stylus.

Ehrlich, E., & Hawes, G. R. (1984). *Speak for success.* New York: Bantam Books.

Forsyth, D. R. (1999). *Group dynamics.* Belmont, CA: Wadsworth Publishing Company.

Gareis, E. (2006). Virtual teams: a comparison of online communication channels. *Journal of Language for International Business, 17,* 6–21.

Hall, E. T. (1977). *Beyond culture.* Garden City, NY: Anchor Press/ Doubleday.

Hollowell, C. (n.d.). 4 tips to success small group learning. *Lightspeed.* Retrieved from https://www.lightspeed-tek.com/lightspeed-classroom-audio-blog/lightspeed-classroom-audio-blog/4-tips-to-success-small-group-learning1/category/blog/view-all/

Janis, I. (1982). *Groupthink,* 2nd Ed. Boston: Houghton Miff lin.

Kilbane, K. (2016, July 15). Nuns on the Bus group inspired by work, clients of Vincent Village. *The News-Sentinel.* Retrieved from http://www.news-sentinel.com/news/local/Nuns-on-the-Bus-group-inspired-by-work--clients-of-Vincent-Village

Kreps, G. L. (1990). *Organizational communication: theory and practice,* 2nd Ed. New York: Longman.

Lewis, R. D. (2006). *When cultures collide: leading across cultures,* 3rd Ed. (pp. 27–38). Boston: Nicholas Brealey International.

Lustig, M. W., & Koester, J. (2010). *Intercultural competence,* 9th Ed. (p. 309). Boston: Allyn and Bacon.

Meyers, S. A., Eidsness, M. A., Bogdan, L. M., Zackery, B. A., Thompson, M. R., Schoo, M. E. et al. (2009, June). Dealing with slackers in college classroom work groups. *College Student Journal, 43*(2), 592–598.

Payne, Brian K., Monk-Turner, Elizabeth, Smith, Donald, & Sumter, Melvina. (2006). Improving group work: voices of students. *Education, 126*(3), 441–448.

Ross, R. S., & Ross, J. R. *Small groups in organizational settings.* Englewood Cliffs, NJ: Prentice-Hall.

Steimel, S. J. (2013). Community partners' assessment of service learning in an interpersonal and small group communication course. *Communication Teacher, 27*(4), 241-255.

REFERENCES

Stevenson, L. (2016, July 16). Local gamers enjoying Pokémon Go. *The Marion Star*. Retrieved from http://www.marionstar.com/story/news/2016/07/15/local-gamers-enjoying-pokmon-go/87093974/

Tubbs, S. L. (2011). *A systems approach to small group interaction*, 11th Ed. New York: McGraw-Hill.

Wagner, K. (2016, July 13). How many people are actually playing Pokémon Go? Here's our best guess so far. *Recode*. Retrieved from http://www.recode.net/2016/7/13/12181614/pokemon-go-number-active-users

Watson, W. E., Kamalesh, K., & Michaelson, L. K. (1993). Cultural diversity's impact on interaction process and performance: comparing homogeneous and diverse task groups. *Academy of Management Journal, 36,* 590–602.

Winter, J. K., & Neal, J. C. (1995). Group writing: student perceptions of the dynamics and efficiency of groups. *Business Communication Quarterly, 58*(2), 21–24.

Zeff, L. E., & Higby, M. A. (2002). Teaching more than you know. *Academic Exchange, Fall,* 155–160.

INDEX